# Roman Law and the Origins of Civil Law Tradition

George Mousourakis

# Roman Law and the Origins of the Civil Law Tradition

 Springer

George Mousourakis
Faculty of Law
University of Auckland
Auckland
New Zealand

ISBN 978-3-319-12267-0     ISBN 978-3-319-12268-7 (eBook)
DOI 10.1007/978-3-319-12268-7
Springer Cham Heidelberg New York Dordrecht London

Library of Congress Control Number: 2014956262

Printed on acid-free paper

Springer is part of Springer Science+Business Media (www.springer.com)

*To Sumi, Eli and Kent*

# Preface

The civil law tradition is the oldest and most prevalent legal tradition in the world today, embracing the legal systems of Continental Europe, Latin America and those of many African and Asian countries. Despite the considerable differences in the substantive laws of civil law countries, a fundamental unity exists between them. The most obvious element of unity is the fact that the civil law systems are all derived from the same sources and their legal institutions are classified in accordance with a commonly accepted scheme existing prior to their own development, which they adopted and adapted at some stage in their history. The civil law tradition was the product of the interaction among three principal forces: Roman law, as transmitted through the sixth century codification of Emperor Justinian; Germanic customary law; and the canon law of the Church, which in many respects derived from Roman law but nevertheless constituted a distinct system.

Roman law is both in point of time and range of influence the first catalyst in the evolution of the civil law tradition. The history of Roman law is divided into two great phases. The first phase spans more than a thousand years, from the formation of the city-state of Rome to the codification of Justinian in the sixth century AD. During its long history, Roman law progressed through a remarkable process of evolution. It advanced through different stages of development and underwent important transformations in substance and form as it adapted to the changes in society, especially those derived from Rome's expansion in the ancient world. During this long process the interaction between custom, enacted law and case law led to the formation of a highly sophisticated system gradually developed from layers of different elements. But the great bulk of Roman law, especially Roman private law, derived from jurisprudence rather than legislation. This unenacted law was not a confusing mass of shifting customs, but a steady tradition developed and transmitted by specialists who were initially members of the Roman priestly class and then secular jurists. In the final stages of this process when law-making was increasingly centralized, jurisprudence together with statutory law was compiled and 'codified'. The codification of the law both completed the development of

Roman law and evolved as the means whereby Roman law was subsequently transmitted to the modern world.

The second phase of Roman legal history (occasionally labelled the 'second life' of Roman law) commenced in the sixth century, yet only acquired true significance in the eleventh century when Roman law was 'rediscovered' in Western Europe. This law was initially the object of academic study and then later engaged for a far-reaching reception in large parts of Continental Europe. Particularly important in this process was the work of the medieval jurists who systematically studied, interpreted and adapted Roman law to the conditions and needs of their own era. From the fifteenth century onwards the relationship between the received Roman law, Germanic customary law and canon law was affected in varying degrees by the rise of the nation-state and the increasing consolidation of centralized political administrations. The rise of nationalism precipitated the move towards the codification of the law, which engendered the great European codifications of the eighteenth and nineteenth centuries. When new civil codes were introduced in the various European states, Roman law ceased to operate as a direct source of law. But as the drafters of the codes greatly relied on the Roman system, elements of Roman law were incorporated in different ways and to varying degrees into the legal systems of Continental Europe. Moreover, through the process of legal borrowing or transplanting these legal elements permeated the legal systems of many countries around the world.

This book begins with an overview of the historical and constitutional framework of Roman law in antiquity. The need to place Roman law in its historical setting was recognized by the Romans themselves. For instance, the jurist Gaius wrote that the person who omitted reference to historical causes was one who took up his subject-matter with "unwashed hands." (D. 1. 2. 1.) In Chap. 2 the focus of the discussion is on the sources of law (the ways in which law was created), the mechanisms whereby the various sources were effectuated and the way each legal source influenced the progress of law. Special attention is accorded to the development of legal science, which emerged as the most productive element in Roman legal life by the end of the first century BC. Then follows an exposition of the principal institutions of Roman private law: the body of rules and principles relating to individuals in Roman society and regulating their personal and proprietary relationships. Private law greatly overshadowed public law in both its intrinsic merit and subsequent influence. This is because private law had a dominant role in the development of legal norms and was the chief interest of the jurists, the shapers of Roman law. In this part of the book I have tried to describe and elucidate the fundamental assumptions and distinctions of Roman private law and to delineate some of its most characteristic institutions. In doing so I have examined several of its detailed rules, but have omitted much that seemed to me to be, in a work of this kind, of secondary importance. Special attention is given to the Roman law of things, which furnished the foundations of much of the modern law of property and obligations in civil law systems. Furthermore, emphasis is laid on the classical era and the age of Justinian, the most important periods in terms of the development and documentation of Roman law. Chapter 4 offers an account of the history and principal features of Roman criminal law and procedure. It should be noted that it was not until the imperial age that Roman juridical literature began giving serious attention to matters of criminal law. Prior to that we have to rely mainly on literary sources, whose focus of attention is largely on the upper social classes. This leaves us in the dark as to how the ordinary citizen fared, in particular when prosecuted for common (as opposed to political) offences. Nevertheless, even with this qualification, the sources give valuable insight into how the Romans thought about crime and criminal justice. Chapter 5 appraises the move towards the codification of law in the later imperial epoch, which culminated in the final statement of Roman law: the *Corpus Iuris Civilis* of Emperor Justinian. The final three chapters of the book offer an overview of the history of Roman law from the early Middle Ages to modern times and illustrate the way in which Roman law furnished the basis of contemporary civil law systems. In this part, special attention is given to the factors that warranted the preservation, resurgence and subsequent reception of Roman law as the 'common law' of Continental Europe.

The guiding aim of this book is to introduce law students to the history, fundamental principles and major institutions of Roman law. There are few, if any, legal subjects that can properly be studied without some grasp of their historical context, least of all Roman law, where the student has to take on board the legal development of the system over a vast time scale. This poses particular problems to the teacher of Roman law at the present time, when the decline of classical studies in the schools has led to a generation of students who are generally unfamiliar with the landmarks of Roman history. The book is therefore designed to offer students and general readers an accessible and comprehensive introduction to the subject, by combining the perspectives of legal history with those of political, constitutional and social history. To give the reader a better insight into the character of Roman law, I have included representative materials from a variety of Roman juridical sources and have tried as best I could to make the meaning of the ancient texts intelligible. At the end of the book there is an extensive bibliography for further reading on the topics discussed, together with the titles of those studies that have furnished the basis of my work. Although the book does not purport to provide a detailed account of the development of particular legal doctrines or branches of law, the careful examination of central themes will hopefully emphasize that Roman law deserves to be studied not merely as an important part of the intellectual background of civilian legal systems, but also as an essential part of the history of civilization.

The impetus of this book grew from a series of lectures and seminars that I gave at universities in New Zealand, Australia, Europe and Japan. I would like to thank in particular my students and colleagues at the University of Auckland for their support and constructive criticism when the themes of this book were discussed in class and seminar presentations. Many thanks go to my former students Miss L. Stroud and Mr. I. MacIntosh, who have been superb editors and have made a number of helpful suggestions for improvement. Finally, I wish to thank Professor T. Duve, Director of the Max Planck Institute for European Legal History in Frankfurt, Professor R. Zimmermann of the Max Planck Institute for Comparative and International Private Law in Hamburg, Professor M. Avenarius, Director of the Institute of Roman Law at the University of Cologne, Professor A. Bürge of the Leopold Wenger

Institute at the University of Munich, Professor D. Gottardi of the University of Verona, Professor S. Riondato of the University of Padova, Professors B. Santalucia and R. Bartoli of the University of Florence, Professor S. Hama of Doshisha University and Professor N. Yoshinaka of Hiroshima University for their generosity in allowing me access to the library resources and other research facilities of their institutions.

Auckland, New Zealand                                                    G. Mousourakis

# Abbreviations

| | |
|---|---|
| Bruns, *Fontes* | *Fontes iuris romani antiqui*, ed. C. G. Bruns, Tübingen 1909, repr. Aalen 1969 |
| C. | *Codex* of Justinian |
| C. Th. | *Codex Theodosianus* |
| D. | *Digest* of Justinian |
| FIRA | *Fontes Iuris Romani Anteiustiniani*, I-III, ed. S. Riccobono, J. Baviera and V. Arangio-Ruiz, Florence 1940–1943, 2nd edn, 196. |
| G. | *Institutes* of Gaius |
| Girard, *Textes* | *Textes de droit romain*, ed. P. F. Girard and F. Senn, 7th edn, Paris 196. |
| *Inst* | *Institutes* of Justinian |
| *Nov* | *Novels* of Justinian |
| XII T | *Law of the Twelve Tables* |

# Contents

# Chapter 1
# The Historical and Constitutional Context of Roman Law: A Brief Overview

## 1.1 Divisions of Roman Constitutional and Legal History

The history of Roman law in antiquity spans a period of more than eleven centuries. Initially the law of a small rural community, then that of a powerful city-state, Roman law became in the course of time the law of a multinational empire that embraced a large part of the civilized world. During its long history Roman law progressed through a remarkable process of evolution. It advanced through different stages of development and underwent important transformations, both in substance and in scope, adapting to the changes in society, especially those derived from Rome's expansion in the ancient world. During this long process the interaction between custom, enacted law and case law led to the formation of a highly sophisticated system, gradually developed from layers of different elements. But the great bulk of Roman law, especially Roman private law, was not a result of legislation but of jurisprudence. This unenacted law was not a confusing mass of shifting customs, but a steady tradition developed and transmitted by specialists, initially members of the Roman priestly class and later secular jurists. In the final phases of this process when law-making was increasingly centralized, jurisprudence together with statutory law was compiled and 'codified'. The codification of the law both completed the development of Roman law and evolved as the means by which Roman law was subsequently transmitted to the modern world.

Roman history is traditionally divided into three major periods that correspond to Rome's three successive systems of political organization: (1) the Monarchy, from the founding of Rome in the eighth century BC to 509 BC; (2) the Republic, from 509 BC to 27 BC; and (3) the Empire, from 27 BC to AD 565. The republican era is subdivided into two phases: the early Republic, from 509 BC to 287 BC, and the late Republic, from 287 BC to 27 BC. The imperial era is likewise subdivided into two parts: the early Empire or Principate, from 27 BC to AD 284, and the late Empire or Dominate, from AD 284 to AD 565. According to some Romanist scholars, Roman

© Springer International Publishing Switzerland 2015
G. Mousourakis, *Roman Law and the Origins of the Civil Law Tradition*,
DOI 10.1007/978-3-319-12268-7_1

legal history follows these divisions as the various legal institutions adapted to the type of government in power.

Roman legal history may also be divided into periods by reference to the modes of law-making and the character and orientation of the legal institutions that prevailed in different epochs. In this respect, the following phases are distinguished: (1) the archaic period, from the formation of the city-state of Rome to the middle of the third century BC; (2) the pre-classical period, from the middle of the third century BC to the early first century AD; (3) the classical period, from the early first century AD to the middle of the third century AD; and (4) the post-classical period, from the middle of the third century AD to the sixth century AD. The archaic period covers the Monarchy and the early Republic; the pre-classical period largely coincides with the later part of the Republic; the classical period covers most of the first part of the imperial era, known as the Principate; and the post-classical period embraces the final years of the Principate and the late Empire or Dominate, including the age of Justinian (AD 527–565).[1]

Although the above divisions facilitate the study of Roman law, one must recall that Roman law evolved gradually and therefore no distinct lines separate the different stages of its development. The sources of law were, in varying degrees of strength from period to period, all present and in force at the same time, and in diverse ways qualified the influence of each other.

During the early archaic period, Roman society was governed by a body of customary norms with a largely religious character. Their formulation and articulation was mainly determined by the priestly college of the pontiffs. Only the pontiffs were acquainted with the technical forms employed in the typical transactions of private law and were entitled to offer authoritative advice on questions of law. Resembling the law of other primitive societies, the Roman law of the archaic period was characterized by its extremely formalistic nature. A legal transaction or procedure could not produce its desired effects unless it was performed in accordance with strictly prescribed rituals. A momentous event of this period was the codification of the customary norms that governed the life of the Roman citizens by the Law of the Twelve Tables, enacted around 450 BC. This law embodied the first written record of the rules and procedures for the attainment of justice and it entailed a new source of law, in addition to the unwritten customary law. In the years after the enactment of the Law of the Twelve Tables, legal development was based largely on the interpretation of its text, a task carried out by the pontiffs and, in later times, by secular jurists. Moreover, later in this period the office of praetor was introduced (367 BC)—a new magistracy entrusted with the administration of the private law. In the course of time the praetor's edict became one of the strongest formative forces in the development of Roman law, furnishing the basis for a distinct source of law known as *ius praetorium* or *ius honorarium*.

---

[1] Some modern Romanist scholars consider Justinian's age to constitute a distinct phase in the history of Roman law in its own right.

The legal history of the pre-classical period is marked by the emergence of the first secular jurists (*iurisconsulti* or *iurisprudentes*), who, like the pontiffs, were members of the Roman governing aristocracy. The main focus of their activities was presenting legal advice on difficult points of law to judicial magistrates, judges and parties at law, and the drafting of legal documents. Towards the end of this period the first systematic treatises on civil law emerged—a development reflecting the influence of Greek philosophy and science on Roman legal thinking. The legal history of this period is marked also by the development of the *ius honorarium*, or magisterial law, as a distinct source of law. As noted, early Roman law was rigid, narrow in scope and resistant to change. As a result of the changes generated by Rome's expansion, the Romans faced the problem of how to adjust their law to address the challenges created by the new social and economic conditions. In response to this problem the law-dispensing magistrates, and especially the prae-tors, were granted the power to mould the law in its application. Although the magistrates had no legislative authority, they extensively used their right to regulate legal process and thus in fact created a new body of law that was progressive, flexible and subject to continual change and development.

Roman law reached its full maturity in the classical period and this emanated mainly from the creative work of the jurists and their influence on the formulation and application of the law. From the early years of the Principate age the emperors customarily granted leading jurists the right to present opinions on questions of law (*ius respondendi*) and deliver them by the emperor's authority. In the later half of the second century it was recognized that when there was accord between the opinions of the jurists who had been granted this right, these opinions operated as authoritative sources of law. Besides dealing with questions pertaining to the practical application of the law, the jurists were also engaged in teaching law and writing legal treatises. The main fabric of Roman law, as we know it today, was established upon the writings of the leading jurists from this period. During the same period, the resolutions of the senate and the decrees of the emperors came to be regarded as authoritative sources of law. On the other hand, the role of the magisterial law (*ius honorarium*) gradually declined as praetorian initiatives became increasingly rare. The final codification of the praetorian edict in AD 130 terminated the development of the *ius honorarium* as a distinct source of law.

In the post-classical period the only effective source of law was imperial legislation, largely concerned with matters of public law and economic policy. Moreover, as jurisprudence had ceased to be a living source of law, earlier juristic works were regarded as a body of settled doctrine. At the same time, custom again played a part as a secondary source of law. During this period, as the body of imperial legislation grew, there emerged the need for the codification of the law. In addition, direction was required for the use of the classical juridical literature—a vast body of legal materials spanning hundreds of years of legal development. The process of codification commenced with the publication of two private collections of imperial law, which appeared at the end of the third century AD: the *Codex Gregorianus* (AD 291) and the *Codex Hermogenianus* (AD 295). These were followed by the *Codex Theodosianus*, an official codification of imperial laws published in AD 438. The process of codification ceased in the middle of the sixth century AD with the great codification of the Roman law, both juristic law and imperial enactments, by Emperor Justinian.

## 1.2   The Archaic Period (Monarchy and Early Republic)

### 1.2.1   General Historical Background

Ancient legend and modern archaeology converge in the story of the Palatine Hill. On this hill, situated in the lower valley of the Tiber River on the central Italian plain of Latium, tradition asserts that Romulus founded the city of Rome on the 21st April of 753 BC. Archaeology confirms the settlement of a pastoral community on the Palatine Hill in the eighth century BC. At some time in the seventh century BC the Etruscans, a highly civilized people who occupied the neighbouring territory of Tuscany, crossed the Tiber River and conquered Latium. It would have been now that the villagers of the Palatine Hill joined up with other clans (*gentes*) in the area to form a larger political entity in the form of an autonomous city-state, according to the Etruscan system of political organization.[2]

The earliest Rome was an agricultural community: the mass of the population was composed of small freeholders and economic life was based on cattle-raising and the cultivation of the land. Political power was in the hands of a landowning aristocracy, the patricians, who dominated the most important political body, the senate, out of which the highest magistrates of the state were chosen. Social life revolved around the family (*familia*), the basic social unit, whose head (*paterfamilias*) had absolute authority over all persons and all property in his family group. A turning-point in the history of this period was the overthrow of the monarchy, Rome's earliest system of government, at the close of the sixth century BC and the establishment of an aristocratic republic. During the period from the sixth to the mid-third century BC Rome's social and political organization underwent a series of important changes derived from the so-called 'struggle of the orders': the internal political strife between the old aristocracy, the patricians, and the lower classes, the plebeians. By the middle of the third century BC a precarious equilibrium between the classes had been established and the Roman state came to be dominated by a new nobility composed of both patrician and wealthy plebeian families.

Rome's social and political development during the early republican age was directly related to her steady expansion throughout Italy. In 493 BC, Rome

---

[2] In early times, the clan (*gens*) was the most important element in society as it performed most of the political, religious and economic functions that were only later gradually assumed by the state. A clan was composed of households (*familiae*) that traced their lineage back to a common male ancestor (real or legendary). Although in time the central state organization supplanted the earlier clan system, the latter continued to play an important role in social and religious life for a considerable time to come.

concluded a treaty with a league of Latin cities whereby each party undertook to aid the other in the event of war. Thereafter, the Romans concentrated on quelling the power of opposing tribes to the north while gradually dominating the Latin cities. During the fourth and early third centuries, the Romans fought a series of wars against the Samnites (a tribe from the Apennine area); the Latins who rose in revolt; the Celts and the Etruscans; and finally the Greek city-states of southern Italy. By the time these wars were over in 272 BC the Romans had gained control over most of the Italian peninsula. This did not entail the formation of a single state; rather, the various Italian communities were more or less allowed to govern themselves but they were made subordinate to Rome in different ways.

## 1.2.2   The Constitutional Framework

According to Roman tradition, a succession of seven kings had governed Rome in the first two and a half centuries after the city's establishment.[3] Although knowl-edge of the political history of the regal period is scarce, its institutions must almost certainly have included a council of elders, or senate, in which the heads of the noble patrician families had a seat, and a popular assembly, where the voice of the people could make itself heard from time to time. The king (*rex*) wielded much of the same power over his subjects as that of a Roman head of family over his household, including the right to inflict capital punishment. He was also responsible for foreign relations and for war, public order, justice and the maintenance of Roman state religion. In carrying out his various duties the king would usually seek the advice of the senate, which was taken to represent the collective opinion of the patrician class. One of the matters that came before the senate was the choice of a king, for the Roman monarchy seems to have been elective rather than heredi-tary.[4] The royal power appears to have significantly expanded in the late seventh century BC with the introduction, under Etruscan influence, of the principle of *imperium* or supreme command.

The kingship came to an end in 509 BC when King Tarquinius Superbus was overthrown and replaced by two annually elected magistrates. Apparently, the fall of the Monarchy was devised by the patricians who, chafing under high-handed foreign monarchs who did not respect their prestige (*dignitas*) or their advice, led a movement that wrested control of the state from the king. The uprising was probably inspired by similar movements in neighbouring cities and precipitated by the general weakening of the Etruscan power in Italy.

---

[3] The first four of these kings (Romulus, Numa Pompilius, Tullius Hostilius and Ancus Marcius) are believed to have Latin or Sabine origins, whilst the last three (Tarquinius Priscus, Servius Tullius and Tarquinius Superbus) were Etruscans.

[4] The senate was also entrusted with the task of governing the state during the period between the death of a king and the election of another (*interregnum*) through a succession of senators acting as temporary kings (*interreges*).

Roman writers describe the end of the monarchy as one of the fundamental events of Roman history. However, the constitutional change from monarchy to republic was gradual and the political machinery of the Roman state underwent a long and complicated process of development and adjustment. Of particular importance was the gradual shift of power from the exclusive control of the patrician class towards the plebeians. This was reflected in the creation of political institutions specifically designed to safeguard plebeian interests and the opening up of offices that had traditionally been the preserve of the patricians. However, the plebeians' success in the so-called 'conflict of the orders' did not entail the eradication of socio-economic inequalities and the fundamentally aristocratic character of the Roman state did not change. What changed was the composition of the aristocracy in power: the old patrician aristocracy was replaced by a new and exclusive patricio-plebeian nobility (*nobilitas*) based on wealth and office-holding.[5]

By the middle of the third century BC, the Roman constitution comprised three major components: the magistrates (*magistratus*), the senate (*senatus*), and the assemblies of the people (*comitia*).[6]

### 1.2.2.1  The Magistrates

The magistrates represented the executive. Their functions were carefully prescribed, and their powers limited by two important constitutional principles: annuality and collegiality. Annuality meant that a magistrate held office for a year only; collegiality denoted that there were at least two magistrates of equal

---

[5] The term *res publica* (from which the word republic is derived) is usually translated as 'state' or 'commonwealth'. It should be noted that at no time was Rome a democracy in the Greek sense, i.e. a state ruled by the people. Its society was always rigidly divided by legal status and by class. Free persons were classified, for example, by reference to whether they were so by birth or by release from slavery, were independent or subject to the authority of a father or guardian, or were Roman citizens or persons holding 'imperfect citizenship' (e.g. the members of some Latin communities).

[6] The most noteworthy feature of the republican constitution at the height of its development (3rd century BC) was the balance of powers it presented. The Greek historian Polybius (*Historiae* VI. 11), drawing upon the work of Aristotle, described the Roman constitution as a mixed constitution: partly monarchic, partly oligarchic or aristocratic, and partly democratic. This, he argued, was why the Roman constitution was stable and didn't have to change on a cyclic pattern the way Aristotle had predicted constitutions should. As Polybius saw it, the monarchic element in the Roman constitution was represented by the magistrates; the oligarchic or aristocratic element was represented by the senate; and the democratic element was represented by the Roman people and their assemblies. There was an elaborate system of checks and balances between each of the three components and in the stability that this system produced Polybius saw one of the principal factors in Rome's rise to world empire. However, this approach to the Roman constitution can be misleading, for Polybius' frame of reference was mainly Greek, not Roman. Thus, at no time was Rome a democracy in the Greek sense of rule of the *demos* or 'people'. The Roman republic began, and finished, as a state largely dominated by the upper classes in society, i.e. the senators and the equestrians.

power in the same office. Furthermore, after leaving office, a magistrate could be held liable for any offences he committed while in office.

The magistrates were elected by the assemblies of the people, which also invested them with *potestas* or executive power and, in the case of higher magistrates, *imperium* or supreme command. In exercise of his *potestas* a magistrate could issue executive orders (*edicta*) and employ any coercive measures deemed necessary for the enforcement of his orders (*coercitio minor*). From the *imperium* a magistrate derived the power to assume command of an army, convene and preside over the assemblies of the people (*ius agendi cum populo*) and summon and preside over the senate (*ius agendi cum senatu*). Moreover, only a magistrate with *imperium* had the full power of *iurisdictio*, i.e. the power of prescribing the legal principles for determining legal disputes,[7] and could impose severe penalties for violations of their orders, including capital punishments (*coercitio maior*).[8]

The highest executive office of the state was held by two annually elected magistrates, the consuls (*consules*). Their functions were very broad and included the administration of the state, leadership of the army and holding supreme command in war. Moreover, they convened the senate and the assemblies of the people, presided over them as chairmen and introduced matters for senate discussion and legislative proposals for assembly voting. Before the introduction of the praetorship in 367 BC, they also governed the administration of justice in relation to both civil and criminal matters.

In 367 BC the *Leges Liciniae Sextiae* introduced the office of praetor—an office of particular importance for the development of Roman law. The praetor's function was the administration of civil law, which had hitherto belonged to the consuls. From *c.* 242 BC a second praetor was appointed to exercise civil jurisdiction in disputes between foreigners (*peregrini*) and between foreigners and Roman citizens. The new praetor (*praetor peregrinus*) was distinguished from the original official whose jurisdiction was normally restricted to disputes between Roman citizens (*iurisdictio urbana*) and was thus termed *praetor urbanus* or *praetor urbis*. In the course of time a number of additional praetors were appointed for various purposes, for example, to act as provincial governors or as chairmen of the newly established standing criminal tribunals (*quaestiones perpetuae*).

---

[7] The jurisdiction of the higher magistrates embraced the resolution of disputes between citizens (*iurisdictio inter cives*) and the confirmation of personal legal acts, such as adoptions, emancipations and such like (*iurisdictio voluntaria*). The lower magistrates (*magistratus minores*) who lacked *imperium* had only limited jurisdiction.

[8] As magistrates remained in office for a limited time only, it would have been difficult for them to carry out their duties efficiently without the help of advisers and experienced technical staff. Thus, when discharging his judicial functions, a magistrate was usually assisted by a council of experts (*consilium*). The daily routine and most of the clerical work was carried out by salaried civil servants (*apparitores*) or slaves (*servi publici, ministeria*). Moreover, a magistrate could perform some of his duties through delegates acting in his name, but could not appoint another person in his place.

From 443 BC two censors were elected for the purpose of taking the census, a function that hitherto had pertained to the consuls. Censors were elected every 5 years, but held office for 18 months, which was an exception to the annuality principle. On the occasion of the taking of the census, these officials were entitled to inquire into the private and public life of citizens and to stigmatize those whose behaviour violated generally accepted moral norms.[9] They could also promulgate general measures for repressing modes of behaviour or living (e.g. excessive luxury) they considered to be contrary to the public interest or the moral traditions of the community.

From 367 BC, two *aediles curules* were elected each year to oversee law and order and to attend to the care and upkeep of the city. Their functions included the supervision of public works, streets and buildings in Rome, the maintenance of essential food supplies and the organization of certain public games. They also controlled public markets, laid down rules governing the sale of goods therein and exercised jurisdiction with respect to market disputes and matters of public order.[10]

From the middle of the fifth century BC, quaestors were elected annually to supervise the state treasury (*aerarium*). These officials were also entrusted with the collection of public revenues derived from taxation and other sources and the financing of public works and military operations.[11]

At the beginning of the fifth century BC, the plebeians decided to elect their own officials, called tribunes (*tribuni plebis*),[12] to safeguard their interests.[13] The tribunes had the right of affording aid (*ius auxilii*) to members of the plebeian class who were the victims of oppression at the hands of patrician magistrates. In time, the tribunes were endowed with a general power of veto (*intercessio*), which they might exercise against practically any act of a state organ and so bring about a deadlock in the machinery of government.[14] When the political differences between the patrician and the plebeian classes disappeared the tribunes were regarded as magistrates for all the Roman people and by the third century BC they had become the chief proponents of legislation.

---

[9] The censor's disapproval was expressed in the form of a note added next to the culprit's name in the register (*nota censoria*). Conduct likely to incur the censors' disapprobation included, for example, maltreating one's family members or clients, neglecting one's religious duties, acting against good faith in private transactions or being engaged in a disreputable trade.

[10] The edicts of the aediles concerning market transactions played an important part in the development of the Roman law of sale.

[11] In discharging these duties the quaestors acted under the authority of the senate, which exercised general control over the administration of public finances.

[12] *Tribunus* was originally a military title probably used to describe the commander of the armed forces of a tribe (*tribus*).

[13] The original number of the tribunes is believed to have been two (as in the case of the consuls), but that number was subsequently increased to five and, around the middle of the fifth century BC, to ten.

[14] As the tribunes were regarded as being inviolable and sacrosanct (*sacrosancti*), any person who impeded or assaulted a tribune in the execution of his duties could be declared an outlaw and put to death without trial.

### 1.2.2.2 The Senate

The senate (*senatus*), the great council of the state, was the most important stabilizing factor in the republican system of government. This was largely due to its prestige and influence in society and the permanence of its constitution. Its resolutions, referred to as *senatus consulta*, although not legally binding, carried special weight in the eyes of the magistrates and the assemblies of the people. In particular, it was the constitutional practice for magistrates to seek the advice and cooperation of the senate on the formulation and implementation of laws and other important matters of the state. In addition, resolutions passed by the assemblies of the people could not acquire the full force of laws without their ratification by the senate (*patrum auctoritas*).[15] The senate had control of public finances, which placed the magistrates, whose activities entailed expenses for the state, in a position of dependence. It also exercised control over foreign policy: it received envoys of other states, conducted negotiations with foreign powers, appointed ambassadors (*legati*) out of its own ranks, concluded treaties and alliances and intervened in disputes between cities in alliance with Rome.[16] Finally, it fell upon the senate to ensure that acts of state organs were carried out in accordance with the prescribed religious forms. In times of crisis the senate could declare a state of emergency, passing a special resolution (*senatus sonsultum ultimum*) by virtue of which the consuls were authorized to apply any extraordinary measures deemed necessary to avert the danger.

At the beginning of the republican period the senate was composed of 300 members, chosen exclusively from the patrician class.[17] Leading plebeians began to be admitted to the senate after the passing of the *leges Liciniae Sextiae* in 367 BC. From that time the senators were drawn from among those who had occupied the highest offices of the state (notably, former consuls and praetors)[18] and held their office for life. Although there is no evidence that during the Republic admission to the senate depended upon the possession of certain amount of property, there is no doubt that the senatorial class (*ordo senatorius*) as a whole represented the wealthiest element of society.

---

[15] The *lex Publilia Philonis* of 339 BC provided that the approval of the senate had to be given in advance (i.e. before a proposal was put to the vote of the people). Under the *lex Maenia* (early third century BC) candidates for the highest offices of the state had to be approved by the senate before they were formally elected by the assembly.

[16] With the senate appears to have rested the ultimate responsibility of declaring war and concluding peace, although in principle this power belonged to the people.

[17] The senators were selected first by the consuls and, from 443 BC, by the censors (*censores*). The latter were entrusted with the task of drawing up the senators' list (*album senatorium*), filling up vacancies caused by the death or the expulsion of senators.

[18] According to the *lex Ovinia de senatus lectione*, enacted in the late fourth century BC.

### 1.2.2.3   The Assemblies of the People

Legislative power vested in the assemblies of the people, whose principal functions were the enactment of statutes and the election of magistrates. All male Roman citizens with the right to vote (*ius suffragii*) had a seat in these assemblies. The assemblies met when convened by the appropriate magistrate, who would place a proposal before them. This proposal could then be approved or rejected and this was done on a block vote system, not by the method of one man, one vote. The voting took place either by *curia*, a unit going back to very early times, or by *centuria* (century) or by *tribus* (tribe) or, in later times, by geographical unit.

Depending on whether voting was done by *curia*, *centuria* or *tribus*, there were three types of assembly: the *comitia curiata*, the *comitia centuriata* and the *comitia tributa*. Alongside these assemblies was the *concilium plebis*, which was reserved for the plebeians.

The earliest popular assembly in Rome was the curiate assembly (*comitia curiata*), based on the division of the Roman people into 30 *curiae*, or brotherhoods of men.[19] The principal function of this assembly during the Republic was to vote on the *lex de imperio*, the special law whereby the *imperium* was vested to the higher magistrates. Furthermore, twice a year it was convened to witness and confirm certain ceremonial acts of private law, such as the making of wills and *adrogatio* (the adoption of a person not subject to paternal control).[20]

The *comitia centuriata*, the greatest of all Roman assemblies, consisted of the citizens organized on a timocratic basis into classes and centuries (*centuriae*).[21] Of the political functions of this assembly the most important was the election of the higher magistrates of the state (the consuls, praetors and censors). Within its province fell also the enactment of legislation.[22] Originally, it seems, legislative measures were regularly brought before it, but eventually this assembly, presumably because of its cumbrous nature, was seldom convened for legislative purposes—after the enactment of the *lex Hortensia* (287 BC), practically all legislative measures were brought before the *concilium plebis*. The *comitia centuriata* operated also as a court of justice hearing appeals against sentences involving death and other severe punishments imposed by magistrates.

---

[19] The *curiae* originated from the prehistoric organization of the Italian tribes into groups of clans, probably bound together by blood ties and united for common defence. Besides kinship, territorial proximity between different clans must also have played a part in the formation of these groups.

[20] When it was summoned to perform these functions the curiate assembly was referred to as *comitia calata*.

[21] This assembly originally consisted of the citizens in military array. As time went on, however, its military basis was deprived of all reality and the century became merely a voting group that might be of any size, the literal significance thereof, as a body of a hundred men, being entirely lost.

[22] Legislative proposals were submitted to the assembly by the consuls or the praetors by whom it was convened. Depending on the magistrate by whom they had been proposed, laws (*leges*) were referred to as *leges consulares* or *leges praetoriae*.

The *comitia tributa* was the assembly of the citizens organized into groups according to their place of residence. This assembly possessed the important political function of electing the lower magistrates of the state, such as the aediles and the quaestors. Another task of this assembly was voting on laws proposed by higher magistrates, although generally these laws were less politically important than those enacted by the centuriate assembly. However, the relatively uncomplicated proceedings in the tribal assembly often inspired the senate, in emergencies or for expediency, to request magistrates to submit bills to this assembly rather than the *comitia centuriata*.

The *concilium plebis* was the assembly of the plebeians alone, and the voting unit therein was the tribe.[23] This assembly passed resolutions (*plebiscita*), which originally had no binding effect outside the plebeian class. After the plebeians' success in the struggle of the orders, the *plebiscita* were recognized (by the *lex Hortensia de plebiscitis* of 287 BC) as having the full force of laws binding on both patricians and plebeians alike. Besides its legislative functions, the *concilium plebis* acted as a court of justice to hear cases involving violations of the plebeians' rights.[24] From the time of the *lex Hortensia* onwards, this assembly, sitting under the presidency of a *tribunus plebis*, was by far the most active legislative organ of the state, and the great majority of the laws of which we have record were, strictly speaking, *plebiscita*.[25]

## 1.3   The Pre-classical Period (Late Republic)

### 1.3.1   General Historical Background

The late republican period witnessed Rome's ascendancy as the dominant power in the Mediterranean world. By the middle of the third century BC the Romans had conquered most of the Italian peninsula and, by the end of the first century BC, they held sway over the entire Mediterranean basin.[26] It was during this period that the

---

[23] The assembly of the plebeians (*concilum plebis*) was created in 471 BC, following the recognition by the Roman senate of the plebeians' right to hold meetings to elect their leaders (the *tribuni plebis*) and discuss matters concerning their class.

[24] The jurisdiction of the plebeian assembly also captured appeals against decisions of the tribunes imposing fines and other minor penalties.

[25] Although the formal distinction between the *concilum plebis* and the *comitia tributa* was retained until the close of the Republic, the differences between the two bodies, regarding their composition and the laws they enacted, gradually faded away. This mainly emanated from the elimination of the political division between the patricians and the plebeians and the rapid increase of the plebeian population.

[26] The third century BC is marked by Rome's two great wars for control of the Western Mediterranean against Carthage, an old Phoenician colony in North Africa and a great maritime power. Despite the initial successes of her armies, Carthage was finally overwhelmed by the

Romans came into direct contact with the Greek world and were fully exposed to the influence of the Greek and Hellenistic culture. The massive influx of Greek ideas and practices had a profound impact on every aspect of Roman life, including education, religion, art and science. As the demand for instruction in Greek language, rhetoric and philosophy increased, schools began to be established under the patronage of prominent men.[27] Furthermore, Rome's expansion was accompanied by profound changes in economic life. In the course of the second century BC the city of Rome emerged as an important commercial centre and private businesses of all kinds were set up that provided services and manufactured goods.[28] Rome's increasingly sophisticated economic life required enterprising men to direct her trade, undertake the construction of public works, manage war contracts and collect taxes. This entailed the emergence of an important new class of merchants and entrepreneurs, which were known as the equestrian class (*ordo equester*).[29]

However, Rome's dramatic expansion also brought about severe problems and upheavals in the Roman state. The central problem was to devise a suitable government for the territories conquered. The republican system of government, originally designed for a small city-state, was inadequate to meet the organizational and administrative requirements of the vast empire that evolved. This central issue was accompanied by acute economic, social and political problems at home, as Roman society was transformed from a relatively small, closely-knit and

---

Romans and was reduced to the position of a client-state of Rome. In 188 BC, after a four-year war, the Romans broke the power of Antioch III, King of Syria and Asia Minor, and extended their control over the Eastern Mediterranean. In 148 BC, following a protracted struggle, Macedonia was defeated and turned into a Roman province. With the dissolution of the Achaean confederacy and the sacking of Corinth in 146 BC, the whole of Greece fell under Roman domination. The same year marks the end of the Third Carthaginian or Punic War (149–146 BC), which resulted in the complete destruction of Carthage and the annexation of her territory as part of the Roman province of Africa. In 88 BC Rome embarked on a series of wars in the East against King Mithridates of Pontus, who had declared himself liberator of the Greeks and launched a campaign aimed at expelling the Romans from Asia Minor and Greece. After Mithridates' defeat in 63 BC, Rome regained control of Greece and a continuous belt of Roman provinces was created along the coasts of the Black and Mediterranean Seas from Northern Asia Minor to Syria and Judaea. This phase of Roman expansion ceased with the conquest of Gaul by Julius Caesar (58–53 BC) and the annexation of Egypt by Octavian in 30 BC.

[27] Greek philosophical thinking, especially Stoic philosophy, attracted many followers among the members of Rome's upper classes. The success of Stoicism was to a large extent due to the fact that it reflected best the cosmopolitan ideals of the times. In particular, the Stoic ideal of a world state based on the brotherhood of men exercised a strong influence on Roman thought and furnished one of the foundations on which the political philosophy of the empire was built.

[28] The increase in economic activity during this period is manifested by the development and widespread use of currency and the establishment of financial institutions in Rome and other cities in Italy and overseas.

[29] An active and visible minority within the equestrian class acquired their wealth by entering into contracts with the Roman state for the collection of public revenues. These contractors, referred to as *publicani*, assumed the risk and expense for exploiting the state's assets and paid an annual fixed sum to the Roman state treasury. The wealth and influence of this class of businessmen grew rapidly as Rome's territory and revenues expanded.

homogenous grouping into a complex stratified society with diverse and often competing interests. At the same time, the influx of Greek models had an erosive effect on the long-established moral and ethical norms on which the unity of Roman society hinged. As the ideological underpinnings of the Roman state began to crumble with the weakening of the old value system, the governing senatorial nobility found it increasingly difficult to achieve satisfactory solutions to the problems generated by Rome's expansion. The oncoming crisis manifested itself in the intensification and widening of factional political strife within the ruling class. This, combined with growing social unrest, gave to ambitious political and military leaders an opportunity to attain power by gaining the support of discontented social groups demanding various kinds of reform. The problems and tensions in the Roman state found expression in a series of civil wars and rebellions, which became the norm by the first century BC. Out of this strife there emerged, in 31 BC, Octavian, who became the sole master of the Roman world. In the period that followed, the senate and the assemblies legitimised his *de facto* control of the state by bestowing upon him a range of powers that placed him in a unique position. Armed with these powers, Octavian, who assumed the honorary title Augustus Caesar, ushered in a new form of government known as the Principate.

## 1.3.2   The Constitutional Framework

During the period under examination the Romans tenaciously clung to the constitution and accompanying traditions they had established in the early republican age. The senate retained its central role in political life and, in the course of the second century BC, evolved from a mere advisory body to the magistrates into an executive body with a wide range of customary powers over foreign policy, public finance, legislation and the administration of justice. The magistrates and the people showed themselves ready to follow its lead and, although only the assemblies had the constitutional right to enact legislation, senatorial resolutions (*senatus consulta*) were regarded, for all practical purposes, as having the force of laws. Political contest took place mainly within the senate, where a number of rival groups of allied families were striving to increase their political influence.

However, by the close of the second century BC the unavoidable fact emerged that the Roman constitution, devised in the days when Rome was a small agricultural community, could not achieve the centralized and cohesive control required to govern a world empire. It became impossible for the entire citizen body to assemble to debate and vote on the passing of laws and the election of magistrates. The senate had by this time lost much of its former vigour and, with its authority and prestige undermined by the corroding influences of wealth and luxury, increasingly failed to fulfil the role assigned to it. This failure aggravated political instability and enabled powerful and unscrupulous men to gain control of the state by manipulating the magisterial offices and the assemblies of the people. Thus, although the outward forms of the republican constitution were retained, the republican system of government was inexorably undermined by forces alien to the traditional framework.

The erosion of the traditional constitutional structure was accompanied by an increasingly violent internal strife, both between rival factions and individuals within the ruling class, and between the aristocracy and various disadvantaged groups. During the revolutionary period of the first century BC, these circumstances degenerated into an almost permanent state of civil war, which prompted the disintegration and eventual collapse of the republican system of government.

## 1.4 The Classical Period (Early Empire or Principate)

### 1.4.1 General Historical Background

When Octavian gained control of the state in 31 BC, the Roman world was still in a state of confusion. The main demand of the age was the return to the stability that only a properly functioning system of government could provide. But the whole administration of the state was so inextricably bound up with the republican constitution that political stability was virtually impossible without upholding the republican traditions. Based on this realistic appraisal of the situation, Octavian–Augustus, through a series of masterful manipulations, established a constitution that artificially preserved the republican institutions but in fact created a new monarchical power and a new system of government for the provinces. This constitution, referred to as the Principate, made possible for more than 200 years the peaceful development of the Roman empire and its civilization. The work of Augustus was continued and developed further by his successors: the Julio-Claudians (Tiberius AD 14–37, Caligula AD 37–41, Claudius AD 41–54 and Nero AD 54–68); the Flavians (Vespasian AD 69–79, Titus AD 79–81 and Domitian AD 81–96); and the Antonines (Nerva AD 96–98, Trajan AD 98–117, Hadrian AD 117–138, Antoninus Pius AD 138–161, and Marcus Aurelius AD 161–180).

For nearly a century and a half after the establishment of the Principate the Roman empire continued to expand territorially until it included all the countries within the natural boundaries outlined by Augustus: Thrace, the Rhine regions, Britain, Armenia and Mauretania. During the same period the Roman world enjoyed an unprecedented degree of peace and the Greco-Roman civilization continued to spread throughout the provinces. The conditions of peace and security that prevailed promoted economic development and produced high levels of prosperity throughout the empire. This prosperity was to a large extent based on an enormous increase in industry and commerce that was precipitated by the expansion of the Roman road network, the security of transport and the establishment of a currency system for the whole empire.[30] The cultural and economic basis of the

---

[30] In the second century AD, regular commercial contacts were established with lands as distant as India, China, Arabia, central and southern Africa, and the Scandinavian regions. Of far more importance was the trade conducted within the empire itself, between different provinces and cities.

empire was a vast network of city-states spread throughout the provinces. These enjoyed a large measure of autonomy, and all had a share in the same civilization and favourable economic conditions.[31] Moreover, from the early years of the Principate age Roman citizenship began to spread in the provinces. From the time of Emperor Claudius on, provincial aristocrats were admitted as members of the senate, and by the reign of Hadrian they filled nearly half of this body. By the second century AD, the provincials shared in all the privileges of Rome and even the office of emperor itself was opened to persons of Roman descent whose families lived in the provinces. The process of Romanization of the empire was completed in AD 212, when Emperor Caracalla issued an edict, the *constitutio Antoniniana*, by which he bestowed Roman citizenship on all the free inhabitants of the empire who were members of organized communities. Caracalla's edict was a milestone in the history of the Roman Empire: it signified the triumph of the idea of a supra-national world empire over the old idea of the city-state and led to the gradual leveling of the inhabitants of the empire with respect to their legal and political rights. The republican traditions, which Augustus had artificially preserved and which in the course of time had become an empty shell, were ripe for collapse.

In the later half of the second century AD, several forces began to gather to complete the transformation of the empire from its previous structure under Augustus. The most important among these forces originated from the conditions present in the socio-political milieu of the times: the increasing reliance of the emperors on the army as a means of maintaining control of the state; the creation of a vast administrative apparatus that, in the long run, could not be supported by the resources of the empire; the perpetuation of a class structure that failed to give the producing classes rewards equal to the burdens imposed on them; and the sharp decline of public spirit in a state where servility to imperial authority had replaced active participation in public affairs. With the final abandonment of the principle of diarchy (the double rule of the emperor and the senate) during the reign of Emperor Septimius Severus (AD 193–211) and the further militarization of the administration, the army discarded its position as the empire's servant and became its master. From AD 235, the collapse of the central government authority entailed disorder and civil war as different field armies proclaimed their generals as emperors and used their own strength to plunder the lands of the empire. The continuous military mutinies and struggles between different pretenders to the throne weakened the state's defences at a time when new external enemies increasingly threatened its frontiers. In the wake of the devastation caused by war and plunder, the civilian populations and the economies were severely damaged; law and order disintegrated; commerce and industry came to a standstill; and once flourishing urban centres fell into decay. In the closing years of the third century, the crisis was

---

[31] An outstanding social by-product of the empire's prosperity was the emergence of a numerically small but significant middle class in the provincial cities and towns, which was composed largely of landowners, merchants, bankers, and private contractors. This class furnished the members of the municipal councils (*decuriones*) who, after their election, became citizens of Rome.

finally checked under a succession of capable emperors but only at the cost of establishing a despotic government and a rigidly regulated society.

## 1.4.2   The Constitutional Framework

As previously noted, in the new system of government inaugurated by Augustus there was no sharp break with the past. The powers he was invested with were conferred upon him in forms compatible with republican precedents, and the Republic itself still functioned. The assemblies and senate still met, the regular magistrates were elected each year, and the senate continued, as in the past, to be recruited from ex-magistrates. Augustus was successful because he was able to establish a stable regime, a disguised kind of monarchy cleverly hidden behind a constitutional, republican façade. But the new political system was heavily encumbered by its contradictions between façade and reality. However successful Augustus' programme proved to be, neither he nor his successors resolved the contradictions inherent in the elective theory supporting the new regime and its dynastic practice. In the course of time, the absolutism inherent in the imperial system became progressively more pronounced and, inevitably, the relics of the republican state (senatorial independence of action and the sovereignty of a people legislating and electing magistrates in popular assembly) withered away.

### 1.4.2.1   The Republican Elements in the Augustan Constitution

The Popular Assemblies

During the early years of the Principate age, the assemblies of the people continued to function as legislative and elective bodies. However, from the beginning of the new order, the political role of the assemblies was destined to wither away yielding to the necessities of a society transformed from a city-state into an empire in which leadership had shifted from short-term magistracies to the supremacy of a single ruler. Thus, as early as the time of Tiberius, the election of magistrates was transferred to the senate and by the end of the first century AD, popular legislation was superseded by the decrees of the emperor and the resolutions of the senate.[32] As a result, the assemblies lost their significance as independent political bodies, although they continued in existence in an honorary or ceremonial capacity until the end of the third century AD.

---

[32] The last law passed by the *comitia* was a *lex agraria* enacted under Emperor Nerva (96–98 AD). This law is mentioned in the Digest of Justinian in an extract of the jurist Callistratus (D. 47. 21. 3. 1.).

## The Senate

In contrast with the people's assemblies, the senate received a considerable accession of dignity, as well as electoral and legislative powers. Officially, the senate had become a full partner in the government. Theoretically, it was even more: the ultimate source of the emperor's power, as his *imperium* and legitimacy on accession was derived from the senate's approval of his nomination. In reality, however, the senate was much under the control of the emperor, who regulated its composition, dominated its proceedings and prescribed its tasks. Elections of magistrates always corresponded with the wishes of the emperor; legislative proposals brought before the senate by the emperor or his representatives were accepted without much debate[33]; the conduct of foreign policy was in the hands of the emperor, who also controlled all the politically important provinces; and the management of public finances was gradually assumed by the emperor following the establishment of the imperial treasury (*fiscus*). Thus, in the end, the division of government between the emperor and the senate (diarchy) was more apparent than real; although the emperors owed all their powers to the senate, once these powers were given the senate became virtually impotent and unable to retract them, even if it had desired to do so.

## The Magistrates

After the establishment of the Principate, the old republican magistracies continued to exist and their apparent importance was shown by the fact that the emperors forged their power by relying on the most important of these, such as the consulship and the tribunate. In fact, however, the authority of the magistrates was now considerably limited. The consuls no longer directed the political life of the state, nor did they hold military command as these functions were transferred to the emperor. Nevertheless, the consulship remained until the closing years of the Empire an important status symbol and a gateway to the highest offices in the imperial administration.[34] The praetors retained the civil and criminal jurisdiction they had held during the Republic.[35] However, their role in the administration of

---

[33] In the first century AD the procedure leading to the enactment of a *senatus consultum* was initiated by the emperor himself, or a magistrate acting in his name, through a speech containing the emperor's legislative proposal (*oratio principis in senatu*). From the second century AD the emperor's proposals were approved by the senate as a matter of course and, in most cases, without discussion.

[34] Whereas during the Republic the office of consul was normally held by two persons in the course of one year, it now became common practice to appoint several pairs of consuls during one year, and this number varied according to the number of persons on whom the emperor wished to bestow the title.

[35] During the Principate the number of praetors was increased, initially to twelve and later to eighteen. Of these the *praetor urbanus* and the *praetor peregrinus* had general jurisdiction, whilst

justice gradually decreased in importance following the expansion of the emperor's judicial functions, and the establishment of new civil and criminal courts under the jurisdiction of imperial officials.[36] The tribunes continued to exist down to the fourth century AD, but their authority was considerably diminished by the decline of the popular assemblies and their complete dependence on the will of the emperor.

### 1.4.2.2    The Emperor and Imperial Administration

Under the Augustan constitution, the powers of the emperor were those exercised by the higher magistrates of the Republic, now combined and concentrated in one person. In the course of time these powers were gradually extended, although their legal basis remained largely unchanged. A great deal of the emperor's authority emanated from his *tribunicia potestas*, the power the tribunes had held under the republican constitution. This enabled him to veto acts of the magistrates and other state organs (*intercessio*); it allowed him to call together and submit proposals to the senate and the assemblies of the people; it afforded his person inviolability (*sacrosanctitas*), so that any indignity offered to him could be treated as a criminal offence; and it allowed him to present himself as the protector of the common man's interests. The *imperium proconsulare*, the overriding authority of a proconsul, gave the emperor supremacy over the key frontier provinces and secured his position as commander-in-chief of the army. Yet it should also be noted that much of the emperor's authority derived from sources quite beyond the traditional republican institutions. Thus, the emperor was seen as enjoying *auctoritas*: supreme political prestige, moral authority and social influence.[37] In 27 BC the senate granted Octavian the title *Augustus*, signifying grandeur and majesty, but also meaning holy or worshipful. Despite of all his powers and titles, Octavian refrained from assuming the position of king, professing to be no more that a *princeps*, a term simply meaning 'the first citizen of the state'.[38] He boasted that he had not taken a single magistracy in conflict with ancestral custom and that the official powers he possessed were not greater than those of his colleagues in the office concerned. The

---

the jurisdiction of the rest was limited to certain matters only. Thus, in the Augustan era the management of the public treasury (*aerarium*) was entrusted to two praetors, referred to as *praetores aerarii*; from the time of Claudius a special praetor was appointed to deal with cases concerning trust estates (*praetor de fideicommissis*); under Nerva a special praetor was entrusted with the resolution of disputes that arose between private individuals and the imperial exchequer (*praetor fiscalis*); and in the time of the Antonine emperors the appointment of guardians and the resolution of disputes which arose between guardians were consigned to a special praetor known as *praetor tutelarius*.

[36] The office of *praetor peregrinus* disappeared after the Roman citizenship was granted to all the free inhabitants of the empire in the early third century AD.

[37] Subsequent emperors regarded their *auctoritas* as the ultimate source of their acts in the legislative, judicial and administrative fields (*ex auctoritate nostra*).

[38] From the word *princeps* arose the term 'principate', by which the new system of government became known.

truth, however, is that as the powers of the *princeps* were not subject to the limitations traditionally imposed on magisterial authority, initiative passed from the senatorial oligarchy to one man and the whole system functioned under the autocratic control of an emperor.

As the true master of the state, the emperor marshalled a huge administrative machine: a vast civil service composed of trained, paid and permanent officials. These new officials gradually assumed those duties the emperor deemed impossible or undesirable for the old republican magistrates to perform. The imperial officials differed from the magistrates of the Republic in some important respects: they were chosen by the emperor himself, without the approval of the senate or the popular assemblies, and reported directly to him; they were appointed for an indefinite period, although the emperor could dismiss them at any time at his pleasure; and they were not invested with *imperium* or *potestas*—their only powers were those delegated by the emperor who could approve, reverse or modify their decisions as he thought fit. The most important imperial officials were the praetorian prefect (*praefectus praetorio*) and the city prefect (*praefectus urbi*). The former was originally the commander of the special military units that served as the emperor's personal bodyguard (the praetorian guard). The office evolved into one of the most powerful in the state, and the praetorian prefect became the emperor's chief adviser and executive officer in military and civil matters. From the late second century onwards, he also assumed important judicial functions. The city prefect was responsible for maintaining public order in Rome with the Roman police (the urban cohorts) at his disposal. He had extensive jurisdictional powers as he headed the chief criminal court in Rome and the surrounding area, and also dealt with civil matters connected with his criminal jurisdiction. Other important officials of this period were the prefect of the grain supply (*praefectus annonae*),[39] and the prefect of the watch (*praefectus vigilum*).[40] Another category of officials with a varying extent of power embraced the procurators (*procuratores*). Acting as agents of the emperor, procurators carried out a number of tasks within the civil administration, such as the collection of taxes, the management of state revenues and the supervision of public buildings and factories. When dealing with important administrative and legal matters the emperors consulted a body of advisors (*consilium principis*) composed of trusted friends, senior state officials and experts. By the middle of the third century AD, this body had assumed most of the functions and duties of the Roman senate. The administrative apparatus of imperial Rome included also a complex network of offices (*scrinia*): these were manned initially by slaves and freedmen, and then by members of the equestrian class in later eras (from the second century AD). The *scrinium a rationibus* dealt with matters relating to public finance; the *scrinium a libellis* responded to petitions from private citizens; the

---

[39] The *praefectus annonae* had general jurisdiction in matters connected with the supply and trade of foodstuffs.

[40] This official was the head of Rome's fire brigades (*cohortes vigilum*) and his duties included policing the city by night and dealing with fires and any other natural emergencies that might arise.

*scrinium ab epistulis* handled the emperor's official correspondence; the *scrinium a cognitionibus* investigated judicial disputes referred to the emperor; and the *scrinium a memoria* performed the secretarial work on all decisions, letters, appointments and orders issued by the emperor. State revenues derived from taxation and other sources were deposited in the central state treasury (*fiscus*) managed by the *procuratores a rationibus* or *fisci*.[41]

Probably the weakest point of the constitutional regime of the Principate was that it did not provide for an orderly system of succession to the imperial throne. This weakness stemmed from the contradiction between the emperor's constitutional position as a Roman magistrate whose tenure derived from the senate and the people, and his *de facto* status as a monarch whose maintenance of power ultimately depended on army support. Aware that he could not legally nominate a successor, Augustus (and then the Antonines) adopted the most apparently effective means of ensuring the peaceful succession to imperial power: the designation of a successor by the incumbent emperor, the adoption of the individual designated as the emperor's son, and then the training of the successor for his future duties (by sharing in the government of the state). The system of adoptive emperorship broke down in the late second century AD, and thereafter emperors were made and unmade at the will of different field armies that each backed its own general to power.

## 1.5   The Post-classical Period (Late Empire or Dominate)

### 1.5.1   General Historical Background

The assassination of Emperor Alexander Severus in AD 235 marks the beginning of a long period of crisis during which the Roman Empire came close to disintegration. But in the later part of the third century a succession of capable emperors[42] began the work of restoring the crumbling empire. The work of these so called 'soldier emperors' paved the way for the systematic changes of structure that took place during the reigns of Diocletian and Constantine the Great in the late third and early fourth centuries AD. Diocletian (AD 285–305) succeeded in re-establishing peace and regular government within the realm, and in strengthening the imperial frontiers against foreign foes. Constantine completed the work of Diocletian, infusing the empire's organization with the basic characteristics it retained until the fall of

---

[41] In the course of time the *fiscus* assumed a special legal personality and, from the late second century AD, it began to be represented in the courts when disputes arose between the *fiscus* and private individuals concerning debts. Distinct from the *fiscus* was the personal property of the emperor, referred to as *patrimonium Caesaris*, which was administered by officials known as *procuratores patrimonii*.

[42] Claudius Gothicus AD 268–270, Aurelian AD 270–275, Probus AD 276–282.

the Empire in the West and its transition to the Byzantine Empire in the East. Constantine's reign is marked by two dramatic new developments: the rise of Christianity as the dominant religion of the empire and the establishment of a new imperial capital, Constantinople, in the East (AD 330).[43] The reforms of Diocletian and Constantine marked a significant stage in the abandonment of the outward forms and guiding spirit of the Augustan system of government. As the autocratic tendencies that had strengthened over the previous years prevailed, the republican façade of the Principate was replaced by an unconcealed and unlimited monarchy supported by a complex and ever-growing bureaucratic apparatus. During the same period, the predominance of Rome and Italy in the empire faded and the eastern, Greek-speaking provinces came to be seen as a separate, and possibly as the predominant part of the empire. The transformation of the Roman state and society that transpired under Diocletian and Constantine inaugurated the last phase of Roman history, known as the 'Dominate' (*dominatus*), and in many respects it ushered in the medieval world as well.

The development of the imperial society during the Dominate age was a direct continuation of the process of change that had began as early as the late second century AD. Clear indications of the altered structure and direction of the late Roman society embrace: the polarization between the impoverished masses and the concentrated wealth and power of privileged dignitaries; the power consolidation of the senatorial land barons and the growing inability of the central government to control them; the institutionalization of rigidly defined and closely regulated hereditary castes, each with a definite rank in society; and the rapid decay of the cities' governing classes (*decuriones, curiales*) owing to the incessant and excessive demands imposed upon them by the government. The transformation of the Roman state into a machinery of power supported by relatively small groups and the consequent absolutization of state demands provoked the refusal of large sections of the population to identify themselves with the state. Thus, the rule of the emperor and his machinery of power, exalted to unprecedented heights by an artificial enhancement of the system's brilliant façade of display, finally became an end in itself: a pure burden that only oppressed society with its coercive measures and impositions. With mounting indifference to the state's fate and few individuals prepared to sustain the regime, the forces of dissolution acquired momentum and the demise of the empire appeared unavoidable.

After a breathing spell in the first half of the fourth century, the difficulties of the empire began to mount. In particular, the external pressures on the imperial frontiers increased. Finally, after several years of intense fighting against the Germanic tribes in the North, the Rhine–Danube frontier gave way: in AD 378, the Visigoths and Ostrogoths crossed the Danube River, and simultaneously the Franks, Vandals and Burgundians poured across the Rhine River into Gaul and the western provinces. These invasions exacerbated problems within the empire

---

[43] Constantine's decision to establish a new capital city testifies to the fact that the empire's political and economic centre of gravity had shifted inexorably to the East.

itself, in particular those deriving from the continued failure to establish a firm system of succession to the imperial throne; the shortage of manpower as citizens and officials fled from the tasks imposed upon them; the heavy burden of taxation imposed to set up and maintain new armies for the conduct of war; and the overall demoralisation of the Roman society. In the face of these problems, the division of the empire into western and eastern halves was seen as a necessary remedy. Although imperial unity was in theory preserved, in reality the empire was split into two independent states and from the late fourth century this division became permanent.

The fifth century witnessed the complete disintegration of the Roman Empire in the West, in the face of continuous barbarian invasions and the permanent, large-scale settlement of Germanic tribes in its territories. During the same period, the political power of the central government faded as the western emperors depended entirely on the support of Germanic war bands and warlords who, as 'king-makers', actually ruled the state. Western Roman emperors continued to rule in name until AD 476, when Emperor Romulus Augustulus was overthrown by the Germanic troops which had placed him on the throne.[44] By the close of the fifth century, the western provinces of the empire were in the hands of various Germanic tribes: the Ostrogoths controlled Italy; the Visigoths ruled Spain and south-western Gaul; the Burgundians were settled in the Rhine River area; the Franks established themselves in northern Gaul; the Angles and Saxons were settled in England; and the Vandals had established their own kingdom in northern Africa. The effect of this was that the civilization and forms of social and economic life characteristic to the ancient Greco-Roman world gradually faded away. The public institutions of the Roman Empire in the West gave way to the more primitive personal loyalty of the barbarians to their tribal chiefs and political conditions shifted towards the decentralized localism associated with the feudal system; once flourishing urban centres were destroyed or abandoned, giving way to forms of habitation constructed around fortified manors and small village communities; and trade and industry declined as economic life reverted to an agricultural and pastoral type geared to maintaining local self-sufficiency.

While the Empire in the West succumbed to the control of Germanic warlords, the Eastern Empire survived the crisis with its institutions and frontiers largely intact. The emperors at Constantinople successfully guarded their territory in Asia Minor against the restored power of Persia and resisted the infiltration of the Germanic tribes and the decentralizing influence of the great landlords and gener-alissimos. The Empire in the East survived as its socio-economic circumstances were more favourable. In fact, the Eastern Empire underwent a considerable economic revival; a certain amount of flexibility returned to its society; urban life remained strong; and, particularly during the reign of Emperor Theodosius II (AD 408–450), it experienced a remarkable cultural rebirth. From this base, the gifted ruler Justinian worked for the restoration of the empire to its former greatness.

---

[44] This date is traditionally regarded as marking the end of the Roman Empire in the West.

## 1.5.2   The Constitutional Framework

The Roman Empire in the third century had been dogged by two interconnected problems: the weakness of the imperial authority and the inadequacy of the empire's administrative structure. Politically, the emperor was in the hands of the army, which had become the real master of the state. Administratively, the government was incapable of ruling the empire efficiently and of defending its frontiers against external enemies. The character of the new order created by Diocletian is reflected in the solutions he devised for these problems: the transformation of the imperial power into an absolute monarchy; the institution of the system of co-regency or 'tetrarchy'; and the reorganisation and transformation of the empire's administrative machine into a rigid bureaucratic system.

Diocletian sought to bolster his authority by imbuing the imperial ideology with a new form and content. The emperor was elevated to the position of an absolute monarch and invested with the dignity and grandeur of the oriental god-kings.[45] Secluded in his palace and set apart by a framework of complicated ceremonial and court etiquette, he demanded divine veneration from his courtiers, officials and community.[46] His powers were now unashamedly unlimited and were seen to pervade every sphere of government, administrative, military, legislative and judicial. He appointed and dismissed the public officials, who were now regarded as servants of the throne rather than as servants of the state as an abstract entity; directed foreign policy; exercised control over Church matters; and regulated economic policy. He was also the sole author of laws and their final interpreter. His unchallengeable legislative supremacy conformed to the nature of an absolute monarchy whose omnipotence precluded constitutional or any other limitations on the emperor's law-making power.[47] The emperor was also the supreme judge and all other judges were deemed his representatives.

Diocletinan's answer to the empire's administrative problem was the introduction of the system of the 'tetrarchy'. Recognising that the empire could not be governed efficiently by a single ruler, or from a single administrative centre, he devised a system whereby imperial rule was divided whilst, at the same time, the principle of imperial unity remained unaffected. In AD 285 he appointed Maximian, one of his ablest generals, as Caesar and co-ruler. In AD 286 Maximian was promoted to Augustus and was made ruler of the West, while Diocletian himself took over the rule of the East. In AD 293 each Augustus appointed as his assistant

---

[45] He was referred to as *dominus* (lord), and so this era has become known as the Dominate.

[46] In later years, the recognition of Christianity as the state religion compelled an adaptation of the imperial cult to the demands of a stringent monotheism. The emperor was installed by the grace of God and his empire existed as a reflection of the heavenly kingdom; both were deemed divinely inspired and protected, and everything remotely connected with the imperial personage partook of imperial sanctity.

[47] The emperor was held to exist above the laws, in the sense that he could not be held responsible for his legislative and administrative acts; however, he was bound to respect the laws and abide by his own edicts as his authority rested on obedience to them.

and successor a Caesar and the four ruled jointly, each having control over one quarter of the empire. From Nicomedia, his capital city, Diocletian ruled over Asia, Egypt and Thrace, while his Caesar, Galerius, governed the Balkan peninsula. Maximian, whose seat of government was at Mediolanum (Milan), had control over Italy, Africa and Spain, while his Caesar, Constantius Chlorus, ruled over Britain and Gaul.[48] This proliferation of the imperial summit was designed not only to facilitate the administration of the empire but also to discourage attempts at usurpation by establishing a stable succession mechanism.

As the imperial government assumed the characteristics of an Eastern despotism, the remaining republican institutions became mere shadows of their former selves or were entirely abandoned. The assemblies of the people had long disappeared. Some of the old republican magistracies continued to exist, but they were divested of all their former powers. The consulship was still regarded as a high honour and was frequently held by the emperor himself. However, it was now a purely honorary office without political importance. The praetors and quaestors also continued to exist but only in an honorary capacity. The senate was retained and, in fact, a second senate was established in Constantinople (c. AD 340). This body retained a certain prestige and dignity, and its members formed the highest rank of imperial subjects from which the heads of the imperial civil service and army were chosen. However, the actual administration of Rome and Constantinople was in the hands of the urban prefects and their subordinates, and the only political role the senate played was in the inauguration of a new emperor.

When carrying out the various responsibilities of his office, the emperor relied upon a machinery of official and non-official confidants who proffered him advice and assisted him in the formulation of policy decisions. He also depended upon an apparatus of execution that translated his decisions into the realities of the political process. Among the most important civil functionaries of this period was the *magister officiorum* (master of the offices): he was chief of the imperial secretariats (*scrinia*), supervised the division of the various imperial offices and regulated imperial audiences. Another key official was the *quaestor sacri palatii* (magistrate of the sacred palace) who was the emperor's Minister of Justice. This official prepared the drafts of laws and answers to petitions, and presided over the imperial Council of State when the latter met in the absence of the emperor. The Council of State (*sacrum consistorium*) consisted of the highest officials of the imperial civil service that acted as the emperor's advisory council in legislative, administrative and judicial matters. It also operated as an imperial court of justice, usually dealing with appeals from decisions of the lower courts.[49] Besides the officials resident at the central imperial court, an important branch of the administrative apparatus consisted of officials engaged in provincial rather than central government. The

---

[48] In later times the city of Ravenna in Italy was chosen as the new home of the Western emperors, while the administration of the East centred around the eastern emperor at Constantinople.

[49] The *sacrum consistorium* developed from the earlier *consilium principis* as organized by Emperor Hadrian in the second century AD.

latter formed a separate administrative hierarchy whose structure was linked with the territorial division of the empire into prefectures, dioceses and provinces. The highest-ranking civil official of the provincial administration was the praetorian prefect (*praefectus praetorio*), the officer heading the administration of each of the four prefectures (Gaul, Italy, Illyricum and the Orient) into which the empire was divided. Subordinate to the prefects were the chiefs of dioceses, called vicars (*vicarii*), and the provincial governors. The cities of Rome and Constantinople were exempt from diocesan government and each was administered by a city prefect (*praefectus urbi*). The complex administrative machinery of the Late Empire was designed to secure efficient administration, and maintain order and regularity for revenue collection and judicial proceedings. Despite the tight controls that theoretically existed, the system was rife with corruption as office holders sought career advancement and self-enrichment at the expense of civilians. In AD 368, the newly created office of *defensor civitatis* was entrusted with the protection of the lower classes within the population against abuses committed by state officials and great landowners.[50]

## 1.6   The Reign of Justinian (AD 527–565)

### 1.6.1   General Historical Background

In 527 AD a vigorous new ruler, Justinian, ascended the throne at Constantinople. Imbued with the Roman imperial tradition, Justinian directed all his energies to fulfilling his essential ambition: the restoration of the Roman Empire to its earlier grandeur. Thus he inaugurated a programme that focused on three interrelated goals: the re-establishment of imperial rule throughout the Mediterranean basin; the restoration of unity in the Church through the enforcement of religious orthodoxy; and the systematic restatement and consolidation of the law.

After concluding a peace agreement with the Persian Empire in the East, Justinian mounted an expedition under general Belisarius against the Vandal kingdom of North Africa in AD 533. Within a year the Vandals were defeated and Africa was restored to its former position as a province of the empire. The invasion of Sicily in AD 535 marked the initiation of the reconquest of Italy. After a bitter struggle that endured for more than two decades, the Ostrogothic kingdom was overthrown and Rome, the empire's ancient capital, was recaptured. In AD 554 Justinian's ambitions directed him to the far western Mediterranean, where southern Spain was wrested from the Visigoths and adjoined to the empire. By exploiting the diplomatic isolation of his opponents in the West and assuming a

---

[50] However, the institution of the *defensor civitatis* ultimately failed to achieve its declared goal as many of those individuals who held the office often committed abuses themselves or were prone to manipulation through bribery or intimidation.

defensive stance in the East, Justinian succeeded in converting the Mediterranean once more into an imperial lake. However, the reconquest of Africa, Italy and Spain entailed mixed blessings for their inhabitants; their initial acceptance of imperial rule was soon tempered by misgivings prompted by the obligations placed upon the population by the imperial authorities.

Within the empire, Justinian introduced a series of administrative reforms designed to protect his subjects against the rapacity of government officials and soldiers, and to curb the oppression of the rural population by powerful land barons. Moreover, he adopted measures devised to revitalize commerce and industry; embarked on an extensive architectural and artistic program, furnishing the empire with churches, public buildings and fortifications; and accomplished his ambitious tasks of codifying the law and transforming legal education. However, he encountered impediments when endeavouring to restore religious orthodoxy within the Church, whose unity was threatened by various schisms.

Modern historians are generally divided as to their assessment of Justinian and his work. Some point to his authoritarianism and his ruthless suppression of all internal opposition, and to the fact that his reconquest of the West proved ephemeral and exhausted the empire both economically and militarily (after his death in AD 568 renewed attacks by Germanic tribes reduced imperial authority in the West to a few strong points). Others draw attention to his undeniable military successes and to his tremendous internal achievements, notably in the fields of art and law. They point out that at a time when the ancient world was ending, Justinian did succeed in finally assembling and preserving for posterity the heritage of Roman law—an immense body of legal materials spanning hundreds of years of legal development.

## *1.6.2  The Constitutional Framework*

The government and administrative structure developed in the later imperial age continued in operation, except for certain minor changes.[51] The administration of the Eastern Roman Empire continued as before, while the reconquered provinces in the West were placed under the control of viceroys, with full civilian and military power, who ruled in the name of the emperor from the centres of Ravenna in Italy and Carthage in North Africa.

---

[51] For example, the office of consul was abolished by imperial decree in AD 541.

# Chapter 2
# The Sources of Roman Law

## 2.1 Introductory

The Romans called their own law *ius civile*: the legal order of the Roman citizenry (*cives Romani*). Like other peoples in antiquity, the Romans observed the principle of personality of law, according to which the law of a state applied only to its citizens.[1] Thus the Roman *ius civile* was the law that applied exclusively to Roman citizens.[2] However, Roman law underwent an important expansion in the course of time. With the gradual enlargement of the Roman city state and the increasing complexity of legal life, Roman jurisprudence adopted the idea of *ius gentium*: a body of legal institutions and principles common to all people subject to Roman rule regardless of their *civitas*. By the introduction of the *ius gentium* within the body of Roman law, the scope of the law was considerably enlarged. Nevertheless, technically the position remained that some legal institutions were open only to Roman citizens. Such institutions were classified as belonging to the *ius civile*, while other institutions were regarded as belonging to the *ius gentium* in the sense that they were applicable to citizens and non-citizens alike. After the extension of the Roman citizenship to all free inhabitants of the empire by the constitution of Emperor Caracalla in AD 212, this technical distinction in effect vanished: in principle every free man within the empire was now a citizen, subject to the same law.

The term 'sources of law' denotes the ways in which law is created or comes into being. The Roman jurists, notwithstanding their liking for classification, were never

---

[1] In a broader sense, the term *ius civile* denoted the law peculiar to a particular state or political community. According to Gaius, 'the rules enacted by a given state for its own members are peculiar to itself and are called civil law' (G. 1. 1.).

[2] Hence the description of the Roman *ius civile* as '*ius proprium Romanorum*'. It should be noted here that from an early period, communities affiliated with Rome were granted limited rights under the Roman *ius civile*. The members of these communities occupied an intermediate position between Roman citizens and foreigners (*peregrini*).

© Springer International Publishing Switzerland 2015
G. Mousourakis, *Roman Law and the Origins of the Civil Law Tradition*,
DOI 10.1007/978-3-319-12268-7_2

very subtle in their approach to this term and different sources were highlighted as they existed in different historical epochs to reflect their predominance as vehicles of legal development. Reference may be made to a number of statements in which the sources of Roman law are listed, apparently without any specific order. In his *Institutes*, the second century AD jurist Gaius states that Roman law consists of statutes (*leges*), plebiscites (*plebiscita*), senatorial resolutions (*senatus consulta*), enactments of the emperors (*constitutiones principum*), edicts of the magistrates (*edicta*), and answers of those learned in the law (*responsa prudentium*).[3] Gaius' treatment was adopted by the drafters of Justinian's *Institutes* in the sixth century AD, with the exception that the latter make a preliminary distinction between written and unwritten law.[4] In Justinian's textbook the specific sources mentioned by Gaius are subsumed under the category of written law (*ius scriptum*), while unwritten law (*ius non scriptum*) or custom is discussed briefly a few paragraphs below.[5] The view that custom (also referred to as *mos* or *consuetudo*) was a source of law can also be found in the work of the first century BC orator and philosopher Cicero, who also included in his list of sources equity (*aequitas*) and decided cases.[6] It should be noted, however, that Cicero's conception of custom differed from that of the drafters of Justinian's *Institutes*. Whilst for Cicero the term custom denoted ancestral tradition (*mos maiorum*) in the context of the Roman *ius civile*, the same term in the *Institutes* referred to regional and local variations on the law of the Roman Empire. The omission of custom from Gaius' and other classical jurists' accounts can probably be explained on the grounds that these authors did not view custom as a source of law distinct from jurisprudence, but regarded it as being connected with jurisprudence as "a special form of civil law that is founded without writing solely on the interpretation of the jurists."[7]

---

[3] G. 1. 2.

[4] *Inst* 1. 2. 3: "Our law is partly written, partly unwritten. The written law consists of statutes, plebiscites, decrees of the senate, enactments of the emperors, edicts of the magistrates and answers of the jurists." It should be noted that the Roman distinction between *ius scriptum* and *ius non scriptum* was based on the Greek distinction between written law (*nomos eggraphos*) and unwritten law (*nomos agraphos*), which goes back to Aristotle (*Rhetorica* 1. 10. 1368b). The Greek distinction, however, was normally used to depict a contrast very different from what the Romans had in mind; namely that between the (written) positive law of a particular state and (unwritten) natural law. Only in exceptional cases did the Greeks employ the term unwritten law to describe the unformed positive law of a particular people. When the Romans came to borrow the relevant Greek terms, inasmuch as they possessed a Latin equivalent for the term natural law, namely *ius naturale* (usually identified with *ius gentium*), they restricted unwritten law, or *ius non scriptum*, to the exceptional Greek usage, i.e. to customary law.

[5] *Inst* 1. 2. 9: "The unwritten law is that which usage has approved, for all customs established by the consent of those who use them obtain the force of law."

[6] *Topica* 5. 28: "The civil law is to be found in statutes, resolutions of the senate, decided cases, opinions of the jurists, edicts of the magistrates, custom and equity." Other rhetorical writers of the early imperial age likewise regard custom as one of the sources of law. See, e.g., Quintilian, *Inst. Orat.* 12. 3. 6.

[7] D. 1. 2. 2. 12. (Pomponius).

## 2.2 Sources of Law in the Archaic Age

### 2.2.1 *Customary Law and the* Leges Regiae

The earliest source of Roman law was unwritten customary law, comprising norms (referred to as *mores maiorum*: the ways of our forefathers) that had grown from long-standing usages of the community, as well as from cases that had evolved from disputes brought before the clan patriarchs or the king for resolution. However, archaic Roman law was not marked by uniformity, since the two classes, the patricians and the plebeians, which made up the bulk of the population, appear to have been distinguished not only by the possession of different political privileges but also by the possession of different systems of customary law.[8] A further divergence of practice in the primitive society out of which the city-state of Rome gradually evolved derived from the considerable amount of autonomy in legal relations that existed in the clans (*gentes*) out of which the earliest Roman community was formed. One might perhaps say that the earliest phase of Roman history is marked by a fundamental dualism: the *civitas* (in the sense of state or political community) on the one hand and the *gentes* on the other. Rome evolved politically as a unitary state when the gentile organization declined and the sense of unity among the population intensified. Thus, the initially diverse customs of the different *gentes* underwent a process of assimilation that engendered a common body of customary norms for governing the whole community. Furthermore, as the Roman state evolved, an attempt was made to create a uniform system by making the law of the patricians approximate as closely as possible to that of the plebeians.

Although the Romans themselves never analysed the concept of customary law and the classical jurists did not regard custom as a distinct source of law, there is no doubt that Roman law was almost entirely customary in its origin. Rome owed to custom an essential part of her family organization, such as the norms prescribing the rights and duties of family members and the position of the head of the family (*paterfamilias*); the rules regulating the formation of marriage; the earliest forms of property ownership and transfer; and a great deal of the formalities employed in legal procedure. Many of the relevant customary norms went back to the remote past of the Roman people, while others emerged later, during the formative years of the Roman city-state. The rules and procedures created in this way were characterized by extreme formalism, indeed ritualism: the casting of all juridical acts into an

---

[8] This seems to be evidenced by the existence of dual forms for the attainment of the same end in some areas of Roman law. E.g., we have the marriage by *confarreatio* (a form of marriage involving an elaborate religious ceremony) side by side with marriage by *usus* (an informal variety requiring simply mutual consent and evidence of extended cohabitation); and the testament in the *comitia curiata* (now referred to as *comitia calata*) (*testamentum calatis comitiis*) side by side with the testament '*per aes et libram*' ('with the copper and the scales') or mancipatory will. The exclusion of the plebeians from political office and the priesthood and the denial to them of the right of *conubium* (marriage, intermarriage) with members of the patrician class also point in the direction of a fundamental division between the two classes.

unchangeable form where successful completion depends upon strict adherence to a set ritual engaging certain words or gestures. This kind of formalism has a socio-psychological explanation: public opinion and, subsequently, public authority, refused to recognize rights or allow their enforcement, unless the act that created them had been performed with such publicity and formality as may draw the attention of society and leave no possibility of doubt as to its existence. In this respect it appeared fitting that the material signs (words or gestures) that accompanied the relevant act should be so precise that no doubt could arise with respect to its nature and object. It should be noted, further, that for a long time law (*ius*)[9] was hardly distinguished from religion, being entirely a matter of ritual, and that the pontiffs (*pontifices*), the priests who were the first regulators of customary law, maintained in it this ritual and symbolic character.[10]

In the course of time, as Roman society continued to grow both in numbers and complexity, the role of custom as the principal source of law gradually diminished, for the customary norms, often vague and limited in scope, could not provide the certainty that a more intricate system of social and economic relations required. Thus, with the rise of the Roman city-state, the need emerged for the development of all-embracing legislation, i.e. the organization of law by public authority. While sanctioning the majority of customary norms already in existence, the state reserved to itself the right of making law in the future, and this opened the way to the ascendancy of written law (*ius scriptum*), initially in the form of statute. In later times, when law became subject to authoritative interpretation by the jurists, custom ceased to be regarded as a formal source of law having been incorporated into a variety of other sources, such as statutory law, the edicts of the magistrates and the responses of the jurists. However, customary norms continued to indirectly affect both the content and scope of laws. For instance, many transactions of private law became enforceable by actions with respect to which the judge was instructed to take into consideration matters relating to good faith (*bona fides*), a legal concept relating to the enforcement by legal means of what was generally viewed as social or moral obligations. Furthermore, it must be noted that the Romans did recognize local custom (*mos regionis*), especially in connection with customary usages prevailing in the provinces. In the post-classical period, well-established local customs were acknowledged as a supplementary source of law and exercised a considerable influence on both legislation and the administration of justice.

In the archaic period, legislation in the modern sense and as the Romans understood it in their politically mature eras, was practically unknown. The law

---

[9] Originally, the term *ius* (plural, *iura*) referred to a course of conduct that the community would take for granted and in that sense endorse. The existence of a *ius* was determined by securing, probably through ordeal, the sanction of the gods. And see relevant discussion in Chap. 3 below.

[10] The rules of law, consisting of fact-decision relationships, could not be argued for; similarly, a minister of religion was unable to present a rational justification for his prophesies. In each case the link between the facts (the judicial proof, the flying bird) and the decision (a legal judgment or a statement concerning divine law – *fas*) remained an inexplicable norm. This perspective emphasizes the *irrational* aspect of archaic legal procedure.

was mainly construed as a sacred custom and thus not subject to change by direct legislative means. The classical jurist Pomponius describes the state of the law during this period as featuring a series of laws, referred to as 'laws of the kings' (*leges regiae*), which supposedly emanated from some of the early kings. According to Roman tradition, these laws were collected and recorded at the end of the regal era by Sextus Papirius, a *pontifex maximus*.[11] The *ius civile Papirianum*, as this collection was known, if it ever existed, is lost to us, but a number of rules ostensibly promulgated by kings have been preserved in the works of later Greek and Roman authors. The *leges regiae* were probably little more than a gloss on the prevailing customary law that assumed the form of declarations composed by the kings and publicly announced during an assembly. The surviving fragments of these laws, as far as they are authentic, attest to the close connection between law and religion that marks the character of archaic law. For the most part, the kings' laws were prescriptive or condemnatory in character. Examples of prescriptive laws, i.e. laws prescribing 'correct' behaviour, include a law of Romulus, Rome's first king, prohibiting a wife from divorcing her husband[12]; and a law of King Numa according to which a *pater familias* could not sell a son to slavery after he had given him permission to marry.[13] Condemnatory laws, on the other hand, laid down penalties for various forms of wrongdoing. These penalties sometimes consisted of private redress against the wrongdoer; e.g. retaliation (*talio*) was allowed in some circumstances as satisfaction for certain forms of personal injury. However, offences of a particularly serious nature, such as certain religious crimes, entailed more public forms of punishment, including ritual execution. Such punishments were primarily expiatory in character: they were aimed at eliminating the state of collective impurity created by the commission of the offence.[14]

---

[11] D. 1. 2. 2. 1–2: "At the outset of our state, the citizen body decided to conduct its affairs without fixed statute law or determinate legal rights; everything was governed by the kings under their own hand. When the state had subsequently grew to a reasonable size, then [King] Romulus himself, according to tradition, divided the citizen body into thirty groups, and called them *curiae* on the ground that he improved his curatorship of the commonwealth through the advice of these groups. And accordingly, he himself enacted for the people a number of statutes passed by advice of the *curiae* ... [and] his successor kings legislated likewise. All these statutes have survived written down in the book by Sextus Papirius, who lived in the time of Superbus. This book is called the Papirian Civil Law, not because Papirius added anything of his own to it, but because he compiled in a single work laws that had been passed without observing any order."

[12] Plutarch, *Romulus* 22.

[13] Dionysius 2. 27.

[14] See relevant discussion in Chap. 4 below.

## 2.2.2   The Law of the Twelve Tables and the Growth of Statutory Law

As previously noted, archaic Roman law initially consisted of a body of unwritten customary norms, the nucleus of which had its origins in the period when the gentile organization of society was still effective. These norms were characterized by a high degree of uncertainty and, when a legal question arose, it fell to the college of the pontiffs to give an authoritative answer thereto. As the members of this college, like all state magistrates, were at this time exclusively patricians, it is reasonable to suppose that the plebeians frequently accused them of showing class bias in their determinations. It is thus unsurprising that one of the plebeians' chief demands during the struggle of the orders was that the customary law in force be written down and made public so that it could no longer be applied arbitrarily by the pontiffs and other magistrates charged with the administration of justice. After several years of strife, it was agreed that a written code of laws applicable to all citizens should be compiled. The idea of codification was probably borrowed from the Greeks, who had established colonies in Southern Italy and Sicily and with whom the Romans had from an early period come into contact.

According to the traditional account, before embarking on the work of codification, the senate dispatched a three-member commission to Greece to study the laws of the famous Athenian lawgiver Solon, and those of other Greek city-states.[15] On the return of this commission it was decided that the constitution should be virtually suspended and that the reins of government should be placed in the hands of an annually appointed board of ten magistrates (all of them patricians). In addition to their regular governmental functions, these magistrates were to be assigned the special task of drafting a written code of laws (*decemviri legibus scribundis*).[16] In 451 BC the decemvirs produced a series of laws inscribed on ten tablets (*tabulae*). These laws were considered unsatisfactory, which prompted the election of a second commission of ten men (now incorporating some plebeians) to complete the work.[17] In 450 BC two further tablets of laws supplemented the existing ten and, after it was ratified by the centuriate assembly (*comitia centuriata*), the work was published under the name *lex duodecim tabularum*. According to Roman tradition, the second decemviral board refused to resign after completing their legislative work and endeavoured to retain their office by ruling as tyrants. Eventually, however, they were deposed following a popular revolt and the constitutional order of the Republic was restored.

The traditional account of the events leading to the enactment of the Law of the Twelve Tables, embellished with myths and legends, contains several

---

[15] Livy 3. 31. 8. and 32. 6. 7.

[16] Livy 3. 32–33; Dionysius 10. 55–57. See also D. 1. 2. 2. 4. (Pomponius). The idea of a suspension of the constitution and the temporary conferment of supreme authority on a law-giver, seems likewise to have been borrowed from the Greeks.

[17] Dionysius 10. 58. 4.

inconsistencies and anachronisms. In modern times, the queries over the origin and nature of the decemviral legislation have generated much controversy. Some scholars have challenged the historicity of the second decemvirate and argued that the work of the original commission was probably completed by the consuls of the following year. Moreover, historians contend that the dispatch of a commission to Greece is highly unlikely and, even if such a mission existed, it may have visited only Greek cities in Southern Italy. The preserved fragments of the Law of the Twelve Tables reveal scant material that could be directly traced to a Greek influence, although certain parallels with the laws of other early societies can be observed.[18] A Greek influence on the code, slight though it may have been, was the inevitable result of the prolonged influence of the Greek civilization, through its outposts in Southern Italy and Sicily, on Rome from the days of her infancy. But, in spite of the fact that a few of its ideas may have been borrowed from Greek sources, the Law of the Twelve Tables was basically a compilation of rules of indigenous Roman customary law, designed not to reform but to render the existing law more certain and more clearly known to the populace. Only the most important of these rules were included, while the general framework of the customary law was taken for granted. At the same time, an important objective of the compilers was to eliminate, as far as possible, the divergence in legal systems within the state and to make a common law for Roman society considered as a whole. In pursuance of this goal, certain disputed or controversial points must have been settled and some innovations made.

With regard to the nature of the particular rules themselves, the vast majority were concerned with matters of private law, in other words, with the rights and duties of individuals amongst themselves (not with the relationship between the individual citizen and the state). Special attention was given to matters of procedure in court actions and enforcement, as in this area the unskilled parties to a dispute, usually plebeians, could be misled by those conversant with the law. This was especially because the bringing of legal suits at this time was surrounded by a host of forms and technicalities. One can detect in these procedural rules the origins of the Roman state: they were in many ways a form of regulated self-help.[19] There

---

[18] The Law of the Twelve Tables does have some elements in common with Athenian law, but these are not of the kind that could suggest a direct influence. The relevant provisions that, according to Cicero, were extracted from the laws of Solon, pertain mainly to the settling of disputes between neighbours, the right of forming associations (*collegia*) and restrictions on displays at funerals. Cicero, *de leg.* 2. 23. 59.; 2. 25. 64.

[19] Table I prescribes the way a defendant could be summoned by the plaintiff to appear before a jurisdictional magistrate: if the defendant refused to go to court, force may be employed to secure his appearance; but if he was ill or aged, the plaintiff was required to provide a means of transportation. Table II lays down the amounts that had to be deposited in court by the parties prior to the commencement of certain forms of action. Finally Table III is concerned with the enforcement of judgments: a debtor was allowed 30 days after the judgment to pay the debt; if he failed to do so, he could be seized by the creditor and brought before the court; if the debt was not discharged, the debtor could be detained by the creditor who, after keeping him in bonds for sixty days, was entitled to put him to death or sell him into slavery.

were also rules prescribing the monetary penalties required to be paid for wrongs done, and rules concerning family, property and succession rights. The treatment of private wrongs shows that the law had reached a phase of transition between a primitive state of permitted self-redress and the state at which the appropriate remedy had to be sought by legal process. It was provided, for example, that if a person was caught stealing by night, he might be lawfully slain on the spot[20]; but a man whose limb had been fractured might only revenge himself by inflicting the like injury on his assailant provided that no agreement had been reached for rendering compensation, in which case the remedy would be to take legal action against the wrongdoer if the promised ransom was not paid.[21] With respect to other offences the law itself fixed the amount of compensation that could be demanded for the wrong done, and the victim was restricted to claiming that redress, thus being placed in the position of creditor rather than an avenger. In these provisions one might trace the origins of what was eventually to become a contractual obligation, a relatively advanced notion that was virtually unknown at the time of the Twelve Tables. The family law of the Twelve Tables revolves around the notion of *patria potestas*: the absolute power of the head of the family (*paterfamilias*) over his children and other family members.[22] With respect to the law relating to property, the Law of the Twelve Tables shows the rigidity and formalism that prevailed, but rights in both movables and immovables were clearly recognized.[23] During this early age a mere expression of intention was not enough to create liability or covey rights from one individual to another; some visible formality was necessary, by which the requisite intention was manifested to witnesses. Table V of the Law contained rules dealing with matters of succession and guardianship. It provided, among other things, that if a person died intestate, or if his will was found to be invalid, his property should pass to his nearest agnates (*agnati, sui heredes*) or, in the absence of agnates, to the members of the clan (*gentiles*) to which he belonged. The Law of the Twelve Tables contained also some provisions of a constitutional or religious character. For example, Table IX rendered it unconstitutional for a magistrate to propose a law imposing penalties or disabilities upon a particular person only, and declared that no one should be put to death except after a formal trial and sentence. It stated, moreover, that only the assembly of the centuries could pass laws affecting the political rights of citizens, and that no citizen should be condemned on a capital charge without the right of appeal

---

[20] Table VIII 12.

[21] Table VIII 2.

[22] See e.g. Table IV.

[23] Table VI includes provisions regulating the acquisition and transference of property. It is stated, among other things, that a person would acquire ownership upon two years of uninterrupted possession of landed property, or one year in the case of other property (this mode of acquiring property was termed *usucapio*). The transference of property by *mancipatio* (a formal transaction involving an imaginary sale and delivery) is also recognized together with an early form of contract known as *stipulatio* (a verbal contract consisting in a formal question and an affirming answer: 'do you solemnly promise to do X?' – 'I solemnly promise').

(*provocatio*) to the assembly. Table X addressed sacral law and matters relating to the burial or cremation of the dead.[24] Finally Tables XI and XII contained certain provisions of general character, such as the prohibition of intermarriage between patricians and plebeians (Table XI)[25] and rules relating to the liability of a master of a slave for offences committed by the latter (*noxae deditio*).

The Law of the Twelve Tables is a highly casuistic, case-oriented (in contradistinction to generalizing, principle-oriented) piece of legislation reflecting the life of a fairly primitive agricultural community. However, even though archaic in form and content, it contains elements indicative of a legal system that had advanced considerably beyond its original, primitive stage. Of particular importance for the subsequent development of the law were the rudiments of inter-organ controls to prevent excesses in the administration of justice. But the significance of the Law of the Twelve Tables lays not so much in its contents as in the fact that it opened up new possibilities. Considered from a political angle, its main achievement was vindicating the monopoly of state authorities over all acts of judicial administration. As it produced a common body of law for the populace regarding the legal matters most important for daily life, private citizens and magistrates alike were made subject to the sovereignty of the law and members of the plebeian class were no longer exposed to the vagaries of customary rules administered by patrician officials. At the same time, the process towards the secularization of the law was accelerated: conduct patterns that were in the past shrouded in religious ritualism were rationalized by general rules of substantive and procedural law in a written form, and thus ascertainable by all people. As the law was now publicized, it began to lose the immutable quality of a religious mystery and evolved into a conventional, human form that was therefore subject to change.

Later generations of Romans felt the greatest veneration for the Law of the Twelve Tables, which was described as the 'foundation of all public and private law'.[26] Indeed, for a thousand years, this enactment remained the only attempt by the Romans to comprehensively record their laws. This first attempt ushered in the history of Roman law as discernible today and for a thousand years it formed the basis of the whole legal system, despite changes in social, economic and political conditions. Legal development in the succeeding centuries was effected without directly repealing the provisions of the Law of the Twelve Tables, but mainly

---

[24] It contained provisions forbidding burial and cremation within the city; the immoderate wailing or tearing of their faces by women at funerals; and the burial of gold ornaments with the dead.

[25] This was a highly controversial measure that was repealed within a few years.

[26] Livy, 3. 34. 6. Cicero states: "It seems to me that the small booklet of the Twelve Tables, if one looks to the origins and sources of law, surpasses the libraries of all the philosophers in weight of authority and wealth of utility. . . .It is the spirit (of Rome), the customs and the principles that first ought to be remarked; both because this country is the parent of all of us and because that wisdom which went into the establishment of her laws, is as much to be counted as it was in the acquisition of the vast might of the empire." (*De oratore* 1. 44. 195–196).

through their interpretation by trained jurists, who adapted them to the changed conditions of later eras.[27]

In the period following the enactment of the Law of the Twelve Tables, legislation by popular assembly evolved as a generally acknowledged source of law. However, in contrast to the role of legislation in the Greek world, Roman legislation remained largely underdeveloped. Controversy still prevails as to the extent (or the exact time) it was deemed legally viable to modify the ancient *ius civile*. The Romans' disinclination to apply legislation derived from their conservative attitude towards law and the deeply rooted conception of the merits of their ancient customs reinforced by the special position accorded to the Law of the Twelve Tables. It was not easy to frame statutes in a way that avoided infringement of these established norms, especially in the field of private law. Therefore, the necessary reforms were fashioned in an indirect manner by means of interpretation. Accordingly, statutes remained relatively rare and dealt only with certain special matters. Statutes were enacted, for instance, to incorporate in the constitution the gains forged by the plebeian movement and to create new magistracies. In matters of social concern, legislation was occasionally relied upon to instigate reforms or merely to appease the populace. Some legislation had a hybrid character displaying a political basis and also elements that affected the private relations of citizens— this embraced specific laws relating to civil procedure, marriage, debts and testamentary benefits.

Important statutes of this period in the field of public law encompass: the *lex Valeria Horatia* (449 BC), which recognized the inviolability of the plebeian tribunes; the *lex Canuleia* (445 BC), which removed the rule prohibiting intermarriages between patricians and plebeians; the *leges Liciniae Sextiae* (367 BC), which admitted plebeians to the office of consul and established the praetorship; the *lex Publilia Philonis* (339 BC), which removed the rule directing that the legislative enactments of the popular assemblies had to obtain senate approval after their passage; and the *lex Hortensia de plebiscitis* (287 BC) that rendered the resolutions

---

[27] The original text of the Law of the Twelve Tables has not been preserved (the tables on which it was written were probably destroyed during the sack of Rome by the Gauls in 387 BC). Our knowledge of its contents is based on various later sources (the oldest source dates from the period of the late Republic). However, the contents were not recorded in their entirety by the relevant authors like Livy, Dionysius, Cicero, Aulus Gellius and Gaius. They only reproduced fragments that were relevant to them, modernizing the text in language and consciously or subconsciously adapting it to the conditions of their own times. The precise quantity of missing text is unknown as is the arrangement of the original provisions of the enactment. Thus, the reconstructions by contemporary Romanist scholars that draw on the extant literary sources are largely hypothetical. Modern reconstructions of the Law of the Twelve Tables include: H. Dirksen, *Übersicht der bisherigen Versuche zur Kritik und Herstellung des Textes der Zwölf-Tafel Fragmente* (Leipzig 1824); R. Schöll, *Leges duodecim tabularum reliquiae* (Leipzig 1868); E. H. Warmington, *Remains of Old Latin* III, Loeb Classical Library (Cambridge, Mass. 1938), 424 ff. FIRA I, 23 ff. Bruns, *Fontes* I, 15 ff. A. C. Johnson, P. R. Coleman-Norton and F. C. Bourne, *Ancient Roman Statutes*, (Austin, Texas 1961), 9 ff. P. F. Girard and F. Senn, *Les lois des Romains* (Naples 1977), 25–73; M. Crawford (ed.), *Roman Statutes* (London 1996).

of the plebeian assembly binding on all citizens. In the fourth century BC a number statutes were passed that established a limit on the interest rate charged on debts for borrowed money, such as the *lex Duilia Menenia* of 357 BC and the *lex Genucia* of 342 BC. Other statutes eased the debtors' burden with respect to the securities they could be requested to provide against the risk of non-payment, as well as pertaining to the sanctions they incurred for non-payment. Thus the *lex Poetelia Papiria* of 326 BC forbade the private imprisonment of the debtor by the creditor, which entailed the former becoming a slave of the latter.

### 2.2.2.1  Law-Making in the Roman Assemblies

As elaborated in the previous chapter, the Roman popular assemblies existed in two forms: those including all citizens, who voted either according to wealth (*comitia centuriata*) or tribe (*comitia tributa*); and the assembly of the plebeians (*concilium plebis*), which excluded the patrician upper class from its membership. Statutes (*leges*) enacted by the *comitia centuriata* and the *comitia tributa* were binding on all citizens, whilst the resolutions of the plebeian assembly (*plebiscita*) were initially only binding on the plebeians.[28] Since the enactment of the *lex Hortensia* in 287 BC, at the latest, the *plebiscita* were considered as complete laws binding on the entire citizenry.[29] Thereafter, the *concilium plebis*, convened under the presidency of a *tribunus plebis*, became the most active legislative body and the great majority of the statutes that we can observe in the sources were, strictly speaking, *plebiscita*.

The Roman assemblies could only meet to discharge their functions when formally summoned by a magistrate empowered to convene and preside over a popular assembly (*ius agendi cum populo*).[30] When a magistrate submitted a proposal to an assembly he was said to ask or request (*rogare*) the people. Thus,

---

[28] As Gaius observes, "A law [*lex*] is what the people orders and ordains. A plebiscite is what the plebs orders and ordains. The difference between the people and the plebs is that by the term 'people' all the citizens are meant including the patricians, by the term 'plebs' the other citizens without the patricians. For this reason the patricians in the old days declared that they were not bound by plebiscites, because they were made without their authority." G. 1. 3. And see *Inst.* 1. 2. 4: A law [*lex*] is what the Roman people ordered on the proposal of a senatorial magistrate, e.g. a consul. A plebiscite is what the plebs ordered on the proposal of a plebeian magistrate, e.g. a tribune of the plebs. The plebs differs from the people as species from genus. For all the citizens are meant by the term 'people', the other citizens excluding senators and patricians by the term 'plebs'."

[29] Aulus Gellius, *Noctes Atticae* 15. 27. 4: "He who does not require the presence of all, but only of a portion of the people, must proclaim not a *comitia* but a *concilium*. The tribunes cannot summon the patricians, nor refer to them concerning any matter, so that measures passed on the proposal of the tribunes of the plebs are not called *leges* but *plebiscita*, by which bills the patricians were not bound formerly, until Quintus Hortensius, dictator, passed a law, that whatever law the plebs should pass should be binding on all citizens." And see D. 1. 2. 2. 8; G. 1. 3.

[30] The assembly of the centuries (*comitia centuriata*) was convened usually by a consul; the assembly of the tribes (*comitia tributa*) by a consul or praetor; and the plebeian assembly (*concilium plebis*) by a tribune.

his proposal was called *rogatio legis* and the resultant laws were identified as *leges rogatae*.[31] Custom and eventually law dictated that the full text of a proposed measure must be publicly posted 24 days before its formal submission to the assembly (*promulgatio, promulgare rogationem*). During this interval the citizens had the opportunity to discuss the bill and recommend changes, or even its withdrawal, to the magistrate in informal gatherings (*contiones*). It should be noted that legislative measures proposed by magistrates were normally debated in the senate before promulgation. This debate was much more important than any public discussions that might occur in *contiones*. Once the bill was presented to the assembly it could not be modified; the assembly could either accept (*iubere rogationem*) or reject the bill as a whole and in the precise form it was delivered by the magistrate.[32]

In all Roman assemblies voting was by group rather than by individual suffrage. For example, in the assembly of the centuries (*comitia centuriata*) decisions were reached by considering the number of centuries that voted in favour of or against a proposal; the vote of each century was determined by the majority of the individual voters it comprised.[33] During the early republican age voting was done orally. The method of voting by ballot (*per tabellas*) was introduced in the later Republic by a series of laws referred to as *leges tabellariae*.[34] When an assembly was summoned to decide on a legislative proposal, each voter-member was given two wooden tablets (*tabellae*). The tablet representing a positive vote was inscribed with the letter *V*, which stood for the phrase *uti rogas* ('as you propose', 'as you ask')[35]; the other tablet bore the letter *A*, which stood for the word *antiquo* ('I maintain things as they are'), and indicated a vote against the proposed measure. After the vote of each group (*centuria* or *tribus*) became known, it was reported to the presiding magistrate who made a formal announcement. When the votes of all the groups had thus been reported and counted the magistrate notified the final result to the assembly.

---

[31] The *leges rogatae* were distinguished from the *leges datae*: laws that were introduced by magistrates on special occasions after obtaining the permission of the senate. In the category of *leges datae* belonged, for example, the various *leges coloniae* and *leges provinciae* by which new colonies and provinces were created.

[32] What are today referred to as 'private members bills' were not permitted, for the magistrate alone decided what motions should be put to vote.

[33] The number of citizens needed to be present for holding a lawful meeting was not fixed by law. It appears, however, that if the number of the citizens in attendance was very low the presiding magistrate could postpone the meeting.

[34] The *lex Gabinia* of 139 BC introduced the secret ballot in elections of magistrates. This was followed by the *lex Cassia* in 137 BC, which provided that the secret ballot should be used in all cases heard before the assemblies when these operated as courts of justice (*iudicia populi*), except in those involving treason (*perduellio*). In 131 BC the *lex Papiria* introduced the use of the ballot in voting on legislative matters. Finally, the *lex Caelia* of 107 BC extended the use of the ballot to trials for treason, thus removing the exception provided for by the *lex Cassia*.

[35] See, e.g., Cicero, *ad Att.* 1. 14; *de leg.* 3. 17. In judicial assemblies (*iudicia populi*) the tablet with the letter *L* (*libero*: 'I absolve') was used to indicate a vote for acquittal; the tablet with the letter *D* (*damno*: 'I condemn') expressed a vote for condemnation.

According to tradition, a law passed by the people could not come into force until it received the senate's approval (*patrum auctoritas*).[36] This rule was reversed by the *lex Publilia Philonis* of 339 BC that stipulated that the *patrum auctoritas* must be issued before, not after, a legislative proposal was submitted to the people. Thereafter, laws usually had immediate effect following the formal announcement of the assembly's decision endorsing the magistrate's proposal. After their passing, laws were inscribed on tablets of wood, copper or stone and retained in the state treasury (*aerarium populi romani*) under the supervision of the quaestors.

A statute was composed of three parts: (1) the preamble (*praescriptio legis*) that embodied the name of the magistrate who had proposed it (and after whom it was named), the place and time of its enactment, and the name of the group (*centuria* or *tribus*) that had cast the first vote in the proceedings[37]; (2) the text of the law (*rogatio*) that was usually divided into sections; and (3) the ratification of the law (*sanctio*). The *sanctio* specified the penalties that would be imposed if the law was violated, and stated the rules governing the relation between the new statute and earlier and future legislation.[38] A distinction was drawn between 'perfect laws' (*leges perfectae*), 'imperfect laws' or laws without any sanction at all (*leges imperfectae*) and 'less than perfect laws' (*leges minus quam perfectae*). Acts performed in violation of a perfect law were deemed null and void.[39] The infringement of an imperfect law, on the other hand, did not affect the validity of the relevant act.[40] Similarly, when a less than perfect law was violated the relevant act itself remained valid, but the transgressor was liable to punishment. Laws containing unrelated or superfluous provisions were designated *leges saturae* or *per saturam* and were forbidden under early law.[41]

---

[36] The period between the formal enactment of a law and its coming into force was termed *vacatio legis*.

[37] Sometimes the preamble also included certain words indicating the subject-matter of the statute; examples include the *lex Hortensia de plebiscitis* (287 BC), providing that the resolutions of the plebeian assembly were binding on all citizens; the *lex Sempronia agraria* (133 BC), concerning the distribution of public lands (*ager publicus*); and the *lex Sempronia de provocatione* (123 BC), confirming the right of citizens convicted of capital offences to appeal to the people's assembly (*ius provocationis*).

[38] For example, the *sanctio* could state that a previously enacted statute remained fully or partially in force despite the introduction of the new law.

[39] An illustration is the *lex Falcidia delegatis* (40 BC), mentioned by Gaius (2. 227), according to which legacies (*legata*) should not exceed three-quarters of the testator's estate. The part of the legacy exceeding three-quarters was deemed void.

[40] An example is the *lex Cincia* of 204 BC. This plebiscite prohibited the issue of gifts for the performance of tasks when such performance was regarded as a sacred duty. Gifts promised in violation of this law were not void, but the donor could raise a defence (*exceptio legis Cinciae*) if he was sued for payment. The category of *leges imperfectae* was abolished in the post-classical period (AD 439) by an enactment of Emperors Theodosius II and Valentinian III.

[41] The *lex Caecilia Didia* of 98 BC renewed this prohibition.

## 2.2.3  The Pontiffs and the Beginnings of Jurisprudence

The central role of the pontiffs in the interpretation and application of customary law shows the interconnection of religion and law in the archaic age. During this period all legal knowledge was confined to their college and was handed down to new members by tradition and instruction. As guardians of ancestral tradition, the pontiffs alone knew all the laws, the forms of actions and ritual techniques, the court calendar and the authoritative opinions their predecessors had rendered in the past. Thus, it was to them that private citizens had to go to obtain advice on whether specific rules of law applied to their particular case and the correct procedure in litigation.[42]

In the period following the enactment of the Law of the Twelve Tables, the population mass and intricacy of Roman society proliferated. Thus, the old rules proved increasingly inadequate for fulfilling the requirements of social and commercial life. But the Romans did not respond to the need for legal change by replacing the Law of the Twelve Tables with fresh legislation. As noted, the Romans were conservative and extremely careful in their approach to legal matters. They were attached with great tenacity to the Law of the Twelve Tables, which they considered as the foundation of their legal system. Although legislation introduced some new rules, interpretation was the chief means of changing the law (especially in the field of private law). Because a close connection still prevailed between the legal and religious spheres, it is unsurprising that the interpretation of the law and its deriving actions lay in the hands of the pontiffs. Through skilful interpretation of the provisions of the Twelve Tables and later statutes, the early jurists filled the gaps in the law and also succeeded in infusing the old rigid rules with new substance, thus adapting them to changed conditions.

The influence of the pontiffs on legal development was also connected with their role in the administration of justice. The Romans construed the term *lex* as a formal act of the people that required or permitted a magistrate to enforce a right (*ius*), which was demanded in a particular way by a particular procedure. In the archaic period the principal method for obtaining a *ius* was the *legis actio* (literally, an action based on the law)—a ritual procedure that was conducted orally and divided

---

[42] According to Roman tradition, the college of pontiffs was created by the priest-king Numa Pompilius in the late eighth century BC. Originally, this religious body was made up of five members drawn exclusively from the patrician class (four ordinary *pontifices* headed by a *pontifex maximus*). The pontiffs were, in effect, state officials who, in addition to their duties as senators or magistrates, were responsible for the religious branch of public administration. As guardians and interpreters of the divine law (*ius divinum*), these priests exercised general supervision over a wide range of matters associated with public religion and set the rules governing the conduct of religious ceremonies and rituals (*ius sacrum*). They gave instructions to state officials on the performance of public acts of a religious nature and punished wrongdoings regarded as disrupting the *pax deorum* – the harmony between the community and its gods. Moreover, the *pontifex maximus* was entrusted with the regulation of the calendar, the fixing of the dates of public ceremonies and festivals (*dies festi*), and the setting of the days of each month on which alone legal transactions, litigation and other business could take place (*dies fasti*).

into two distinct phases. The first phase (*in iure*) originally proceeded before a pontiff or, according to some scholars, a consul. This official determined on the basis of the applicable law whether the plaintiff could initiate legal action and, if so, its required form.[43] In the second phase (*apud iudicem*) a private judge (*iudex*), appointed by both the pontiff or magistrate and the relevant parties, considered the evidence and decided the case within the frame set by the pontiff or magistrate. In the *in iure* phase of the proceedings the plaintiff had to couch his claim in set words, and the defendant also replied in set words—this formed the actual *legis actio*. If a party used the wrong *legis actio* or departed from the set form, his claim was rejected. The pontiffs possessed knowledge of the word forms that could be admitted as efficacious. They could expand or restrict the scope of a *legis actio* by construing it broadly or narrowly as required by the needs of the relevant case. This was rendered possible by the fact that, despite the emphasis that archaic law attached to the letter of the law and the forms of action based on it, there was a tendency to permit a slightly greater degree of freedom in legal proceedings than was allowed in purely religious ceremonies—at least in the era when the *legis actio* emerged as a definite form of procedure.[44]

A well-known illustration of law-making through interpretation is the method devised for releasing a son (*filiusfamilias*) from his father's control (*patria potestas*). As Roman society developed in complexity, cases emerged where a son's absolute dependence on the father regarding his legal position had to be overcome so as to sustain the healthy functioning of economic life. Originally, the power of the *paterfamilias* over his children (and also over his grandchildren and more remote descendants) entailed complete control over them. Only the father had any rights in private law—he alone was entitled to own property, including all the acquisitions of the subordinate family members. As economic conditions changed, this rigid system could not be absolutely sustained in practice. The problem was resolved by the constructive interpretation of a certain clause of the Twelve Tables that was apparently designed to protect a son against a father who misused his power. A father could consign a son to another person for money on the

---

[43] After the enactment of the *leges Liciniae Sextiae* in 367 BC, this task was entrusted to the praetor.

[44] D. 1. 2. 2. 5–7 (Pomponius): "When these statutes (the Twelve Tables) were enacted discussion in the forum became necessary – as naturally is wont to happen, that interpretation requires the guidance of those learned in the law. This discussion and this law, which without writing was developed by the learned, is not specifically named – as the other parts of the law have been designated by names, since special names have been given to other parts – but is referred to by the general term *ius civile*. Then from these statutes, at about the same time, actions were devised by which men might litigate, and lest these actions be indiscriminately brought by the people, they were required to be in certain and solemn form; and this part of the law is called *legis actiones*, that is, statutory actions. Accordingly, these three branches of law appeared at about the same time: the law of the Twelve Tables, from these came the *ius civile*, and from the same the *legis actiones* were devised. Moreover all of these, both the science of interpretation and the (conduct of) actions were vested in the college of pontiffs, from among whom one was appointed each year to preside over private causes. And for nearly a hundred years the people conformed to this custom."

understanding that the son obtained manumission upon completion of work for that person. Following the manumission, the son returned automatically into the *potestas* of his father and the sale process could be repeated. Table 4.2 limited this right of the father by stating that if a father sold his son three times, the latter acquired freedom. The pontiffs seized on this provision and engaged the pretence of interpretation to introduce the rule that if a father completed a fictional threefold sale of his son to another person, the son after the third alienation and manumission gained release from the *partia potestas* and became *sui iuris* (in control of his own affairs).[45] This example displays how a legal provision was utilized to achieve a purpose quite different from that originally contemplated by the legislator and how, through interpretation, a new norm was created as required by altered conditions.[46] While the pontiffs retained their monopoly in legal matters, it was mainly through their interpretations that innovations in the field of private law could be effected. At the same time, the pontiffs' activities as interpreters of the law forged the groundwork for the subsequent development of Roman legal science.

According to Roman tradition, the pontifical monopoly of legal knowledge came to an end after the publication in 304 BC by a certain Gnaeus Flavius, clerk of Appius Claudius (a prominent patrician who was appointed censor in 312 BC), of a collection of formulas and ritual words that were recited in court when litigation took place (*ius civile Flavianum*). Although any alert citizen must have known a great deal of the information embodied in the *ius Flavianum*, it was now rendered official and the jurisdictional magistrates could no longer refuse what all the people would know to be the law. From the late third century BC, an increasing number of leading Roman citizens adopted the practice of proffering legal advice without being members of the pontifical college. Around 200 BC one of these jurists, Sextus Aelius Paetus Catus, consul in 198 BC, published a book containing the text of the Twelve Tables, the interpretations of its rules by the pontiffs and secular jurists and a list of the legal forms employed in civil procedure. This work, known as *ius Aelianum*, marks the beginning of Roman legal literature and the transition from the unsystematic approach of the earlier priest-jurists to a new approach that may be termed scientific.[47]

---

[45] However, usually after the third manumission the 'buyer' sold the son back to his father, who at once manumitted him. In this way, the father acquired the status of patron over his son and thus retained rights of succession with regard to him.

[46] Another example of a rule developed through juristic interpretation is the rule relating to the guardianship of freed persons. According to Gaius: "The same law of the Twelve Tables assigns the guardianship of freed men and freed women under puberty to the patrons and their children. This form of guardianship is called statutory, not because it was expressly stated in that body of law, but because it has been accepted by interpretation as if it had been introduced by the words of the statute. For, by reason that the statute ordered that the estates of freed men and freed women who died intestate should go to the patrons and their children, the early jurists deemed that the statute willed that tutories also should go to them, because it had provided that agnates who were heirs should also be tutors." See G. 1. 165.

[47] D. 1. 2. 2. 6–7 (Pomponius): "Both the science of interpretation and the [conduct] of actions were vested in the college of pontiffs, from among whom one was appointed each year to preside

## 2.3  Sources of Law in the Late Republic

### 2.3.1  *Legislation*

As previously noted, in the period following the enactment of the *lex Hortensia* (287 BC) the term *lex* in a broad sense denoted not only a statute voted in the *comitia* on the proposal of a higher magistrate but also a *plebiscitum* passed in the *concilum plebis*. This period is rich in statutory enactments, but the *leges* that were passed encroached on the field of private law only with hesitation and within narrowly defined limits. As it was not easy to frame statutes in such a way as to avoid infringing long-established legal principles and customs (especially those embodied in the Law of the Twelve Tables), changes in this field were effected indirectly, primarily by means of praetorian action and juristic interpretation. Changes in the field of public law, on the other hand, were difficult to effect indirectly, since these were largely dictated by new situations or socio-political developments. It is thus unsurprising that the great majority of the statutes enacted during the later republican epoch fell in this field. Some statutes had a hybrid character, having a political basis but at the same time affecting the private relations of citizens. To this category belonged, for example, statutory enactments concerned with the distribution of land, release from debt, testamentary benefits and court procedure. As a whole, legislation was employed to deal with specific problems rather than to establish rules and principles governing social policy or constitutional arrangements in a comprehensive and permanent manner. Statutes were enacted, for example, to create new magistracies or to define the nature of public crimes and the procedures for dealing with them. In the field of private law statutes were relied on as a means of supplementing or limiting private rights, or instigating changes in civil procedure when juristic interpretation or magisterial action were deemed unable to produce the desired effect.

Among the statutes relating to private law of special importance were: the *lex Aquilia* (286 BC), which set general rules of liability for damage caused to another person's property; the *lex Atinia* (second century BC), which excluded stolen property (*res furtivae*) from *usucapio* (the acquisition of ownership through possession of a thing for a prescribed period of time); the *lex Laetoria de minoribus* (passed early in the second century BC), which aspired to protect persons under 25 years of age from fraud; the *lex Cincia de donis* (204 BC), which prohibited gifts in excess of a certain (unknown) amount with the exception of those in favour of

---

over private causes. Afterwards, when Appius Claudius had pronounced and fixed the form of these actions, Gnaeus Flavius, his secretary, the son of a freedman, stole the book and delivered it over to the people, and this service was so gratifying to the people that he was made tribune of the plebs, as well as senator and curule aedile. This book, which contains the actions, is called *ius Flavianum*, as that other, the *ius civile Papirianum*; nor did Gnaeus Flavius add anything of his own to the book. Since, with the expansion of the state, certain forms of action were lacking, not long afterwards Sextus Aelius compiled additional actions and gave the book to the people which is called the *ius Aelianum*."

near relatives and certain privileged persons; the *lex Voconia* (*c.* 169 BC), which imposed limitations upon the testamentary capacity of women; and the *lex Falcidia* (40 BC), which specified the amount of legacies that could be bequeathed.


### 2.3.1.1  The Role of the Senate in the Legislative Process

As previously observed, during the later republican period the senate became the centre of government and the most important stabilizing factor in the republican constitution. In domestic administration it was consulted by the magistrates on all important matters of the state; in foreign policy it directed negotiations with foreign powers, concluded treaties and appointed commissioners to oversee the organization of conquered territories; in finance it determined the use of public revenues and authorized public works; and in military affairs it prescribed the sphere of operations of the military commanders and their supplies of men and funds.

Even though under the constitution the senate had no direct power to enact laws, it played an increasingly active role in the legislative process, largely by virtue of its influence over the magistrates. As was previously noted, it was customary for the higher magistrates of the state to seek the senate's opinion on legislative proposals before submitting them to the assembly. Although the magistrates had the liberty to ignore such opinion, so great was the senate's power and prestige that they would normally defer to its authority and follow its lead. Ordinarily, the senate thoroughly discussed the drafts of legislative proposals and, if necessary, amended these drafts in accordance with the views of the senate's majority. A finally approved draft would then be incorporated in a resolution (*senatus consultum*) advising the magistrate concerned to submit it to the assembly, whose subsequent action virtually amounted to nothing more than a formal ratification of the terms of the *senatus consultum*. In this way, it was possible for the senate to bring about what amounted to indirect legislation as a result of which changes in the law could be effected, even though a *senatus consultum* could not be put into effect until it was adopted by a magistrate and had technically become part of a statutory enactment. Furthermore, in circumstances of emergency the senate could encroach on the power of the assemblies by claiming the right of suspending the constitution and of overriding the law by issuing a special resolution (*senatus consultum ultimum*)[48] that authorized the consuls to apply any extraordinary measures deemed necessary to avert the danger.

Besides playing a part in the formulation of legislative proposals, the senate exercised a lawmaking influence by advising the praetors and other jurisdictional magistrates to implement certain lines of policy. In such cases its recommendations would normally be incorporated in the edict (*edictum perpetuum*) issued by each magistrate at the commencement of his year of office. In this way, the senate

---

[48] Also referred to as *senatus consultum de re publica defendenda*: decree of the Senate on defending the Republic.

contributed to the development of magisterial law (*ius honorarium*), i.e. the law that derived its formal force from the authority of magistrates, as opposed to the *ius civile* construed as the law that derived its formal force from statute (*lex*) and juristic interpretation (*interpretatio*).

In the last century of the Republic, when the Roman state was embroiled in a political and administrative crisis and the influence of the assemblies declined, it sometimes happened that a legislative proposal sanctioned by the senate was not presented to the people, but immediately entered into force. Moreover the senate at times assumed the power to declare statutes null and void based on some alleged irregularity or violation of an established constitutional principle.[49] As the government transformed into the bureaucratic administration of a world empire during the early Principate era and the mode of creating law by vote of the people gradually withered away, the legislative function passed to the senate, whose enactments thus acquired the full force of laws.

## 2.3.2   The Rise of Magisterial Law

The Roman law of the archaic period was built around a relatively simple system of rules for a community of farmers and large landowners and its scope of application did not extend beyond the boundaries of the city-state of Rome. Like other primitive systems of law, it was closely bound up with religion and custom and was characterized by its formalism, rigidity and limited field of application. As a result of Rome's transformation from a small agrarian community into a vast transnational empire during the later republican era, the Romans faced the problem of how to adjust their law so that it might meet the challenges imposed upon it in this new era. In response to this problem, Roman law broke through the barrier of archaic formalism and formed a highly flexible system that could constantly adapt to the changing demands of social and commercial life. Important factors in this development encompassed the nascent contacts with other cultures and the increasingly intricate economic relations between Roman citizens and foreigners (*peregrini*). The transition to a more flexible system was made possible by the practice of granting wide powers to the jurisdictional magistrates who declared and applied the law, thus enabling them to mould the law in its application.

We observed earlier that the praetor was the official who supervised the administration of justice. In civil cases his role was to conduct a preliminary investigation where he determined the admissibility of the plaintiff's claim, i.e. whether the plaintiff had an action at law. If he was satisfied on this point, the praetor appointed the judge (*iudex*) before whom the case would be heard; in the opposite scenario, the plaintiff could not proceed to enforce his rights. In archaic Roman law, legal

---

[49] It is thus not surprising that both the *senatus consulta* and the *leges* are mentioned as sources of law by Cicero. See *Topica* 5. 28.

suits had to fit into certain set actions and comply with certain strict formalities. If the correct form of action was identified and the requisite formalities were adhered to, the magistrate had little choice but to grant the action and appoint a judge. However, in the later republican period there emerged a far more flexible procedure for initiating legal actions that allowed the magistrate greater discretion and freedom of action. Under this system, litigants could raise claims and concomitant defences that were not provided in the recognized actions. The admissibility of these claims and defences was determined in an informal procedure before the magistrate. The main reason behind this development was that as social and economic life grew in complexity there increasingly emerged cases where a right should clearly have been recognized, but this right and an appropriate legal action were not accommodated by the traditional *ius civile*. The magistrate was thus empowered to proceed beyond the strict letter of the law and admit or reject an action when he considered this right or equitable, even where this was not in accordance with the *ius civile*. He did not accomplish this step by introducing fresh legal rights (magistrates had no formal law-making authority), but by promising the applicant a remedy. He would inform the plaintiff that he now had an action on which to proceed in the subsequent hearing before the judge, and that success at that hearing meant his claim would be enforced by a remedy the magistrate granted. Ultimately, the end result was largely the same: though no civil law right existed, there was a praetorian remedy and hence a praetorian right. At the end of the proceedings before the magistrate, the latter composed a written document (*formula*) that prescribed the direction for the investigation and determination of the case by the judge appointed to try the case. In this document, he authorized the judge to condemn the defendant if certain facts were proven or to absolve the defendant if they were not proven. It must be assumed that the innovations in substantive law introduced through this system were gradual and organic. Whenever possible, the new *formula* was fitted into the system of actions recognized by the *ius civile*; in other cases the magistrate emancipated himself entirely from the established law by instructing the judge to decide the case on the basis of the factual situation, thus in essence functioning as a law-maker.

Every magistrate at Rome was in the habit of notifying to the public the manner in which he intended to exercise his authority, or any change which he contemplated in existing regulations, by means of a public notice (*edictum*).[50] With respect to magistrates who were merely concerned with administrative work, such notices were often occasional (*edicta repentina*). With respect to magistrates concerned with judicial business, they were of necessity valid for the whole period during which the magistrates held their office (*edicta perpetua*). The edicts of the praetors were necessarily of this latter type.[51] Although a newly elected magistrate was in

---

[50] Initially, an edict consisted in a verbal announcement before a public meeting (*contio*); in later times edicts were written on wooden tablets and were set up in the Forum (the market-place).

[51] D. 1. 2. 2. 10 (Pomponius): "During the same period magistrates also administered the laws and published edicts in order that the citizens might know what rule each magistrate would pronounce on each question, and take corresponding precaution."

theory free to introduce any measures he saw fit, over time it was expected that he would absorb the bulk of his predecessor's edict and make only limited alterations (that part of the *edictum perpetuum* adopted from year to year was referred to as *edictum tralaticium*). No legal obligation was imposed on the magistrate to adhere to the directions set out in his edict, for that was taken for granted. However, the breakdown of good government in the closing years of the Republic prompted the enactment of the *lex Cornelia* (67 BC) that forbade the praetors departing from their *edictum perpetuum*.[52]

The *edictum* of the praetor, in the sense in which this word is commonly used, is really a colloquial expression for the *album*, or great notice board exhibited by that magistrate, which contained other elements besides the *edicta* in their true and proper sense. It contained the *legis actiones* (actions provided by statute) and the *formulae* of the traditional *ius civile*, probably preceded by certain explanatory headings, but by no ruling in law (for the praetor did not create the rulings on which these civil actions and *formulae* were based). But the edict contained also model *formulae* for each promised remedy created by a praetor and his predecessors. Each of these *formulae* must have been preceded, at least eventually, by the ruling in law, which might have grown out of the *formula*, but finally served as its basis and justification.[53] Thus the edictal part of the *album* was really a series of separate *edicta*, each edict being followed by its own *formula*; it was regarded as being a supplement to that portion which specified the actions of the *ius civile*; and it really had this character of being a mere supplement in so far as praetorian actions were rarely granted where a civil action would have sufficed. But its supplementary role had far-reaching implications for the development of the law. This is because the edicts might take cognizance of cases not provided for by the *ius civile* at all; they might replace the mechanism provided by the civil law for attaining a legal end; and they might alter the character of the end itself. The edict of the peregrine praetor (*praetor peregrinus*)[54] was necessarily still more of a substitute for the *ius civile*

---

[52] Dio Cassius, *Historia Romana* 36. 40. 1–2: "The praetors were accustomed to compile and publish the edicts according to which they would grant actions, for those concerning agreements had not yet been fully set forth. Since they were not accustomed to do this once for all and did not observe the written rules but often made changes, many of which were introduced in order to favour or in order to defeat some person, he (C. Cornelius) moved that they should announce at the beginning of office the rules they would follow and not depart from them."

[53] In the course of time, the *formulae* used in specific types of cases became relatively fixed and the collection of established *formulae* was constantly augmented by new *formulae*. The number of established *formulae* had become so great by the end of the Republic that there appeared to be a *formula* for every possible occasion. According to Cicero: "There are laws, there are *formulae* established for every type of case, so that no one can be mistaken as to the kind of injury or the mode of action. Based on the loss, on the distress, on the inconvenience, on the ruin, or on the wrong suffered by anyone, public *formulae* have been set forth by the praetor, to which private controversy may be adapted." (*Pro Roscio comoedo oratio* 8. 24)

[54] As previously noted, this praetor exercised civil jurisdiction in disputes between foreigners (*peregrini*) and between foreigners and Roman citizens.

than that of his urban colleague (*praetor urbanus*).[55] For, as the actions of the civil law could not (at least in many cases) be employed by foreigners, the peregrine praetor was obliged to devise equivalents for these actions and the forms by which they were accompanied.[56]

The various rules and remedies by which the magistrates were actually transforming the old *ius civile* furnished the basis for the development of a new body of law that was ultimately designated honorary or magisterial law (*ius honorarium*)—because it proceeded from the holders of offices (*honores*)—and that existed in contradistinction with the narrowly defined *ius civile*. The magisterial law served a vitally important function in the Roman legal system in various ways. Firstly, it aided the *ius civile* as the magistrate introduced remedies in addition to those that the civil law provided for the person who possessed a civil law right. For instance, the edict would state that an individual recognized as the owner of property under the civil law might be granted, in addition to the normal action, a speedier magisterial remedy. Secondly, it supplemented the *ius civile* as the magistrate granted remedies to persons who had no rights or remedies under the civil law. For instance, the wife of a deceased person who died intestate without leaving children or relatives had no rights to his estate. However, the edict would grant the widow a remedy to acquire possession of the estate. Thirdly, it amended or corrected the civil law as persons who had no rights or remedies under the civil law were granted remedies by the magistrate at the detriment of those who did have such rights. For instance, the edict might provide that the magistrate would uphold certain wills that did not meet the requirements of the civil law and he would grant a remedy to the person nominated as heir in such a will at the detriment of the intestate heir who would have succeeded under the civil law.[57] Through these means, the magisterial law became the living voice of the law of the Romans. Alongside the rigid and formalistic *ius civile* there emerged a body of law that was

---

[55] The original praetor who had jurisdiction over disputes involving only Roman citizens (*iurisdictio urbana*).

[56] Another perpetual edict valid in Rome was that of the curule aediles. As pertaining to the limited civil jurisdiction these magistrates exercised in the market place, this edict played a part in the development of the Roman law of sale. By far more important, however, was the edict issued by the provincial governors (proconsuls or propraetors). These officials issued notices of their intentions with respect to jurisdiction, similar to those of the praetors at Rome as regards their permanent character and the possibility of their transmission, but peculiarly applicable to the particular governor's domain. One important point in which the governor of a province differed from the praetor at Rome was that he was an administrative as well as a judicial official. Hence the provincial edict had to contain a good many rules of administrative law not to be found in its counterpart at Rome. The rest of the edict covered the procedure the governor promised to apply for the recovery of certain rights by individuals such as, for example, those entailed in inheritance or the seizure of a debtor's goods. Although these rules were based on Roman law, they were mere outlines capable of adaptation to the local customs of the subject communities.

[57] D. 1. 1. 7. 1 (Papinianus): "*Ius praetorium* is that which the praetors have introduced from the purpose of aiding, supplementing or correcting the *ius civile* to the public advantage. It is also called *ius honorarium* after the office (*honos*) of the praetors."

progressive and free, and subject to continual change and development.[58] It is germane to note at this point that the magistrates were not solely responsible for the creation of the *ius honorarium*. Since magistrates very often possessed little knowledge of the law, most of the techniques they engaged to produce the required legal innovations were demonstrated to them by expert jurists (*iurisconsulti* or *iurisprudentes*). The jurists explained the law to magistrates and offered guidance in framing their edicts and drafting the *formulae* used in legal proceedings. Thus, the legal norms incorporated in the *edictum perpetuum* at any given time represented the consensus of opinion of the best-qualified legal minds of the day.

But how did the praetor choose which rights to protect? The main basis for this choice appears to have been the social and ethical values generated by the conditions of the times. These values materialized in appropriate guidelines that emphasized the importance of fairness and honesty in business practices, accorded preference to substance over form in transactions and refused to uphold obligations arising from promises elicited by fraudulent means. An important factor was the growing role of contractual good faith (*bona fides*) as a legal concept relating to the enforcement by legal means of what had been previously viewed as merely social or moral obligations.[59] The classical jurists used the term *aequitas* (equity) when referring to the basis or the qualifying feature of praetorian measures granted on a case-by-case basis and promised in the edict.[60] There are two ways to understand

---

[58] According to the classical jurist Marcianus, "the *ius honorarium* is of itself the living voice of the *ius civile*." (D. 1. 1. 8) A parallel may be drawn between the Roman *ius honorarium* and English equity. Unlike the English common law and equity, however, the *ius civile* and *ius honorarium* did not operate as two separate systems administered by different courts but were regarded as two sides of the same legal system.

[59] The concept of good faith (*bona fides*) probably had a Roman origin and initially appeared to be linked with the notion of *fas*, or divine law. However, a Greek influence cannot be ruled out. In the sphere of private law *bona fides* was perceived in two ways: a) from an objective point of view, *bona fides* was associated with the general expectation that persons should behave honestly and fairly in legal transactions; b) from a subjective point of view, *bona fides* pertained to a person's belief that his actions were just and lawful and did not violate another person's legitimate interest. Several general rules based upon the concept of *bona fides* are included in the sources, e.g. '*bona fides* requires that what has been agreed upon must be done' (D. 19. 2. 21. – Iavolenus), '*bona fides* demands equity in contracts' (D. 16. 3. 31. pr. – Tryphoninus).

[60] Aristotle defines equity (*epieikeia*) as a principle of justice designed to correct the positive law where the latter is defective owing to its universality (*Nic. Ethics*, 5. 10). As constituting a 'mean', or 'intermediate', i.e. a kind of compromise, the law must be expressed simply and in general terms. But while framing the law generally and simply, the lawmaker exposes it to deficiencies that produce injustice. A general rule is considered deficient and lacunary because it cannot precisely cover every potential case as the human condition is imbued with complexities. Thus, a case may arise where one acted against the rule but no injustice was committed. To exclude such a case from the field of application of a broadly framed law, a new norm must be formulated to govern a determination of the case. The judge then has to allow equity to guide his discovery of the most appropriate solution, i.e. the one that best conforms to the justice that inspires the law. Furthermore, the law has a decisive form and can only evolve from sporadic attempts that are often too late. Once more, the judge assumes the task of correcting and completing the law. In contrast to positive law that is only a rough or incomplete reflection of justice, equity is the precise reflection

the connection of equity with positive law: first, *aequitas* may be construed as the substance and intrinsic justification of the existing legal norms; secondly, it may be conceived as an objective ideal the law aims to effectuate and which determines the creation of new legal norms and the modification of those that do not conform with society's sense of justice nor accomplish the requisite balance in human relations. This second understanding of *aequitas* served as the basis of the innovations produced by jurisdictional magistrates and jurists. However, according to classical jurists, what has positive force is not *aequitas* as such, but *ius*, or law in a broad sense. Thus, until *aequitas* is transfused into a positive norm it remains confined to a pre-legal sphere. Once this transfusion has occurred, *ius* has notable significance while *aequitas* exists as the matrix.[61] The incorporation of equity into the administration of the law is attributable to the praetorian edict and the interpretations of the jurists. This redressed the formalism and rigidity of the traditional *ius civile*, and enabled the creation of new law that could fulfill the needs of a changing society.

The following two examples provide good illustrations of the techniques engaged by the praetor for surmounting the difficulties arising from the rigidity of the *ius civile*.

The idea that legal obligations could materialize from anything other than a strict form was strange to the original structure of Roman law established in the Law of the Twelve Tables. Such obligations could only arise from transactions executed in a few solemn forms and rites that had a predominantly public and partly sacred character. Consider *stipulatio*, for example. This formal transaction consisted of a solemn question posed by one party to the other as to whether the latter would

---

of justice. Therefore, the judge must constantly correct the errors or fill the gaps in the positive law by appealing to equity as a form of justice that extends beyond positive law.

[61] Cicero's definition of the *ius civile* as 'the equity constituted for those who belong to the same state so that each may secure his own' (*Top.* 2. 9.), and the renowned aphorism of the jurist Celsius '*ius est ars boni et aequi*': 'the *ius* is the art of the good and just' (D. 1. 1. 1. pr.), are obviously inspired by the concept of equity as an abstract ideal of justice and as a touchstone of the norms of positive law. Linked with this perception of equity is the distinction between *ius strictum* and *ius aequum*. The distinction was created on a philosophical-moral basis in order to differentiate the rigorous and inflexible rules of the operative law from the flexible norms inspired by the superior criteria of *aequitas*. In the early imperial epoch Roman jurisprudence, drawing upon the philosophical conception of *aequitas* as true justice, started to speak in some cases of superior equity, from which the jurisdictional magistrates drew inspiration and which, in turn, led to the development of *ius honorarium*. Thus, Roman jurisprudence laid the basis for the distinction between legal institutions conforming with or diverging from the principles of ideal justice. After the Christianization of the Roman Empire in the fourth century AD, the concept of *aequitas* was interpreted in light of Christian ethical principles. This new approach to the meaning of *aequitas* is reflected in the Justinianic codification where *aequitas* is connected with values such as piety (*pietas*), affection (*caritas*), humanity (*humanitas*), kindness (*benignitas*) and clemency (*clementia*). This entailed the tendency of the notion of *ius aequum* to coincide with the Christian conception of *ius naturale*. In this respect, the abatement or derogation of laws in force was justified by reference to an *aequitas* construed as an expression of a law superior to the law in force because it was inspired by God – a law whose principal interpreter was deemed to be the emperor. Thus, for the first time, equity was perceived as a benign rectification of strict law rather than as an objective equation between conflicting interests.

render specific performance, followed by a solemn affirmative answer from the other party. This exchange of question and answer created an actionable obligation of the answering party under the *ius civile*. Circumstances could exist that made it unfair for the creditor to enforce the transaction. However, no remedy was provided by the *ius civile* in such a case. If the parties had observed all the prescribed formalities, the validity of the contract could not be questioned. To rectify the situation, the praetor could use his own authority to include an additional clause (*exceptio*) in the relevant *formula* that enabled the defendant to render the plaintiff's claim ineffective by showing grounds for denying judgment in the plaintiff's favour. When the *exceptio* was based on the allegation that the plaintiff had acted fraudulently (*dolo*), it was designated *exceptio doli*.[62] Granting exceptions was an ingenious device that enabled the praetor to deliver appropriate relief in individual cases without questioning the validity of the relevant legal rule. Thus the *exceptio doli* left the principle of the *stipulatio* intact, i.e. the obligation to act as one had promised by responding in a particular way to a specific question posed. The *form* of the transaction still created the legal obligation, although the recognition that intention had priority over form was implicit in accepting the *exceptio doli*.

An important distinction in the early Roman law of property existed between *res mancipi* and *res nec mancipi*. *Res mancipi* included land and buildings situated in Italy, slaves and draft animals, such as oxen and horses. All other objects were *res nec mancipi*. The ownership of *res mancipi* could be transferred only by means of a highly formal procedure called *mancipatio*. The ownership of *res nec mancipi*, on the other hand, could be passed informally, e.g. by simple delivery (*traditio*).[63] If a *res mancipi* was transferred to someone in an informal manner, the transferee did not acquire title under the *ius civile*.[64] In such a case, if the transferee lost possession of the property he could not recover it from the person with the current holding. While retaining possession of the property he could be challenged by the transferor who remained the lawful owner (*dominus*). As economic relations grew more complex, the strictness of the law proved detrimental to many legitimate interests. To rectify the situation, the praetor intervened and placed the transferee in the factual possession of a civil law owner. The property was then regarded as *in bonis* (hence the concept of 'bonitary' ownership) and such a 'bonitary' owner could acquire true ownership by *usucapio* (i.e. through lapse of a certain period of time).[65] If the bonitary owner lost possession of the property, he could recover it by

---

[62] The *bona fides* requirement that existed as the basis of the system of consensual contracts was virtually incorporated into the Roman *ius civile* by the *exceptio doli* and the *actio doli*.

[63] The origin of the distinction between *res mancipi* and *res nec mancipi* remains obscure, although it may be related to the fact that the *res mancipi* were extremely valuable in the archaic period when agriculture formed the basis of Roman economic life. In later times, the formal methods for transferring ownership diminished in importance and, by Justinian's era, the distinction between *res mancipi* and *res nec mancipi* no longer existed.

[64] Only Roman citizens or persons vested with the *ius commercii* could acquire ownership under the *ius civile* (*dominium ex iure Quiritium*).

[65] G. 2. 41.

means of the *actio Publiciana*.[66] This action was granted to all *bona fide* possessors in the process of acquiring ownership by *usucapio*, and was based on the fiction that the period required for obtaining the property by *usucapio* was completed. If the original owner endeavoured to claim the property, the bonitary owner could raise the defence of *exceptio rei venditae et traditae* (defence of a property sold and delivered by *traditio*),[67] or the *exceptio doli*. The praetor engaged these devices to create a new type of property right that supplemented those recognized under the traditional *ius civile* and this generated a considerable improvement in the Roman law of property.[68]

The above examples present a sketch of the techniques the praetor used to invent not merely supplementary but often superseding rights that galvanized the development of the *ius honorarium*. The descriptions expose two interrelated characteristics of the Roman legal system: a pervasive dualism, perhaps even a dialectic relationship between old and new; and a tendency towards gradual adaptation. There is the dualism between *ius civile* and *ius honorarium*, between an adherence to past forms and an admirable ingenuity in designing ways to address new situations and problems. This system is even more remarkable as both the aspects of respecting the past and adapting to the new were combined in the praetor. The praetor used all his creativity to construct devices that tackled the problems arising from novel socio-economic circumstances, and also acted as a guarantor of the basic forms and principles of the old law. Such a system seemed to satisfy the people's desire to believe that things remained the same as long as they were ascribed the same labels. It created the comfortable illusion that nothing really had changed. The reluctance to abandon the fundamental principles of the traditional legal system is aptly illustrated by the institution of the *patria potestas*, which was recognized by the Romans as a characteristic element of their system. Despite the enormous inconveniences generated by this institution, it survived until as late as the fourth century AD. Devices were designed to mitigate its unwanted consequences in a new era that no longer required a family structure based on the traditional *patia potestas*; yet, these devices did not affect the essence of that institution. Although several aspects were modified, like the power to prevent the marriage of a daughter, it had a longevity that virtually resembled that of Roman law. The practice of the praetor to grant exceptions to defendants illuminates the same tendency for observing the old rules. Granting exceptions was a cautious device that retained the essence of the rules, while providing relief in a particular case or type of case. Indeed, classifying a particular case as exceptional would appear to confirm the validity of the relevant rule. Similarly, the use of fiction

---

[66] Introduced by Publicius, a *praetor urbanus*, probably in the first century BC. See G. 4. 36.

[67] D. 21. 3. 3.

[68] Fictions were not an exclusively praetorian device used to adapt the legal system to changing socio-economic conditions. They were also embodied in statutes, such as, for example, the *lex Cornelia* (first century BC). According to this law, a citizen who died in captivity should be deemed to have died at the moment he was taken prisoner, i.e., as a free Roman citizen, so that his will made prior to captivity could be regarded as valid (*fictio legis Corneliae*).

helped the victim of bad faith or error in cases where the requirements of strict law were not fulfilled. However, it did not diminish the validity of the legal principles that applied under the old *ius civile*. For example, the fiction of a completed *usucapio* in the *actio Publiciana* did not affect the basic principles of the *ius civile* relating to the acquisition of ownership over *res mancipi*. Fictions and other praetorian devices facilitated the cautious and gradual adaptation of the rules insofar as this was deemed necessary, but did not appear to change any elements on the normative level. On closer observation, it is not difficult to discern that these devices produced important changes to the law. This evokes the Hegelian idea that a change in quantity may lead to a change in quality. Although the form of this change suggested that only a minor detail of a rule was affected, a major principle of the Roman *ius civile* was actually rendered ineffectual or set aside. The relationship between the *ius civile* and the *ius honorarium* (or between law and equity) clearly exhibits the Romans' commitment to the two notions of stability and change, of preservation of the past and efficient adaptation to new needs.

### 2.3.2.1 Relationship with Non-Roman Communities and the Concept of *Ius Gentium*

The development of the *ius honorarium* in the later republican era was closely connected with the dramatic increase in contacts between the Romans and non-Roman communities, and the growth in economic relations between Roman citizens and foreigners (*peregrini*). As the granting of Roman citizenship had not kept pace with Rome's expansion, a growing mass of foreigners residing in Roman territory had no access to the Roman *ius civile*.[69] However, the development of foreign trade and the proliferation of foreigners living in Rome prompted the need to formulate rules applicable to disputes between foreigners, and between foreigners and Romans. The Romans responded to this need by appointing (from c. 242 BC) a special praetor, the *praetor peregrinus*, to handle cases involving foreigners. The peregrine praetor enjoyed greater liberty than his urban colleague did as no law limited his operations. Thus, when formulating remedies he could consider the new needs created by the ever-changing social and economic conditions. Governors in the provinces were also granted jurisdiction over disputes concerning Roman citizens settled there and provincials; and, occasionally, over cases involving foreigners. The edicts of the *praetor peregrinus* and, to a lesser extent, those of the provincial governors engendered a new system of rules governing relations between free men without reference to their nationality.

---

[69] As already noted, according to the principle of the personality of laws, the Roman *ius civile* was only for Roman citizens and non-citizens were unable to share therein. Thus, a foreigner could not easily engage in legal transactions and, if aggrieved by another person, could not defend himself or prosecute a claim before the authorities of the city unless he secured personal protection from a Roman citizen.

Although this body of law was Roman in origin, it became known as *ius gentium*:
the law of nations.[70]

From an early period the Romans realised that certain institutions of their own
*ius civile* also existed in the legal systems of other nations. As contracts of sale,
service and loan, for example, were recognised by many systems, it was assumed
that the principles governing these were everywhere in force in the same way.
These institutions which the Roman law had in common with other legal systems
were thought of by the Romans as belonging to the law of nations (*ius gentium*) in a
broad sense. But this understanding of the *ius gentium* was of little practical value
for the Roman lawyer, for the specific rules governing the operation of such
generally recognised institutions differed from one legal system to another. When
the Romans began to trade with foreigners they must have realised that their own
*ius civile* was an impossible basis for developing trading relations. Foreigner traders
too had little inclination to conform to the tedious formalities of domestic Roman
law. Some common ground had to be discovered as the basis for a common court,
which might adjudicate on claims of private international law, and this common
ground was found in the *ius gentium*, or the law of nations in a narrow, practical
sense.

Although little information exists on the methods employed by the peregrine
praetor in performing his functions, we may surmise that he adopted the *ius civile*
when applicable to the relevant case. Moreover, the customary norms common to
many nations must have been relevant to determining whether or not a claim was
acceptable. For example, a magistrate could easily fathom that many nations
transferred titles to land and property by mere delivery and payment, and not by
the formal methods familiar to Rome. This entailed an increasing recognition by
jurisdictional magistrates of the validity of informal agreements or consensual
contracts based on good faith (*bona fides*) in commercial transactions—contracts
where Romans and foreigners alike could engage.[71] However, an important note is
that when a magistrate addressed a dispute involving foreigners he had to recall that
his solutions must accord with what was considered proper and reasonable from a
Roman citizen's viewpoint. Thus the *ius gentium* might be described as a complex

---

[70] According to Gaius: "Every people that is governed by statutes and by customs observed partly
its own particular law and partly the common law of all mankind. That law which any people
established for itself is peculiar to it and is called *ius civile* as being the law of its own citizenry,
while the law that natural reason establishes among all mankind is observed by all peoples alike
and is called *ius gentium*. So the laws of the people of Rome are partly peculiar to itself, partly
common to all nations..." (G. 1. 1.).

[71] Where *bona fides* was accepted as the basis of a legal obligation, the intention of the parties to
the contract rather than the form observed was decisive for the generation of legal consequences.
However, the recognition of the role of *bona fides* as a basis of liability did not entail abandonment
of the *stipulatio* that existed as the principal formal contract of the *ius civile*. Instead, both
consensual contracts and *stipulatio* existed for a long time alongside each other. Neither did this
mean that consensual contracts were only relevant to transactions involving foreigners. Roman
citizens among themselves increasingly used informal agreements as the role of ritual in concluding agreements decreased.

system of generally observed customs and rules that embodied elements the Romans regarded as reflecting the substance of *ius*, or law in a broad normative sense; in other words, 'that which was good and fair' (*bonum et aequum*).[72]

Attending to disputes involving people of diverse national backgrounds would have been difficult without employing rules based on common sense, expediency and fairness that were confirmed by general and prevalent usage among many communities. In contrast to the *ius civile*, the *ius gentium* was thus characterized by its simplicity, adaptability and emphasis on substance rather than form. The absence of any rigid rules in the procedure implemented by the peregrine praetor created sufficient elasticity for its adjustment to the demands of the relevant case. For that reason, not only foreigners but also Roman citizens increasingly resorted to the procedure as a means of resolving legal disputes. The elastic technique of the *praetor peregrinus* was gradually adopted by the *praetor urbanus*, the magistrate in charge of the administration of the Roman domestic law (*ius proprium Romanorum*), when deciding cases between citizens that fell outside the scope of the traditional *ius civile*. As a result of this development, the urban praetor was no longer bound by the old statutory forms of action (*legis actiones*) and had freedom to devise new remedies and corresponding procedural formulae to tackle *ad hoc* controversies engendered by novel socio-economic circumstances. Such measures were not restricted to the application of the laws in force, but could be used to modify or replace existing law. Although in principle neither praetor had legislative authority, they actually created new law by extensively engaging their right to regulate the forms of proceedings accepted in court. A new body of law thus emerged that incorporated the norms of private law derived from the edicts of the praetors and other magistrates: the *ius honorarium*.

## 2.3.3  The Jurists of the Late Republic

As previously noted, during the archaic era knowledge of the law and the rules governing legal procedure was confined to the priestly college of the pontiffs. After the enactment of the Law of the Twelve Tables and the introduction of the system of *legis actiones* the authoritative interpretation of statutory law and the conduct of the actions at law remained within the province of these priests.[73] According to Roman tradition, the pontiffs' monopoly of legal knowledge ended in 304 BC when Gnaeus Flavius published a manuscript containing the procedural formulas and ritual words employed in litigation. In *c.* 253 BC Tiberius Coruncanius, the first plebeian *pontifex*

---

[72] One might declare that the *ius gentium* was not entirely a technical name for a body of legally recognized rights, but a means of justifying the introduction of new ones. The fact that an institution was discovered to exist in many nations was *prima facie* evidence that it was equitable and hence could be invoked in the praetor's court.

[73] D. 1. 2. 2. 6.

*maximus*, began to discuss cases and to give legal advice in public (*publice profiteri*) in such a way that the knowledge he imparted became common to all.[74] Thereafter, an increasing number of secular jurists (*jurisprudentes* or *iurisconsulti*)[75] engaged in furnishing legal advice and by the end of the second century BC they had supplanted the original interpreters of the law. These jurists were members of the Roman aristocracy and were actively involved in politics. Like the pontiffs before them, they received no remuneration for their services for they considered it their civic duty to assist citizens who sought their legal advice. Although jurisprudence did not become a profession through which one could earn a living, it provided an important outlet for members of the nobility who sought to distinguish themselves in social and political life. Because of the respect and honour they gained through their activities, these individuals were able to increase their influence among their fellow citizens and, by widening the circle of their friends and dependants, to win their way to high office.

Cicero declares that jurists had to be skilled in three respects in matters of law: *agere*, *cavere* and *respondere*.[76]

*Agere* (literally, to act) meant managing a legal cause or suit. The jurists gave help on matters of procedure and prepared the forms that had to be used by the parties to lawsuits. As noted previously, in the archaic era a person initiating a lawsuit was required to fit his claim within one of the set forms of action prescribed by the law. The rigidity of this system considerably limited the scope of juristic intervention. However, a new flexible system of procedure for initiating legal actions emerged in the second century BC. Under this system, the final settling of the plaintiff's statement of claim was an extremely technical process and this provided broad scope for the intervention of the jurists in litigation. It is important to note, however, that the jurists very rarely argued cases in the courts—this task was left to the *oratores*.[77]

*Cavere* (literally, to take precautions) meant the drafting of legal documents, such as contracts and wills, designed to preserve a person's interests by protecting them against certain eventualities. This cultivation of forms was one of the most important contributions of the jurists to the development of legal thinking and

---

[74] D. 1. 2. 2. 35 and 38.

[75] *Jurisprudentes*: those possessing the knowledge of the law; *iurisconsulti*: those who were consulted on legal matters.

[76] *De oratore* 1. 48. 212.

[77] Although trained in law, advocates often relied on the help of jurists in difficult cases to ensure that their clients' claims were properly stated according to the prescribed *formulae*. Moreover, an advocate might seek a jurist's advice when he intended to request the granting of a new form of action from a magistrate (at the *in iure* stage of the proceedings), and when he pleaded the case before the judge (*apud iudicem*). See, e.g., Cicero, *Topica* 17. 65: "For private actions involving important issues, indeed, seem to me to depend on the wisdom of the jurisconsults. For they frequently attend [trials] and are turned to in council and furnish the weapons to advocates who choose them seeking their knowledge. In all suits, then, ... they are bound to be ready [with their advice]."

language. It was mainly through this work of form development over the centuries that Roman legal speech attained its perfection.

*Respondere* (literally, to answer) meant giving advice or opinions on questions of law. A practice applicable to every field of Roman life was that an individual would elicit the advice of competent and impartial persons when contemplating a serious decision. Thus, the jurists gave *responsa* or replies to private citizens involved in lawsuits or other legal business that required attention, and to jurisdictional magistrates and the judges (*iudices*) appointed to decide particular cases.[78] The *responsa* were expressed in a casuistic form: the jurist restated the factual aspects of the case in such a way to illuminate the legal question presented to him. By drawing on the wealth of legal principles applied in the past or encountered within his own experience, he rendered a decision that only obliquely referred to the principle or rule that supported it. It should be noted that the casuistic form in which the *responsa* were expressed entailed considerable differences of opinion among individual jurists with respect to certain matters.[79] In many cases, opposing points of view were adopted by contemporary or later jurists. Many of these controversies persisted for decades or even centuries.[80]

Besides the practical activities outlined above, the jurists were occupied by two further tasks that were instrumental in the development of Roman law: the education of those aspiring to enter the practice of law, and the composition of legal works.

Legal education in republican Rome had a largely practical orientation; there was neither theoretical nor academic legal training or educational institutions where law was formally taught.[81] Upon completion of their basic education, young men would enter the household of a jurist to live with the family. They would attend consultations when clients sought legal advice, and accompany the jurist to the marketplace where they observed him imparting legal advice, drafting legal documents and assisting parties in legal proceedings. In this way, students acquired knowledge of the law through contact with legal practice and professional tradition.[82] Sometimes, the jurists gave opinions when their students raised purely

---

[78] The jurists presented their replies verbally or in writing and the audience which received them was by no means confined to those who sought the jurists' advice.

[79] According to Cicero, "as for that law which is unsettled among the most learned [jurists], it is not difficult for the orator to find some authority for whichever side he is defending, and having obtained a supply of thronged spears from him [the jurist], he himself will hurl these with the vigor and strength of an orator." (*De oratore* 1. 57. 242)

[80] The only proof of the validity of a juristic opinion was its acceptance by a court. But even this was but a slender proof, for different jurisdictional magistrates or judges might be under the sway of different jurists.

[81] Systematic instruction by professional law teachers was not introduced until the later imperial age.

[82] Cicero, *Orator* 42. 143: "It was sufficient for the [law students] to listen to those responding, as those [jurists] who taught set aside no special time for that purpose, but at the same time satisfied both the students and the consultants."

hypothetical cases for discussion. These opinions were almost equal in influence to those given on real facts, and possibly helped to develop Roman law in new and unique directions.

From the second century BC, prominent jurists began to compile books of *responsa* that they had issued and were applied in practice (especially those ratified by virtue of a judicial decision). The need to create such collections derived from the fact that in Rome the administration of private law was not closely regulated by the state and hence judicial decisions were not formally collected on behalf of the state. In their collections the jurists sometimes included summaries of important cases, and recorded the relevant court decisions and the opinions rendered to the parties concerned. The jurists also composed various commentaries or treatises on different branches of the law and, over time, a large body of legal literature materialized. The emergence of legal literature is associated with the influence of the Greek culture and science on the Roman aristocracy that encompassed the jurists. It is important to note that the contributions of the jurists are not evenly distributed over the whole field of law; private law and civil procedure patently dominate, whereas many areas of public law were never the object of the same intensive analysis and constructive development.

As the foregoing discussion suggests, Roman jurisprudence evolved largely from legal practice with a notable contribution from the discussion of individual cases. A distinction is usually made between two types of juristic method: the *empirical* or *casuistic* and the *deductive*. The Roman jurists were typical representatives of the former method. When dealing with legal problems, they resorted primarily to topical rather than axiomatic argument. If a legal rule or concept is formed by logical reasoning from basic principles or axioms, it invokes axiomatic argument. Topical or problem reasoning, on the other hand, occurs when one proceeds from the case to identify the premises that would support a solution, and then formulates guiding principles and concepts as a basis for attaining a solution. The rules and concepts devised in this manner are not rigid and inviolable but are subject to change, depending on the circumstances of the relevant case. Moreover, it is generally believed that the Roman jurists reached their conclusions intuitively. This intuitive grasp of the law is attributed to the Romans' innate sense for legal matters, and to the jurists' experience with the everyday practice of the law. However, one should not construe Roman jurisprudence as a merely pragmatic, unprincipled case law or believe that Roman decision-making was based solely on free and creative intuition. The greatest achievement of the Roman jurists was their ability to extend beyond the accidental elements of the relevant case to illuminate the essential legal problem as a *quaestio iuris*. As the jurists gradually acquired familiarity with Greek philosophy and the intellectual methods and tools the Greeks had created, they developed a systematic approach to legal knowledge and to handling legal problems. Thus, acquaintance with the logical syllogism (or reasoned conclusions) enabled them to construct legal concepts in a deductive manner. The jurists engaged the dialectical method: a form of logical analysis that both distinguished between various concepts and subsumed those sharing the same essential characteristics under common heads. This fostered their learning to divide (into *genera* and *species*) and define juridically relevant facts, and thereby distinguish and categorize juridical concepts. Moreover, awareness of the sociological function of law led the jurists to attach more emphasis on equity (*aequitas*), good faith (*bona fides*) and other general guiding principles.[83] The jurists' tendency towards systematization not only allowed them to present their casuistic approach in a more simple and elegant manner, but also helped to improve their decision-propositions. This improvement in decisions was closely connected with the requirement for integration in the growing empire and the need to adapt the legal system to its deriving socio-structural changes.

A celebrated jurist of the later republican period was Quintus Mucius Scaevola, *pontifex maximus* and consul in 95 BC. Scaevola is declared to have been the first jurist who endeavoured to systematize the existing law in a scientific fashion. Unlike earlier jurists, he did not confine himself to the discussion of isolated cases or questions of law. Rather, he made great efforts towards a higher level of generalization and ventured to introduce more definition and division. In his comprehensive treatise on the *ius civile*, he assembled related legal phenomena and principles under common headings. He also distinguished the various forms of appearance of these broader categories. For instance, he first defined the general features of possession, tutorship and so on, and then described their various individual forms (*genera*) existing in the legal system. He also seems to have written a book that featured brief definitory statements (*horoi*) indicating the decisive factual moment (*horos*) of a certain legal consequence or decision.[84] Scaevola is also attributed with formulating certain standard legal clauses and presumptions, such as the *cautio Muciana* (a promise by a legatee that he would return the legacy if he acted against the attached condition) and the *praesumptio Muciana* (the presumption that all the property a married woman possessed was furnished by her husband, until the contrary was proved). As governor of the province of Asia, Scaevola also composed a provincial edict (*edictum provinciale*) that was used as a model by other provincial governors. Scaevola's work was an

---

[83] Quintilianus, *Institutio oratoria* 12. 3. 7: "Those laws which are written or established by the custom of the state present no difficulty, since they call for knowledge, not reasoning. But those matters which are explained in the responses of the jurists are founded either upon the interpretation of words or on the distinction between right and wrong."

[84] The scheme appeared in the following style: X is the essential characteristic when the choice between D or non-D must be determined; X is present in the combination of facts A; X is not present in the combination of facts B; X is the *differentia specifica* between the classes A and B, which leads to the conclusion that A→D, whilst B→non-D. This scheme was elaborated further by the great Augustan jurist M. Antistius Labeo. Labeo had adopted the Stoic mode of expressing Aristotelian definitions in the form of implicative statements. His 'hypotheses' (*pithana*) very much resembled legal norms: if F then D; if non-F, then non-D and so on. Such statements were later conceived as and called norms: *regulae iuris*. They were also often designated *definitiones* or *differentia* – terms that reflect their origin in Aristotelian philosophy.

important step forward as it introduced a scheme of law conceived as a logically connected whole alongside the collections of precedents and isolated legal rules. It had enduring influence and commentaries on it were still written as late as the second century AD.[85]

Other distinguished jurists of the later republican period included: Manius Manilius, consul in 149 BC, whose work *venalium vendendorum leges* ('conditions of sale for things capable of being sold'), mainly elaborated model *formulae* relating to contracts of sale[86]; M. Porcius Cato Censorius, consul in 195 BC and censor in 184 BC, whose work *de agricultura* ('on agriculture') comprised forms and precedents for drafting agrarian contracts; the latter's son, M. Porcius Cato Licinianus, who authored a celebrated treatise on the *ius civile* (*de iuris disciplina*)[87]; M. Junius Brutus, praetor in 142 BC, who wrote books on the *ius civile*[88]; Gaius Aquilius Gallus, praetor in 66 BC, who introduced the action and exception of *dolus* (a term that merges the ideas of fraud, abuse of right, and the general concept of tort)[89]; C. Trebatius Testa, a friend of Cicero's, whose work on the *ius civile* was highly regarded by the classical jurists[90]; P. Alfenus Varus, consul in 39 BC, who produced an extensive work (*Digesta*) in 40 books[91]; Servius Sulpicius Rufus, consul in 51 BC, whose writings included an important commentary on the praetorian edict[92]; and P. Rutilius Rufus, consul in 105 BC, who devised the bankruptcy procedure described by Gaius (*actio Rutiliana*).[93] Only a few

---

[85] Cicero, *Brutus* 39. 145–46: "Scaevola was considered the most eloquent of those learned in the law. He was an exceedingly acute legal thinker; his language very terse and admirably suited to legal discussion. An incomparable interpreter of the law, but in the matters of emotional appeal, oratorical embellishment and debate a formidable critic rather than a marvellous orator." And see D. 1. 2. 2. 41–42 (Pomponius): "Quintus Mucius, pontifex maximus, son of Publius, was the first to compile the *ius civile*, which he arranged according to *genera*, in eighteen books. (42) The pupils of Mucius were many, but those of the greatest authority were Aquilius Gallus, Balbus Lucilius, Sextus Papirius, Gaius Iuventius ...".

[86] Cicero, *de orat.* 1. 246; D. 1. 2. 2. 39.

[87] D. 1. 2. 2. 38.

[88] Cicero, *pro Cluent.* 141; *de orat.* 2. 142. 224; D. 1. 2. 2. 39.

[89] D. 4. 3. 1. 1. This had far-reaching implications, as it introduced equitable considerations into determining the validity of transactions. In practice, it enabled equitable defences to be pleaded in almost any action.

[90] D. 1. 2. 2. 45; *Inst.* 2. 25. pr.

[91] D. 1. 2. 2. 44.

[92] According to Cicero, Servius was the first jurist to apply the dialectic method in the study of legal problems (*Brut.* 152 ff.). And see D. 1. 2. 2. 43.

[93] G. 4. 35.

scattered and fragmentary traces of these jurists' works survive through the writings of jurists from the classical period embodied in the Digest of Justinian.[94]

### 2.3.4  *The Role of Custom*

In the later republican era, custom (*consuetudo*) no longer operated as a direct source of law. However, it prevailed as a component in the formulation of the norms of positive law as found in statutory enactments, the edicts of the magistrates and the interpretations of the jurists.[95] Thus, many forms of action devised by the praetors to address situations not covered by the existing *ius civile* reflected customary norms endorsed by public opinion and actually observed by the people (*opinio necessitatis*).[96] As previously explained, the principal duty of the praetor when faced with a legal dispute was to determine whether the plaintiff's claim was admissible and, in doing do, the magistrate was to a large extent guided by current public opinion and the general sentiment as to what was right and proper in the circumstances. Similar considerations informed the jurists when formulating their *responsa*.

## 2.4  Sources of Law in the Principate Era

### 2.4.1  *The Decline of Popular Law-Making*

After the establishment of the Principate, the assemblies of the people continued to operate. However, their significance as constitutional organs was greatly diminished as the laws they enacted were all part of imperial policy and expressed the emperor's will. Abiding by a tradition that accepted comitial enactment as the exclusive source of legislation, Augustus used the assemblies to procure the enactment of several important laws. Some of these laws were passed directly on the emperor's motion while others were passed on the motion of higher magistrates, though obviously the emperor was their real promoter. In this way, statutes were passed concerning legal procedure (*leges Iuliae iudiciorum publicorum et*

---

[94] For a reconstruction of works of the late republican jurists see O. Lenel, *Palingenesia iuris civilis*, 2 vols (Leipzig 1889, repr. Graz 1960). See also F. Bremer, *Iurisprudentiae ante-hadrianae quae supersunt*, I (Leipzig 1896).

[95] According to the classical jurist Paulus, "custom is the best interpreter of statutes." See D. 1.3. 37.

[96] Consider Cicero, *de invent.* 2. 22. 67; D. 1. 3. 32. 1; D. 1. 3. 35.

*privatorum*)[97]; marriage and divorce (*lex Iulia de maritandis ordinibus, lex Papia Poppaea*)[98]; adultery (*lex Iulia de adulteriis coercendis*)[99]; the repression of elec-toral corruption (*lex Iulia de ambitu*)[100]; and the operation of the senate (*lex Iulia de senato habendo*).[101] Other noteworthy enactments of this period were the *lex Fufia Caninia* (2 BC) and the *lex Aelia Sentia* (AD 4) that introduced restrictions on the testamentary manumission of slaves; and the *lex Claudia de tutela mulierum*, a law passed under Emperor Claudius, that abolished agnatic tutelage over women.[102]

However, almost since the emergence of the new order, popular legislation was destined to wither away. It succumbed to the necessities of a community transformed from a city-state into a world empire, and a political system where the leadership shifted from short-term magistracies to the supremacy of a single ruler. As the political functions of the assemblies declined rapidly, this form of legislation soon became obsolete and ceased to exist at the end of the first century AD—the last known *lex* was an agrarian law passed in the time of Emperor Nerva (AD 96–98).[103]

---

[97] These laws were enacted in 17 BC and completed the transition from the *legis actiones* to the formulary procedure.

[98] The *lex Iulia de maritandis ordinibus* was passed in 18 BC and was supplemented by the *lex Papia Poppaea* in 9 AD. Both laws aspired to promote marriage and the procreation of children, and to check the decline of traditional family values. The earlier statute introduced several prohibitions on marriage (it prohibited marriages between members of the senatorial class and their former slaves, and between free-born men and women convicted of adultery). At the same time, various privileges were granted to married people who had children whereas severe social and economic disadvantages were imposed on unmarried and childless persons. The later law excluded unmarried men aged between twenty-five and sixty, and unmarried women aged between twenty and fifty from succession under a will. Both laws were referred to as *leges Iulia et Papia Poppaea*.

[99] Under this law enacted in 18 BC, adultery (*adulterium*) was classified as a public crime (but only when it was committed by a married woman). The father of the adulteress was permitted to kill her and her partner if he caught them in his or her husband's house. A husband whose wife had committed adultery had to divorce her, otherwise he could be found guilty of match-making (*lenocidium*). He (or the woman's father) could also launch an accusation against her before a court of law within two months after the divorce. Thereafter and for four months, any citizen could initiate a criminal charge. The punishment for a woman declared guilty of adultery was banish-ment, accompanied by confiscation of one-third of her property and loss of part of her dowry. Under the same enactment, the illicit intercourse with an unmarried woman or a widow (*stuprum*) was also made subject to criminal prosecution. See D. 48. 5. 13–14; D. 48. 5. 30. 1; D. 23. 2. 44.

[100] Enacted in 18 BC.

[101] This law was enacted in 10 BC and contained provisions regulating the voting procedure in the senate.

[102] G. 1. 157.

[103] D 47. 21. 3. 1.

## 2.4.2   The Consolidation of Magisterial Law

After the establishment of the Principate, Roman law still comprised the *ius civile* and the *ius honorarium*: the original core of the civil law and the law derived from the edicts of the jurisdictional magistrates (especially the praetors). However, since the inception of this period the productive strength of the magisterial edict started to weaken. As the republican magistrates' authority faded away and their cardinal functions were increasingly assumed by the emperor and his officials, magisterial initiatives became increasingly rare and the magistrates' right to alter the edicts on their own authority eroded. Any changes made in the edicts largely embraced measures introduced by other law-making agencies (*leges* or *senatus consulta*). Finally, pursuant to Emperor Hadrian's orders in the early second century AD the permanent edict of the praetors and the aediles was recast, unified and updated by the jurist Salvius Iulianus (probably during the latter's praetorship). The codified edict was ratified by a *senatus consultum* in AD 130 and thereafter magistrates were bound to administer justice in individual cases exclusively on the basis of the reformulated edict.[104] Although edicts were still annually issued by magistrates, the latter had no control over their content. For all practical purposes, the *edictum perpetuum* thus evolved as established law; any further necessary changes had to be initiated by imperial enactment.[105]

Although the magisterial edict was no longer a source of new law, for a long period it was still regarded as an important source of law for legal practice. Moreover, the distinction between *ius civile* and *ius honorarium* persevered as long as the judicial system allied to these bodies of law still operated. As new forms of dispensing justice gradually replaced the republican system of legal procedure, the distinction between the two bodies of law (existing as one of form rather than substance) was obliterated. The fusion of *ius civile* and *ius honorarium* was also precipitated by the Roman jurists who gradually removed the boundaries by developing both masses of law in common. In the later imperial era the resultant combination of these two sources of law was designated *ius*, in contradistinction to the body of rules derived from imperial legislation known as *lex*.

---

[104] The text of the codified edict has not been preserved in its original form. Modern reconstructions are based on commentaries and interpretations of later jurists, especially those of Pomponius, Gaius, Ulpianus and Paulus. See O. Lenel, *Das Edictum perpetuum*, 3rd ed. (Leipzig 1927, repr. Aalen 1956).

[105] Emperor Hadrian declared that any new point not contemplated in the codified edict should be decided by analogy with it. It is probable that such new points were still drawn attention to in successive edicts, for there is no doubt that the edict still continued to be published annually. Iulianus' work could, therefore, never have been intended to be unchangeable in an absolute sense. Such invariability would have been inconceivable, for although changes in law were now made primarily by means of imperial enactment, yet these very changes would entail related changes in the details of the edict. The fixity of Iulianus' edict was to be found mainly in its structure and in its guiding principles – in the way in which the various legal norms were ordered and in the general import of these norms.

### 2.4.3   The Senatorial Resolutions as a Source of Law

As previously noted, during the republican epoch the senate had, in theory, no law-making powers. Its resolutions (*senatus consulta*) were largely advisory in nature and had no legal effect unless they were incorporated into a statute or magisterial edict. The last century of the Republic featured a decline in the political role of the assemblies and occasionally a magistrate's proposal approved by the senate came into effect immediately without popular ratification. After the establishment of the Principate, an increasing number of laws originated in this way and, in time, the *senatus consultum* rather than the *lex* became the chief means of legislation.[106] Resembling the pattern followed under the Republic, the *senatus consulta* were couched in the form of instructions addressed to magistrates and were assigned the name of the magistrate who proposed them rather than the reigning emperor. However, from the start, the senate was virtually a tool of the emperor and had no free hand in the matter of legislation any more than it had in other matters. Indeed, most senatorial decrees were passed on the initiative of the emperor or at least with his acquiescence. From the time of Emperor Claudius (AD 41–54), senatorial decrees were increasingly composed by imperial officials and the relevant proposal was presented in the senate by or in the name of the emperor (*oratio principis*). The senators were then invited to express their views and a vote was conducted. However, the emperor's influence on the senate entailed the latter never failing to agree with the main premises of the proposal. As the movement towards absolute monarchy advanced, the terms of the emperor's proposal were increasingly adopted as a matter of course by the senate without even the pretence of a discussion. By the end of the second century AD, this practice was so routine that it was customary to label a *senatus consultum* as an *oratio* of the emperor on whose initiative the *senatus consultum* was passed. In the third century, emperors no longer submitted their proposals to the senate for approval and thus the senatorial resolutions formally ceased to exist as a source of law.

In the first two centuries of the Principate numerous *senatus consulta* were issued that effectuated important changes in the areas of both public and private law. An early senatorial decree of this period was the *senatus consultum Silanianum* of AD 10 that aspired to repress the frequent killing of masters by their slaves.[107] Other important senatorial resolutions of this period embraced: the *senatus consultum Vellaeanum* (AD 46) that forbade women from assuming liability for

---

[106] According to Gaius: "A *senatus consultum* is that which the Senate orders and establishes, and this is assimilated in force to a statute, although this was formerly disputed." (G. 1. 4.) And see D. 1. 3. 9. (Ulpianus): "There is no doubt but that the senate can make law."

[107] It provided that when a master of slaves was killed and the identity of the murderer or murderers remained unknown, all slaves who lived with him had to be tortured and eventually killed. A slave who revealed the identity of the killer was declared free by the praetor's order. See Tacitus, *Ann.* 14. 42–45.

debts of others, including those of their husbands[108]; the *senatus consultum Libonianum* (AD 16) that imposed the penalties of the *lex Cornelia de falsis* for the forging of testaments[109]; the *senatus consultum Trebellianum* (*c.* AD 56) and the *senatus consultum Pegasianum* (AD 73) that concerned the acceptance of inheritances subject to *fideicommissa*[110]; the *senatus consultum Iuventianum* (AD 129) that addressed matters such as claims of the Roman public treasury (*aerarium populi Romani*) against private individuals for the recovery of vacant inheritances; the *senatus consultum Macedonianum* (second half of the first century AD) that prohibited loans to sons who remained subject to *partia potestas*[111]; and the *senatus consultum Tertullianum*, passed in the time of Hadrian, that granted mothers the legal right of succession to their children's inheritance.[112]

## 2.4.4  *The* Princeps *as a Lawmaker*

As previously observed, Augustus exhibited deference to the traditional republican institutions he claimed to have restored by consistently refusing to accept direct law-making powers that could supplant those of the established organs of legislation. So long as the principles of the Augustan system of government retained their vitality, the emperor achieved his legislative goals indirectly by regularly using the popular assemblies and then the senate. However, the emperor not only controlled legislation but since the start of the Principate period had diverse methods for creating new legal norms directly without appearing to legislate. The emperor's law-making authority was initially based on his magisterial powers, especially the *imperium proconsulare maius*, and his tribunician *potestas*. As the imperial power increased over time at the expense of the old republican institutions, the enactments of the emperors (*consitutiones principum*) were recognized as possessing full statutory force (*legis vigorem*) and functioning as a direct source of law alongside the *leges* and the *senatus consulta*.

The direct law-making power of the *princeps*-emperor was justified on the ground that the law that conferred *imperium* on the emperor (*lex de imperio*) transferred to him the authority to legislate in the name of the Roman people. According to the jurist Gaius, "a constitution of a *princeps* ... has the force of law, since the emperor himself receives his *imperium* by a law".[113] This statement

---

[108] D. 16. 1. 2. 1. The relevant transaction remained valid unless the woman sued by the creditor raised the *exceptio senatus consulti Valleiani*. She could also demand the return of the sum she had paid in fulfillment of her obligation.

[109] D. 48. 10.

[110] On the first of these see G. 2. 253; on the second see G. 2. 254.

[111] Such transactions were not invalid but the son could raise against the lender's claim an *exceptio senatus consulti Macedoniani*. See D. 14. 6. 1; C. 4. 28.

[112] However, priority was accorded to the children's progeny and their father. See D. 38. 17.

[113] G. 1. 5; see also *Inst.* 1. 2. 6; D. 1. 4. 1 pr.

implies nothing less than whatever the emperor decreed as law possessed the validity of a formal statute (*lex*), i.e. a statute like those that were formally enacted by a popular assembly and sanctioned by the senate.[114] But the true foundation of the emperor's legislative authority is not discovered in legal rationales but in political reality: the emperor's socio-political power evolved so that his assumption of a direct legislative role could not be challenged. It should be noted that the growth of imperial legislative authority was gradual. The imperial office in the late Principate age displayed a far more autocratic nature than in the Augustan period, operating as the ultimate source of all administrative, legislative and judicial activity.

Imperial law-making, like the magisterial law-making of the later Republican age, formed a new source of equitable rules that unravelled the rigidity of the Roman legal system, thereby adjusting it to the socio-economic conditions of an evolving society. However, the multiplicity of the emperor's law-making functions precluded the formation of a homogenous body of law until the later imperial era when attempts were made to introduce order into the mass of imperial constitutions claiming validity in the empire.

Imperial legislation was designated the common name of imperial constitutions (*constitutiones principis*) and assumed diverse forms: *edicta*, *decreta*, *rescripta* and *mandata*.[115]

### 2.4.4.1   *Edicta*

As holder of the magisterial *imperium*, the *princeps*-emperor had the right to issue edicts (*edicta*) that publicized his orders and intentions. But as the emperor surpassed all other magistrates in authority and his sphere of competence was virtually unlimited, his edicts embraced the whole business of the state, dealing with such divergent matters as criminal law and procedure, private law, the constitution of the courts, and the bestowal of citizenship.[116]

---

[114] D. 1. 2. 2. 11–12 (Pomponius): "Therefore, a first citizen (*princeps*) was established, and the power was given to him that whatever he laid down was binding. Hence, in our state a rule depends upon law, that is, upon a statute (*lex*) … or the imperial constitution, that is, what the emperor himself decrees and is observed as a statute (*pro lege*)."

[115] According to Ulpianus: "whatever the emperor determines by *epistula* or by *subscriptio*, or has decided after hearing or has pronounced without hearing or has prescribed by *edictum*, is clearly law. These are what we commonly term *constitutiones*." (D. 1. 4. 1 pr.-1) See also G. 1. 5.

[116] See, e.g., the edict of Augustus in D. 48. 18. 8 pr. (Paulus): "The edict of divus Augustus, which he posted during the consulate of Vibius Habitus and Lucius Apronianus (AD 8), is extant as follows: 'I do not think that torture should be inflicted in every case and upon every [slave] person [of the family]; but when capital and atrocious crimes cannot be detected and proved except by the torture of slaves, I believe that it is most effective for ascertaining the truth, and I hold it is to be employed'." Probably the best-known example of an imperial edict is the *constitutio Antoniniana de Civitate* (AD 212) whereby Emperor Caracalla granted the Roman citizenship to all the free inhabitants of the empire: "Imperator Caesar Marcus Aurelius Severus Antoninus

The edicts of the *princeps* were, like those of the praetor and other jurisdictional magistrates of the Republic, technically interpretations of law; but, like the praetor, the *princeps* could alter or supplement the law under the guise of interpretation and his creative power, as exercised by his edictal authority, was very extensive. An emperor's edict did not necessarily bind his successors; but if it had been recognized as valid by a succession of emperors, it was deemed to be part of the law, and its subsequent abandonment had apparently to be provided by some definite act of repudiation. It should be noted that Augustus and his immediate successors used their power of issuing edicts sparingly. Only during the late Principate age when the imperial system moved closer to an absolute monarchy did the emperors regularly employ edicts to achieve aims that, according to the spirit of the Augustan constitution, called for the enactment of legislation by a popular assembly or by the senate. By that time, both comitial and senatorial legislation had disappeared and the capacity of the emperor to create law directly had been recognized as an essential attribute of his office.

### 2.4.4.2   *Decreta*

The *decreta* (decrees) were decisions issued by the emperor in exercise of his judicial powers on appeal and, on occasions, as judge of first instance.[117] Under normal circumstances, the *princeps*-emperor rarely interfered with the course of ordinary judicial proceedings. Yet from the start, an extraordinary jurisdiction was bestowed to him and those officials to whom he delegated his powers. Over time, the extraordinary jurisdiction of the emperor and his delegates assumed greater significance until it ultimately superseded the jurisdiction of the regular magistrates and courts.[118]

Cases referred to the emperor's tribunal were decided in accordance with the existing law. However, as the highest authority in the state, the emperor granted himself considerable freedom in interpreting the applicable legal rules. He could even venture to defy some hitherto accepted rule if he felt that it failed to produce an equitable outcome. Although theoretically the emperor's decision on the point at issue was only binding in the particular case, in practice it was treated as an authentic statement of the law and binding for all future cases. In this way, the

---

proclaims: …Therefore I believe that magnificently and reverently I can render proper service to their [the gods'] majesty if I bring to the worship of the gods as many foreigners as have entered into the number of my people. Therefore I now grant Roman citizenship to all the foreigners who are residents of the Empire, there remaining [the rights of the city-states], except the *dediticii*." See FIRA I No. 88. Consider also D. 1. 5. 17.

[117] The emperor's appellate jurisdiction was justified on the following ground: as the emperor received his powers from the people and hence acted in their name, an appeal to him was the exercise of the age-old citizen's right of appeal from a magistrate's decision to the judgment of the people in the assembly.

[118] I.e. the *praetor urbanus* and the *praetor peregrinus* with respect to civil matters, and the *quaestiones perpetuae* regarding to criminal matters.

emperor in his judicial capacity contributed to the development of fresh legal principles and rules, and a doctrine of judicial precedent evolved. It should be noted in this context that as the emperor lacked expertise in legal issues, an important point of law invoked in a case before the emperor's tribunal would usually be debated at a meeting of the *consilium principis*. From the second century AD, this council embodied the most eminent jurists and thus the relevant decision represented the best legal opinion of the day.[119]

### 2.4.4.3   *Rescripta*

The *rescripta* were written answers given by the emperor to petitions raised by state officials and private citizens. Such petitions might relate to all sorts of matters, but the present context focuses on those that invoked questions of law. There were two types of imperial rescripts: *epistulae* and *subscriptiones*. The former were embodied in a separate document and were addressed to state officials in Rome or in the provinces. The latter were responses to petitions from private citizens written on the margin or at the end of the application itself.

Rescripts were particularly important for the development of private law in the second century AD, when it became customary for judges and private citizens to petition the emperors for decisions on difficult questions of law. The emperor would articulate the legal position that applied to a certain stated factual situation and if the judge confirmed the veracity of these facts as stated, he was bound by the imperial decision. Moreover, the emperor's ruling on a point of law contained in a rescript was treated in practice as a binding statement of law for all future cases. In this way, a new body of legal rules developed that had assumed voluminous proportions by the end of the second century AD.[120] Jurists of this period formed private collections of imperial rescripts, large parts of which have come down to us

---

[119] The following is an example of an imperial *decretum* from the Digest of Justinian. D. 48. 7. 7 (Callistratus): "Creditors who proceed against their debtors should demand back through a judge what they allege is owed to them. Otherwise, if they enter upon the property of the debtor without permission having been given them, divus Marcus decreed that they no longer had the rights of creditors. The words of the *decretum* are these: 'It is best, if you think you have certain claims, that you seek them judicially by actions; in the mean time the other party ought to remain in possession, for you are but a claimant.' And when Marcianus declared: 'No force had been employed', the emperor replied: 'Do you think there is force only if men are wounded? Force exists as often as anyone thinks he can take what is owing him without demanding it though a judge. Moreover, I do not think it conformable to your character or dignity or respect to permit something illegal. Therefore, when it shall have been proved to me that any property of the debtor, not delivered by him to the creditor, has been unauthorizedly possessed without any trial, and it is alleged that he [the creditor] has a right to that property, he shall not have the right [to sue] as a creditor'."

[120] It should be noted that the authors of the imperial rescripts were, in most cases, the jurists who served as members of the imperial chancery.

through the codification of Justinian and other post-classical compilations of law.[121]

### 2.4.4.4 *Mandata*

The *mandata* (instructions) were internal administrative directions given by the emperor to officials in his service. The most important *mandata* were addressed to provincial governors and concerned provincial administration (especially its financial side), while others dealt with matters of private and criminal law and the administration of justice.[122] Based on the emperor's *imperium proconsulare*, a *mandatum* was originally strictly personal and remained in force only as long as both the emperor who issued it and the official to whom it was addressed remained in office. When the emperor died or the official was replaced, the *mandatum* had to be renewed. Gradually, the successive renewals established a body of standing instructions (*corpus mandatorum*) that acquired general validity for not only state officials but also with respect to the contacts of private citizens with the administrative authorities.[123] As officials were virtually bound to implement all the received instructions from the emperor, and citizens could invoke these instructions

---

[121] The following are examples of imperial rescripts.

C. 4. 44. 1: "'The Emperor Alexander to Aurelius Maro, soldier: if your father sold the house under compulsion, the transaction will not be upheld as valid, since it was not carried out in good faith; for a purchase in bad faith is invalid. If therefore you bring an action in your own name, the provincial governor will intervene, especially since you declare that you are ready to refund the buyer the price that was paid."

D. 1. 15. 4 (Ulpianus): "The Emperors Severus and Antoninus rescripted to Iunius Rufinus, praefect of the watch, as follows: 'You can also order to be beaten with sticks or flogged those occupants of apartments who have kept their house-fires carelessly. But those who have been found guilty of wilful arson, you shall remit to our friend Fabius Cilo, praefect of the city. You ought to hunt down fugitive slaves and return them to their masters'."

D. 19. 2. 19. 9 (Ulpianus): "When a scribe leased out his labour and his employer then died, the Emperor Antoninus together with the deified Severus replied by rescript to the scribe's petition in these words: 'Since you allege that you are not responsible for your not providing the labour you leased to Antonius Aquila, it is fair that the promise of wages in the contract be fulfilled if during the year in question you received no wages from anyone else'."

[122] According to Dio Cassius, "the emperor gives certain instructions to the procurators, the proconsuls and the propraetors, in order that they may proceed to their offices with fixed conditions. Both this practice and that of giving salary to them and to the remaining officials of the government became customary at this period." (*Historia Romana* 53. 15. 4) And see D. 29. 1. 1; D. 1. 18. 3; D. 48. 3. 6. 1.

[123] In the course of time, various compilations of imperial *mandata* were produced that were referred to as *libri mandatorum*. An important collection of imperial mandates is the *Gnomon* of the *Idios Logos*, a work dating from the second half of the second century AD. This work is partially preserved in a papyrus and contains instructions pertaining to the financial administration of Egypt; it also includes several provisions that deal with matters of private law. See FIRA I, no. 99.

in their favour, the imperial *mandata* operated in practice as a distinct source of law.[124]

## 2.4.5   The Culmination of Roman Jurisprudence

As previously elaborated, the legal history of the late republican era is marked by the emergence of the first secular jurists (*iurisprudentes, iurisconsulti*). The work of the jurists attained great heights of achievement by the end of the republican age and formed the most productive element of Roman legal life during the Principate, as evidenced by the volume and quality of the juridical literature of this period. The jurists' authority in legal matters derived from their highly specialized knowledge, technical expertise and primarily the esteem the general populace held towards them. In a deeply conservative and traditionalistic society (like that of the Romans), the public actions of private citizens and state organs required the support of religious, political and legal authority. In legal matters, private parties and public authorities (including jurisdictional magistrates) thus relied upon the advice from the 'oracles of the law'—the jurists. Both legislation and magisterial law were stimulated and moulded by the jurists, who provided guidance to magistrates in the composition of their legislative proposals and edicts. Furthermore, the jurists contributed to the development of the law through their activities in the day-to-day practice of law, the education of students and the writing of legal works.

The administrative and judicial authorities in the Principate age faced new demands generated by the empire's ever-increasing administrative complexity, the expansion of the Roman citizenship in the provinces and the proliferation of legal transactions prompted by the growth of trade and commerce. These new demands could not be adequately addressed without the active assistance of learned jurists. It is thus unsurprising that not only did the jurists' advisory role increase in importance, but they also commenced a direct involvement in governmental tasks. The emperors employed jurists to assist them in executing the multiplying tasks of administration from as early as Augustus' era with increasing regularity in the later Principate period. Many leading jurists occupied important state posts, from various magisterial positions right up to the prefecture of the praetorian guard. Moreover, distinguished jurists were among the members of the emperor's *consilium* that evolved under Hadrian (AD 117–138) to resemble a supreme council of the state. In this way, the Roman jurist was gradually transformed from a member of the ruling class in an aristocratic republic into a servant of the imperial government. But the jurists' increased participation in governmental affairs did not entail that the

---

[124] It is germane to mention that Gaius and other classical jurists do not include the *mandata* among the imperial constitutions but mention them as a special category of imperial enactments. See G. 1. 5. and C. 1. 15. Modern writers almost invariably treat the mandates as a form of imperial law-making, because they sometimes contained new rules of law.

primary focus of their interests shifted away from private law. In this field, the jurisprudence of the Empire absorbed all the legal questions that had arisen in the republican age. These questions, enriched by the emergence of new issues, were categorized and often adequately answered for the first time.

Continuing the role of their republican predecessors, the jurists of the Empire were engaged in diverse activities in the legal field: they presented opinions on questions of law to private citizens, magistrates and judges (*respondere*); helped litigants on points of procedure, interpreting laws and formulas in their pleas and occasionally arguing cases as advocates themselves (*agere*); and drafted legal documents, such as contracts and wills (*cavere*). However, composing new *formulae* for use in the formulary procedure was no longer a regular task of the jurists. The reason is that by the beginning of the Principate era the contents of the praetorian and aedilician edicts were largely fixed and adequate legal remedies existed. The jurists were also engaged in the systematic exposition and teaching of law. In performing this task, they composed opinions when their students raised questions for discussion based on hypothetical cases. These opinions were almost equal in terms of influence to those formulated for questions arising from actual cases and indirectly helped to develop Roman law in new directions.

In the Principate age, the giving of opinions on legal questions (*respondere*) evolved as the most important aspect of the jurists' work. An important change regarding this task occurred in the early years of this period, when the *princeps*-emperor began to grant certain jurists the right to present opinions and deliver them by the emperor's authority (*ius publice respondendi ex auctoritate principis*). During the Republic, the jurists' *responsa* had not been legally binding but the judge trying a case would normally accept the opinion of a jurist. By the end of this period, the number of jurists practicing in Rome had greatly increased and it was difficult to ascertain precisely which opinions should be relied upon when they all carried the same weight. As a result, the practice of law was thrown into a state of confusion. Partly to resolve this problem and partly to establish some imperial control over the jurists, Augustus is said to have issued an ordinance investing the opinions of certain pre-eminent jurists with increased authority.[125] The granting of this privilege did not curtail the activity of the unpatented lawyers, although it

---

[125] Amongst the earliest of the patented jurists was Masurius Sabinus, who lived in the time of the Emperor Tiberius. D. 1. 2. 2. 48–49 (Pomponius): "Massurius Sabinus was in the equestrian order and was the first to respond publicly; afterwards, this privilege began to be given, which, however, had been granted to him by Tiberius Caesar. (49) And we may observe in passing, before the time of Augustus the right of responding publicly (*ius publice respondendi*) was not given by the emperor, but he who had confidence in his studies responded to his consultants; nor were *responsa* always given under seal, but often they themselves wrote to the judges or were testified to by those who consulted them. The deified Augustus was the first to decree, in order to ensure greater authority of the law, that they might respond upon his authority; and from that time on this began to be sought as a favour. And therefore the excellent Emperor Hadrian, when praetorian men sought leave to respond, rescripted that this was not to be sought but was wont to be earned, and accordingly, if anyone had faith in his own ability he himself decided if he was qualified to give *responsa* to the people."

doubtlessly diminished their influence. However, it gave the response of its possessor as authoritative a character as though it had proceeded from the emperor himself. Although judges were not in principle obliged to accept the opinions of the jurists with the *ius respondendi*, in practice it was very difficult for a judge to ignore the advice of a jurist whose *responsa* were reinforced by the emperor's authority.[126] It may have been understood that the opinion of only one patented jurist was to be sought in any single case, for in the early Principate there seems to have been no provision determining the conduct of a judge when the opinions of his advisers differed. Later it must have been possible to elicit the opinion of several patented jurists on a single legal question. In the early second century AD, Emperor Hadrian issued a rescript ordaining that if the opinions of the jurists possessing the *ius respondendi* were unanimous they had the same force as a statute. If there was no unanimity among the jurists, the judge was free to adopt any opinion he thought fit.[127] The emperor devised this rescript to establish clearly and definitely that if a uniform agreement existed between the authorized jurists their unanimous opinion must be followed as binding. However, Hadrian concurrently abandoned the practice of granting the *ius respondendi* to individual jurists. Thereafter, opinions were presented in the form of imperial rescripts prepared, with supervision from distinguished jurists, by the two imperial chanceries: the *scrinium ab epistulis* that attended to the correspondence with state officials and persons of high social status; and the *scrinium a libellis* that dealt with petitions from private citizens.

From a historical perspective, probably the most important of the jurists' activities was the writing of legal works. The great majority of juristic works had a casuistic and practical nature: they were developed from legal practice and written primarily for legal practitioners. Only their expository works, such as elementary textbooks and manuals, exhibited the jurists' adoption of a more theoretical approach to law. Depending upon their subject-matter and structure, the literary works of the classical jurists may be classified as follows:

(a)  *Responsa, quaestiones, disputationes, epistulae*—collections of opinions or replies delivered by jurists with the *ius respondendi*. Works of this kind were generally written for practitioners and usually embodied two parts: the first part contained juristic opinions arranged according to the rubrics of the praetorian edict (*ad edictum*), while the second part linked the opinions with the *leges, senatus consulta* and *constitutiones principum* that they addressed.

---

[126] The jurists who had been granted the *ius publice respondendi* were referred to as *iurisconsulti* or *iurisprudentes*, although the same terms were sometimes also used to describe any prominent jurist irrespective of whether or not he enjoyed this privilege. The term *iurisperiti*, on the other hand, was used to denote less important jurists, especially jurists practicing in the provinces. Such lesser jurists were particularly active in Egypt and other Roman provinces in the East.

[127] In the words of Gaius: "The *responsa* of the learned in the law are the decisions and opinions of those to whom it has been permitted to lay down the law. If the decisions of all of these are in accord, that which they so hold has the force of statute. If, however, they differ, the judge is permitted to follow the decision he pleases; and this is expressed in a rescript of divus Hadrianus." (G. 1. 7.)

The responses in these collections were set forth in a casuistic form and dealt with an immense number of problems, sometimes in connection with the opinions of other jurists. The adaptation of the original *responsa* for publication occasionally necessitated the further elaboration of the adopted views, especially when the opinions of other jurists were challenged.[128] Some works in this category, especially the *quaestiones* and the *disputationes*, explored the real or fictitious cases discussed by the jurists in their capacity as law teachers. The juristic works known as *epistulae* contained legal opinions delivered in writing by jurists to judicial magistrates, judges, private citizens or other jurists. The *responsa*, the *quaestiones*, the *disputationes* and the *epistulae* (collectively designated 'problematic literature') are among the most instructive juristic works that reveal the acumen of the authors' legal thinking and the strength of their criticism towards divergent opinions.

(b) *Regulae, definitiones, sententiae*—short statements of the law that originally related to specific cases, but were later reformulated in the form of legal principles with a more general nature. Couched in terms easily recalled, these works were 'rules of thumb' manuals intended for use by legal practitioners and probably also students.

(c) General works on the *ius civile*. Some of these works were known as *libri ad Sabinum* or *ex Sabino* as they were modelled on the systematic treatise on the *ius civile* (*Libri* III *iuris civilis*) written by Massurius Sabinus, a famous jurist of the early first century AD and head of the school of the Sabinians. Others drew upon the earlier work of the jurist Q. Mucius Scaevola, who lived in the first century BC. Essentially, these works were based on the jurists' interpretation of the provisions of the Law of the Twelve Tables together with the later development of the institutions of the civil law.

(d) Commentaries on the *ius praetorium* (or *ius honorarium*), referred to as *libri ad edictum*. These works examined the edicts of the magistrates and offered commentaries pertaining to those aspects of the *ius civile* they were intended to supplement or correct.[129]

(e) *Digesta*—comprehensive treatises on the law dealing with both the *ius civile* and the *ius honorarium*.

(f) *Institutiones* or *enchiridia*—introductory or expository textbooks written primarily for students at the beginning of their formal legal education.[130]

The jurists also wrote treatises on individual *leges* or *senatus consulta*, handbooks describing the functions of various imperial officials, and commentaries on the works of earlier jurists. Among the juristic literature of the classical period, the

---

[128] Sometimes responses relating to one theme were collected in one volume. Examples include the *liber singularis* of Modestinus that addressed the institution of *manumissio*, and the book of Paulus on the office of the proconsul (both these works were published in the early third century AD).

[129] A renowned illustration is Ulpian's commentary on the edict (*libri ad edictum*) in eighty-three books.

[130] An illustration of this type of work is the Institutes of Gaius that dates from around AD 160.

Institutes of Gaius is the only work that survives in its original form. The remaining literature is discoverable chiefly in the citations that appear in the Digest of Justinian and other later compilations of law.[131]

As previously noted, a distinctive feature of Roman jurisprudence was its strictly legal and predominantly casuistic nature. The jurists did not consider it part of their tasks to critique the law from sociological, ethical, historical or other broader points of view. Nor were they interested in the laws and customs of other nations, save insofar as these could be incorporated into the conceptual framework of their own legal system. In general, their attitude towards the law was conservative: they endeavoured to preserve the system in which they worked while at the same time developing it by exploring new ways to put its institutions to satisfactory, practical use. In the Principate era, the need arose to further systematize the casuistic method adopted by the republican jurists. In response to this need, the jurists of this period created a system and a science that enabled them to develop the law in new directions in line with changing socio-economic circumstances. The starting-point of a systematic statement of law was often a settled case that was then compared with other real or fictitious cases. Other elements contributing to the process were norms (e.g. statutes and juristic *regulae*) as well as various standards used in the normative discourse (e.g. *bona fides*). The function of such elements was mainly explanatory, pedagogical or informative rather than persuasive (especially in juridical treatises): the jurists sought to illustrate the relevant norm or principle through cases demonstrating its actual operation, without immersion in theoretical argument. But Roman jurisprudence did not stop at the level of a purely pragmatic casuistry. As already noted, a remarkable quality of the jurists was their ability to look beyond the accidental elements of the individual case, the *species facti*, and to define the relevant legal problem as a *quaestio iuris*. Their legal genius was exhibited in their ability to render their decisions or decision-propositions in concrete cases sufficiently flexible for future synthesis into new principles when subsequent experience showed that change was desirable. Although they kept strictly to the doctrines of their law, they understood the sociological import of its rules. The combination of a sure instinct for the necessities of life with the conscious application of firm principles imparted eternal value to the accomplishments of the jurists.

Like their republican predecessors, the jurists of the Empire attached particular importance to the concept of *aequitas* and its role in correcting or expanding the existing body of law so it could meet the demands of social and commercial life. This is reflected in the definition of *ius*, or law in a broad sense, attributed to the jurist Celsus as the art of doing equity (*ius est ars boni et aequi*) or, in other words, a

---

[131] In the Digest each extract is preceded by an *inscriptio*, which includes the name of the jurist from whose work the extract is taken. These extracts, as well as references by one jurist to another, have made it possible for modern scholars to obtain a good idea of the nature and structure of the original works. The date of the individual works is deduced largely on the basis of information in the surviving fragments, such as references to emperors, legislative enactments or events whose dates are verified by other sources. For a reconstruction of the juristic literature of the classical period see O. Lenel, *Palingenesia iuris civilis*, 2 vols (Leipzig 1889, repr. Graz 1960).

technical device for obtaining that which a good man's conscience will endorse.[132] The test of the *bonum et aequum* in this era was still the *ius gentium*, the norms governing civilized society as construed by the Romans. But the Roman *ius gentium* was now declared binding because it was also natural law (*ius naturale*), based on natural reason.[133] The 'law of nature' was a familiar concept to many philosophical systems of antiquity but acquired a more concrete form with the Stoic school of philosophy. The Stoics' starting-point was the idea that the world is an organic whole, an intimate combination of form and matter and an order of interdependent tendencies, governed by a divine, rational principle (*Nous, Logos*) and moving towards a pre-determined end (*telos*).[134] The word 'nature' (*physis*) is used to refer to this cosmic order and to the structures of its component parts. Natural law, as founded in the natural order of things, exists as a reflection of right reason (*recta ratio*) and is universally valid, immutable and has the force of law *per se*, i.e. independently of human positivization.[135] Compliance with its rules is a prerequisite for attaining justice (*iustitia*), as the essence of law (*ius*) in its broadest sense. Although the Stoics' philosophical views on the ideal law or the ultimate nature of justice apparently had no profound effect on the way the Roman jurists executed their traditional tasks, the concept of *natura* provided an important device for the articulation and systematization of the law. However, the jurists did not

---

[132] D. 1. 1. 1 pr.; D. 4. 1. 7; D. 50. 17. 183.

[133] However, the assumed connection between *ius gentium* and *ius naturale* is far from clear as no generally accepted definition of natural law is revealed in juridical literature. According to the jurist Ulpian: "Private law is threefold: it can be gathered from the precepts of nature, or from those of the nations, or from those of the city. Natural law is that which nature has taught all animals; for this is not peculiar to the human race but belongs to all animals ... From this law comes the union of male and female, which we call marriage, and the begetting and education of children ... The law of nations is that law which mankind observes. It is easy to understand that this law should differ from the natural, inasmuch as the latter pertains to all animals, while the former is peculiar to men." (D. 1. 1. 1.) A few paragraphs below this quotation from Ulpianus we find the following statement of the jurist Gaius: "All peoples who are governed by law and by custom observe laws which in part are their own and in part are common to all mankind. For those laws which each people has given itself are peculiar to each city and are called the civil law ... But what natural reason dictates to all men and is most equally observed among them is called the law of nations, as that law which is practiced by all mankind." (D. 1. 1. 9; and see G. 1. 1 and *Inst*. 1. 2. 11.) In the next few paragraphs appears this definition of law attributed to Paulus: "We can speak of law in different senses; in one sense, when we call law what is always equitable and good, as is natural law; in another sense, what in each state is profitable to all or to many, as is civil law." (D. 1. 1. 11.) The divergences between these three accounts are evident: Ulpianus asserts that there is a clear difference between natural law and other human laws, the former being regarded as pertaining to the natural drives that men and animals have in common; Gaius and Paulus, on the other hand, perceive the reason for the universal validity of certain principles in their rational character and their recognition by all mankind, as well as in their inherent utility and goodness.

[134] The Stoics sought to effect a reconciliation between the seemingly conflicting principles of form and matter by dialectically linking them under one principle: *Nous* or cosmic *Logos*. They perceived meaning to exist in the material world, not in a realm beyond it.

[135] If all men, irrespective of race, nationality, social standing and such like, share in the divine reason in the same way, then in principle all are equal and together form one grand universal community, a *cosmopolis*, governed by natural law.

juxtapose the law governing social relations in everyday life to a code of ideal natural law functioning as a master model. They developed the content of *natura* in close connection with the practical aspects of legal life and always in response to concrete needs and problems emerging from actual cases. From their viewpoint, discovering the appropriate legal rule or devising an acceptable solution to a legal problem presupposed a reasonable familiarity with both the nature of practical reality and the ordinary expectations that social and legal relations entailed. In this respect, the postulates of nature did not emanate from metaphysical speculation but from the findings of common sense and the need for order in human relations. Thus, in the eyes of the jurists, certain methods of acquiring ownership were 'natural' or derived from natural law as they appeared to follow inevitably from the facts of life such as *traditio* (the most usual form for transferring ownership, involving the informal transfer of actual control over an object on the basis of some lawful cause, e.g. a contract of purchase and sale); and *occupatio* (the acquisition of the actual control of a *res nullius*, an object belonging to no one). Of course, such methods of acquisition were regarded as universal and therefore as facets of the *ius gentium*: the law actually observed by all humankind. The fact that the Roman jurists regarded natural law, in the manner described above, as juridically valid is implied by their identification of *ius naturale* with *ius gentium*. This prevailed even though the former term referred to the supposed origin of a rule or institution and the latter to its universal application. If natural law is interpreted as law that ought to be observed, the identification of *ius naturale* and *ius gentium* is untenable as certain institutions of the law of nations clearly conflicted with natural law precepts. Thus while according to natural law all people were born free, slavery was widely recognized in antiquity as an institution of the law of nations. In view of this detail, the most one can say from a moral-philosophical perspective is that the universal recognition of an institution as part of the law of nations could be regarded to constitute *prima facie* evidence that such an institution originates from natural reason. The Roman jurists, however, never drew a clear distinction between positive law and law as it ought to exist, nor did they adopt the philosophical conception of natural law as a higher law capable of nullifying positive law. They were not social reformers and their conception of natural law does not embrace anything resembling a revolutionary principle to support those rights that are termed in the modern era as 'inalienable human rights'. Thus, no matter how such institutions as slavery or the division of property appeared contrary to natural law they were still perceived as perfectly justified and legal. *Ius naturale* significantly contributed to Roman legal thought, but as a professional construction for lawyers it had little relevance to moral philosophy. It was not viewed as a complete and ready-made system of rules but primarily as a means of interpretation existing in conjunction with the *ius gentium* to enable the Roman jurists to test the equity of the rules they applied.[136] In this way, *ius naturale* played a key part in the process of adapting positive law to changing socio-economic conditions and shaping the legal system of an international empire.

---

[136] See, e.g., D. 50. 17. 206 (Pomponius): "It is just (*aequum*) by the law of nature (*lex naturae*) that no one, by the commission of a wrong, can be enriched at the expense of another."

The group of jurists responsible for the development of Roman legal science in the early imperial epoch was always small in scale at any particular time. Nevertheless, over the course of nearly three centuries their total attained a considerable scale. Today we are aware of many jurists from fragments of their works incorporated in post-classical compilations of law and from references located in various historical sources. Important sources of our knowledge on the lives of the classical jurists are Pomponius' *Enchiridium*, embodied in the Digest of Justinian and containing a survey of jurisprudence until the time of Hadrian; various literary works by authors such as Tacitus, Aulus Gellius, Pliny the Younger and Cassius Dio; and a number of inscriptions. At this point, it is important to identify the most important jurists and the period of their activity. The examination may be divided into three time periods: the early period (27 BC to *c*. AD 80), the high classical period (*c*. AD 80 to *c*. AD 180) and the late period (*c*. AD 180 to *c*. AD 235).

The jurists of the early Principate period hailed from urban Roman families or from the Italian municipal aristocracy, and so they possessed a thoroughly Roman background. According to Pomponius, the jurists of this period divided themselves into two schools (*sectae*) that formed around two political rivals: Marcus Antistius Labeo and Gaius Ateius Capito.[137] An opponent of the Augustan regime, Labeo never progressed further in his public career than the office of *praetor* and the traditional account holds that he declined an offer of the consulship from Augustus because of his republican convictions.[138] Reputedly an innovator and an exceptionally gifted jurist, he composed numerous highly influential works that included commentaries on the Law of the Twelve Tables and the praetorian edict, a treatise on pontifical law and collections of *responsa* and *epistulae*. At the time of his death, his written works amounted to 400 volumes. The school established by Labeo was named after the jurist Proculus, and so was designated the School of the Proculians (*Proculiani*). Capito, elevated to the position of consul by Augustus who he supported, was known for his adherence to traditional juristic sources.[139] He produced relatively few works that included a book *de officio senatorio*; collections of *epistulae*; and treatises on pontifical and public law. The school founded by Capito was named after his successor Marcus Massurius Sabinus and so was known as the Sabinian School. However, the meaning of the term '*sectae*' used by Pomponius is not clear as very little is known about the organization and functions of the two schools. It appears that these schools were not places of instruction in law, although it is very probable that young lawyers were mainly educated within the framework of the 'school' community. In all likelihood, the schools were in the nature of aristocratic clubs with their own techniques and courses of training, and each centered around a succession of distinguished jurists. In this respect, they

---

[137] See D. 1. 2. 2. 47 and D. 1. 2. 2. 52; Pliny, *Ep*. 7. 24; Tacitus, *Ann*. 3. 75.

[138] D. 1. 2. 2. 47. Compare with Tacitus, *Ann*. 3. 75; Aulus Gellius, *N. A*. 13. 12.

[139] Tacitus, *Ann*. 3. 75.

resembled the Greek philosophical schools that had existed since the republican era as organized quasi corporations whose direction and management were transferred by one master to his successor. Information reveals that the two schools differed on a great array of individual questions of law. However, the surviving examples do not display the alleged conservatism of the Sabinians or the reformatory spirit attributed to the Proculians. In contrast to the Greek philosophical schools, there were apparently no deep-rooted theoretical differences that separated the two schools.[140] This induces the conclusion that the schools differed only with respect to the techniques they adopted for dealing with concrete questions of law rather than in their general attitudes or principles. From the little we know, it appears that the Sabinians tended to adhere to the letter of the law while the Proculians emphasised the importance of considering the purpose or spirit of the relevant law in the interpretive process. The doctrines of each school must have derived from the accumulated opinions of their successive heads on different questions of law, perpetuated by tradition and adopted on account of conservatism and a sense of loyalty.[141] The Sabinian and Proculian schools seem to have disappeared by the end of the second century AD, as no evidence indicates that the leading jurists of the third century were members of either school.

Massurius Sabinus, whose name is attached to the earlier school of Capito, occupies an exceptional position amongst the jurists. He was not a member of the senate nor did he make his career in politics, and he only gained admittance to the equestrian class later in life. Nevertheless, Emperor Tiberius granted him the *ius publice respondendi* in recognition of his outstanding ability as a lawyer.[142] His chief work was a comprehensive treatise on the *ius civile* in three books that exercised a strong influence on Roman legal thought and was subjected to extensive commentary by later jurists in works known as '*ad Sabinum*'.[143] Other works attributed to Sabinus included a commentary on the edict of the *praetor urbanus*; a collection of *responsa*; a monograph on theft (*de furtis*); and a commentary on the *lex Iulia de iudiciis privatis*.[144] Another leading jurist of this period was C. Cassius Longinus, a student of Sabinus whom he succeeded as head of the Sabinian

---

[140] Some scholars expressed the view that the two schools espoused different philosophical theories: the Sabinians were adherents of Stoicism, while the Proculians adopted the principles of Aristotelian (peripatetic) philosophy.

[141] In the words of W. Kunkel, "Roman traditionalism and the inclination to form relationships of loyalty of the most diverse kinds – or in other words, the *pietas* of the pupil towards the person and opinions of his master – were probably the principal motives which bound together many generations of jurists in consciously cultivated school traditions." *An Introduction to Roman Legal and Constitutional History*, 2nd ed. (Oxford 1973), 115.

[142] D. 1. 2. 2. 48; 1. 2. 2. 49–50.

[143] Although no direct reference to Sabinus' work exists in the Digest, its structure and general nature is known to us from the works of other jurists who used it as a framework for their own work, such as Pomponius, Paulus and Ulpianus.

[144] Aulus Gellius, *N. A.* 14. 2. 1.

School.[145] He attained the urban praetorship and the consulship (AD 30), and served as governor of Asia and Syria several times between the years AD 40–49. His chief work, an extensive treatise on the *ius civile*, is known to us mainly from references and fragments integrated in the writings of later jurists.

The jurists of the high and late Principate periods (AD 90–180 and AD 180–235 respectively) were predominantly natives of the provinces and descendants of Roman and Italian families who had settled outside Italy. A notable feature of this age was the increasingly close connection between the jurists and the imperial government. This link, originally established through the *ius respondendi*, was strengthened under Hadrian's reign (AD 117–138) and an increasing number of jurists joined the imperial administration as holders of high state offices. The first major jurist of the high classical period was Iavolenus Priscus, who was born about AD 55 and still alive during Hadrian's age. He had an illustrious military and political career: he was consul in AD 86, served as governor of Upper Germany, Syria and Africa and was a member of the imperial council from the time of Nerva (AD 96–98) to the early years of Hadrian's reign. Iavolenus is best known for his *Epistulae*, a collection of opinions in 16 books. He also published commentaries on the works of earlier jurists (*libri ex Cassio, ex Plautio*) and a collection of texts from Labeo's posthumous work *posteriora*. Fragments of these works were included in the Digest of Justinian. Another leading jurist was Publius Iuventius Celsus (*filius*) who succeeded his father, a little known jurist of the same name, as head of the Proculian School. He held the praetorship (AD 106) and consulship (AD 129), served as governor of Thrace and Asia Minor, and was a member of the *consilium principis* under Hadrian. His works include a set of 39 books of *Digesta* as well as collections of *epistulae* and *quaestiones*. He was held in high esteem by his contemporaries and was frequently cited by later jurists. Probably the most important jurist of the second century was Salvius Iulianus, believed to have been born in Hadrumentum in the province of Africa. Like other distinguished jurists, he held a rich succession of offices (tribune, praetor, consul, pontifex, governor of Germany, Spain and Africa) under the emperors Hadrian, Antoninus Pius and Marcus Aurelius. He also served as a member of the imperial councils of Hadrian and Antoninus Pius. The most important works he composed were the consolidation of the praetorian Edict (*c*. AD 130) and his *Digesta*, a collection of *responsa* in 90 books. The *Digesta* exercised a potent influence on the legal thinking of the imperial period, as exhibited by the numerous references to this work by later jurists and the mass of fragments embodied in the Digest of Justinian.

Two more jurists of this period deserve mention with a focus on their activities as writers and teachers rather than their innovative contribution to Roman legal thinking: Sextus Pomponius and Gaius.

---

[145] D. 4. 8. 19. 2. Thus this school is sometimes referred to as *schola Cassiana*.

Pomponius lived in the time of Hadrian and Antoninus Pius and was a man of great knowledge and an enormously prolific writer. Yet, his work is characterized by clarity rather than by originality or depth. He appears to have acquired notoriety as an antiquarian rather than as a lawyer, even though some of his doctrinal writings are mentioned by later jurists and numerous fragments were included in the Digest of Justinian. No evidence indicates that he ever held public office and it is unknown whether he was granted the *ius publice respondendi* as no *responsa* of his are mentioned. His works included three treatises on the *ius civile* written in the form of commentaries on earlier juristic writings (*ad Quintum Mucium, ad Plautium, ad Sabinum*); an extensive commentary on the praetorian edict (discoverable in citations by later jurists); two comprehensive collections of casuistic material (*epistulae* and *variae lectiones*); and a series of monographs on various subjects (*stipulationes, fideicommissa, senatusconsulta* and such like). Pomponius' best-known work is the *Enchiridium* that embodies a short outline of Roman legal and constitutional history that spans the period from the kings through to his own day. The relevant fragment has been preserved in its entirety in Justinian's Digest, under the title '*de origine iuris*' ('on the origin of law') and, despite its gaps, constitutes an important source of information on the historical development of Roman law.[146]

Although Gaius is one of the most renowned jurists of the Principate period, there is scant information on his life except for the material emerging from his writings.[147] Internal evidence suggests that he lived during the reigns of Hadrian (AD 117–138), Antoninus Pius (AD 138–161) and Marcus Aurelius (AD 161–180), and that he was a Roman citizen.[148] His style of writing and his knowledge of Eastern laws and customs have been construed to suggest that he was a teacher of law in a province within the eastern half of the empire, probably Asia. However, presently no convincing evidence exists to support this hypothesis. Since he refers to the leaders of the Sabinian school as 'our teachers', it is very likely that he studied law in Rome, and was thoroughly familiar with Roman law as practiced and taught by the leading lawyers of the capital. In contrast to his contemporary Pomponius, who was held in great respect and frequently cited by classical writers, Gaius is not mentioned by any of them. This suggests that he was not accepted as a member of the select group of jurists who possessed the *ius respondendi*. He was probably one of the many lesser jurists outside this select group, rescued from oblivion by the later recognition of his elementary treatise, the Institutes, as a major document of classical Roman law.[149] The Institutes (*Institutiones*), was designed as an introductory textbook for students and was written about AD 160. Until the 1816

---

[146] D. 1. 2. 2.

[147] Even his family name is unknown – Gaius is only a *praenomen*, or first name.

[148] See D. 34. 5. 7. pr; G. 1. 7; 1. 193; 1. 55; 3. 134; 4. 37.

[149] His works only started to be treated as authoritative in the later imperial period many years after his death. Thus Gaius is one of the five jurists whose authority was recognized by the Law of Citations of AD 426. In the Institutes of Justinian he is affectionately referred to as '*Gaius noster*' ('our Gaius'). See *const. Omnem* 1, *Inst.* 4. 18. 5.

discovery of the Institutes text in Verona,[150] only fragments of the juristic literature from this period survived through later compilations of law such as the Digest of Justinian. Although the manuscript unearthed at Verona dates from the fifth or early sixth century AD (more than three centuries after Gaius' time), it is now generally perceived as a faithful reproduction of Gaius' original work. The importance of the Institutes is twofold. In the first place, it is the only juristic work from the Principate era that we have inherited nearly in its original length and form. Therefore, the work is an important source of classical Roman law. Secondly, the relative simplicity and lucidity of Gaius' style made the Institutes ideal for the ordinary lawyer and the student; thus it was heavily relied upon in later Roman law. Gaius' textbook was used as a model by the compilers of Justinian's Institutes, which played an important part in the reception of Roman law in Western Europe since the High Middle Ages.[151] Gaius also published commentaries on the Law of the Twelve Tables, the provincial edict (*edictum provinciale*) and the edict of the *praetor urbanus*; monographs on various legal institutions; and collections of opinions.

The most highly esteemed jurists of the late Principate period (AD 180–235) were Aemilius Papinianus, Iulius Paulus and Domitius Ulpianus.

Generally regarded as the greatest of the late classical jurists, Papinianus was a lifelong friend of Emperor Septimius Severus (AD 193–211).[152] In AD 203, the emperor elevated him to the position of prefect of the praetorian guard (*praefectus praetorio*)—the emperor's chief of staff, principal adviser and executive officer in civil and military matters.[153] Emperor Caracalla ordered the murder of Papinianus in AD 212 because, it was rumoured, he had refused to devise a justification for Caracalla's murder of his own brother and co-regent Geta. Papinianus did not compose general treatises and his works were mainly collections of opinions and discussions of special topics. These works included 37 books of *quaestiones* and 19 books of *responsa* that also contained references to opinions of other jurists and to judicial decisions adopted by the emperor and the prefects. He also composed a collection of *definitiones* (in two books) and a monograph on adultery. In keenness,

---

[150] The German historian B. G. Niebuhr discovered in the cathedral library of Verona a manuscript containing the epistles of St Jerome, dating from the seventh or eighth century AD. This manuscript was identified as a palimpsest, i.e. a manuscript where two or more texts are written on top of each other. Suspecting that the manuscript had some writing of special interest, Niebuhr presented his discovery to Friedrich Karl von Savigny, one of the most eminent legal historians of the time. The latter detected the text of Gaius' Institutes underneath that of St Jerome. Although about one tenth of the Gaius' text was lost or proved impossible to decipher some of the missing parts were reconstructed after the discovery of more fragments from Gaius' Institutes in Egypt in 1927 and 1933.

[151] On the later influence of Gaius' work see P. H. Birks and G. MacLeod B. (trs), *The Institutes of Justinian* (London 1987), Introduction. Recent translations of Gaius's Institutes include: Francis de Zulueta, *The Institutes of Gaius* (New York 1946, Oxford 1985); W. M. Gordon and O. F. Robinson, *The Institutes of Gaius* (London 1988).

[152] See *Hist. Aug., Carac.* 8. 2.

[153] He also held the office of head of the chancery *a libellis* and was a member of the *consilium principis* by virtue of his important role in the imperial administration.

breadth of reasoning and clarity of presentation his works were unsurpassed, and his authority settled the law for centuries on many controversial issues.[154] Numerous fragments of Papinianus' works were preserved in the Digest of Justinian and other post-classical compilations of law.

Like other leading jurists of this period Iulius Paulus, a contemporary of Papinianus, had a brilliant career in the imperial civil service: he was head of the chancery *a memoria*, member of the *consilium principis* during the reigns of Septimius Severus and Caracalla, and *praefectus praetorio* under Alexander Seve-rus. He was an enormously prolific writer and presented great commentaries on earlier legal works. His best-known work is a comprehensive commentary on the praetorian edict in 80 books (*ad edictum*). Among his writings are also a treatise on the *ius civile* in 16 books (*ad Sabinum*); commentaries on various *leges, senatus consulta* and the works of other jurists (Iulianus, Scaevola, Papinianus); two collections of *decreta*; and numerous monographs on various subjects in public and private law. An extensive collection of extracts from Paulus' works, known as *Pauli sententiae*, was widely used during the later imperial period.[155] The authority of Paulus' writings was confirmed in the Law of Citations (AD 426) where he is listed as one of the 'important five' jurists of the Principate period.

Domitius Ulpianus, a pupil of Papinianus, held various imperial offices during his lifetime that included head of the chancery *a libellis, praefectus annonae, praefectus urbi* and (from AD 222) *praefectus praetorio*. However, his political influence made him unpopular among the members of the powerful praetorian guard and this led to his assassination in AD 223. Ulpianus is probably the most industrious of all the Roman jurists. His contribution to juristic literature includes 51 books on the *ius civile* (*ad Sabinum libri LI*); 83 books on the edict (*ad edictum libri LXXXIII*); 2 books of *responsa*; a legal manual for beginners in two books (*institutiones*); collections of *regulae* and *definitions*; and numerous monographs on individual statutes, various state offices and matters of legal procedure. A thorough assessment of Ulpianus' ability as a jurist is difficult as only fragments of his many works exist. Yet, modern scholars regard him as one of the most learned and elegant writers on the law, if not the most brilliantly original. The extent of his influence can be judged by the fact that almost half of Justinian's Digest (about 42 %) is comprised of fragments extracted from his writings.

In the later half of the third century, Roman jurisprudence lost its vitality and rapidly approached its end. The chief reasons were the collapse of the *Pax Romana*, the demise of the political system of the Principate and the accompanying swift move towards absolutism. As long as private jurists were members of a senate that retained some authority, their *responsa* carried sufficient weight and played a part

---

[154] Scholars of late antiquity, including the compilers of Justinian's codification, attribute special importance to Papinianus' works and often refer with admiration to his exceptional qualities as a lawyer. C. 6. 42. 30; 7. 45. 14; *Const. Omnem* 1.

[155] Consider E. Levy, *Pauli Sententiae: A Palingenesia of the Opening Titles*, (Ithaca, New York 1945).

in the administration of justice alongside the emperor's rescripts. However, the jurists' *responsa* ceased to be regarded as authoritative when the senate lost all its power and authority in the third century AD to the emperor and his bureaucracy, and the senators no longer had any influence in the *consilium principis*. In the third century AD, as imperial government increasingly assumed the characteristics of an absolute monarchy, the *responsa prudentium* ceased to function as a living source of law, having been superseded by the emperors' rescripts on legal and judicial matters.[156]

### 2.4.6 The Influence of Customary Law

Although the classical jurists did not count custom (*usus, consuetudo*) among the sources of law,[157] custom continued to play a part as an important basis of the law that applied in the provinces. The local systems of law, both written and customary, that prevailed in the provinces prior to the Roman conquest remained in force and continued to govern the social and economic life of the provincial communities save insofar as they might prove embarrassing to Roman rule. References to customary law can thus be found in imperial constitutions, as well as in the juridical literature of this period.[158] As far as Roman law proper was concerned, custom continued to exert an influence on both lawmaking and the application of the law through the interpretations of the jurists, who regarded certain long-established norms as so traditional as not to need any specific legal authority.[159] After Roman law became the common law of the empire, following the enactment of the *constitutio Antoniniana* in AD 212, many of the earlier local laws continued to apply in the form of custom if sanctioned by imperial legislation.

---

[156] The last of the great jurists are considered to include Herennius Modestinus and Aelius Marcianus. Modestinus, a student of Ulpianus, authored many works that embraced an extensive collection of *responsa* in nineteen books; a work on *differentiae* (controversial questions) in nine books; a collection of *regulae* (rules of law); and a treatise, written in Greek, on the exceptions from guardianship. The authority of his works is confirmed in the Law of Citations where he is listed as one of the 'important five' jurists of the early imperial age. Marcianus' most renowned work is the *Institutiones*, an elementary treatise on law in sixteen books that is frequently cited in the Digest of Justinian.

[157] Consider, e.g., G. 1. 2; D. 1. 1. 7; D. 1. 2. 3. 12.

[158] See, e.g., the *rescriptum* of Emperors Septimius Severus and Caracalla of AD 199 in FIRA I, 84 & 85. The jurist Ulpianus speaks of custom as a direct source of law in the provinces in those cases involving disputes that cannot be resolved on the basis of an existing written law. See D. 1. 3. 33.

[159] According to the jurist Iulianus, rules derived from custom ought to be relied upon in those cases not covered by written law, or where the relevant statute has been repealed by salient agreement of the people through desuetude (D. 1. 3. 32.). It is not clear, however, if this view reflects the classical approach, as the relevant passage might have been inserted by post-classical writers.

## 2.5   Sources of Law in the Later Imperial Era

### 2.5.1   The Development of Imperial Law-Making

During the later imperial age, the 'pluriformity' that characterized legislative activity during the Republic and the Principate no longer existed. With the transformation of the Roman government into an absolute monarchy, the emperor emerged as the sole source of laws and also their final interpreter. The unchallengeable legislative supremacy of the emperor conformed to the essence of the new regime, whose absolutist nature barred constitutional or any other legal limitations.[160] Nevertheless, the emperor actually exercised his governmental functions and powers with guidance from established substantive and procedural norms. Though he might change these norms at his discretion, he was bound to observe them to ensure that his decisions produced the intended practical results. In the final analysis, it may be declared that the observance of these norms constituted a kind of intra-organ control over an authoritarian regime.

The imperial enactments (*constitutiones*) with their diverse appellations of *edicta*, *rescripta*, *decreta* and *mandata* were now collectively designated *leges*—this signified legal norms with the highest validity. These enactments furnished the basis for the formation of a new body of law (*ius novum*) distinct from the old law (*ius vetus*) as traditionally interpreted by the classical jurists. The principal fields of operation of the imperial laws were public administration and socio-economic policy, but they also introduced numerous changes in other areas, such as family and criminal law. Many imperial laws were not strictly Roman in character but exhibited the influence of foreign (especially Greek) institutions. Moreover, since the era of Constantine the Great, imperial legislation was also moulded by ideas derived from Christian ethics. Generally, the legislation of this period displays elements of so-called the 'vulgar law': statutes are composed in an inflated, grandiose style while their provisions have an ill-arranged, vague and unrefined form; and these laws are often deficient in affording an exhaustive and unambiguous determination of the relevant issues. While the quality of the imperial laws declined, their quantity rapidly increased as often conflicting enactments were produced in great profusion entailing a chaotic mass that had little practical use. Since the late third century AD, the Roman government endeavoured to install some order to the mass of laws claiming validity in the empire.

Depending on their form and scope of application, the majority of imperial enactments fell into two categories: *edicta* or *leges generales* and *rescripta* or *leges speciales*.[161]

---

[160] The theoretical assumption that the emperor was also bound by the laws was nullified by the fact that he was above the law (*princeps legibus solutus*) and equally so by his legislative omnipotence (*quod principi placuit legis habet vigorem*).

[161] As regards the *mandata* and the *decreta*, these essentially fell into disuse during this period (the former were superseded by the edicts while the latter were replaced by the rescripts).

An edict was usually issued in the form of a letter addressed to a high official (generally a praetorian praefect), who had a duty to publicise its contents; it could also be addressed to the people or some section thereof (e.g. to the inhabitants of a particular city), or to the senate (either of Rome or of Constantinople, depending on the circumstances).[162] When an edict was addressed to the senate, no *senatus consultum* was passed to confer formal validity to the emperor's wishes that now existed as law *per se*. Simply, the terms of the statute were recited in the senate, recorded and retained in the archives of that body. Edicts were usually prepared by the minister of justice (*quaestor sacri palatii*) with the assistance of legal experts and discussed in the imperial council (*sacrum consistorium*). After the division of the empire, they were almost invariably issued in the name of both *Augusti* even when they emanated from only one of them (obviously they had no effect within the realm of the other *Augustus* without the latter's consent).[163] This type of imperial enactment is illustrated by the famous Edict of Prices (*edictum de pretiis*) promulgated by Emperor Diocletian in AD 301 that set maximum prices for a wide range of goods and services, and prescribed penalties for profiteering.[164]

The rescripts (i.e. the emperor's answers to legal questions invoked by actual cases and submitted to him by private citizens or state officials) remained an important source of law until the time of Diocletian.[165] In AD 315, Emperor Constantine decreed that a rescript must be deemed invalid if it deviated from a *lex generalis*.[166] Moreover, a law issued by Arcadius and Honorius in AD 398 stipulated that a rescript was only binding in the individual case that it concerned.[167] However, Emperors Theodosius II and Valentinian III in AD 426 sought once more to confer imperial rescripts an indirect law-making force. Thus they decreed that as

---

[162] It should be noted that a *lex generalis* always operated in the same way irrespective of to whom it was formally addressed.

[163] This served to emphasize that the empire remained politically united, despite its administrative partition.

[164] See M. Giacchero, *Edictum Diocletiani et Collegarum de pretiis rerum venalium* (Genoa 1974); H. Blümner, *Der Maximaltarif des Diokletian* (Berlin 1958); S. Lauffer, *Diokletians Preisedikt* (Berlin 1971); A. C. Johnson, P. R. Coleman-Norton, F. C. Bourne, *Ancient Roman Statutes* (Austin 1961, repr. 2004), 235–237.

[165] During Diocletian's reign, when elements of classical legal science still survived, the imperial chancery *a libellis* issued, in the emperor's name, a large number of individual case decisions in the form of rescripts that addressed diverse legal points.

[166] C. Th. 1. 2. 2. & 3: "Rescripts that are contrary to law shall not be valid, in whatsoever manner they may have been impetrated. For the judges must rather follow what the public laws prescribe. (3) When We are persuaded by entreaty to temper or to mitigate the rigor of the law in a special case, the regulation shall be observed that rescripts that were impetrated before the posting of the edict shall have their own validity, and a prior rescript shall not be derogated by a later one. But rescripts which were elicited thereafter shall have no force unless they are in conformity with the public laws, especially since it is necessary and permitted that We alone shall investigate an interpretation that has been interposed between equity and the law."

[167] C. Th. 1. 2. 11: "Rescripts which have been issued or which will in the future be issued in reply to references of cases to the Emperor shall assist only those lawsuits for which they shall be proved to have been issued."

a rescript constituted a declaration of a general principle in an individual case, it could be considered generally binding. This view seems to have prevailed during the late fifth and sixth centuries.[168]

In the later imperial period two new kinds of imperial constitution emerged, namely the *sanctio pragmatica* and the *adnotatio*. The former generally consisted of a reply by the emperor to a petition, but it apparently ranked as a more formal manifestation of the emperor's will than an ordinary rescript and practically had the same effect as a *lex generalis*. Accordingly, it was commonly used in replying to petitions that requested the settlement of matters of general public interest or the issuing of decisions with a scope of application that extended well beyond the interests of the parties involved. A *sanctio pragmatica* might be employed, for example, to effect administrative reform; regulate the operation of government bodies or corporations; or confer important privileges to certain groups.[169] The term *adnotatio* was probably used to denote a decision of the emperor in response to a petition or any other communication directly addressed to him and written in the margin of the petition.[170] Finally, a form of subordinate legislation that originated from the late Principate period was embodied in the edicts of the praetorian prefects (*edicta praefectorum praetorio*).[171] The provisions of such edicts mainly addressed administrative matters and were binding within the prefecture of their author, provided that they did not conflict with the general law of the empire.

## 2.5.2  The Law of the Jurists

As previously observed, by the middle of the third century jurisprudence entered a period of rapid decline and the *responsa prudentium* soon ceased to be a living source of law. This development was generated by a combination of factors: the social and economic decay precipitated by the catastrophes of the third century AD; the crisis of the political system of the Principate and the growing absolutism of the emperor who sought to make himself the sole source of legal progress; the growing influence of Christian thinking that had an ethical orientation with little use for the subtleties of the secular jurisprudential techniques; and the gradual abandonment of the Roman tradition of distilling legal norms from the body of individual cases in favour of a system where decisions in individual cases were controlled by

---

[168] C. 1. 14. 3.

[169] A good example of such an enactment is the *sanctio pragmatica pro petitione Vigilii* (AD 554) that embodies the response of Emperor Justinian to a petition from Vigilius, a bishop of Rome. It addressed problems concerning the legal order in Italy, which Justinian had recently recaptured from the Goths. By the same enactment, the Emperor ordered that his legislation should be in force in Italy. And see C. 1. 23. 7. 2.

[170] Originally, the *adnotatio* seems to have been a written instruction from the emperor for the drafting of a rescript by the imperial chancery *a libellis*.

[171] These were also known as *formae, programmata, praecepta* or *commonitoria*.

previously formulated general rules. However, it cannot be asserted that the decline of classical jurisprudence was tantamount to a collapse of legal culture in general. Lawyers were still essential in the imperial court, the various government departments, and those agencies in Rome and in the provinces charged with the administration of justice. In the late third and early fourth centuries AD, many state officials in Rome were men steeped in the classical tradition and they sought to defend this tradition against the inroads of eastern and vulgar legal influences.[172] However, it is clear that in the late imperial era the social position of the lawyers and the character of their work had radically changed. The new lawyers no longer worked as individuals who, as members of the senatorial aristocracy, experts in law and representatives of a great and living tradition, presented opinions on legal problems and recorded them in writing. These lawyers were mere state officials, anonymous members of a vast bureaucratic organization, who simply prepared the resolutions for issue in the name of the emperor.

As already noted, during the Dominate epoch imperial legislation became the principal source of law and the sole means for modifying the current body of law. The old law (embodied in *leges, senatus consulta, edicta magistratuum*), created and developed by the former agencies of legislation, remained valid. However, it was customary to cite this law not by reference to the original sources, but by reference to the classical jurists' commentaries on them. Moreover, the past emphasis on the development of new law through interpretation of extant legal materials evaporated. The focus now attached to the study and elucidation of the jurists' writings from the Principate era. As jurisprudence ceased to exist as a living source of law, annihilated at its source by the absolutism of the imperial system, literary production in the legal field sank to the level of merely compiling, editing and abridging earlier juristic works. The latter were now treated as a body of finally settled doctrine that could be applied in a case at any time. This body of law was designated *ius* or 'jurists' law' in contradistinction to the body of law derived from the enactments of the emperors, known as *lex*.

However, serious problems beset the application of *ius*—problems that were intensified by the general passivity of the judges in an age of absolutism, who shied away from seeking original solutions and preferred to rely essentially on established authority. But the sheer vastness of the classical juridical literature made it virtually impossible for the average lawyer to familiarize himself with the material. Furthermore, the classical works contained an extensive range of opinions that often reflected incompatible or contradictory viewpoints. Judges, who were expected to base their decisions upon established authority, often faced the problem of choosing between two or more conflicting sources that in principle were deemed equally authoritative. The problem was exacerbated by the fact that at a time when legal texts circulated only in manuscript copies, many works attributed to classical jurists were actually not written by them. This situation generated a

---

[172] A last effort to preserve the fruits of the classical jurisprudence is reflected in the imperial rescripts that were transmitted to us from the reign of Diocletian (AD 284–305).

great deal of confusion as to the state of the law and also opened the door to abuse, as advocates often sought to deceive judges by producing captious quotations from allegedly classical texts. This prompted the urgent need to discover a way for identifying those works that formed part of the authoritative juridical literature and the appropriate solution to adopt if the classical authorities displayed conflicting opinions. The government's response was a series of legislative enactments prescribing the juristic works that should be relied upon by the courts and fixing the degree of authority accorded to different sources. Thus, in AD 321, Emperor Constantine decreed that the critical comments (*notae*) that the jurists Paulus and Ulpianus had made in connection with the *responsa* collection of Papinianus were no longer to be used.[173] However, a year later Constantine issued another enactment confirming the authority of Paulus' other works (especially the *Sententiae*).[174] In the end, such measures proved inadequate. Theodosius II (Eastern emperor, AD 408–450) and Valentinian III (Western emperor, AD 423–455) thus formulated a new law on the subject in AD 426. The effect of this so-called Law of Citations was that the works of Gaius, Papinianus, Paulus, Ulpianus and Modestinus were made the primary authorities and the only ones that could be cited in a lawsuit. Gaius was the only jurist of the middle Principate period to be chosen, probably because his work was popular and well known. The other jurists belonged to the later Principate period and so manuscript copies of their works must have been readily available. If the authorities adduced on a particular issue disagreed, then the majority view prevailed; if numbers were equal, then the view of Papinianus had to be followed and only if Papinianus was silent was the judge free to make a choice himself.[175] Although the Law of Citations did not provide a

---

[173] C. Th. 1. 4. 1: "Since We desire to eradicate the interminable controversies of the jurisconsults, We order the destruction of the notes of Ulpianus and Paulus upon Papinianus, for, while they were eagerly pursuing praise for their genius, they preferred not so much to correct him as to distort him."

[174] C. Th. 1. 4. 2: "All opinions which are contained in the writings of Paulus, since they have been accepted by duly constituted authority, shall be confirmed and shall be given effect with all veneration. Therefore, there is not the least doubt that his Books of Sentences, characterized by the fullest lucidity, a most finished style of expression, and a most reasonable theory of law, are valid when cited in court."

[175] C. Th. 1. 4. 3: "We confirm all the writings of Papinianus, Paulus, Gaius, Ulpianus and Modestinus, so that the same authority shall attend Gaius as Paulus, Ulpianus and the others, and passages from the whole body of his writings may be cited. We also decree to be valid the learning of those persons whose treatises and opinions all the aforesaid jurisconsults have incorporated in their own works, such as Scaevola, Sabinus, Iulianus, and Marcellus, and all others whom they cite, provided that, on account of the uncertainty of antiquity, their books shall be confirmed by a collation of the codices. Moreover, when conflicting opinions are cited, the greater number of the authors shall prevail, or if the numbers should be equal, the authority of that group shall take precedence in which the man of superior genius, Papinianus, shall tower above the rest, and as he defeats a single opponent, so he yields to two. As was formerly decreed, We also order to be invalidated the notes which Paulus and Ulpianus made upon the collected writings of Papinianus. Furthermore, when their opinions as cited are equally divided and their authority is rated as equal, the regulation of the judge shall choose whose opinion he shall follow. . .".

definite solution, it imparted a measure of certainty to the administration of justice and remained in force until the time of Justinian.

In the fifth century, legal scholarship experienced a period of revival centred around the law schools of the empire. The first law school was probably founded in Rome in the late second century and a second such school was later established in Beirut during the third century. As the administrative needs of the empire grew (especially after Diocletian's reorganisation of the administration), new law schools were established in places such as Alexandria, Caesaria, Athens and Constantinople in the East; and Carthage and Augustodunum in the West. Initially, tuition at the law schools was delivered in Latin but from the early fifth century Greek replaced Latin as the language of instruction. The teaching was conducted by professional law-teachers (*antecessores*), and the courses offered were components of a fixed curriculum that focused entirely on the systematic study of classical juristic works and imperial constitutions. First, the Institutes of Gaius were discussed and then followed the study of the classical jurists' opinions *ad ius civile* and *ad edictum* embodied in collections (with special attention to the works of Papinianus and Paulus). In the final year, the focus converged on the study of current law and this involved an examination of imperial constitutions dating from the middle of the second century AD. The method of instruction was similar to that used in the schools of rhetoric: a classical work was discussed and clarified step by step and, when possible, compared or contrasted with other relevant works. In this way, general legal principles were formulated and applied to resolve specific problems of law arising from actual or hypothetical cases. At the end of their studies that spanned a maximum of 5 years, students were awarded a certificate that entitled them to serve as advocates in the courts or to join the imperial civil service. Over time, the professional lawyers educated in the law schools (*causidici, advocati*) replaced the earlier orators (*oratores*) whose training in law was usually only elementary.[176]

Besides training people for functions in the civil service, the law schools cultivated a scholarly approach to law with a focus on the study and elucidation of the juristic works from the classical period that had evolved into a unitary and peculiar body of law (*ius*). The extent to which the ideal of a full education in classical law was realized naturally varied in different periods and places. In the early years of the Dominate period (late third and early fourth centuries AD), a substantial scholarly interest in law apparently existed in the West, with most of this interest probably revolving around the law school in Rome. Since Constantine's era and especially after Constantinople became the seat of government, the empire's intellectual centre and thereby the centre of legal culture gradually shifted to the East.[177] In the fifth century AD the study of the classical authorities particularly at

---

[176] An edict of Emperor Leo I, issued in AD 460, ordained that postulants for the bar of the Eastern praetorian prefecture had to produce certificates of proficiency from the law professors who instructed them. This requirement was soon extended to the inferior bars, including those of the provinces. See C. 2. 7. 11.

[177] From the middle of the fourth century AD legal culture in the West exhibited a sharp downward trend – a decline precipitated by the deteriorating socio-economic conditions, political instability and the constant threat of barbarian invasions.

the law schools of Beirut and Constantinople engendered a new type of theoretical jurisprudence (as opposed to the largely practical and casuistic jurisprudence familiar to the classical and earlier periods). The East-Roman law professors were admiringly termed the 'teachers of the universe', and the most celebrated encompassed Cyrillus, Patricius, Eudoxius, Leontius, Amblichus and Demosthenes. It is established that these men composed a diversity of works: commentaries on imperial constitutions and texts of classical jurists; summaries (*indices*); annotations; and collections of rules on particular legal questions. These works were concerned not so much with developing new legal ideas but with helping novices and practitioners acquire a sound knowledge and understanding of the material imparted by the classical Roman jurists. They were also concerned with adapting the classical materials to the demands and conditions of their own times.[178] Despite its lack of originality and its tendency towards simplification, post-classical legal science did succeed in resurrecting genuine familiarity with the entire classical inheritance and facilitating its adaptation to the conditions of the times. The new insight into the essence of the classical law enabled court lawyers trained at the law schools to enhance the technique of imperial legislation and successfully tackle the task of legal codification. The improvement of legal technique is manifested by the fact that the imperial laws of the late fifth and sixth centuries were superior in clarity and style to those of the early post-classical period. It was largely through the work of the late imperial jurists that the spirit of classical legal science was preserved and found its way into the codification of Justinian and thereby into modern law.

As previously elaborated, in the later imperial epoch the problems surrounding the application of *ius* were magnified by the fact that the manuscripts containing the works of the classical jurists were few and scarce. Thus these materials were not easily accessible to legal practitioners, especially those working in the provinces. Moreover, as a result of the general decline of legal culture, especially in the West, lawyers encountered increasing difficulties with handling and comprehending the language of the classical texts. Connected to these problems was the appearance of legal works that mainly embodied compilations of assorted extracts from the works of the classical jurists and intended primarily for use by students and legal practitioners. The authors of these works (whose names remain largely unknown) selected parts from the original texts that would appear interesting to contemporary readers, whilst other parts were reproduced in a summary form or altogether omitted if they were deemed useless or superfluous. Occasionally passages were replaced with those composed by the authors or entirely new passages were added to render the material more intelligible or adapt the classical texts to transformed conditions. From the point of view of a modern scholar, this tampering distorted rather than improved the texts. However, it must be acknowledged that from the

---

[178] After the *constitutio Antoniniana* (AD 212) granted Roman citizenship to all the free inhabitants of the empire, knowledge of Roman law was requisite for those engaged in the practice of law, especially in the provinces where the newly admitted citizens had to conduct their affairs according to an unfamiliar system of law.

perspective of the post-classical lawyers the classical works were largely outdated and in need of 'modernization'. Irrespective of its form, the juridical literature of the later imperial period patently reveals one aspect: the extent to which legal thinking remained under the spell of classical jurisprudence. The legal science that existed at that time was concerned exclusively with the classical jurists, whose works were regarded with an almost religious awe by legal practitioners and judges.

Probably the most important post-classical collection of juristic writings is the so-called 'Vatican Fragments' (*Fragmenta Vaticana*) discovered in 1821 in the Vatican library. This work contains extracts from the writings of the jurists Papinianus, Paulus and Ulpianus who lived in the late second and early third centuries. It also includes imperial rescripts dating from the period AD 205–372 that were reproduced from the Gregorian and Hermogenian Codes. The texts are arranged in titles according to the subject-matter, with each title preceded by a note indicating the name of the jurist from whose work the materials were extracted or, if the text is a rescript, the name of the emperor who issued it.[179] Another work, dating from the early fourth century, is known under the title of *Collatio Legum Mosaicarum et Romanarum* or *Comparison between Mosaic and Roman Laws* (sometimes abbreviated to *Collatio*). This work closely resembles the Vatican Fragments with respect to its content and composition but differs from that text as sentences from the first five books of the Old Testament (especially the sayings of Moses) are embodied at the beginning of every title. In addition, it includes texts not only by Paulus, Ulpianus, Papinianus, but also by Gaius and Modestinus. Ostensibly, the purpose of this work was to compare some selected Roman norms with related norms of Mosaic law to show that basic principles of Roman law corresponded with or possibly derived from Mosaic law.[180] Two other works originating from the same period must also be mentioned: the *Pauli Sententiae* and the *Ulpiani Epitome*. The first mainly consists of brief pronouncements and rules attributed to the third century jurist Paulus. It covers a broad range of topics relating to both private and criminal law, and was probably used as a handbook by legal practitioners. As it is not certain whether Paulus himself ever wrote a book called *Sententiae*, this work is now generally assumed to be a brief presentation of Roman law extracted from the writings of Paulus by an unknown author from the latter part of the third century. We have not discovered this work directly; it exists only through citations in the Digest of Justinian and other post-classical compilations of law.[181] The *Ulpiani Epitome* was probably an abridgment of Ulpianus' work *liber singularis regularum* (Rules of Law in One Book). It was composed in the late third or early fourth century and, like the *Pauli Sententiae*, was probably

---

[179] For the text, see FIRA II, pp. 461–540. A critical edition of this work was produced by Th. Mommsen in (1860) – see P. Krüger, Th. Mommsen & G. Studemund, *Collectio librorum iuris anteiustiniani* III (Berlin 1927).

[180] The standard modern edition of the *Collatio* is that of Th. Mommsen included in his *Collectio librorum iuris anteiustiniani* III (Berlin 1927). And see FIRA II, pp. 541–89.

[181] See FIRA II, pp. 317–417, 419–432.

used by practitioners. This work has reached us in an incomplete form through a manuscript dating from the tenth or eleventh century.[182] Two important works from the East have survived: the Syrio-Roman book of law and the *Scholia Sinaitica*. The first was composed in Greek by an unknown author in the late fifth century and used as a textbook for students in the law school of Beirut.[183] The second was a collection of fragments from a commentary in Greek on the work of Ulpianus' *libri ad Sabinum* that was probably composed at the law school of Beirut where it was used for instructional purposes.[184]

## 2.5.3    Custom and the Growth of 'Vulgar Law'

After the enactment of the *constitutio Antoniniana* (AD 212) that extended Roman citizenship to all the inhabitants of the empire, the old distinction between *ius civile* and *ius gentium* dissolved as the distinction between *civis* and *peregrinus* vanished: every free man within the empire was now a citizen, subject to the same Roman law. In fact, however, the imposition of a uniform legal system did not entail the adoption of Roman law pure and simple by the peoples of the empire nor did it result in the disappearance of local systems of law that continued to apply as customary law. In the eastern Mediterranean, in particular, the common Greek culture and language had produced a distinct body of law, whose origins are located in the Greek city-states as well as the Hellenistic monarchies of Syria and Egypt. This body of law operated alongside Roman law and was enforced by officials like the latter law. It did not merely sustain itself in a half-submerged condition, but it contributed distinct elements to the Roman system through a process of cross-fertilization. This process had been operative for centuries but accelerated after the intellectual centre of the empire shifted from Rome to Constantinople in the fourth century AD. This entailed the 'orientalization' or 'Hellenization' of Roman law, and the 'Romanization' of Greek-Hellenistic and other local bodies of law. Similar processes featured in the Western provinces of the empire, but also in Italy and Rome itself. This precipitated a phenomenon that is generally labelled the 'vulgarization' of Roman law.

The term 'vulgar' law refers to the legal views and practices of lay people—a body of 'popular' or 'folkish' law untouched by the artifices of the legal experts. This genuine customary law was initially regarded as supplementary and unofficial.

---

[182] See FIRA II, pp. 261–301.

[183] FIRA II, pp. 751–98. See also K.G. Bruns & E. Sachau, *Syrisch-Römisches Rechtsbuch* (Leipzig 1880, repr. Aalen 1961); P. E. Pieler, *Byzantinische Rechtsliteratur* in H. Hunger, *Die hochsprachliche profane Literatur der Byzantiner*, Bd. 2 (Munich 1978), 393 ff.

[184] FIRA II, pp. 635–52; P. E. Pieler, *Byzantinische Rechtsliteratur* in H. Hunger, *Die hochsprachliche profane Literatur der Byzantiner*, Bd. 2 (Munich 1978), 391 ff. N. van der Wal & J. H. A. Lokin, *Historiae iuris graeco-romani delineatio. Les sources du droit byzantin de 300 a 1453* (Groningen 1985), 20–24.

Finally, in the fifth century AD it attained recognition as an authentic source of legal norms on a par with imperial legislation.[185] The increasing ascendancy of customary or 'vulgar' law, that is, legal solutions adopted by practitioners at a local or regional level, may partly be attributed to the fact that imperial legislative enactments reached local magistrates and courts, if at all, with great delay and in a piecemeal fashion due to the uncertainty of communications. Moreover, at a time when printed books did not exist, local courts and practitioners had no access to the bulk of the classical legal sources. The enhanced role of custom as a source of law was also reinforced by the fact that while the emperor and his bureaucracy created all law, they were often unfamiliar with the prevailing conditions in the provinces. Thus, many imperial enactments were at variance with local practices and conceptions of justice. Setting aside long-established local customs was not easy and thus the actual implementation of imperial legislation in the provinces sometimes proved an impossible task.[186] But vulgar law did not pertain only to customary law. An important source of vulgar law was also the imperial enactments, which were often influenced by foreign legal ideas and practices. Another factor emerged after the recognition of Christianity in the fourth century AD, when Christian ethics started to exercise considerable influence on certain branches of Roman law, such as family and criminal law.

The body of law that evolved from the interaction between Roman and foreign elements was markedly inferior to the classical system in terms of logic and abstract refinement. Yet, it was closer to the prevailing conditions of life and thus had some practical advantages. Non-Roman influences are detected at many points of the legal system. For example, the importance of the written document (a heritage of the Hellenistic tradition) as a prerequisite for a binding agreement was now generally recognized. At the same time, freedom of contract was promoted by the abandonment of the cumbrous formalism that existed previously. Under the influence of Greek-Hellenistic law, which adopted a narrower conception of paternal authority than Roman law, Emperor Constantine introduced restrictions to the traditional Roman institution of *patria potestas* by conceding that persons *in potestate* could have proprietary rights in certain circumstances. Thus, it was recognized that a child was entitled to the property a mother bequeathed to them, even if the child remained under the *potestas* of their father.[187] The influence of

---

[185] According to the jurist Hermogenian, an established customary norm had the same force as written law because it was based upon the tacit consent of the citizens ('*tacita civium conventio*'). D. 1. 3. 35; see also D. 1. 3. 32. 1. This view was endorsed by imperial legislation, under the condition that a customary norm did not contradict a written law and had a logical basis. C. 8. 52. (53.) 2 (Constantine): "The Emperor Constantine to Proculus. The authority of custom and long-continued usage should not be treated lightly, but it should not of its own weight prevail to the extent of overcoming either reason or statute."

[186] For example, the institution of *abdicatio* (pertaining to the right of the head of a family to renounce a child) was still implemented during the later imperial period, despite the fact that it was abolished by a *rescriptum* of Emperor Diocletian. See C. 8. 46. (47.) 6.

[187] C. 6. 60. 1. Justinian finally adopted the position that a child *in potestate* could claim ownership over everything he acquired, except when he acquired property from his father. C. 6. 61. 1.

certain Greek customs is also reflected in Justinian's decision to replace the quite complicated *adoptio* procedure of the *ius civile*[188] with a simpler procedure that merely required the father, child and intending adoptor to appear before an official and have the *adoptio* inserted in the court roll.[189] A feature alien to old Roman law that was adopted from the customs of the near East was the *donatio propter nuptias*: a donation by the husband to the wife before the marriage to provide for the wife's domestic needs and to ensure that she had an estate should the marriage be dissolved by divorce or by the husband's death. In the course of time, the tendency developed to regard the *donatio propter nuptias* as existing in the interests of the children rather than the wife. The influence of Christian principles concerning the sanctity of marriage is exhibited in legislative enactments of Constantine and some of his successors that sought to curtail, by imposing severe penalties, the freedom of spouses to declare a divorce without proper justification.[190] Moreover, the prevalence of Christian ethical principles during the fourth century AD entailed disrepute for the institution of concubinate (*concubinatus*), a permanent union between a man and a woman not legally married. Concubinate was discouraged through the introduction of various restrictions on the rights of children born out of such a union (*liberi naturales*). To avert such restrictions, the parents or in some cases the children resorted to some form of legitimation such as legitimation by the subsequent marriage between the parents of such children.[191] In the field of criminal law, the influence of Christian ethics is displayed in the abolition of certain cruel forms of punishment such as crucifixion and gladiatorial combat. This influence is also evident in the introduction of new criminal offences pertaining to the suppression of heretical cults and practices. The list of pertinent illustrations could be easily enlarged.

---

[188] This procedure entailed the transfer of a person governed by the paternal power of the head of his family to the *patria potestas* of another (*pater adoptans*).

[189] *Inst* 1. 12. 8.

[190] According to a law of Constantine, a wife who divorced her husband without good reason was punished by deportation and loss of her dowry. A husband who did the same was not allowed to remarry. If he did remarry, his former wife could seize the new wife's dowry. However, these penalties did not affect the validity of the divorce. See C. Th. 3. 16. 1.

[191] C. 5. 27. 10.

# Chapter 3
# The Private Law

## 3.1 Introduction

From an early stage in the development of Roman society, the term *ius* (plural, *iura*) signified that which is due in human relations—the rightful power of a community member to act in a certain manner vis-à-vis his fellow citizens. It referred to a course of conduct that the community would take for granted and in that sense endorse. The community had a general awareness of the circumstances when acts would be construed as *iura* and these were established by custom. Originally, the exercise of *ius* had no connection with state organization and thus *ius* was defined as any instance of approved self-help. After the consolidation of the state and the establishment of a formal system of justice, *ius* denoted the rules or norms capable of enforcement with the consent of those responsible for safeguarding and maintaining the norms governing community life. Thus the holders of *imperium* had the essential functions of pronouncing the *ius* and assisting those with rights to obtain their entitlements through formal channels. The earliest form of legal procedure was the act whereby a person who possessed or claimed a *ius* against another requested a jurisdictional magistrate to both confirm his *ius* and enable its exercise by effectively suppressing an opponent's resistance. Roman law developed primarily as a private law that was devised as a system of rights or claims bolstered by causes of action and specific procedural remedies.

When Roman legal thinking evolved to perceive the various protected powers as a system, the term *ius* resembled our modern meaning of the word 'law' in a broad sense: the entire system of norms by which the rights and concomitant powers of community members are defined, protected and enforced. Furthermore, *ius*, or law in a broad sense, was construed to embody a strong normative element reflecting the

© Springer International Publishing Switzerland 2015                                        95
G. Mousourakis, *Roman Law and the Origins of the Civil Law Tradition*,
DOI 10.1007/978-3-319-12268-7_3

relationship between law and justice (*iustitia*).[1] In this broad normative sense *ius* is not the same as morality nor as positive law; rather, it is right law, or positive law as it ought to exist in light of what morality and justice ordain.[2] *Ius*, as defined above, was distinguished from *lex* (plural *leges*). The latter term signified a law created by a competent legislative organ of the state in conformance with a prescribed procedure. A *lex*, which by definition pertained to a specific type of legal relationship, drew upon *ius* but was not identified with it. The normative principles of *ius* that determined the question of lawfulness or unlawfulness were not reducible to the body of formally enacted laws. These principles were regarded as pre-existing and transcending the enacted law, which merely prescribed the method for implementing *ius* under certain circumstances. Unlawfulness was defined primarily in relation to *ius*, for an unlawful act was deemed to encroach upon the principles of *ius* that informed the particular legislative enactment encompassing the act. From this viewpoint, the word *iniuria* signified any infringement of the law comprised of an act performed '*contra ius*'. Furthermore, the application of a *lex* was typically strict as an act or dispute was tackled according to the letter of the law without reference to the circumstances of the individual case. On the other hand, the norms of *ius* were construed as flexible and thus adaptable to the circumstances of each particular case. Whereas the implementation of a *lex* was based on formal criteria, the implementation of *ius* was anchored in its intrinsic rightness.

As previously noted, the term *ius civile* or 'law of the state' was used to denote the law that each state had established for itself and was peculiar to it. The law peculiar to the Roman state was originally that derived from custom and legislation, and applied only to Roman citizens. However, as the Roman state expanded and social and economic relations grew more complex, the law that applied in Rome came to be derived from a great variety of sources, including the edicts of the foreign and urban praetors. Nevertheless, although Roman law expanded in scope, some traditional legal institutions (such as conveyance by *mancipatio*) remained open only to Roman citizens. Such institutions were deemed to belong to *ius civile* in a narrow sense, while other institutions (such as conveyance by *traditio* or simple delivery) were considered to belong to the law of all peoples (*ius gentium*) in the sense that they were open to non-citizens and citizens alike. As earlier observed, this technical distinction disappeared after the extension of the Roman citizenship to all free inhabitants of the empire in the early third century AD. A further contrast mentioned by the classical jurists is that between *ius civile* and *ius honorarium*, the law derived from the edicts of the magistrates. In this context, the term *ius civile* was understood as encompassing not only the rules derived from custom and

---

[1] Thus, *ius* was defined by jurists of the classical era as 'the art of good and equitable' (Celsus: D. 1. 1. 1.), and as that which is always 'just and fair' (Paulus: D. 1. 1. 11.). According to Ulpianus, *ius* requires living honestly, harming no one and giving each one his due' (D. 1. 1. 10. 1; see also *Inst* 1. 1. 3.). The connection between law and justice is also reflected in Ulpianus' definition of jurisprudence as 'the knowledge of things divine and human, and of what is just and unjust' (D. 1. 1. 10. 2; see also *Inst* 1. 1. 1.).

[2] This meaning of *ius* is better conveyed in English by the word 'right' as a noun.

legislation, but also those that emanated from the interpretations of the jurists, the resolutions of the senate and the constitutions of the emperors.

With respect to the subject matter of law, the Roman jurists recognized a distinction between public law (*ius publicum*) and private law (*ius privatum*). Public law was concerned with the organization and administration of the state and the interests of the Roman people as a whole. Under the heading of public law fall criminal law, constitutional law, administrative law and the law governing the conduct of religious affairs (*ius sacrum*). Private law, on the other hand, comprised those branches of law concerned with the rights and duties of individuals and regulating their personal and proprietary relationships.[3] Although the classification appears intelligible and convenient, there are points at which public law and private law overlap. Such overlap occurred, for instance, when a general public interest concurred with a private one. It should be noted that private law greatly overshadowed public law in both its intrinsic merit and subsequent influence. This is because private law had a dominant role in the development of legal norms and was the chief interest of the jurists, the most creative element in Roman legal life.

Private law is classified by the compilers of Justinian's Institutes into three branches: the law of persons, the law of things and the law of actions.[4] This classification, which has permeated all subsequent legal thinking, is repeated from the Institutes of Gaius[5] and was in all likelihood entrenched by tradition. The law of persons, sometimes described as the law of status, denotes that part of the law concerned with the legal position of the human being, their rights, capacities and duties. It encompasses much that in modern law is termed family law, as well as the rules governing marriage and guardianship. The law of things is concerned with the rights and obligations generated by the use and exploitation of economic assets and covers what in modern law is termed the law of property, the law of contract, the law of delict and the law of succession. Finally, the law of actions deals with the remedies by which legal rights were protected and the procedures by which the relevant legal judgments were enforced.

## 3.2  The Law of Persons

The Roman law of persons was concerned with the status or legal position of the human being. It can be defined as the body of legal rules relating to a person's rights, capacities and obligations as an individual, as a member of the community and as a member of a particular family. It dealt with the issues of liberty and

---

[3] See *Inst* 1. 1. 4: "Public law is that which regards the state of Rome; private law is that which concerns the well-being of individuals." And see D. 1. 1. 1. 2.

[4] *Inst* 1. 2. 12.

[5] G. 1. 8.

slavery, citizenship, family status, as well as other factors such as age, sex or mental state that were relevant to determining a person's legal position.[6]

In classical law the term person (*persona*) denoted simply a human being (*homo*), and hence even slaves were considered persons, despite the fact that a slave was a legal object or object of rights and duties, in contrast with a free person who was a legal subject or bearer of rights and duties.[7] A *persona* originated at birth and terminated on death.[8]

### 3.2.1   Status Libertatis

At the centre of the Roman law of persons lay the distinction between those who were free (*liberi*) and those who were slaves (*servi*).[9]

Liberty, enjoyed by those who were either freeborn or freed persons, was defined as "the natural ability to do anything one pleases unless it is prohibited by force or law."[10]

It is important to note here that the Romans were deeply aware of the limitations imposed on individual liberty by their collective existence and considerations of public welfare (*salus publica*). The scope of liberty was conditioned by the need to safeguard the social order to which each citizen had to subordinate his own rights. Liberty was perceived by the authority-minded Roman community as freedom within the established socio-political order and not outside, let alone against it. The all-pervading notion of authority (*auctoritas*) was the natural and indispensable complement of liberty, setting limits to the free expression of individual impulses or choices. From a Roman moral perspective, submitting to the authority of one who manifested the ability to lead was considered the test rather than the negation of liberty. Where the authority of the leader was reciprocated by the genuine loyalty (*fides*) of the follower, order with liberty or liberty within order could prevail. This relationship supplied the foundation of the Roman concept of discipline: subordination by free will and reason rather than by force or compulsion. To the Romans discipline was the indispensable basis of order and liberty. In this respect, differences of rank and social status were considered to be the natural consequences of a well-ordered society by no means incompatible with liberty. The

---

[6] According to the jurist Paulus, "there are three positions a man may have: liberty, citizenship and family status." D. 4. 5. 11.

[7] Although Roman law also knew and recognized non-human subjects of rights and duties, such as municipalities and private bodies, these were not regarded as *personae* and fell outside the scope of the law of persons.

[8] Under certain circumstances, an unborn child was regarded as already born. This is known as the '*nasciturus* fiction', and was usually applied where it would have been to the advantage of the unborn child to have been born at the relevant stage.

[9] G. 1. 9; *Inst* 1. 3 pr; D. 1. 5. 3.

[10] *Inst* 1. 3. 1.

notion of civil liberties as a private sphere protected against interference by the state was wholly alien to the Romans, for it was incompatible with a civilization that attributed the highest value to the state. And yet, on the whole, Roman society during the republican and early imperial epochs was far from totalitarian. Instead, it presents the picture of a *laissez-faire* society in which each law-abiding citizen could lead the life that his talents, means and desires dictated. In many respects, the Roman citizen enjoyed a security of existence equal to any modern constitutional order: he was protected against illegality by the scrupulous observance of the rule of law enjoined on all state officials; he could neither be arrested nor convicted arbitrarily; and his private property rights were upheld. The magistrates' power of enforcement could be exercised only to secure obedience to lawful demands and the autonomy of private life was generally respected.

### 3.2.1.1   Slavery

The most vulnerable group in Roman society were the slaves (*servi*).[11] In the early republican period a relatively small number of slaves lived in Rome; but from the mid-third century BC the slave population expanded rapidly and, by the end of the Republic, slave labour was the predominant factor in economic life.[12] The living conditions of slaves varied considerably, depending on their personal skills, education and place of work.[13] In general, urban slaves were treated better than rural slaves and were more frequently released from slavery. But the vast majority of slaves, especially those working on the large estates, lived in misery and were treated harshly by their masters.[14]

Slavery could arise in a number of ways, the principal of these being birth from a slave woman,[15] capture in war[16] and as a punishment. A slave was considered to be both a person (*persona*) and a form of property (*res*) legally existing as the object rather than the subject of rights and duties. As he was the property of his master (*dominus*), he lacked legal capacity and this theoretically entitled the master to govern the slave as he pleased.[17] A slave could not contract a lawful Roman

---

[11] Slavery is defined as "an institution of the law of nations (*ius gentium*) whereby one man is, contrary to nature, subject to the dominion of another." See *Inst* 1. 3. 2.

[12] By the end of the republican period, it is likely that more than one third of Italy's entire population consisted of slaves.

[13] Educated slaves were often employed as instructors, clerks or physicians. On the estates an educated slave could become estate manager, work supervisor or book-keeper.

[14] The deep resentment felt by slaves against their Roman masters erupted in a series of large-scale slave revolts during the late second and early first centuries BC.

[15] *Inst* 1. 3. 4; D. 1. 5. 5. 1.

[16] *Inst* 1. 3. 4; D. 1. 5. 5. 1.

[17] G. 1. 52: "Slaves are in the power of their masters, a power recognized by the law of nations (*ius gentium*), for in all nations masters are invested with power of life and death over slaves; and (by the Roman law) the owner is entitled to everything acquired by the slave". In the Principate

marriage, had no standing in the courts and their offspring immediately became the property of the slave's master. However, slaves had limited contractual capacity attached to the condition that whatever they acquired accrued to their masters.[18] It should be noted also that initially a slave could not impose legal duties on his master by his actions. From the republican period, however, the praetor could intervene and grant certain praetorian actions, labeled *actiones adiecticiae qualitatis* (such as the *actio de peculio* and the *actio de in rem verso*), against the master and in favour of third persons who had entered into dealings with a slave. Furthermore, a master could be rendered liable for the delicts of his slave on the grounds of an *actio noxalis*.

A slave could be released from slavery (*manumissio*) in three ways: by a formal announcement by the master in public and before a higher magistrate (usually a praetor) that the slave was free (*vindicta*); after the enrolment of a slave as a Roman citizen by the censor, according to the master's request (*censu*); and under his master's will (*testamento*). Besides these legally recognized ways of manumission, there were other informal ways of liberating slaves, e.g., when a master in the presence of his friends declared his slave to be free (*manumissio inter amicos*); or when he expressed such a wish in a letter (*manumissio per epistulam*); or even when he shared his table with his slave (*manumissio per mensam*). Although these methods of liberation provided little security for the slave, if he could prove that the relevant actions transpired he could then refuse to return to slavery by appealing to the praetor.[19] Liberated slaves or freedmen (*libertini, liberti*) were Roman citizens, but enjoyed fewer social and political rights than those with no slaves in their ancestry. Nevertheless, many freedmen successfully earned a steady living through their involvement in trade, industry and the arts; some even gained access

---

era, legislation was enacted restricting the masters' right to mistreat or arbitrarily slay their slaves. See G. 1. 53; D. 40. 8. 2; D. 48. 8. 11. 2; D. 1. 6. 2; D. 48. 8. 4. 2; C. Th. 9. 12. 1; *Inst* 1. 8. 2.

[18] An interesting element connected with the slave's contractual capacity was the *peculium*, a form of private property comprised of assets such as a sum of money or an object granted by a master to his slave for the slave's use, free disposal or use in commercial and other transactions. Although, the *peculium* theoretically remained the master's property it was considered in the eyes of the community to belong to the slave himself.

[19] The freedperson retained a special legal relationship with their former master, now termed patron (*patronus*), in relation to whom he was referred to as *libertus*. A *libertus* was expected to behave toward his patron in a respectful manner (*obsequium*), and so he could not act to the detriment of the patron. He could not bring certain actions entailing infamy against the patron, and could bring other civil suits only with the consent of a magistrate. Moreover, he could not prosecute the patron for criminal offence (except for treason). The *libertus* could also be required to offer his patron *munera*, which were gifts on special occasions, and owed him various services (*operae liberti*) suitable to the status and age of the freedperson. See, e.g., D. 37. 15. 2; C. Th. 9. 6. 4; D. 38. 1. 7. 3; D. 37. 14. 6. 1; D. 38. 1. 16. 1. However, the relationship between the *libertus* and his *patronus* was not entirely one-sided, as it involved several factors that worked to the advantage of the freedperson. For instance, the patron was expected to provide for his freedperson if the latter was impoverished. Consider D. 37. 14. 5. 1.

to positions of power, especially in the last century of the Republic and during the Principate.

### 3.2.2   Status Civitatis

Roman citizenship (*civitas Romana*) was that status whereby a person was entitled to the rights and was subject to the duties of Roman law. The issue of citizenship may be more appropriately addressed in a discussion of constitutional law, yet, in the field of private law, it had important consequences for those individuals who were privileged to occupy the status of a Roman citizen (*civis Romanus*).

Roman citizenship was usually acquired by means of conception during a Roman marriage or birth from an unmarried Roman mother. Furthermore, citizenship could be acquired by the formal liberation of a slave by his master (*iusta ac legitima manumissio*) and by law or decree by the authorities. During the Republic, the citizenship was initially granted to individuals and whole communities in only special instances and after the Social War (91–87 BC) it was granted *en masse* to all Italian allies. Augustus attempted to put a brake on the expansion of citizenship by designing a population policy that sought to preserve the Roman and Italian stock as the core of the empire. This entailed the sparser granting of individual naturalizations to foreigners whilst attempting to stem the flood of emancipated slaves. However, the realities of a coalescing empire forced upon his successors standards that were more elastic. Once Rome, Italy and the provinces had entered the stage of mutual assimilation, the citizenship was granted with increasing frequency to individuals or whole communities, often following the concession of the *ius Latii* (the intermediate legal status between citizen and foreigner given to members of Latin colonies). At the end, rather than being a conscious method for furthering Romanization, the extension of the citizenship to the provincials was its unavoidable result. It may seem, therefore, merely the logical culmination of a process in the making for centuries that Emperor Caracalla issued an edict, the celebrated *constitutio Antoniniana* (AD 212), by which he bestowed Roman citizenship upon all the free inhabitants of the empire who were members of organized communities. The *constitutio Antoniniana* signified the final transformation of the traditional *civitas* into empire citizenship and led to the extension of Roman law to the whole empire.

Depending on their age, gender and mental capacity, freeborn Roman citizens (*cives Romani ingenui*) enjoyed a number of legal capacities or rights. In public law, these citizens had the right to vote in the popular assemblies (*ius suffragii*); the right to stand for public office (*ius honorum*); and the right to occupy military offices in the Roman legions. In private law, they had the right to contract a legal Roman marriage (*ius conubii*); the right to enter into legal transactions and conclude valid legal acts relating, for example, to the conclusion of contracts and the acquisition of property (*ius commercii*); and the right to litigate before the Roman courts. In addition, certain financial rights and privileges were reserved for freeborn citizens only. A person entitled to all the rights of the citizenship (*ius civitatis*) was referred to as *civis optimo iure*. However, not all Roman citizens were *cives optimo iure*. Roman women, for example, did not possess the *ius honorum* and the *ius suffragii*, and their contractual capacity initially depended on whether or not they fell under the authority (*manus*) of their husband. Similarly, freedpersons (*libertini*) were subject to various restrictions: they were excluded from all the important offices of the state, could not serve in the legions and could not contract a lawful marriage with a member of the senatorial aristocracy.[20] Furthermore, only some of the relevant rights were held by persons granted by law limited citizenship, such as the members of certain communities or individuals in Italy and overseas.[21]

### 3.2.3   Status Familiae

The cornerstone of Roman society was the family (*familia*), a closely-knit unit corresponding very largely to the nuclear family of our own times. The *status familiae*, one's position in or out of a family unit, was the factor that determined the question of whether a person was independent (*sui iuris*) or subject to the control of another (*alieni iuris*). The *alieni iuris* persons were under the authority of the father of the family (*paterfamilias*), the oldest male member of the family, who was entitled as a person *sui iuris* to enjoy the maximum number of rights or capacities that a Roman citizen could possess. The *paterfamilias* was the pivot of the Roman family system, as his power and authority (*patria potestas*) over the members of his family was the tie that held the family together. Usually, the *paterfamilias* had authority over his wife (*uxor*), provided that she had been married to him by virtue

---

[20] See D. 23. 2. 44 pr.

[21] During the early republican era, members of Latin communities in Italy, who were racially akin to the Romans, were granted some share in the rights of Roman citizenship and, up to the second century BC, received full citizenship on migration to Rome. The privileged status of these communities was referred to as *ius Latii*. Later, colonies were founded in Italy by Romans and Latins which were granted internal autonomy, but were subject to Roman foreign policy, to financial obligations to Rome and to military service in time of war. Although legally strangers (*peregrini*), the members of these communities enjoyed approximately the same rights as the old Latins, which included the right to acquire property in Rome (*ius commercii*), and the right to conclude marriages with Romans (*ius conubii*), when specifically granted. Moreover, they could obtain full citizenship through domicile in Rome. In the early imperial age, numerous individuals and also whole communities or even provinces were accorded the *ius Latii*. Reference should also be made here to the so-called 'Iunian Latins' (*Latini Iuniani*): slaves who had been manumitted informally or in a manner that was not recognized by the law. Under the *lex Iunia* of AD 19, such slaves became free but did not acquire full Roman citizenship, only Latin status without political rights – see G. 1. 22. More specifically, they enjoyed the right to acquire property, to enter into contracts, to adopt and to act as witnesses to civil law wills. However, they did not have the right to contract a Roman civil law marriage and also lacked testamentary capacity and the capacity to serve as guardians. When an Iunian Latin died, his property went to his patron just as if he had remained a slave. The status of *Latini Iuniani* was finally abolished during the reign of Justinian.

of a *cum manu* marriage[22]; his children[23]; his grandchildren and further descendants from marriages of sons in his *potestas*; his legitimized and adopted children; as well as slaves or other individuals similarly dependent on him.[24] The term *agnatio* denoted the relationship between all persons under the *potestas* of the same *pater*, or persons who would have been under such *potestas* if their common *paterfamilias* had still been alive.[25] Regarding persons under the *patria potestas*, it should be noted that a blood relationship (*cognatio*) was irrelevant in early Roman law but gradually evolved as a factor of central importance in the time of Justinian (especially in the field of intestate succession).

Originally, the power of the *paterfamilias* over his dependants was theoretically almost unlimited. He had the power of life and death (*ius vitae necisque*), that is, the power to kill his children, sell them into slavery or simply abandon them if he so wished. Furthermore, he could marry-off or forbid the marriage or divorce of a dependant as well as give them away for adoption or emancipate them. Finally, his dependants were financially completely dependant on him, since they could not own or acquire any property of their own. Everything a dependant acquired or already had in his possession was deemed the property of the *paterfamilias*. However, an exception to this rule emerged in respect of the male descendants of the *paterfamilias*—the *filiifamilias*.[26] Like competent slaves, the *filiifamilias* were allowed *de facto* enjoyment of a *peculium*, a term denoting an estate consisting of various forms of property that gradually became considered, for all practical purposes, the property of the *filiifamilias*.

The *patriapotestas* came to an end in a number of ways. The most common mode was the death of the *paterfamilias* or a change in his status following a *capitis deminutio* (e.g. loss of citizenship).[27] Moreover, when a daughter entered into

---

[22] The authority or marital power a man had in respect of his wife was referred to as *manus*. As a family member, a wife under the *manus* of her husband stood in the position of a daughter (*filiae loco*) with respect to him. On the other hand, if the marriage was without marital power (*sine manu*) the wife remained under the authority of her own *paterfamilias* or *sui iuris*.

[23] In the classical period, there was a rebuttable presumption that children conceived during a marriage were the legitimate children of the husband and thus in his *potestas* – see D. 2. 4. 5. Moreover, daughters-in-law married *cum manu* with sons *in potestate* were in the *potestas* of the *paterfamilias*. Illegitimate children were at all times regarded as persons *sui iuris*.

[24] More specifically, under the *paterfamilias'* authority fell persons *in mancipio*, i.e. persons who had been under the authority of a certain *paterfamilias* and had subsequently been transferred by such *paterfamilias* to the authority of another person. The status of these persons was in many respects similar to that of slaves, although they retained certain rights.

[25] Such persons were referred to as *agnati*, in contradistinction to the blood relatives (*cognati*).

[26] Upon attaining full age, a *filiusfamilias* was accorded in public law the right to vote in the assemblies, stand for public office and serve in the army, but in private law he remained subject to his father's *potestas* and hence had reduced proprietary capacity.

[27] G. 1. 127: "When a father dies, his sons and daughters always become *sui iuris*." And see G. 1. 128: "Since one who for some crime loses Roman citizenship, it follows that his children cease to be in his *potestas* exactly as if he had died; for it is against principle that a man of foreign status should exercise paternal power over a Roman citizen."

marriage *cum manu* she immediately fell under her husband's authority. The *patriapotestas* also terminated when the *paterfamilias* gave his child to another for adoption (*in adoptione*),[28] or when he released such child from his paternal power by means of the formal *emancipatio* process.[29]

As Roman society evolved over the course of time, the power of the *paterfamilias* over his dependants considerably decreased. The *ius vitae necisque* became obsolete and was abolished[30] together with the father's power to sell his dependants into slavery.[31] At the same time, various duties were placed on the head of the family with regard to his dependants, such as the duty to provide maintenance and the duty to give his daughter a dowry (*dos*) when she entered into marriage.[32]

---

[28] The institution of adoption had great importance to the ancient Romans, especially the members of the upper classes concerned with the continuation of the family line, family name and cult of their ancestors. Two forms of adoption existed: *adrogatio* and *adoptio*. *Adrogatio* occurred when a *sui iuris* person was brought under the *patriapotestas* of another. The effect of the *adrogatio* was that all persons in the power of the adrogated person (*adrogatus*) as well as his property fell under the *potestas* of the adrogator (*pater adrogans*) as his new *paterfamilias*. Adoption in the form of *adoptio* transpired when a person *alieni iuris*, i.e. under the power of another, was transferred from the *potestas* of one *pater* to that of another. Although originally this form of adoption was not available in early Roman law, the interpretation of certain principles of the Law of the Twelve Tables and the old *ius civile* facilitated the establishment of *adoptio*. The transfer of the adoptee from one *patria potestas* to another broke his agnatic relationship with his old family and cancelled his right of succession in that family whilst establishing a new position as though he had been born into the adoptor's family.

[29] Emancipation (*emancipatio*) was the most common method of terminating paternal power. Just as in the case of *adoptio*, it was derived from the rule of the Law of the Twelve Tables according to which a *paterfamilias* who sold his son three times lost his power over him. In the Principate age this method was effected as follows: the father sold his son by *mancipatio* three times (daughters and grandchildren only once) to a confidant who then granted the son his freedom on two occasions, whereupon he returned to his father's *potestas*, and on the third transaction sold him back to the emancipating father (*pater emancipans*) who in turn freed the son or other dependant. The confidant could grant the son or other dependant his freedom, but this did not usually happen as in such a case the confidant would have acquired certain rights of succession and guardianship over the emancipated person (*emancipatus*) that were generally not intended by the parties involved – it was customary that only the emancipating father himself should be the possessor of such rights. Under Justinian *emancipatio* could be performed by a simple declaration of the parties before a competent official and registration of their agreement in the court register. See *Inst* 1. 12. 6; C. 8. 48. 6.

[30] In the time of Hadrian, a father who killed his son was stripped of citizenship and all its attendant rights, had his property confiscated and was exiled.

[31] Under Justinian, the selling of a child was allowed in the case of extreme poverty of the parents, but the child could redeem himself and become free by paying the buyer the price he had paid to his father.

[32] The *paterfamilias* retained only the right to chastise or inflict moderate and reasonable punishment on his dependants.

### 3.2.4   Capitis Deminutio

The loss or impairment of an individual's social and political rights was known as *capitis deminutio* and entailed a curtailment or change of *status* (*status permutatio*).[33] The Roman jurists distinguished between three forms or degrees of *capitis deminutio*: *maxima*, *media* (or *minor*) and *minima*.[34]

*Capitis deminutio maxima* was the loss of personal liberty, which also entailed a loss of citizenship and family ties. A Roman citizen could be sold into slavery if he committed certain grave offences, including offences connected with military service (such as desertion to an enemy) or for willfully avoiding enrolment in the censor's books in order to evade taxation.[35]

A *capitis deminutio media* (or *minor*) entailed loss of citizenship but no loss of freedom. In early times, this occurred when a man went into exile or became a member of a foreign state. Under the Empire, a sentence of deportation (*deportatio*) to an island had the same effect.[36]

Finally, the *capitis deminutio minima* involved an alteration in a family relationship which occurred when a person's family ties were dissolved either by their entry into another family (by adoption, adrogation or the *cum manu* marriage of a woman) or by becoming *sui iuris* and the head of a new family following his emancipation.

### 3.2.5   Marriage

Marriage in Rome was not a simple institution. There were a variety of different types of marriage that all had varying degrees of recognition and legal impact; and the institution underwent drastic changes in both social and legal senses throughout the ages. Notwithstanding these changes, the institution of marriage always held a central place in community life as it was the foundation of the *familia*, the pivot of Roman society. Its cardinal importance is reflected in the famous definition offered by the jurist Modestinus that is recited at the beginning of the title on marriage in the Digest: "Marriage is the joining of a man and a woman in a general communion of life by virtue of the communication of divine and human law".[37] It is important to

---

[33] The term *caput* primarily meant a person or human being. In a derivative sense the same term denoted an individual's privileges as a free person, as a member of a family and as a holder of certain social and political rights. The term *status* referred to the position a person occupied in the community by virtue of his *caput*.

[34] D. 4. 5. 11.

[35] Under the Law of the Twelve Tables, an insolvent debtor was liable to the same penalty but the relevant rule was abolished in later times.

[36] This must be distinguished from relegation (*relegatio*), which denotes the exclusion of a person from residence in a particular territory and did not result in loss of citizenship.

[37] D. 23. 2. 1.

note at the outset that for a considerable period of Roman history, marriage was not so much a legal institution as it was a simply factual relationship recognized by society. In later times, the influence of Christian dogma and ethics moulded the gradual perception of marriage as a legal relationship with a strong religious character.

Most marriages were preceded by an engagement or betrothal (*sponsalia*), consisting of reciprocal promises by the future husband and wife to contract a legal marriage with each other at a later date.[38] In early times the betrothal assumed the form of an enforceable agreement that was usually concluded between the respective *patresfamilias* by means of the contract of *sponsio*. Before the beginning of the second century BC, however, the promises ceased to be actionable.[39] Nevertheless, betrothal entailed certain legal consequences. From the time it was concluded relatives of the pair were considered to be in-laws, and a sexual involvement by the woman with another man amounted to adultery. By the fourth century AD it became customary for the fiancé to give the woman a gift signifying his earnest intention to marry. This was forfeited if he refused to proceed with the marriage, and was repaid to him in multiple if the breach came from the other side.[40] An engagement could be terminated by mutual consent of the parties or upon the death of one of them. It was likewise terminated if it was revealed during the course of the engagement that the parties did not meet the conditions for a valid marriage.

There were two forms of marriage: *cum manu* and *sine manu*. In the marriage *cum manu* the wife fell into the power (*manus*) of her husband or his *paterfamilias*, if the latter was still alive. In the marriage *sine manu*, on the other hand, the wife remained in the power (*potestas*) of her own *paterfamilias* or, if she had been *sui iuris* before the marriage, she remained independent.

Marriage *cum manu* could be celebrated in one of three ways: *confarreatio*, *coemptio* and *usus*.[41] *Confarreatio* was a religious ceremony that created both *manus* and the marriage itself.[42] It took its name from the cake of spelt (*farreus panis*) that was eaten by the parties in the temple of Jupiter. The relevant ceremony was conducted under the supervision of a priest of Jupiter (*flamen dialis*) and the chief priest (*pontifex maximus*). By the early Principate age *confarreatio* had largely become obsolete, but it possibly remained in existence until the close of the fourth century AD, when Emperor Theodosius abolished pagan sacrifices.

---

[38] D. 23. 1. 1 (Florentinus): "A betrothal is the mention and promise of a marriage to be celebrated hereafter."

[39] See D. 23. 1. 4. Pr; D. 23. 1. 7. 1. Any penalty attached to the relevant agreement was void as "it was considered dishonest that marriage be enforced by the threat of a penalty." See D. 45. 1. 134 pr.

[40] C. 5. 3. 15 (Constantine): "If the man or his parents are unwilling to consent to the marriage, whatever has been donated by him cannot be recovered if it has been delivered." C. 5. 1. 5 (Leo and Anthemius): "A woman who is her own mistress is liable for double the amount of the betrothal gift [if she refuses to proceed with the marriage without a good cause]."

[41] G. 1. 110–115 b.

[42] This ancient form of marriage ceremony originated in the archaic period and was initially intended for the aristocracy.

*Coemptio* consisted of the formal conveyance of the wife to the husband by means of a fictitious sale conducted according to the technical procedure of *mancipatio* (also employed for *adoptio* and *emancipatio*).[43] Like *confarreatio*, *coemptio* created both *manus* and the actual marriage. This type of marriage ceremony appears to have fallen into disuse as early as the first century AD and it disappeared not latter than the third century AD. A wife who was not married with either of the above ceremonies came into the *manus* of her husband by *usus* if she cohabited with him for a year without interruption. This method was analogous to the acquisition of property by prescription. A woman not wishing to come under her husband's power in this way was required to stay away from the matrimonial home for three successive nights in each year (*absentia trinoctium*).[44] As already noted, the principal effect of a *cum manu* marriage was that the woman passed into the power of her husband or, if he was himself *in potestate*, into the power of his *paterfamilias*. This implies that if she had been *sui iuris* she became *alieni iuris* and her property was transferred to her husband or his *paterfamilias*.[45] Everything that she subsequently acquired accrued immediately to her husband or his *paterfamilias*, with the result that she never had property of her own.

Originally nearly all Roman marriages were *cum manu* but during the later republican epoch, as family relationships became less rigid and women acquired a greater degree of independence, marriage *sine manu* evolved as the principal form of marriage.[46] In the imperial age, the latter became virtually the only form of marriage. The marriage *sine manu* was a formless transaction. This means that for the creation of such marriage nothing more was necessary than the intention of the parties to live together as husband and wife (*affectio maritalis*). However, while ceremonies were not essential to the validity of the marriage, celebrations including bridal feasting and songs and the leading of the bride to her husband's home were usual. Such celebrations provided evidence that marriage (not concubinage)[47] was

---

[43] *Coemptio* probably had its origins in the real sale of the wife to the husband that took place in primitive times.

[44] According to Gaius, the *trinoctium* was an innovation of the Law of the Twelve Tables. This suggests that the legislation contained some express provision on the subject. Furthermore, it appears that the emphasis was on the avoidance of *manus* rather than on its acquisition and this indicates that, prior to the introduction of *usus*, the typical form of marriage was marriage with *manus*.

[45] Henceforth she was considered to be in the position of a daughter of her husband or his *paterfamilias* – G. 2. 139. On the death of her husband, she had the same rights of succession as a daughter.

[46] The *sine manu* marriage was probably in existence, even though uncommon, as early as the time of the Law of the Twelve Tables.

[47] Concubinage (*concubinatus*) was a lasting relationship between a man and a woman who lived together without being lawfully married. It bore a great resemblance to regular marriage and as such was not immediately rejected but viewed as an inferior kind of marriage. However, the growing influence of Christian values during the fourth century AD entailed the *concubinatus* falling into disrepute and the imposition of disincentives to these unions in the form of various restrictions placed by the state on the rights of children born out of such relationships (*liberi naturales*).

intended. The *sine manu* marriage had little impact on the status of the parties. The wife did not fall under the power of her husband or his *paterfamilias*. If she had been *sui iuris* before the marriage, she remained so and retained her own property. Everything that she subsequently acquired accrued to her own property. If she had been under *patria potestas* before her marriage, she remained a member of her original family and all that she acquired accrued to her own *paterfamilias*. In general, there were few legal effects of the *sine manu* marriage as the partners stood legally in the same position as strangers to each other. In the course of time, however, the existence of a valid marriage was held to produce certain legal consequences: donations between husband and wife (*donationes inter virum et uxorem*) were prohibited[48]; the parties could not institute defaming actions against each other; and the assumption of liability by a wife for her husband's debt (*intercessio*) was considered null and void.

A number of conditions had to be fulfilled before a valid civil law marriage (*iustae nuptiae* or *iustum matrimonium*) could take place.[49] Firstly, it was required that both parties possessed the capacity to contract a Roman marriage (*ius conubii*). Thus, only marriage between Roman citizens or with someone from a state that had been granted the right of intermarriage with Romans constituted a valid marriage. Secondly, both parties had to be of marriageable age. This usually meant that the man had to be at least 14 years old and the girl at least 12.[50] If the parties were *alieni iuris*, the consent of the *patresfamilias* was required, as was the consent of the parties, although in early times the wishes of the woman were legally irrelevant. A *paterfamilias* could withhold consent for a reasonable cause, but otherwise provision was made for the granting of the requisite consent by a magistrate. Where the woman was *sui iuris*, the consent of her tutor was needed when the marriage was to be *cum manu*. Finally, there were to be no impediments. The most important impediments derived from relationship by blood, marriage and adoption. Thus, ascendants (*adscendentes*) and descendants (*descendentes*) in the direct line could never marry each other.[51] Furthermore, collaterals (*collaterales*) were not permitted to marry each other if they were too closely related, but the forbidden degrees varied through the ages.[52] Originally, second cousins were not permitted to marry, but by the first century BC first cousins could. Uncles and nieces, aunts and nephews could not intermarry, but a *senatus consultum* exceptionally permitted marriage with a brother's daughter so that Emperor Claudius (AD 41–54) could marry

---

[48] During the later imperial age this prohibition gradually fell into disuse.

[49] The term *matrimonium non iustum* (or *iniustum*) denoted a marriage between two persons one or both of whom did not possess the right to contract a legal Roman marriage (*ius conubii*). Children born in a *matrimonium iniustum* were socially legitimate (and not stigmatized as *spurii*), but they were not in their father's *potestas* nor agnatically related to their father. It should be noted, moreover, that the parties intending to form a *matrimonium iniustum* were not hindered by the authorities from forming such a union; they were only denied the effects of a lawful Roman marriage.

[50] See *Inst* 1. 10 pr; C. 5. 4. 24.

[51] G. 1. 59.

[52] G. 1. 61.

Agrippina.[53] The latter exception was repealed in the fourth century AD.[54] Any marriage concluded contrary to these prohibitions was absolutely null and void, and constituted the criminal offence of incest (*incestus*) entailing severe penalties.[55] Moreover, during the course of the centuries a large number of prohibitions against the intermarriage of certain persons evolved from considerations of a social or moral nature as well as related public policy decisions. Differences in respect to social class or rank constituted one of the most important impediments. Marriage between patricians and plebeians was forbidden by the Law of the Twelve Tables but this prohibition was finally removed by the *lex Canuleia* of 445 BC. The *lex Iulia* of Augustus forbade members of the senatorial class to marry freedpersons as well as those connected with the theatrical profession.[56] Further-more, marriage was forbidden between Roman provincial officials and native women of the province, and, in later times, between Christians and Jews.[57] Marriages concluded in conflict with these prohibitions were deemed null and void, and the children born from such marriages were treated as children without a father (*spurii*).[58]

From an early period, a general custom and moral duty for the father required him to bestow upon the bride a fortune or dowry (*dos*) when she entered into marriage. By the time of Justinian this moral duty had developed into a statutorily recognized legal duty.[59] As a general rule, the bride's father supplied the dowry, although the relevant duty could also be discharged by the bride herself (if she was *sui iuris*) or another member of her family or even an outsider. The primary purpose of the dowry was to serve as a contribution to the necessary expenses a marriage involved (*ad onera matrimonii sustinenda*), such as those requisite for the mainte-nance of the common household and the upbringing of children. This emphasis adapted over time to influences such as Christian humanitarian principles, and the chief function of the dowry came to be the protection of the wife and children after the marriage was dissolved by the death of the other spouse or by divorce.

A marriage could be dissolved in various ways: by the death, loss of liberty or loss of citizenship of either party,[60] or by divorce (*divortium*)—the latter existed as

---

[53] G. 1. 62.

[54] See C. Th. 3. 12. 1.

[55] See G. 1. 58–61 and 63–64; *Inst* 1. 10. 1–9 and 12; D. 23. 2. 14 pr and 4.

[56] Emperor Justin permitted marriage of members of the senatorial class with retired actresses, so as to allow his nephew Justinian to marry Theodora, who was an ex-actress – C. 5. 4. 23. 1. Later, Justinian abolished the prohibition altogether – *Nov* 117. 6.

[57] C. 1. 9. 6; D. 23. 2. 63.

[58] See *Inst* 1. 10. 12.

[59] C. 5. 12. 14. The relevant property could be transferred before or after the conclusion of the marriage without any formality.

[60] If one of the parties lost citizenship (e.g. as a result of a *capitis deminutio*), a regular marriage (*iustum matrimonium*) either became an irregular marriage (*matrimonium non iustum*) or was terminated. Whether the marriage was to be dissolved or not was at the discretion of the party whose status remained unchanged. In Justinian's reign, loss of citizenship did not result in the dissolution of marriage.

the most common form of ending a marriage. In early times, divorce was permitted to the husband only on specific grounds: adultery, poisoning a child and tampering with keys. If the husband cast his wife off for any other reason he had to give her half of his property, the remainder being forfeited to the goddess Ceres. This continued until the late third century BC, when it was recognized that a marriage could be dissolved if one or both parties did not want to be married anymore for whatever reason. No action or formalities were required for divorce unless the marriage was *cum manu*, in which case a reverse ceremony (*diffareatio* or *remancipatio*) was needed.[61] In later times, Christian emperors disapproved of unjustified one-sided dissolutions of marriage and imposed financial penalties on the party who divorced in this manner, but the marriage was still dissolved. Good causes motivating divorce included adultery, promiscuous behaviour, attempt on life, sorcery and abuse.[62] Justinian introduced a law prohibiting divorce by mutual consent, except for the purpose of living lives of monastic chastity,[63] and also stipulated certain additional grounds for the justifiable repudiation of marriage by one of the parties.[64]

### 3.2.6   Guardianship and Curatorship

In principle, a *sui iuris* Roman citizen enjoyed all the rights of citizenship and could own property as well as perform legal acts. In practice, however, certain *sui iuris* individuals were wholly or partially unable to conduct their own affairs on account of their immaturity, gender, or mental disability or impairment. Such persons were therefore in need of protection and for this reason were placed under guardianship (*tutela*) or curatorship (*cura*).

Two basic forms of guardianship were recognized: namely, guardianship over persons below the age of puberty (*tutela impuberum*)[65] and guardianship over women (*tutela mulierum*).

---

[61] Although no formalities were required for this declaration of separation (*repudium*), to provide certainty as to whether a divorce had actually taken place it was customary to send a letter of separation (*libellus repudii*).

[62] Consider, e.g., C. Th. 3. 16. 1.

[63] *Nov* 117. 10. This law was repealed by his successor, Justin II, in AD 566.

[64] See C. 5. 17. 10. 11: "We add the following to the causes specifically enumerated by reason of which repudiation can legally take place: namely, when a husband on account of natural impotence is unable to have coition with his wife for two consecutive years; . . .[when] the wife should by her own efforts produce an abortion; or if she should be so lascivious as to date, for the sake of debauchery, to bathe with other men". Consider also *Nov* 117. 13, 14.

[65] In the classical period, the age of puberty was set at fourteen years for boys and twelve years for girls.

From the time of the Twelve Tables a guardian might be appointed by will by the *paterfamilias* to those in his *potestas* who would become *sui iuris* on his death.[66] If a testator failed to appoint a guardian for a child below the age of puberty who was to become *sui iuris* at the testator's death, the nearest agnates (*proximi agnati*)[67] of the child became *ipso iure* (automatically) his or her guardians provided that such agnates were themselves above the age of puberty.[68] The *lex Atilia* (probably late third century BC) allowed the praetor at Rome and a majority of the tribunes of the plebs to appoint a guardian to a child who had none. The *leges Iulia et Titia* (probably late first century BC) extended this to the provinces, and there was additional provision for appointment of a special guardian when there was a lawsuit between the ward (*pupillus*) and the existing guardian.

To serve as a guardian was considered to be a public duty and could not be refused except for specific reasons. Until the fifth century AD, while the ward was an *infans*, literally 'unable to speak', he could not legally act—only the tutor could do that. Where the ward was older, the guardian's consent was required for all legal acts of the ward that might entail loss to the latter. If the ward entered into a bilateral contract without such approval, the result was classified as a 'limping transaction' (*negotium claudicans*): only the other party was bound to the transaction and not the ward, although the latter could not demand performance from the other party unless he was prepared to do likewise.[69] The Law of the Twelve Tables gave an action for theft from the ward's account against an agnatic guardian for double the amount he had embezzled, but such remedy was available only at the end of the guardianship. Another more general action deriving from the republican age was the *actio tutelae*. This was an action based on good faith (*actio bonae fidei*)[70] that the ward could instigate against his guardian after termination of the *tutela* on the grounds of any dereliction of duty by the latter. It should be noted further, that from the time of the Twelve Tables the *tutor* who had acted fraudulently or dishonestly in managing the ward's affairs could always be removed by means of a criminal action brought

---

[66] This appointment usually occurred when the father foresaw that he would die before his children reached the age of puberty.

[67] These were persons related to each other in the paternal line and who were under the *potestas* of the same *paterfamilias* or who would have been if he were still alive.

[68] In the time of Justinian, preference was given to the nearest cognatic relatives (*proximi cognati*). The term *cognatio* (blood relationship) was used to denote persons related through females (*cognati*).

[69] For instance, if a ward had without his guardian's approval agreed to sell part of his estate, he acquired a right to the price but could not enforce that right unless he delivered the property – a delivery which itself required the consent of the guardian. If the ward delivered the property in question without the guardian's *auctoritas*, he could reclaim it. The other party, however, could never take the initiative to enforce the relevant agreement.

[70] An *actio bonae fidei* presented the judge with a greater latitude of discretion, allowing him to take into equitable consideration all facts relating to the case. When such an action was raised the judge was instructed to condemn the defendant to pay a sum equal to 'what he ought to give or do in accordance with good faith'.

against the *tutor* (*accusatio suspecti tutoris, crimen suspecti tutoris*) before the praetor or the provincial governor.[71]

From the earliest times, women who were *sui iuris* and above the age of puberty were also placed under guardianship. The existence of such guardianship (*tutela mulierum*) manifests the essentially patriarchal nature of Roman society where a woman always had to remain under the control of a male.[72] The appointment of a woman's *tutor* occurred in the same manner as that of the *tutor impuberis*: by testament of the person (father or husband) who had power over her; by law (in which case she was placed under the guardianship of her agnates); or by a magistrate. The principal responsibility of the *tutor mulieris* was to grant his authorization (*auctoritas*) in respect of important juristic acts performed by the woman, such as acceptance of an inheritance, preparing a testament and assuming an obligation. As women became progressively more independent over the course of time, this form of guardianship lost its significance and had virtually disappeared from the scene at the end of the Principate age.

Curatorship (*cura*) became relevant where a *sui iuris* person above the age of puberty was incapable of managing his own affairs due to some disability. Curatorship occurred in various forms, the most common being curatorship in respect of juveniles above the age of puberty but under 25 years of age (*cura minorum*), insane persons (*cura furiosi*) and prodigals (*cura prodigi*).

The *lex Plaetoria* (or *Laetoria*) of *c.* 192 BC provided for a fine for anyone who defrauded a person under the age of 25. The same statute gave the minor a defence (*exceptio legis Plaetoriae*) if he was sued by someone who had defrauded him. Where the defrauded minor had entered into a transaction in which he suffered loss, the praetor gave the minor a remedy aimed at restoration of the previous legal position or status *quo ante* (*restitutio in integrum*).[73] Because of the possibility of the praetor's intervention, the practice developed where persons wishing to conduct business with a minor required the magistrate's appointment of an independent adult (a *curator*) to approve the transaction. Originally, the *curator* had no formal legal recognition and this status prevailed for a long time as they were merely deemed someone appointed *ad hoc* when the need arose for a specific transaction. However, from the late second century AD it became possible for a minor to request the appointment of a permanent *curator* to assist him throughout his minority.[74] Under the Law of the Twelve Tables, insane persons and their property were placed

---

[71] D. 26. 10; C. 5. 43; *Inst* 1. 26; G. 1. 182. As the relevant *crimen* was a matter of public law, the *accusatio suspecti tutoris* could be instituted by any person.

[72] According to Gaius, the original reason for the establishment of this form of guardianship (*tutela mulierum*) was the perception that women could be easily manipulated due to their gender 'weakness' (*infirmitas sexus*), natural lack of judgment and intellectual limitations. See G. 1. 144; G. 1. 190.

[73] D. 4. 4. 13. 1.

[74] D. 4. 4. 1. 3. In the later imperial age there was a gradual blurring of the distinction between the *curator* and the *tutor* that culminated in the *cura minorum* almost completely assimilated to the *tutela impuberum* by the time of Justinian.

under the curatorship of their nearest agnates (*proximi agnati*) or kinsmen (*gentiles*).[75] In the absence of such relatives, a *curator* could be appointed by the praetor.[76] Furthermore, a prodigal who wasted away an inheritance that he had received on intestacy, and later any spendthrift person, could be placed under curatorship by the praetor and prohibited from managing his property.

## 3.3 The Law of Property

The Roman law of things (*ius rerum*) or, in contemporary terms, 'property', covered a much broader field than that encompassed by the modern law of property. One of the reasons for this fact is that the Roman jurists linked the thing (*res*) with any legally guaranteed economic interest, any right or rights having monetary value, that a person could hold in respect thereof.[77] The law of things is organized under two broad headings: rights which related to property and which were available against persons generally (*iura in rem*); and rights which related to persons and which were available against specific individuals (*iura in personam*). The Romans divided the rights that existed over property into those acquired over individual objects and those acquired over things in a mass. The law of property in a narrow sense pertained to the former category of rights, whilst the law of succession embraced most of the rules regulating the acquisition of things in a mass. Finally, rights concerned with claims against specific persons were dealt with under the law of obligations. Mainly for reasons of convenience, we will deal with the law of succession and obligations separately and approach the law of property on the same basis as it is done in modern law.

---

[75] The *cura furiosi* came into effect automatically at the manifestation of insanity.

[76] The father of the insane person could also appoint a *curator* by testament. The law of Justinian stipulated that the appointment of a *curator*, irrespective of the method employed, had to be confirmed by a magistrate. *Inst* 1. 23. 1.

[77] The Roman concept of *res* (thing) did not remain fixed but underwent considerable development as its use changed following the evolution of society and economic relations. In the primitive agricultural community of the archaic age, only things a person could perceive with his senses, touch, hold and use were of interest (in short, things that were of service to him). In this context, the term *res* denoted merely physical objects; that is, things that could be touched (*quae tangi possunt*), possessed and used by a person. During the later republican era, however, the evolving complexity of Roman society and economic life meant the notion that there exist things that cannot be touched gained ground. Under the influence of Greek philosophical thought, intangibles and abstract creations of the human mind began to be treated by the Roman jurists as *res*. The practical implication of this evolution was that not only physical objects, but also abstract things (e.g. a debt, a right of way) were regarded as *res*. Eventually everything of economic value or appraisable in money that could be part of a person's estate (in short, all economic assets), whether corporeal or incorporeal, was regarded as *res*.

### 3.3.1  Classification of Things

Before examining property rights over individual objects, it is apposite to consider briefly the kinds of property that existed in Roman law. The various classifications are generally the result of historical development and represent an attempt at systematizing the relevant part of private law.

A first distinction was between things governed by divine law (*res divini iuris*) and those subject to human law (*res humani iuris*).[78] Under divine law were things dedicated by order of the Roman people to the gods above, such as temples and altars (*res sacrae*); things dedicated to the gods of the underworld, such as tombs (*res religiosae*); and things deemed to be under the protection of the gods because of the purposes they served, such as the walls and gates of a fortified city (*res sanctae*).[79] Things under divine law were not susceptible to private ownership (*res extra nostrum patrimonium* or *res extra commercium*). The *res humani iuris* were either public or private. The former were owned by the state and included public roads, bridges, harbors and navigable rivers.[80] Some things were classed not as public but as common to all mankind (*res communes*), such as the air, the sea, and running water.[81] A further category of things were the *res universitatis*: those belonging to a particular city or municipality for the use and enjoyment of its inhabitants, such as theatres, public baths, sports grounds, halls of justice and the like.[82]

Things were further classified into corporeal (*res corporales*) and incorporeal (*res incorporales*). The former were things that could be touched or perceived by the senses such as a garment, an ox, a table or a house; the latter were intangible things or things not capable of sensory perception that the law recognized and protected, such as real and personal rights.[83] Although primarily academic and philosophical in nature, the distinction between *res corporales* and *res incorporales* had some practical importance. This emanated from the fact that only corporeal things could be possessed and consequently several legal concepts with respect to which possession played an essential part were not applicable to *res incorporales*.

---

[78] G. 2. 2: "The principal division of things is into two classes: things subject to divine law and things subject to human law."

[79] G. 2. 3; G. 2. 4; G. 2. 8. Any wrongful act towards *res sanctae* was punishable by death.

[80] Riverbanks were considered private but their use was public.

[81] There was some controversy as to whether the seashore below the high water mark was public or common to all. Members of the public had undefined rights of use and enjoyment of the seashore (e.g. they could erect shelters on it and had ownership over them as long as they remained standing), but this did not give them a permanent right to any part of the shore.

[82] The *res universitatis* may be said to constitute a sub-category of the *res publicae*.

[83] G. 2. 12–14. See also *Inst* 2. 2. 1–2: "Corporeal things are those which, by their nature, can be touched, such as land, a slave, a garment. ...Incorporeal things, on the other hand, are such as cannot be touched but exist in law; for instance, an inheritance, usufruct and obligations." It appears that, initially, only real rights were considered *res incorporales*; it was only at a late stage that personal rights were recognized as also being incorporeal things.

Because incorporeal objects could not be physically seized as required for possession to exist, they thus could not be acquired or transferred by any method involving
the acquisition or transfer of possession.[84]

The principal division of things that could be privately owned (*res in nostro
patrimonio* or *res in commercio*) was between *res mancipi* and *res nec mancipi*. *Res
mancipi*, a category that was early fossilized, were land and buildings situated on
Italian soil[85]; slaves; farm animals of draft and burden, such as oxen, horses, mules
and donkeys; and rustic (not urban) praedial servitudes (*servitutes rusticae*), for
example rights of way and of water over land.[86] Since these were the most
important assets in the early Roman agricultural society, ownership over them
could be transferred only in a formal manner by way of *mancipatio* or *in iure
cessio*. All other things were *res nec mancipi*. With respect to the latter, ownership
could be transferred informally by simple delivery (*traditio*).

### 3.3.2  Ownership

In principle, ownership (*dominium ex iure Quiritium*)[87] was the most complete or
extensive right a person could hold in respect of a corporeal thing. The holder of
such right had the maximum prerogatives a person could have over an object: he
had the right to use, enjoy and even abuse his property (*ius utendi, ius fruendi, ius
abutendi*) as well as to alienate it, in whole or in part, as he saw fit. In short, the
owner (*dominus*) could perform virtually any factual or legal act in respect of his
property. It should be noted, however, that the right of ownership was not as
extensive in early times as it was in later law. The relevant concept underwent a
long process of evolution spanning several centuries until reaching its culmination
in the republican age.[88]

---

[84] Hence, *res incorporales* could not be acquired by prescription nor could they be conveyed by
actual physical delivery (*traditio*).

[85] In later times, lands and buildings situated in certain districts in the provinces were regarded as
*res mancipi*, provided that these districts had the *ius italicum* ('Italic right') and so could be
considered Italian land.

[86] G. 2. 14a–16.

[87] *Dominium* derived from the verb *domo*, meaning to conquer. *Ex iure Quiritium* means
'according to the law of the *Quirites*'. The term *Quirites* originally denoted the inhabitants of
the Sabine town of *Cures*. Around the middle of the seventh century BC, the Romans and the
Sabines merged to form a single nation and this nation was termed *Populus Romanus Quiritium*.
The words Romanus and Quiritium finally came to be used interchangeably and thus ownership by
Roman title was referred to as *dominium ex iure Quiritium*.

[88] In the archaic period, ownership was probably only one of the aspects of the control of the
*paterfamilias* over persons and property assets falling under his *potestas*. It existed as the only real
right, given that possession in the sense of actual physical control over a thing was not clearly
distinguished from ownership; lesser real rights, such as servitudes and usufruct, were viewed as
'partial' ownership. Moreover, it is possible that private ownership as such, especially with respect

As the most extensive of all real rights, ownership had to be acquired in a prescribed manner. Roman law knew several modes of ownership acquisition which all depended on some recognized and public assertion of control of the property. Some of these modes were peculiar to Roman law and, accordingly, derived from the *ius civile*; other modes were also familiar to other peoples and therefore were regarded as originating from the *ius gentium* (identified in this context with *ius naturale*).[89] The modes of acquisition may also be classified into 'original' (or 'natural') and 'derived'. Original modes of acquisition of ownership were those where the person acquired the right of ownership in respect of a thing without intervention by or dependence on another person. The principal modes of original acquisition of ownership were prescription (which assumed various forms), *occupatio* and *accessio*. Derived ownership occurred where a person acquired ownership of a thing from another. In this case, the ownership was transferred or passed from one person to another with the cooperation of the first person. The chief forms of derived acquisition of ownership were *mancipatio, in iure cessio* and *traditio*. The above two methods of classifying the modes of acquiring ownership may be reconciled. The original modes of acquisition of ownership emanated from the *ius gentium*, with the exception of prescription, which was regarded as belonging to the *ius civile*; while the derived modes originated in the *ius civile*, with the exception of *traditio*, which had roots in the *ius gentium*.

An important principle relating to the transfer of ownership was that no one could transfer more rights to another than he himself had (*nemo plus iuris ad alium transferre potest quam ipse haberet*).[90] The practical implication of this principle was that in Roman law a person who was not the owner of a thing could not transfer ownership of that thing to anyone else.[91]

As a mode of acquisition of ownership, *mancipatio* was in form a combination of a formal cash sale and a solemn conveyance of ownership of a *res mancipi*. The formal procedure relating to this legal act required the presence of the transferor, the transferee, five male witnesses who were Roman citizens above the age of puberty, and another person (*libripens*) who held a bronze scale. The transferee grasped the object to be conveyed (if it was movable) or a representation of it (if it was immovable), struck the scale with a bronze ingot, and said: "I declare this object (e.g. a slave) to be mine by the law of the citizens (*ius Quiritium*) and has been bought by me with this bronze and this bronze scale." The transferor said nothing, his silence showing his acquiescence. Assuming that the transferor was owner of the thing, ownership passed to the transferee. The *mancipatio* procedure dated back to a time before the appearance of coined money, and it probably

---

to immovable property, did not exist at all in the earliest period of Roman history but that ownership was vested collectively in the members of a clan (*gens*).

[89] G. 2. 65; *Inst* 2. 1. 11; D. 41. 1. 1.

[90] D. 50. 17. 54.

[91] Consider D. 41. 1. 20 pr: "Delivery ought not to transfer, and cannot transfer, to him who receives more than belongs to the person who delivers. If, therefore, anyone had the ownership of a field, he transfers it by delivery, but if he had not, he transfers nothing to him who receives."

developed from a formal cash sale when brass or copper was in fact weighed out on a scale (*libra*) and handed over simultaneously with the transfer of the object sold. In later times *mancipatio* had no necessary relation with sale at all—it was a general mode of conveyance limited to certain kinds of property, whilst any sale that actually occurred was regarded as a separate transaction furnishing the requisite cause (*causa*).[92] Nevertheless, the relevant formal ceremony was retained in order to stress the seriousness of the parties' intentions. It should be noted, finally, that the person transferring ownership by *mancipatio* had to provide a warranty against the eviction of the transferee from the property. If the acquirer of ownership was evicted after a third person had successfully claimed the property by means of a legal action, the acquirer could instigate the *actio auctoritatis* against the transferor for double the price paid.[93] Furthermore, the transferor was bound by any formal declarations (*nuncupationes*) he made in respect of certain features or characteristics of the property being transferred. By way of illustration, if the transferor had stated in his *nuncupatio* that the land he was transferring had a certain size and it later turned out to be smaller, the transferee could employ the *actio de modo agri* to claim twice the value of the missing portion.[94]

The *in iure cessio* procedure was used for a variety of purposes: to transfer ownership over corporeal property of every kind, whether *res mancipi* or *res nec mancipi*; to create and extinguish praedial servitudes and usufruct; and to transfer incorporeal objects other than obligations, such as an inheritance. As a mode of ownership transfer, *in iure cessio* (literally 'divesting in law') assumed the form of a fictitious lawsuit in front of the praetor in which the transferee claimed to be owner of the object being transferred, the transferor put up no defence, and the praetor adjudged the object to the transferee. In contrast with ordinary lawsuits, the magistrate's decision actually transferred ownership and its effect was not only between the parties. As in the case of *mancipatio*, only Roman citizens or persons possessing the *ius commercii* could employ the *in iure cessio* procedure.[95]

*Usucapio*, the most important original mode of acquisition of ownership, was a form of prescription that occurred when someone had undisturbed physical control of land for 2 years or of movables for one.[96] The acquisition of ownership by

---

[92] Hence Gaius calls *mancipatio* a fictitious sale (*venditio imaginaria*). See G. 1. 119. It should be noted that the transition from the real to the fictitious sale must have been gradual, although nothing is known about the stages leading to this development.

[93] This could happen if the transferor had not actually transferred ownership because he was not the owner of the property. In such a case, ownership did not pass, even if the *mancipatio* procedure was correctly employed.

[94] The institution of *mancipatio* became obsolete in the later imperial age and was an unknown legal relic in the time of Justinian.

[95] Although the *in iure cessio* still existed in classical law, it became obsolete in post-classical times and no longer existed in Justinian's era.

[96] Justinian extended this period for movables to three years and for immovables to ten years where the original owner resided in the same area (*inter praesentes*) and to twenty years where the parties lived in different districts (*inter absentes*). C. 7. 31. 1. 2; *Inst* 2. 6 pr.

*usucapio* presupposed that the property in question was susceptible to private ownership and that it was not stolen or seized by force. Furthermore, it presupposed the existence of a just cause (*iusta causa*) that is, an antecedent event or transaction by virtue of which the possessor would have become owner of the property under normal circumstances.[97] Closely connected with the issue of *iusta causa* was the requirement of good faith (*bona fides*): the person who acquired possession of the property in question had to honestly believe that the relevant transaction (as a just cause) made him owner of the property.[98] If the possessor at a later stage lost his good faith by obtaining knowledge of the true situation, his right to become owner of the property in question by *usucapio* was not affected.[99]

The ownership of *res nec mancipi* could be transferred by *traditio*, the actual physical delivery of a corporeal thing on the grounds of some lawful cause (*iusta causa*). This mode of ownership acquisition originated from the *ius gentium* and was thus available to foreigners. Although *traditio* originally required the acquisition of possession *animo et corpore* ('with soul and body') by the transferee, it was gradually recognized that in certain cases it would be sufficient for establishing possession if the transferee had been placed into a position of control (according to the views of the community) without actual physical contact with the thing. Thus, several methods of fictitious delivery (*traditiones fictae*) developed alongside the actual physical or hand-to-hand delivery. There was *traditio longa manu* ('delivery by the long hand'), when goods stored in a warehouse were sold and the seller gave the purchaser the key within sight of the warehouse; *traditio brevi manu* ('delivery by the short hand'), when the intended transferee was already in possession of the object whose ownership was being transferred[100]; and symbolic delivery (*traditio symbolica*), when a symbol of the thing whose ownership was being transferred rather than the thing itself was delivered.[101]

Important forms of original acquisition of ownership were *occupatio* and *accessio*. The former was the act of taking possession of a thing belonging to no one (*res nullius*) but capable of being *in commercio* with the intention of becoming owner thereof. Things that could be acquired in this way included wild animals, birds, bees and fish; the spoils of war or booty seized from an enemy; an island

---

[97] Examples of such cause or title included purchase and sale, gift, dowry, legacy, discharge of a debt, inheritance and the like.

[98] G. 2. 43: "We may acquire by usucapio, provided that we have received the objects in good faith, believing the deliverer to be their owner." Consider also G. 2. 93; *Inst* 2. 6 pr; D. 41. 3. 33. 1; D. 50. 16. 109.

[99] D. 41. 3. 4. 18; D. 41. 1. 48. 1.

[100] *Constitutum possessorium* was the converse of *traditio brevi manu*. This occurred, for example, when the person who sold a tract of land remained in possession of it because he had agreed with the buyer that he would continue in occupation as a tenant. Once again, the bare will (*nuda voluntas*) of the parties was sufficient to transfer ownership.

[101] This happened, for example, when an agreement for the transfer of ownership over an object was recorded in a document that was later handed over to the transferee as a symbol of the object he acquired.

arising in the sea; and things thrown away by a former owner. Reference may also be made in this connection to treasure trove (*thesaurus*), defined as something valuable hidden away for such a long time that the identity of its owner could no longer be established.[102] According to a legislative enactment of Emperor Hadrian, a person who found a treasure on his own property became the owner of it whilst the ownership of a treasure discovered on another person's property was equally shared between the landowner and the finder as long as the discovery occurred by chance.[103] If the finding was the result of a deliberate search, the owner of the land in which the treasure had been found was entitled to the whole trove. *Accessio* occurred when separate things belonging to different owners were inseparably joined to each other or merged in such a manner that a new entity or object was established. The principle that prevailed was that the owner of the principal object also became owner of the composite thing; furthermore, the owner of the minor object had to be reimbursed for his loss of ownership. A further way of acquiring ownership was *specificatio*, the making of a new thing out of materials belonging to another who did not consent (for example, wine from grapes, or a garment from wool). The Sabinians declared the opinion that the owner of the material should also become owner of the new object or where there were two or more owners, the latter should own the object jointly and in proportion to their contribution. By contrast, the Proculians held the view that the maker acquired ownership of the thing he had created.[104] Justinian adopted a middle course and ruled that if the new product could be reduced to the material from which it had been created (for example, a golden statuette could be melted down to the original lump of gold), the owner of the material also became owner of the new object; if this could not be achieved (for example, wine could no longer be transformed into grapes), the maker became the owner. The party who suffered loss as a result of *specificatio* could institute an action for compensation against the owner of the new object.

Besides *dominium*, Roman law recognized certain lesser forms of property-holding, which placed the holder almost in the position of civil law owner. Probably the best-known example of such ownership occurred when a *res mancipi* had been transferred to someone informally by means of mere delivery (*traditio*) rather than by means of the formal procedures of *mancipatio* or *in iure cessio* as the law required. In such a case, the transferee could not become *dominus ex iure Quiritium* of the property but the praetor intervened and placed such person in the factual position of a civil law owner. The property was then regarded as *in bonis* and the transferee as a bonitary owner who could acquire true Roman law ownership

---

[102] The jurist Paulus defines *thesaurus* as "an ancient deposit of money, of which no memory exists, so that it has no present owner." See D. 41. 1. 31. 1. This definition appears to be too narrow, however, as a treasure is not confined to only money. In a constitution of Emperors Leo and Zeno (AD 474) a treasure is defined as "movables hidden long ago by unknown owners." See C. 10. 15.

[103] *Inst* 2. 1. 39.

[104] The two schools also held different views on the question of what constituted a *nova species* or new thing. The Sabinians followed the Stoic philosophy that accorded priority to matter, whilst the Proculians adopted an Aristotelian approach in giving the primacy to form or essence.

through possession of the thing for a prescribed period by means of *usucapio*.[105] Other lesser forms of ownership included ownership of provincial land and ownership by foreigners (*peregrini*). Provincial land was land under Roman control outside Italy that had not been granted the status of Italian land. *Dominium* of such land in principle vested in the Roman state or the emperor, depending on whether it was situated in a senatorial or imperial province. Although the Roman *ius civile* did not allow private citizens to acquire *dominium* over provincial land, the *ius gentium* allowed the acquisition of extensive control by individuals by natural methods of acquisition. Likewise, although foreigners were unable to utilize the civil law methods of ownership acquisition, the *ius gentium* made possible the acquisition of extensive control of property by *peregrini* by natural law methods. Furthermore, in suits involving rights to property, the law granted to foreigners fictitious actions, with respect to which the court would adopt the fiction that the foreigner was a Roman citizen.[106]

### 3.3.2.1  Protection of Ownership

The most important legal remedies an owner could employ to protect their rights were the *rei vindicatio* and the *actio ad exhibendum*, an action usually employed before an owner initiated the *rei vindicatio*.

The purpose of the *rei vindicatio* was twofold: to determine ownership of the object in question and, once this had been established, to compel the defendant to return the object to its lawful owner or face being ordered to pay a sum of money. It should be noted that this action was directed at the recovery of the property itself and not at the person of the possessor thereof. The *actio ad exhibendum* was a personal action that was used to determine whether a particular person had possession of a thing and, if this was the case, to compel that person to produce it. This action was available not only to the owner who wished to institute a *rei vindicatio* but to any person who wanted a thing to be produced so that he could claim possession of it at a later time.

---

[105] Initially, the transferee's position during the period of *usucapio* was not protected, but the praetor intervened by granting him the *actio Publiciana* and the *exceptio rei venditae et traditae*. The former action was an action *in rem* by means of which the transferee could reclaim possession during the period of *usucapio* from whoever may have held it without lawful title, irrespective of whether or not such person was *bona fide*. The action was based on the fiction that the period required for obtaining the property by *usucapio* was completed. See G. 4. 36. If the original owner endeavoured to claim the property from the transferee during the period of *usucapio*, the transferee could raise the defence of *exceptio rei venditae et traditae* – a special defence based on the claim that the property at issue had been sold and delivered to him. Consider D. 21. 3. 3. By these devices the holder of the property obtained complete protection during the period of the *usucapio* and had all the practical benefits associated with ownership.

[106] G. 4. 37: "If a foreigner sues or is sued on a cause for which an action has been established by our laws, there is a fiction that he is a Roman citizen, provided that it is equitable that the action should be extended to a foreigner."

A further remedy available to the owner was the *actio negatoria*, or 'action of denial'. This action was instituted by the owner of landed property against any person who, without challenging the plaintiff's right of ownership, claimed a servitude or similar right in respect of his land. The aim of such action was to obtain a court order confirming that the plaintiff had full ownership not encumbered by the existence of any right of the defendant and forbidding the latter from arrogating to himself such right or calling upon him to restore the *status quo*.

### 3.3.2.2   Limitations on Ownership

Even though ownership was the most extensive of all real rights, it could still be limited by operation of law or by arrangement.

Several restrictions of the former type were embodied in the Law of the Twelve Tables. There was, for instance, a ruling concerning the branches of trees protruding over the boundary of a neighbour's property. It was provided that the landowner whose property was affected could request a pruning of the overhanging branches to a height of 15 feet from the ground. If this request was not complied with, he could employ the *interdictum de arboribus caedendis*.[107] Analogous remedies were available to an owner when the roots of a plant or tree belonging to a neighbour penetrated into his property. If the fruits of a plant or tree fell on adjoining land, the owner of the plant or tree was allowed to collect his fruit every second day. This right could be enforced by means of the *interdictum de glande legenda*.[108] If a person artificially directed the flow of rainwater onto the property of a neighbour (e.g. by constructing a building or other work), the latter could employ the *actio aquae pluviae arcendae* to demand restoration of the *status quo*.[109] Moreover, if a building or other structure in a dilapidated state threatened to collapse and cause damage to the property of a neighbour, the latter could request the praetor to compel the owner of the defective premises to provide security against possible damage by way of the *cautio damni infecti*.[110]

Furthermore, it was possible for an owner to voluntarily limit his right of ownership by giving a lesser or greater degree of control over his property to another person; for instance, by leasing such property to another person or granting them a servitude over it.

---

[107] D. 43. 27. If the tree owner did not obey the interdictal order, the landowner concerned could cut the branches himself and retain the wood.

[108] D. 43. 28.

[109] D. 39. 3. 1 pr.

[110] Such security was given by means of a stipulation, a formal agreement creating a legal tie between the two parties. In early times, the person concerned could employ the *actio damni infecti* that existed as a remedy probably directed at the payment of a penalty.

*Servitudes*

In Roman law, a servitude (*servitus*) was a real right in property belonging to another (*ius in re aliena*), which restricted the rights and powers of the owner of that property. It therefore, amounted to a burden on property, to which the owner was required to submit.[111] A servitude could be protected by way of a real action that the servitude holder could institute against anyone who infringed upon his right.[112]

A servitude had to fall within a recognized class, and the four earliest—the right to pass through another's land (*iter*), the right to drive draft animals across land (*actus*), the right to use a road on one's land for driving in a carriage or riding on horseback (*via*), and the right to draw water across land by means of an aqueduct or furrow (*aquaeductus*)—were classified as *res mancipi*. Besides the rural praedial servitudes (*iura praediorum rusticorum*), such as the ones mentioned above, a number of urban praedial servitudes (*iura praediorum urbanorum*) were also recognized. The latter were concerned with urban utilization (regardless of whether the relevant immovable property was located in a city or the country) and displayed a more recent date than the rural praedial servitudes. Well-known servitudes of this type included the right to drive a beam into a neighbour's building or wall (*servitus tigni immittendi*); the right to discharge rainwater through a gutter or something similar onto another's land (*servitus fluminis recipiendi*); and the right to prevent a neighbour from obscuring one's light (*servitus ne luminibus officiatur*).

Praedial servitudes could be either negative or positive: the holder of a servitude could either demand that the owner of the servient property should abstain from certain activity (e.g., erecting a building or structure exceeding a specified height), or was empowered by the servitude to conduct a specific task (e.g., draw water). The holder's right was defined by the nature of the servitude and had to be exercised properly according to the standards set by the community. It is important to note, however, that servitudes could not impose a positive obligation on the owner of the servient land.[113] The only exception to this principle derived from the *servitus oneris ferendi* (the right to have a building on the dominant land supported by a wall or building on the servient land), with respect to which the owner of the servient property had the duty to maintain the supporting wall of the building in good condition at his own expense.

Another category of servitudes were the personal servitudes (*servitutes personarum* or *personales*). Like the praedial servitudes mentioned above, the personal servitudes were real rights over another person's property (*iura in re*

---

[111] A servitude was considered to be an incorporeal thing (*res incorporalis*). See G. 2. 14.

[112] If the owner of the property in which the servitude was vested died and the ownership of the property devolved on the heir, or if the owner transferred the ownership of the property in question, this did not affect the relevant right in any way and the servitude holder could enforce his right against the new owner.

[113] The relevant rule was expressed as follows: "the nature of servitudes is not such that someone has to do something, but that he has to permit something or refrain from doing something." See D. 8. 1. 15. 1.

*aliena*). Otherwise than in the case of praedial servitudes, however, these servitudes could be acquired over both movables and immovables, and were designed for the benefit not of a particular property but of their holder in his personal capacity. Furthermore, personal servitudes had limited duration as they were terminated by the death of the holder or the lapse of the period for which they were granted. Usufruct (*ususfructus*) was the earliest and most complete of the personal servitudes. It entailed the right to use the property of another person and to take the fruits thereof without impairing its substance.[114] As a *ius in re aliena*, usufruct could be constituted over immovables, such as land and buildings as well as over movables that could not be consumed by normal use, such as cattle. The personal servitude of *usus* or use may best be described as an offshoot of *ususfructus*. It differed from the latter insofar as the holder of the relevant real right (*usuarius*) was entitled to use another's property without taking the fruits thereof. The servitude of *habitatio* or inhabitation bore a strong resemblance to both usufruct and use. It entailed the real right, also attached to the person of its holder, to occupy and reside in another person's house. Finally, the personal servitude of *operae servorum vel animalium* entailed the real right to use the services of another person's slaves or beasts of burden.

### Real Security

Property could also be burdened by real security: a real right created over the property of another to secure the performance of a debt or an obligation. During the history of Roman law, three forms of real security featured: *fiducia*; *pignus*; and *hypotheca*.

The earliest form of real security known to the Romans was *fiducia*, the transfer of ownership of a *res mancipi* subject to an agreement (*pactum fiduciae*) that when the debt was discharged the creditor would reconvey the thing to the original owner. Originally, the *pactum fiduciae* was not enforceable but based solely on the transferor's trust (*fides*) in the honesty of the creditor. Fairly early, however, the debtor was granted a personal action termed the *actio fiduciae* whereby he could compel the creditor to return the property and to pay compensation for any damage the latter may have caused to it by his fraudulent or negligent conduct.[115] With the abandonment of the *mancipatio* and *in iure cessio* procedures in the later imperial era, *fiducia* as a form of security fell into disuse.

In *pignus*, which could relate to all kinds of property, the debtor delivered possession but not ownership to the creditor. The transfer of the property in

---

[114] *Inst* 2. 4 pr: "Usufruct is the right of using, and taking the fruits of things belonging to others, so long as the substance of the things used remains. It is a right over a corporeal thing, and if this thing perish, the usufruct itself necessarily perishes also." And see D. 7. 1. 1 & 2.

[115] The counterpart of this action was the *actio fiduciae contraria*, which the creditor could institute against the debtor for the recovery of any necessary expenses he had incurred in respect of the property in question.

question was accompanied by an agreement (*pactum*) of the parties that the property would be returned when the debtor paid his debt. The creditor's possession of the object was protected by possessory interdicts against interference by third parties, as well as by the *actio Serviana*. By means of the latter action the creditor could claim possession of the object from any person, including the debtor, who had taken unlawful possession thereof. If after the discharge or extinction of the debtor's obligation the thing was not returned, the debtor could bring the normal action (*rei vindicatio*) for ownership of the security, or a contractual action (*actio pigneraticia*).

*Hypotheca* was a variant on *pignus*, in which the creditor acquired a real right to take certain property on non-payment of a debt, ownership and possession remaining with the debtor.[116] An advantage of the *hypotheca* was that practically any movable or immovable thing and even incorporeal objects (such as a claim or a usufruct) or future things (for instance, a future harvest) could serve as security.[117]

### 3.3.3  Possession

Possession essentially implied the physical control of a corporeal object and the exclusion of other persons from such control. This might be enjoyed by the person who had ownership over the property—one of the principal rights associated with ownership was the right to possess (*ius possidendi*). Despite the close connection between possession and ownership, Roman law drew a clear distinction between the two concepts: ownership was a right; possession was a factual state of affairs. This difference between being entitled to an object and having physical control of it lies at the root of the distinction between ownership and possession. Although possession was essentially a factual relation, it played an important part in the law: it was the foundation of the system of ownership, since it was in most cases possession plus another legal fact that led to ownership. For example, possession plus time entailed ownership by way of *usucapio*; possession plus just cause (*iusta causa*) entailed ownership by way of *traditio*. Furthermore, possession came to be protected in itself by remedies called interdicts (*interdicta*), and in some cases even possession that was not rightfully acquired was accorded protection.

Possession assumed many diverse forms and, from an early period, the Roman jurists set themselves the task of elaborating criteria for distinguishing between protected and unprotected possession. However, they did not develop a general theory of possession as they were mainly interested in the practical questions concerning the acquisition and loss of possession rather than the abstract question of its meaning. In this respect, convenience rather than logical consistency determined the scope of the relevant possessory remedies. In general, protected

---

[116] *Inst* 4. 6. 7.

[117] Obviously, the relevant thing had to be *res in commercio*.

possession had to have two elements: the actual physical control of a thing (*corpus*); and the intention of exercising such actual control, normally as the owner (*animus*).

The introduction of praetorian remedies designed for the protection of possession is related to considerations of public policy. While a person possesses an object, and because he possesses it, the impression is projected that such a person has a right to the object. The law has to consider this factual relationship seriously and ensure that third parties are prevented from interfering with it or taking matters into their own hands until and unless due legal process has transpired.[118] Thus, even the owner was not entitled to eject an occupier from his land. If he did, the latter could bring a possessory interdict to be restored to possession. The owner, on the other hand, could bring a vindicatory action, and if he proved his title, the wrongful occupier would then be lawfully deprived of his possession.

For present purposes a distinction may be drawn between two broad categories of property holding: *possessio* and *possessio naturalis*. The former was juristic possession, protected by praetorian interdicts. This category embraced the possession of an owner; a *bona fide* possessor; a *mala fide* possessor; a holder of a long lease of land (*emphytheuta*); a holder of a long-term right to the enjoyment of a house built on another's land (*superficiarius*); a pledgee; a tenant at will or on sufferance (*precario tenens*); and a person with whom the parties to litigation deposited the object of the dispute, on the understanding that it was to be delivered after the conclusion of the litigation to the party who won the case (*sequester*). The term *possessio naturalis* (also known as *detentio*) denoted the possession of persons who, although they had physical control of a thing, could not seek the protection of possessory interdicts. This category encompassed the possession of a borrower for use (*commodatarius*), a depositee (*depositarius*), a tradesman working on property and a person without capacity (e.g., an insane person or a ward without authority).

### 3.3.3.1 Protection of Possession

In Roman law, possessory protection was achieved mainly by interdicts (*interdicta*), that is, praetorian orders issued on request in duly justified circumstances. Possessory interdicts were classified into three categories: interdicts aimed at obtaining possession (*interdicta adipiscendae possessionis*); interdicts aimed at retaining possession (*interdicta retinendae possessionis*); and interdicts aimed at regaining possession (*interdicta recuperandae possessionis*).[119] The most important interdicts were the *interdictum uti possidetis*, the *interdictum utrubi* and the *interdictum unde vi*. The *interdictum uti possidetis* protected the present possessor

---

[118] The notion that an existing possessory situation must be protected for the time being is expressed by the maxim "*Qualiscumque enim possessor hoc ipso quod possessor est, plus iuris habet quam ille qui non possidet*": "He who has possession has by virtue of his being a possessor a greater right than somebody who does not possess." D. 43. 17. 2.

[119] G. 4. 143.

of immovable property against any disturbance of his possession and thus it had a prohibitory effect in this instance. However, if the present possessor had obtained his possession by force (*vi*), secretly (*clam*) or by request from the other party, then this other party was entitled to the interdict even though he was not in possession. In this instance, the interdict was restitutory, as the present possessor was commanded to return possession to the person from whom he had obtained it.[120] The *interdictum utrubi* protected the party who had been in possession of movable property for the longest period (as against his adversary) in the preceding year, unless he himself had obtained possession by violence, secretly or by grant at will (*vi vel clam vel precario*).[121] As in the case of the *interdictum uti possidetis*, the *interdictum utrubi* was bilateral and prohibitory as well as restitutory where possession of the object was awarded to the party who was not the present possessor. Finally, the *interdictum unde vi* restored the possession of immovables lost by force and was, therefore, solely restitutory. This interdict had to be requested within a year after possession had been lost.

## 3.4   The Law of Obligations

The term obligation (*obligatio*) denoted the legal relationship that existed between two persons, in terms of which one person was obliged towards the other to carry out a certain duty or duties. Obligation may otherwise be defined as a bond recognized by the law (*iuris vinculum*) in terms of which one party, the creditor (*creditor*), had a personal right (*ius in personam*) against the other party, the debtor (*debitor*). It is important to emphasize that the person who bound himself to another as a debtor placed an obligation on only himself and thereby gave the creditor a right against himself, while third parties did not become involved. If the obligation was not properly discharged, the creditor could institute a personal action (*actio in personam*) against that particular debtor with a view to obtaining a judgment that could be executed against such debtor. With this personal action the creditor claimed that the debtor had to perform something for the creditor, i.e. give something to the creditor, do something for him or refrain from doing something.[122]

---

[120] D. 43. 17. 1 pr.

[121] See on this matter D. 43. 31. 1; G. 4. 150 & 160.

[122] According to a well-known definition found in the Institutes of Justinian, "an obligation is a legal bond whereby we are bound as of a necessity to perform something according to the laws of our state." See *Inst* 3. 13 pr. Consider also D. 44. 7. 3 pr (Paulus *libro secundo institutionum*): "The essence of obligations does not consist in giving us ownership of something or entitling us to a servitude, but in binding a person to us to give, do or perform something." As Paulus's statement indicates, although an obligation is a *res incorporalis* and thus belongs to the Law of Things, it invokes a *ius in personam*, i.e., a right available against a specific person, rather than a *ius in rem*, i.e., a right available against any person or, as it is sometimes said, against the entire world. Further, it should be noted that Justinian's (post-classical) definition of obligation is too broad, as it

Gaius, in his Institutes, states that obligations fell into two principal categories: obligations arising from contract (*obligationes ex contractu*), and obligations arising from delict (*obligationes ex delicto*).[123] The term *contractus* was understood to denote any lawful juristic act capable of producing rights and obligations, and enforceable by means of an action at law. As the vast majority of lawful juristic acts creating obligations were transacted because there was agreement on the part of the parties to establish an obligation, it was in time recognized that agreement (*consensus*) was the essence of a contract. The *delictum* was an unlawful act (also referred to as *maleficium*) that was detrimental to the lawful rights and interests of another person and which generated an obligation between such person and the malefactor. The content of such obligation was directed at satisfaction, compensation or a penalty (*poena*). Gaius' original dichotomy of the sources of obligations was subsequently deemed unsatisfactory, since an obligation could also arise from a legal act with respect to which there was no agreement on the part of the parties concerned. Accordingly, a third category of obligations (also attributed to Gaius) appears in the Digest: obligations arising from various causes (*obligationes ex variis causarum figuris*) other than from contract or delict.[124] The phrase *variae causarum figurae* refers to juristic acts that were not based on agreement, yet were deemed wholly lawful. Gaius' final classification was probably the precursor of the fourfold division of the sources of obligations adopted by the compilers of Justinian's Institutes. According to the latter scheme, an obligation may arise: (i) from contract (*ex contractu*); (ii) as if from contract (*quasi ex contractu*); (iii) from delict (*ex delicto* or *ex maleficio*); and (iv) as if from delict (*quasi ex delicto* or *quasi ex maleficio*).[125] The term quasi-contract was used to denote those lawful acts that, although not based on agreement between two or more parties, created an obligation. In contrast, the category of quasi-delict did not differ substantially from that of delict.

A further classification of obligations, recognized from an early period, was that between *obligationes civiles* and *obligationes honorariae* or *praetoriae*. The former derived their authority from the *ius civile* and could be enforced by means of *actiones civiles*, i.e. actions originating from the civil law. The *obligationes honorariae*, on the other hand, arose from the *ius honorarium* and were enforceable by means of *actiones honorariae*, i.e. actions created by the praetor and other jurisdictional magistrates.[126] In this connection reference may also be made to the distinction between obligations of the strict law (*obligationes stricti iuris*) and obligations based on good faith (*obligationes bonae fidei*). An *obligatio stricti iuris*

---

seems to encompass all rights *in personam*. However, obligation in Roman law pertained only to rights *in personam* that could be assessed in monetary terms or belonging to the sphere of proprietary rights. It did not pertain to rights stemming from family relations, or rights created by public law.

[123] G. 3. 88.

[124] D. 44. 7. 1 pr (Gaius *libro secundo aureorum*).

[125] *Inst* 3. 13. 2.

[126] *Inst* 3. 13. 1; D. 44. 7. 25. 2.

arose from a legal act of the strict and formal *ius civile*. An obligation of this kind was enforced by means of an *actio civilis* and in such a case the judge was bound by the strict letter of the law. An *obligatio bonae fidei*, by contrast, derived from a legal act based on good faith (*bona fides*) and was enforced by an *actio bonae fidei*, i.e. an action whose procedural *formula* required the judge to take the requirements of equity and good faith into consideration. Finally, a distinction was drawn between *obligatio civilis* in a wider sense and 'natural obligation' (*obligatio naturalis*). *Obligatio civilis* was an obligation arising from a recognized legal source and enforceable by means of an *actio in personam*. On the other hand, the term *obligatio naturalis* denoted an obligation that was only imperfectly protected by law. Such an obligation was not normally enforceable by an action at law and, in the event of an action being granted, execution was not possible. This fact does not mean, however, that natural obligations had no legal significance whatsoever. Thus, it was possible for a person obliged in terms of a natural obligation to perform such obligation or to subject it to personal or real security. Natural obligations were, for example, those contracted by a slave, or by a *filiusfamilias* under paternal power, or by an *impubes* or a *minor* without the consent of his *tutor* or *curator* respectively.

### 3.4.1   The Law of Contracts

As already noted, in Roman law contract (*contractus*) denoted a legal act based on an agreement by the parties to create a binding obligation. However, in contrast to modern law where, if certain conditions are met, an agreement to perform engenders a legally enforceable obligation, Roman law construed the agreement as only invoking an obligation if the agreement could be classified, on the basis of its form or content, into one of the categories deemed capable of supporting an *actio in personam*. In other words, in order to be enforceable as a contract there was the further requirement that the agreement had an element referred to as *causa contractus* or reason for the contract. Four such *causae* were recognized and in each case a limited number of agreements, involving the requisite *causa*, formed a contract and gave rise to a legally enforceable obligation or obligations. The four *causae* and, consequently, the four categories of *contractus* were: (i) *contractus re*, i.e. contracts that were constituted by agreement and the transfer of a thing; (ii) *contractus verbis*, i.e. contracts that were constituted by agreement and the use of certain formal words; (iii) *contractus litteris*, i.e. contracts that were constituted by agreement and formal writing; and (iv) *contractus consensu*, i.e. contracts constituted by agreement without anything further.[127] Although the last category

---

[127] G. 3. 89; *Inst* 3. 13. 2; consider also D. 44. 7. 1. 1; D. 46. 1. 8. 1. It should be noted that this classification is primarily a classification of obligations rather than of contracts. However, it is commonly applied to the agreements from which the obligations arise, hence the fourfold division of contracts into *re*, *verbis*, *litteris* and *consensu*.

forms an exception to the Roman law approach described above, only four contracts could be concluded by mere agreement between the parties.

### 3.4.1.1 Real Contracts

The real contracts (*contractus re*) were contracts that were constituted by agreement and the transfer of a thing (*res*).

The oldest real contract was *mutuum*, a gratuitous loan for consumption of money or other things that were weighed, numbered or measured (such as wine, oil, corn, gold or silver).[128] A strict contract (*negotium stricti iuris*) dating from the third century BC, it was constituted by agreement and the transfer of property to another person, on the understanding that the borrower would at a later stage return the exact equivalent of what was lent.[129] The contract was unilateral since only the borrower was bound and became operative when the money or other things were transferred to the person to whom the loan was granted. It should be noted that by means of delivery of the property in question ownership passed to the borrower. The lender (who was the creditor) could enforce his personal right by means of a personal action known as *condictio*. The action was termed *condictio certae creditae pecuniae* where the loan consisted of money; *condictio triticaria* in the case of a loan of grain (*triticum*); and *condictio certae rei* in all other cases. No interest could be demanded by the action, although interest could be arranged through a separate contract, namely *stipulatio*.[130] In the first century AD the *senatus consultum Macedonianum* provided that someone who lent to a son in power (*filiusfamilias*) had no remedy, even after the son became *sui iuris* and free from *patria potestas*.[131]

The contract of *commodatum* or loan for use was established when one person lent an object free of charge to another, usually for a fixed period of time and for a specified purpose.[132] This type of contract was introduced by a praetorian edict in the first century BC and was considered to be a *negotium bonae fidei*. As in the case of *mutuum*, *commodatum* was constituted by agreement and the transfer of an object. Otherwise than in *mutuum*, however, the borrower in *commodatum* did not acquire ownership but only detention (*detentio*) over the thing transferred. Thus, he would not suffer the loss if the object were destroyed or damaged unless he had failed to show the degree of care deemed appropriate. *Commodatum* may be

---

[128] These are referred to as '*res fungibiles*': generic things specified according to type or things belonging to a class where all the members thereof are sufficiently similar to be freely interchangeable. In the context of *mutuum*, the rule *genera non pereunt* meant that performance could never become impossible. See G. 3. 90.

[129] See *Inst* 3. 14 pr; G. 3. 90; D. 12. 1. 2 pr-4; D. 44. 7. 1. 2–4.

[130] See relevant discussion under verbal contracts below.

[131] This enactment did not dictate that such a loan would be automatically null and void, but gave the *exceptio senatus consulti Macedoniani* against the action of the lender.

[132] Consider in general D. 13. 6; C. 4. 23.

described as an imperfectly bilateral contract: while in principle it invoked only one obligation (the duty of the borrower to return the same object to the lender after use or at a definite date), a contingent duty might also exist on the part of the lender under certain circumstances. The creditor (i.e. the lender or *commodator*) could enforce his personal right by means of a personal action known as *actio commodati*. On the other hand, the borrower could under certain circumstances institute the *actio commodati contraria* against the lender for the recovery of extraordinary expenses incurred by him in respect of the maintenance of the thing or for damages caused by the thing due to some defect of which the lender was aware. Both the above actions originated from the *ius honorarium* and were, therefore, based on *bona fides*.

The contract of *depositum* came to the fore when one person (the *depositor*) handed over a movable thing to another (the *depositarius*) and the latter undertook to retain the thing in his safe-keeping gratuitously for a given period of time or until the depositor demanded its return. Like the *commodatum*, *depositum* derived from the *ius honorarium* and was therefore a *negotium bonae fidei*. It was constituted by agreement and the actual delivery of the thing.[133] Such delivery caused only physical control or detention (*detentio*) to pass to the *depositarius*, while ownership and protected possession remained with the *depositor*. The *depositarius* could keep the thing but was not entitled to use it; if he did use it, he could be guilty of theft of the use of such thing, unless he had acted in good faith. As in the case of *commodatum*, *depositum* was an imperfectly bilateral contract: although in principle such a contract only created one obligation, under certain circumstances it was possible for a counterclaim to arise. The principal obligation was always the duty of the depositary to return the thing on demand to the depositor in as good a condition as when he received it, together with any produce or accessories. If he failed to do so, the depositor could enforce this obligation by means of the *actio depositi*. On the other hand, the depositary could institute the *actio depositi contraria* against the depositor for compensation of expenses incurred by him in the maintenance of the object in question or for damage he had suffered as a result of *mala fides* on the part of the depositor. Both the above actions derived from the *ius honorarium* and therefore the relevant duties of the parties were determined by reference to the requirements of *bona fides*. A special form of *depositum* was the so-called *depositum necessarium*: a *depositum* created under pressing necessity.[134] This emerged when the depositor was forced to deposit property with someone because of some unforseen emergency (e.g. fire, earthquake or shipwreck), and he thus hardly had the opportunity to choose the depositary. When this event occurred the duties and liabilities of the parties were the same as in the case of an ordinary *depositum*, but if the depositary failed to fulfil his duties and was found to be liable he had to reimburse double of what was due to the depositor.[135]

---

[133] D. 16. 3; C. 4. 34. The *depositum* had to be gratuitous; if there was any remuneration the contract was designated as one of letting and hiring (*locatio et conductio*). See D. 16. 3. 1. 8–10.

[134] The term *depositum necessarium* does not occur in classical literature.

[135] *Inst* 4. 6. 17; *Inst* 4. 6. 26; D. 16. 3. 1. 1–4.

As previously noted, *pignus* or pledge was a form of real security that was established when a debtor or third party handed over a corporeal thing to the creditor as security for a debt on the understanding that the creditor would return the property when the debt was duly paid. The agreement between the debtor or third party and the creditor pursuant to which the security was given constituted a *contractus re* insofar as the transfer of possession constituted the *causa* (*re*) of the contract of *pignus*. Like the contracts of *commodatum* and *depositum*, *pignus* was an institution of the *ius honorarium* and based on *bona fides*. Furthermore, *pignus* was an imperfectly bilateral contract that gave rise to rights and obligations in respect of both the pledgor as well as the pledgee. As long as the pledged object remained in his possession, the pledgee was in principle not allowed to use it unless expressly authorized by the contract. If he did so in bad faith, he could be found guilty of theft. But the principal obligation of the pledgee pertained to his duty to return the pledged thing in a proper condition as soon as the debt was extinguished. If he failed to do so, the pledgor could claim the return of the thing or damages by means of a personal action known as *actio pigneraticia*.[136] On the other hand, the pledgee could institute the *actio pigneraticia contraria* against the pledgor for expenses incurred by him in respect of safekeeping the object or for damages he suffered owing to the *mala fides* of the pledgor. If the secured debt was not satisfied, the pledgee was entitled to sell the pledged object. In such case, the pledgor could claim the residue of the selling price if the price exceeded the debt for which the pledge had been given.

### 3.4.1.2  Verbal Contracts

Verbal contracts (*contractus verbis*) were contracts that were constituted by agreement and certain formal words. *Sponsio*, the earliest verbal contract, is believed to have had a religious origin (it probably began as an oath). Later this contract was superseded by the *stipulatio*, one of the most important juristic acts known to Roman law. Both *sponsio* and *stipulatio* were institutions of the *ius civile* and therefore *negotia stricti iuris*.

*Stipulatio* was a unilateral contract that could be employed in various ways in private or procedural law. It consisted essentially in a formal question by the creditor/promisee (*stipulator*) containing the terms of the proposed promise and a positive reply by the debtor/promisor (*promissor*) accepting them. The same verb had to be used in both the question and the answer, such as "*spondesne centum dare?*" ("do you solemnly promise to pay one hundred?")—"*spondeo*" ("I promise").[137] As this suggests, *stipulatio* could only be concluded where the parties were in each other's presence and where the promisor responded positively to the whole

---

[136] *Inst* 3. 14. 4. And see D. 13. 7. 9. 5; D. 44. 7. 1. 6.

[137] See *Inst* 3. 15 pr-1. Originally, the verb *spondere* (which suggests a sacred origin) had to be used; but in later times other and less formal verbs of promise could also be employed.

question without delay and without qualifying his promise by making it subject to a condition or time clause. As a unilateral contract, *stipulatio* gave rise to only one obligation and one corresponding right: the creditor (*stipulator*) had a personal right against the debtor (*promissor*) while the latter's duty was to perform in favour of the creditor exactly what had been stipulated.[138] The creditor could enforce his personal right with the *actio ex stipulatu*, if performance was undetermined or uncertain (*incertum*); and with the *condictio*, if performance was specific or certain (*certum*).[139]

As *stipulatio* was a *stricti iuris* contract, the parties were supposed to mean what they said and only what they said. Hence it was difficult to imply unspoken terms. Furthermore, the promisor was still bound even if he had entered the contract as a result of fraud or duress. However, in the later republican era the praetor intervened to improve this unsatisfactory situation and gave the person who incurred financial loss as a result of duress an action (*actio metus causa*) for four times the value of the loss. He also granted a special defence of duress (*exceptio metus*) if the wronged promisor was sued. Furthermore, the action for fraud (*actio de dolo*) was made available to the person who had been conned into making a legally binding promise. This action could be employed only if there was no other remedy and was directed at compensation for the actual loss suffered. The defrauded promisor was also given the *exceptio doli* as a defence against an action aimed at enforcing the contract. When the relevant transaction had been executed and loss had already been suffered, the praetor could restore the injured party to the position he would have been in but for the duress or fraud (*restitutio in integrum*).

Not all stipulations were valid. A promise to perform something that was illegal, immoral or physically impossible was void. Moreover, stipulations intended to take effect only after the death of one of the parties were deemed impossible and therefore void. It should be noted, further, that when performance became impossible after the conclusion of the contract, the debtor was in principle discharged from liability. In time, however, a clause was implied by which the debtor undertook that performance would not become impossible owing to his own actions.

*Stipulatio* was the most important contract in Roman law because it was not confined to particular transactions but could be used to render any kind of lawful performance binding. For instance, this form of contract could be employed for the transfer of ownership over a sum of money or some other object; the carrying out of certain work; the constitution of a dowry; the establishment of certain rights on another's property; the transformation of an existing obligation into a new one (*novatio*); and various kinds of promises in the course of judicial proceedings. Moreover, it could be employed to cover all the terms of another type of contract,

---

[138] If the parties entered into a transaction from which they desired reciprocal obligations to arise, they could employ more than one stipulation to cover each performance separately. For example, where the parties wished to purchase and sell something, the seller would stipulate the price the buyer had to pay and the buyer would stipulate that the seller had to deliver the thing purchased.

[139] *Inst* 3. 15 pr;G. 4. 136.

e.g. sale (in which case the contract was one of *stipulatio*),[140] or some terms of another contract, such as warranties against eviction and latent defects in sale. An important application of the *stipulatio* was as personal security, whereby the guarantor promised to pay the same or a lesser debt as the principal debtor, and the creditor could exact from either. The earliest forms of suretyship by *stipulatio* in Roman law were *sponsio* and *fidepromissio*, which were distinguished by the form of words employed by the *stipulator*-creditor in addressing the intended surety. However, both were subject to a number of limitations: they could only be employed when the principal obligation itself was created by *stipulatio*; the obligation of the surety died together with the person who undertook it and, in all cases, was extinguished 2 years after it was established; and where there was more than one surety for the same debt, each was liable only for his *pro rata* share of the debt, even if one or more of his co-sureties were insolvent. These limitations, although largely beneficial to the surety, restricted the scope and usefulness of *sponsio* and *fidepromissio* thereby rendering them unattractive to creditors. Thus, during the later republican age *fideiussio* emerged as a third form of suretyship that was also created by *stipulatio* and not subjected to any of the above-mentioned limitations.[141] This form of suretyship, available to both Roman citizens and foreigners (*peregrini*), gradually superseded the two older forms and evolved as the only form recognized in the time of Justinian's reign.

In early law, performance did not discharge a contract. There had to be a formal verbal acknowledgment of performance, in this case called *acceptilatio*. The stipulatory debtor formally asked his creditor whether the latter had received performance (*habesne acceptum?*), and the creditor formally answered that he had (*habeo*). In the classical period, however, performance by itself had become sufficient, and *acceptilatio* was simply a method of release (when the parties agreed) without performance, the acknowledgment being fictitious.

There were two other forms of *contractus verbis* recognized by Roman law: *dotis dictio* and *iusiurandum liberti*. The *dotis dictio* was a method of constituting a dowry (*dos*) by means of a unilateral promise expressed in prescribed words by the donor (the wife, her *pater* or one of her debtors) and delivered in the presence of the husband.[142] The *iusiurandum liberti* was a solemn promise by which a manumitted slave assumed the duty to render certain services to his patron. Since a slave could not bind himself by a civil law contract, and could refuse to do so after his

---

[140] Where the parties wished to purchase and sell something, the seller would stipulate the price the buyer had to pay and the buyer would stipulate the seller had to deliver the thing purchased.

[141] In the classical era the relevant question was *idem fide tua esse iubes?* (do you pledge your faith for the same?) – to which the person who was to stand as surety replied with *iubeo*. G. 3. 116; D. 45. 1. 75. 6. And see D. 46. 1. 8 pr. However, in Justinian's time the use of formal words was no longer required and the relevant contract was reduced to writing for evidentiary purposes. Consider *Inst* 3. 20. 8.; D. 45. 1. 30.

[142] This method was abolished by an imperial constitution of AD 428, which allowed the creation of a dowry by informal agreement.

manumission, his undertaking was usually secured before he was freed by an oath and this created a religious duty for him. After his manumission the *iusiurandum liberti* was employed to produce a civil, contractual obligation. This type of contract still existed in the time of Justinian's reign.

### 3.4.1.3  Literal Contracts

Literal contracts (*contractus litteris*) were contracts constituted by agreement and a certain form of writing. Much of the detail is uncertain, but it is clear that this contract was a contract of strict law (*negotium stricti iuris*) created by an entry (*nomen transcripticium*) in a creditor's ledger or account book (*codex accepti et expensi*) of a fictitious payment to a debtor.[143] There were two entries (*transcriptiones*) of this nature: *a re in personam* and *a persona in personam*. The first occurred when an existing debt between the parties was entered and thereby transformed into a new debt based on a *contractus litteris*.[144] The second came to the fore when a debt still due was entered as discharged and an equivalent sum was entered as being owed by another person who thus became liable for the debt of the former debtor. This might incidentally also have the effect of transforming an earlier obligation into an obligation *litteris*, but its primary purpose was to substitute one debtor for another. As the above description suggests, the *contractus litteris* was in essence a form of novation (*novatio*) whereby one obligation was terminated and superseded by another.[145] As compared with *stipulatio*, this form of contract was very limited in scope (it was available only for money-debts) but had an important advantage: it could also be concluded *inter absentes*. The form of literal contract based on the *nomina transcripticia* was the only written contract known to Roman law. It presupposed a special system of book-keeping, and when this system fell into disuse in the third century AD the literal contract disappeared.[146]

---

[143] G. 3. 128, 130.

[144] Where the previous claim was based on a *negotium bonae fidei*, this gave the creditor the advantage of a claim based on a *stricti iuris* contract and pursuable by means of the *actio certae pecuniae*.

[145] If an acknowledgment of debt had been obtained by fraudulent means, the alleged debtor could raise the defence that although he had signed the acknowledgement, the money was never paid to him (*exceptio non numeratae pecuniae*).

[146] The compilers of Justinian's Institutes invoke reference to what they claim to be a new literal contract. It is said that if a person acknowledges in writing that he received money when in fact he did not and two years pass, then if he is sued he cannot rely on the defence that he never received the money (*exceptio non numeratae pecuniae*). This is not really a *contractus litteris* but amounts to saying that if a person writes that he has borrowed money, then after a period of time he is precluded from denying that he took the loan.

#### 3.4.1.4 Consensual Contracts

Consensual contracts (*contractus consensu*) were contracts constituted by the mere agreement (*consensus*) of the parties. These contracts were binding as soon as the parties agreed on the basic essentials of the contract. Unlike the other categories of contract, no further formalities were required such as the transfer of a thing, formal words or writing. According to both Gaius and Justinian, there were four types of consensual contract: purchase and sale (*emptio venditio*), letting and hiring (*locatio conductio*), partnership (*societas*) and mandate (*mandatum*). These forms all originated from the *ius gentium* and were, therefore, *negotia bonae fidei*.[147]

*Emptio Venditio*

The contract of purchase and sale (*emptio venditio*) was a bilateral contract whereby one person promised to transfer to another a certain thing (*merx*) and the other on his part promised to pay a price (*pretium*). No set formalities were legally required, but for important transactions evidence could be provided by writing or by giving earnest money (*arra*), which could also serve as part payment. The giving of *arra* was not required for the conclusion of the contract, although the parties could insist on this practice. However, in later law *arra* assumed a greater significance. Thus, Justinian stated that if *arra* had been given and the buyer then refused to complete the contract he forfeited it, while the seller who repudiated the contract was bound to restore the *arra* and pay the same amount in addition.[148] Furthermore, it was recognized that where the parties agreed that the contract was to be put into writing, there was no contract until the relevant document was completed and formalized, and either party could withdraw without penalty provided that no *arra* had been given.

Since agreement was essential to the contract of sale, an error that negated agreement prevented the contract from coming into being. Such error was sufficient if, for instance, it was about the nature of the legal transaction entered into (*error in negotio*), or about the identity of the object of the contract (*error in corpore*). A controversial type of mistake was the so-called *error in substantia*, a mistake about a material characteristic of the object of the contract—for example, the purchaser believed that the item he was buying was composed of gold, but it turned out to be of copper. It was recognized that a mistake of this kind would nullify the contract only if the object at issue differed so widely from what it was supposed to be that it fell into a distinct commercial category. Finally, reference may be made to *error in*

---

[147] *Inst* 3. 22. 1: "The obligation is said to be contracted consensually because [the forms] do not require writing or the presence of the parties nor is it necessary for something to be delivered in order that the obligation should have substance; it is enough that those engaged in the transaction are in agreement." And see G. 3. 135 – 7; D. 44. 7. 2.

[148] *Inst* 3. 23 pr; G. 3. 139.

*pretio* or mistake as to the price of the object of the contract, and *error in quantitate* or mistake regarding the quantity of the contractual object. Such mistakes were only partially operative: neither party could enforce the relevant contract at his own figure; but each could, if he so wished, enforce it at that figure of the other.

The object of the contract of sale (*res* or *merx*) had to be specific (*certum*), in existence or capable of existing and legally capable of being the subject of commercial transactions (*res in commercio*).[149] Any clearly defined thing or even a complex of things or assets (e.g. an inheritance), a right or a servitude, could be the object of a sale. Moreover, for a contract of sale to be valid the price (*pretium*) of the object sold had to be fixed (*certum*) and it had to be seriously intended (a disguised gift was not a sale).[150] It was required, further, that the price should consist of money (*in pecunia*) as otherwise it would be impossible to distinguish sale from exchange or barter[151] as well as buyer from seller (their duties being different). In classical law the principle of free bargaining prevailed and so the amount of the price was left to the unfettered discretion of the parties concerned—the law did not intervene to dictate how they should draw up their sale agreement.[152] However, post-classical law developed the so-called *laesio enormis* ('enormous loss') rule: if land had been sold at less than half its actual value at the time of the sale, the seller could cancel the contract, return the price paid and claim back the land, unless the buyer made up the price to the full value.[153]

The principal duty of the buyer was to pay the agreed price to the seller. In principle, this had to be done on the day of delivery of the object sold, although the parties could agree otherwise. The buyer had to reimburse the seller for expenses incurred by the latter in looking after the thing during the period between the conclusion of the contract and delivery. Moreover, he was liable to pay interest if he had fallen into default (*in mora*) by failing to render payment on the date specified in the agreement. The seller's duties were more complex. He had to keep the thing sold safe until delivery; give free and undisturbed possession of

---

[149] Not only things already in existence at the time of conclusion of the contract but also future things (*res futurae*), for instance a growing crop, could be sold. If the relevant transaction was construed as a purchase of a hoped for object (*emptio rei speratae*), then the contract came into effect only if the thing came into being; if, on the other hand, it was interpreted as purchase of a hope (*emptio spei*), then the expectation was what was bought and the contract was deemed valid even if no thing finally came into being.

[150] No valid contract of sale was concluded if the price was expressed as 'at a reasonable price', or if it was to be fixed by one of the parties. However, there was a sale if the price was ascertainable by reference, for example, to the price of another property or the rate fixed in the market on a particular day. See D. 18. 1. 7. 1.

[151] This was the Proculian view, which finally prevailed and which was adopted by Justinian. The Sabinians, on the other hand, had wished to extend the contract of sale to cover the legally inadequate rules of barter or exchange of one object for another (*permutatio rerum*).

[152] D. 19. 2. 22. 3; D. 4. 4. 16. 4. Even where the purchase price was inadequate or excessive, the contract of sale was valid and binding unless there was a question of fraud (*dolus malus*), in which case the aggrieved party could institute an action (*actio doli*) against the defrauder.

[153] C. 4. 44. 2; C. 4. 44. 8. It appears that the *laesio enormis* rule applied mainly to land.

the thing to the buyer; and provide guarantees against eviction and hidden defects. If the seller was himself owner of the thing sold, the contract of sale was regarded as a *iusta causa traditionis* and in classical law the ownership of the thing passed to the buyer on delivery.[154] On the other hand, where the seller was not the owner of the thing the principle applied that no one could transfer more rights to another which he himself had not possessed (*nemo plus iuris ad alium transferre potest quam ipse haberet*). This meant the buyer did not acquire ownership, although the possibility of acquisition of ownership by *usucapio* remained open. Where the thing sold belonged to a third party, that party could institute the *rei vindicatio* against the buyer to assert his ownership and evict the buyer from the thing. In such a case, the buyer could institute the *actio empti* for damages but only in the case where the seller had fraudulently sold the thing of a third person. In other cases the buyer had to bear the loss. In the course of time, however, it became customary for the buyer to take a stipulation that his use and enjoyment of the object sold would not be legally disturbed, and by a series of steps that culminated in the second century AD this guarantee came to be implied in the sale. Besides an implicit guarantee against eviction, Roman law also recognized the existence of an implicit guarantee against hidden defects, i.e. defects that rendered the thing sold unfit for its ordinary or contemplated purpose. Regarding this protection measure, the law also went through a long process of evolution. In early law, the buyer was not protected against the presence of latent defects unless the seller had fraudulently (*dolo malo*) omitted to disclose a defect known to him but of which the buyer was unaware. In the course of time it was recognized that the parties could enter into *stipulationes* whereby the seller guaranteed that the object being sold was free of certain defects or endowed with certain features. In the late republican era the *aediles curules*, who had control over the streets and markets, introduced special provisions in their edict requiring sellers of slaves as well as beasts of draught and burden to publicly disclose certain temporary or permanent physical and mental defects. If the seller failed to declare any of these defects, the buyer had a choice of two aedilician actions: the *actio redhibitoria* and the *actio quanti minoris*. By means of the former action, the buyer could demand rescission of the sale, return of the purchase price by the seller and the restoration of the thing by the buyer. The latter action pursued affirmation of the sale and restitution of the difference between the price paid and the actual value of the defective slave or animal.[155] Over time the aedilitian remedies were extended to sales of slaves and draught animals outside the market, and by the time of Justinian's reign they encompassed sales of every kind including

---

[154] Under the law of Justinian delivery of the thing did not transfer ownership upon the buyer unless the full price had been paid or security had been provided for payment thereof. D. 18. 1. 19; *Inst* 2. 1. 41.

[155] With respect to both actions the seller's liability was strict: it arose from the mere presence of the latent defects, while the knowledge or ignorance of the seller was irrelevant. If the seller knew of the defect in the thing sold and did not disclose this information to the buyer, or if he made fraudulent declarations about the thing with a view to inducing the buyer to purchase it, he could be held liable by the buyer with the *actio empti* for damages.

land. At the same time, a warranty against latent defects came to be implied in all
sales.[156]

## Locatio Conductio

The contract of letting and hiring (*locatio conductio*) or lease was a bilateral
contract concluded when one person (the lessor or *locator*) had consented to give
another (the lessee or *conductor*) the use and enjoyment of his thing, services or
labour and the latter on his part had consented to pay remuneration. As in the case of
the contract of sale, *locatio conductio* developed from the *ius gentium* and was
therefore based on *bona fides*. A contract of lease became valid and binding as soon
as the parties had reached agreement on three essential elements: to let and to hire,
the subject matter and the price. No formalities were legally required, and the
requisite agreement could be reached in any manner (e.g. by letter or through a
messenger). With respect to the subject matter of the contract, a distinction is made
between three types of *locatio conductio*: *locatio conductio rei*; *locatio conductio
operarum*; and *locatio conductio operis*.

*Locatio conductio rei* was a contractual agreement whereby the lessor agreed to
allow the lessee the use and enjoyment of a particular object for a fixed period of
time or in perpetuity. If the object was not fit for the purpose of the lease, the lessor
was absolutely liable for return of rent and damages irrespective of whether he
knew of the defects or not. Where the lessee suffered damages or was prevented
from use and enjoyment of the thing let owing to fraud or negligence on the lessor's
part, the lessee could institute the *actio conducti* and hold the lessor liable. Furthermore, the lessor bore the risk if the lessee was prevented from using and
enjoying the object leased due to an act of God (*vis maior*). In such case the lessee
was released from his obligation to pay rent and the lessor was obliged to restore the
amount of the rental he had already received.

*Locatio conductio operarum* was an agreement whereby one person consented to
place his services (*operae*) at the disposal of another person, and the latter on his part
consented to pay remuneration. The person letting his services was therefore the
lessor (*locator*) and could claim his wages by means of the *actio locati*; the person
employing such services was the lessee or hirer (*conductor*), and could claim the
services by means of the *actio conducti*. Hire of services was not as common as it is in
present-day law since most labour was performed by slaves, and when the services of
another's slave were hired this would usually be hire of a thing (*locatio conductio rei*).

The contract of *locatio conductio operis* came to the fore when one person
assumed the duty to perform a specific task or work for another person who had
placed such work out on contract and consented to pay in return. In this context, the
object of the contract was not services for a limited time but the completion of a

---

[156] It should be noted that the relevant guarantee could be excluded by agreement, although the
seller might still be liable for bad faith.

piece of work, such as the manufacturing of an object from material supplied by the employer; the building of a house; the cleaning or repairing of clothes; the training of a slave; the teaching of children; or the transport of goods or persons. The party contracting to perform the work was the lessee or contractor (*conductor*), while the party commissioning the work was the lessor (*locator*). The contractor had the duty to produce the specified result (*opus facere*). If he failed to do so due to his own negligence or fraud, he was liable for damages by way of the *actio locati*. Furthermore, the contractor was liable for the loss of or damage to things that had been entrusted to him by the *locator*, even if he were not negligent, unless the injury was the result of external force (*vis maior*).

## *Societas*

The contract of partnership (*societas*) was concluded when two or more persons had reached an agreement to pursue a common purpose with the use of common resources. Partnership had its roots in the early Roman institution of *consortium ercto non cito* (partnership by undivided inheritance), i.e. the community of *sui heredes* who decided to administer the estate of the testator jointly, but not as a result of contract. When consensual partnership emerged during the republican era, the standard case was partnership of all the assets of the partners (*societas omnium bonorum*), in which all partners' current and future property became joint property or part of a common pool. Other forms of partnership were the *societas alicuius negotiationis*, in terms of which the purpose of the partners was to engage in one particular kind of business venture (e.g. the transportation of commodities)[157]; and the *societas unius rei*, concerned with the exploitation of a single joint asset (e.g. a racehorse) for common benefit. Each partner was required to contribute something, whether labour or assets, and each had the right to some share of profits. Unless the partners agreed otherwise, they shared profits and losses equally. They were also liable to each other but only for fraud, since it was regarded as a partner's own fault if he chose a negligent partner.[158]

---

[157] A special form of *societas alicuius negotiationis* was the so-called *societas vectigalis*: a partnership directed at the collection of taxes. Those who formed this partnership entered into an agreement with the state in terms of which they became tax-farmers (*publicani*). Under this agreement they were entitled to collect taxes and keep these taxes for themselves, and in return paid the state the agreed price. Similar rules governed other partnerships contracting with the state, e.g. for the exploitation of mines and quarries. Partnerships engaged in the collection of public revenues were generally referred to as *societates publicanorum*.

[158] If a partner suffered loss or damage as a result of another partner's fraudulent action, he could institute the *actio pro socio* against him for damages. The same action could be launched by one or more of the partners against a partner who failed to comply with his obligations as prescribed in the partnership agreement. In such case, the action pursued damages as well as the adjustment of benefits and liabilities arising from the partnership's activities. A partner condemned in the *actio pro socio* underwent loss of honour (*infamia*), since he was regarded as having betrayed the trust placed upon him.

The *societas*, even in its classical form, had no legal personality.[159] This meant the partnership could not be the owner or possessor of property, debtor or creditor and neither could it litigate, buy or sell, hire or let and such like. Furthermore, a partner had no implicit authority to bind his fellow partners even in matters closely connected with the business of the partnership. Thus, when a partner entered into a legal act with a third party he alone was affected by such act and thus became liable to or acquired rights against the third party. Normally, however, the partners were both entitled and bound to bring their dealings with third parties into the partnership account. Thus, when a partner's share in the profits or losses of the partnership was calculated, the rights and liabilities arising from all his individual transactions were taken into consideration.

A partnership could be dissolved in a variety of ways: by a unilateral express declaration to this effect by one of the partners (*ex voluntate*)[160]; if the period agreed upon expired; if the goal for which it was formed had been accomplished or became impossible; or if the communal property was lost or an essential asset passed out of *commercium*. Moreover, since the relationship between the partners was highly personal, the partnership was dissolved by the death of one of the parties.[161] The *capitis deminutio* or insolvency of a partner or the forfeiture of a partner's entire estate also entailed the dissolution of the partnership.[162] After the termination of the partnership the partners could institute the *actio pro socio* against one another or, where applicable, the *actio communi dividundo* for the liquidation and division of the common property.

### Mandatum

Mandate (*mandatum*) came to the fore when an agreement was reached whereby one person (the *mandator*) gave another person (the mandatary or *mandatarius*) a commission to do something gratuitously for him, and the mandatary accepted the

---

[159] An exception to this rule appears to have been the *societates publicanorum*, i.e. partnerships concerned with the collection of public revenues. The rules governing such partnerships gave them more permanence and stability as well as facilitating them to operate independently of the fate of individual partners. The reasoning was probably linked to the important role the *societates publicanorum* played in the field of public finances.

[160] However, a partner had to fulfil his existing obligations towards the partnership prior to his withdrawal as otherwise his action could be considered fraudulent. If a partner renounced fraudulently (*dolo malo*) or at a bad time for the business, the other partners could hold him liable for damages with the *actio pro socio*.

[161] When a partner died, his rights and liabilities under the contract descended to his heirs, but the partnership was dissolved for all. In such a case the surviving partners might continue without the deceased or admit his heir or another person into the business, but in either case it would be a new partnership.

[162] According to the jurist Ulpianus, partnership is dissolved (i) by causes connected with the person (*ex personis*); (ii) by causes connected with its object (*ex rebus*); (iii) by an act of will (*ex voluntate*); and (iv) by a juridical act (*ex actione*). See D. 17. 2. 63. 10.

commission.[163] If the undertaking was to enter into a contractual relationship with a third party, then any resulting contract was between the third party and the mandatary. Hence mandate was not direct agency. The principal duty of the mandatary was to carry out the mandate properly and to hand over to the mandator all benefits he acquired during its execution. If the mandatary did not comply with his obligations, he could be sued by means of the *actio mandati*. Occasionally, the mandatary incurred certain expenses or suffered loss or damage in the performance of the mandate. Provided that these expenses were necessary and he had not exceeded the mandate, he could institute the *actio mandati contraria* against the mandator to claim reimbursement of expenses or damages. As the mandatary was originally considered to be a trusted friend performing a gratuitous service, he was normally liable only for fraud (*dolus*). The contract of mandate was terminated when the mandate had been carried out or when the prescribed time period for its performance had elapsed. Furthermore, either party could revoke the contract provided that execution of the mandate had not yet commenced.

### 3.4.1.5  Innominate Contracts

As previously observed, Roman law recognized only a limited number of contracts. Although any lawful undertaking could be made binding by means of *stipulatio*, some common daily transactions that fell outside the normal categories of contracts were gradually rendered enforceable. The term 'unnamed' or 'innominate' contracts (*contractus innominati*) was later introduced by jurists to describe enforceable agreements for reciprocal performances which, unlike the recognized types of contract, did not have a name of their own. The most common examples of unnamed contracts encompassed exchange or barter (*permutatio*) whereby the parties agreed that each would transfer something to the other in ownership (e.g. an ox for a horse); the agreement of hawking (*aestimatum*), whereby the owner of goods handed them over to another person on the understanding that the latter would, within a prescribed period of time, either return the goods or pay the sum agreed upon to the former, while retaining any profit he may have obtained from selling them[164]; and the *precarium*, a gratuitous grant of the enjoyment of a thing revocable at will.

The *contractus innominati* were regarded as informal, legally unenforceable agreements (*nuda pacta*) from which no obligations arose. If, however, one of the

---

[163] The gratuitous nature of *mandatum* is explained on the grounds that the mandatary essentially performed a favour for a friend and, according to the moral code of the Romans, it was his duty to help friends free of charge. In the course of time it became an accepted practice to pay the mandatary a fee (*honorarium* or *salarium*) for his selfless service, and this was not considered contrary to the spirit of the mandate.

[164] Such agreements were often made with second-hand dealers who retained the profit when they sold the items they received at a higher price. It was difficult to identify whether the relevant transaction was a sale, or *locatio conductio operarum*, or *locatio conductio operis*, or mandate.

parties had already performed his side of the agreement and the other party did not reciprocate, the former party could in certain cases recover his own performance by means of a legal action (*condictio ob causam datorum*). However, he had no legal action by way of which he could compel the other party to render performance. To address the potential injustice that might arise from this event, the praetor granted in certain cases an *actio in factum*[165] whereby the party who had already performed could force his opposite number to carry out his part of the agreement. By the time of Justinian's reign, this praetorian arrangement was broadened in scope so that a legal action (the *actio praescriptis verbis*) became available in all cases involving a bilateral transaction for reciprocal performances that did not conform to the typical and recognized categories of contracts. This general *bonae fidei* action could be adapted to different legal situations in which a party who had honoured his undertaking claimed performance of the reciprocal duty by the other party.

### 3.4.1.6    Quasi-Contracts

Justinian grouped together a number of situations akin to contract that gave rise to legally enforceable obligations 'as if from contract' (*quasi ex contractu*). Some of these were analogous to particular contracts, while others resembled contracts only in that they did not arise from delicts.[166] The most important quasi-contracts were unauthorized administration (*negotiorum gestio*) and undue payment (*solutio indebiti*). These quasi-contracts arose not from an agreement between parties but from a performance by a person that entailed rights for that person and corresponding duties for another.

*Negotiorum gestio* came to the fore when one person (*negotiorum gestor*) rendered a service to another (*dominus negotii*) without prior authorization or agreement.[167] The service performed might be of any kind: a factual act, a legal act, a single act (e.g. the repair of a building) or a general administration of another's affairs (e.g. becoming a surety), as long as it was not illegal, impossible or immoral. The *gestor* had to have the intention to manage another's affairs and act on the expectation that he would have a legal claim to an indemnity.[168] *Negotiorum gestio* was an imperfectly synallagmatic or bilateral legal act that originated from the *ius honorarium* and was therefore based on *bona fides*. The *dominus* could institute the *actio negotiorum gestorum directa* against the *gestor* to claim recovery

---

[165] An *actio in factum* was an ad hoc action granted on equitable grounds to an aggrieved person where neither the *ius civile* nor *the ius honorarium* offered a satisfactory solution.

[166] *Inst* 3. 27 pr: "Let us also examine those obligations which, properly speaking, cannot be said to arise from contract but which, since they do not derive their existence from delict, are treated as arising quasi-contractually."

[167] Here the relationship between the parties was broadly speaking analogous to mandate, but differed in the aspect that there was no agreement between the parties.

[168] Thus such transaction could not be established if the *gestor* intended to render a gratuitous service.

of the proceeds derived from the *negotiorum gestio* and damages caused by the latter's fault. On the other hand, the *gestor* had recourse to the *actio negotiorum gestorum contraria* whereby he could claim compensation for necessary expenses he incurred or loss or damage he suffered in the execution of the task.[169]

Undue payment (*solutio indebiti*) occurred where a person paid in error what he was not obliged to pay.[170] In such a case, the law laid a duty of restitution upon the person who received payment. Recovery of such payment could be obtained by means of a special personal action, known as *condictio indebiti*. For the successful institution of this action the plaintiff had to prove that he had *bona fide* erred and had performed while labouring under a mistake (*per errorem*).[171] On the other hand, the person who received the money or other property also had to believe, *bona fide*, that the performance was due to him—otherwise he would be held to have committed theft (*furtum*).

## 3.4.2 The Law of Delicts

Modern law draws a distinction between delict and crime. The former is a wrong against an individual, for which the wrongdoer must render compensation following a private action brought by the victim. On the other hand, crime is a wrong deemed to be so serious as to be directed against the state, for which the wrongdoer must be punished. Here the state institutes the action and imposes the penalty. In Roman law the corresponding distinction was between *delictum* and *crimen*. The term *delictum* denoted an unlawful act that caused loss or injury to the person, property, honour or reputation of another. The word *crimen*, on the other hand, signified a wrongful act that was directed against the state. However, Roman law did not clearly distinguish between the law of delicts and criminal law: the law of delicts, besides being concerned with compensation for the victim, sought also to inflict punishment on the wrongdoer. The penal character of the Roman delict was manifested in various ways: first, the sum a wrongdoer was condemned to pay usually far exceeded the cost of the damage suffered by the victim; secondly, if more than one person had jointly committed a delict, each was liable in full and atonement by one did not release the others; and, thirdly, liability *ex delicto* did not

---

[169] It should be noted that expenses incurred by the *gestor* in undertakings that placed an unwanted burden on the *dominus* could not be recovered. For example, if the *gestor* repaired a building that the owner had abandoned because he could not afford the expense, the *gestor* could not claim compensation. Further, it should be noted that the question of expenses was determined by reference to the state of things at the time of the service. Thus, for example, money spent for the treatment of a sick animal could be recovered even if the animal died thereafter.

[170] Payment (*solutio*) embraced any performance whereby one person had been enriched at the expense of another. Such performance must have been undue (*indebitum*) either by civil law or by natural law.

[171] The mistake must have been reasonable in the circumstances.

descend to the wrongdoer's heirs, since against the latter there was no right of revenge. In Roman law the principal point of distinction between delict and crime was that in the former case the victim could recover compensation and inflict punishment on the wrongdoer by means of a private action in civil proceedings and not through prosecution by the state.

Justinian follows Gaius in classifying the principal delicts into four categories: theft (*furtum*), robbery (*rapina*), wrongful damage to property (*damnum iniuria datum*) and insult (*iniuria*).

### 3.4.2.1   *Furtum*

One of the oldest forms of delict known to Roman law was *furtum*, generally translated as theft. However, the Roman concept of *furtum* was broader in scope than the modern concept of theft. It encompassed not only the actual removal of another's thing but also a diversity of acts involving intentional interference with a movable object without the knowledge of, or contrary to an agreement with, the owner of such object.[172]

A distinction was drawn between three basic forms of theft: *furtum rei, furtum usus* and *furtum possessionis*. The first, *furtum rei*, was the unlawful appropriation of another person's movable property. This existed as the most frequently occurring form of theft. *Furtum usus*, or theft of use, consisted of the improper use of a thing belonging to another where the thing was obtained from the owner for a specific purpose and was in the possession of the thief. Examples of this kind of theft included those of the *depositarius* who used an object deposited with him for his own purposes, or of the *commodatarius* who used an object handed over as a loan for a purpose different from that for which it had been lent. The third form of theft, *furtum possessionis* or theft of possession, arose when an owner improperly removed his own thing from the possession of another person who had the right to hold it (e.g. a usufructuary or a pledgee).

Furthermore, as early as the time of the Twelve Tables, theft was divided into manifest (*furtum manifestum*) and non-manifest (*furtum nec manifestum*). The former meant that the thief was caught in the act, and originally if he were a slave, he was flogged and thrown from the Tarpeian Rock; if he was a freeman, he was flogged and allocated to the person he had wronged as a bond servant. The penalties prescribed under the Law of the Twelve Tables fell into disuse as the praetor introduced the *actio furti manifesti*, a penal action for four times the value of the stolen property. For non-manifest theft the relevant action was the *actio furti nec manifesti*, directed at payment of twice the value of the stolen property. Until

---

[172] According to the jurist Paulus: "Theft is the fraudulent handling of anything with the intention of profiting by it; which applies either to the article itself or to its use or possession". See D. 47. 2. 1. 3. In primitive Roman law *furtum* probably referred only to the act of removal of an object (it also included the removal of a person under the *potestas* of another – see G. 3. 199).

the second century AD, by a clause of the Twelve Tables, a thief caught stealing at night could lawfully be killed.[173]

In addition to the *actio furti*, the owner of the stolen property could institute a real action for the recovery of such property or its value. One such action was the *actio rei vindicatio*, by means of which an owner could reclaim the possession of his property from whoever may have held it without right. Alternatively, he could bring the *condictio furtiva*, an attractive action because it could be instituted against the thief and his heirs.

### 3.4.2.2   *Rapina*

*Rapina* (robbery) came to the fore when a person appropriated a moveable corporeal object belonging to another with the use of violence (*vis*). It was instituted as a distinct delict by the peregrine praetor Marcus Licinius Lucullus in 76 BC, with an action (*actio vi bonorum raptorum*) in terms of which the robber was liable for four times the value of the property that had been taken.[174] If there was more than one robber, liability was cumulative and so each robber had to pay the full penalty. In the classical period the victim of robbery could institute, cumulatively with the *actio vi bonorum raptorum*, a real action, such as the *rei vindicatio*, for the recovery of the stolen property or its value.[175]

### 3.4.2.3   *Damnum Iniuria Datum*

*Damnum iniuria datum*, or wrongful damage to property, was dealt with by the *lex Aquilia*, a plebiscite passed probably in the third century BC.[176] The *lex Aquilia* was divided into three sections or chapters. The first and third chapters dealt with wrongful damage to property while the second chapter dealt with the *adstipulator*,

---

[173] The Law of the Twelve Tables provided that a person in whose house a stolen object was detected through a ritual search (*quaestio lance et licio*) was to be regarded as a manifest thief. If stolen goods were found on someone's property without such a formal search, he was liable for a threefold penalty whether he was the thief or not (*furtum conceptum*), although in his turn he could bring an action for the same amount against the person who placed them there. Furthermore, the praetor granted an action for a fourfold penalty where a search was refused.

[174] See *Inst* 4. 2 pr: "A person who seizes another's property is certainly liable for theft ... However, as a special remedy for this offence the praetor has introduced the action for robbery, or the action for things seized by force, which may be brought within a year for four times the value, after a year for simple damages..."

[175] Under the law of Justinian, the action for robbery became a mixed action aimed not only at punishing the wrongdoer but also at recovering the pecuniary loss in one claim. This in practice reduced the punishment to three times the value of the stolen property and the real actions were thus excluded.

[176] Prior to the enactment of this law, the Law of the Twelve Tables and other *leges* provided remedies for several instances of wrongful damage to property. All these specific delicts were superseded by the *lex Aquilia*, which introduced a uniform delict of wrongful damage to property.

a special kind of surety or joint creditor in a *stipulatio*. In the course of time the provisions of the second chapter fell into desuetude, and for present purposes the discussion may be limited to the first and third chapters.

The first chapter of the *lex Aquilia* provided that whoever wrongfully killed another person's slave or four-footed grazing animal (*pecus*)[177] should be condemned to pay the owner the highest value that such slave or animal had in the year preceding the killing.[178] 'Wrongfully' originally meant without rightful cause, but by the end of the republican age it generally meant that the killing was malicious or negligent. In the classical period the action was construed restrictively and lay only if the defendant had killed, not if he had simply furnished a cause of death.

The third chapter provided that if someone wrongfully burned, broke or fractured inanimate or animate things (except slaves and herd animals) belonging to another, the wrongdoer should be condemned to pay to the owner the highest value which the relevant thing had during the preceding 30 days. The damage had to be caused directly by the wrongdoer, by means of a positive act—damage caused indirectly or by way of omission did not fall within the scope of the enactment.

The action provided for by the Aquilian law (*actio legis Aquiliae*) was a mixed action insofar as it aimed at recovering the damage inflicted and also punishing the wrongdoer.

During the imperial age the field of application of the *lex Aquilia* was extended and adapted to the needs of a developed society. This evolution is displayed by the fact that the *actio legis Aquiliae*, which was originally granted only to the owner of the damaged property or to his heir, was later rendered available (usually in the form of a praetorian *actio in factum* or *actio utilis*)[179] to other interested parties who had suffered financial loss, such as the *bona fide* possessor, usufructuary, pledgee, usuary and leaseholder. Furthermore, contrary to the original *lex Aquilia* that provided a remedy for damage only to a tangible thing and not to a person, in post-classical law an *actio utilis legis Aquiliae* was granted for damage resulting from wounding a free person. Thus, although the human body is not a thing, the *paterfamilias* or the injured party himself could claim for the damage that resulted from the wounding.

---

[177] This category of animals encompassed animals normally living in a herd, such as sheep, oxen, horses, mules, donkeys and goats, and later expanded to include pigs and camels. Dogs and wild animals were excluded.

[178] *Inst* 4. 3 pr. And see G. 3. 210; D. 9. 2. 2 pr.

[179] An *actio in factum* was an 'ad hoc' action granted on equitable grounds to a person who suffered injury in circumstances not covered by existing law. When such an action was allowed, the actual facts of the case were incorporated into a new formula (*formula in factum concepta*). An *actio utilis* was devised by the praetor to deal with a case which was not covered by the existing law but which was analogous to another case with an available legal remedy. However, there was probably no difference in practice between these actions. Indeed, many examples can be found in the sources in which the *actio utilis* and *actio in factum* seem to have been used interchangeably.

### 3.4.2.4  *Iniuria*

The term *iniuria*, personal injury, denoted the intentional and unlawful infringement of the body, honour or reputation of a free person. Originally there was no
general delict of *iniuria*, but the Law of the Twelve Tables recognized a diversity of
specific cases in which remedies were granted for attacks on a person's right to his
personal integrity. Thus, for *membrum ruptum*, the mutilation or permanent dis-
ablement of a limb, the victim could inflict the same injury unless a compromise
was reached. For *os fractum*, the breaking of a bone, the action was for 300 *asses*
(copper coins) if the victim were a free man, 150 if he were a slave. For minor
assault the action was for 25 *asses*. Depreciation of the value of money made the
awards absurdly low, and in the third century BC the praetor introduced the *actio
aestimatoria iniuriarum*, a penal action by means of which the victim could claim
an amount assessed in accordance with the circumstances of the case. Originally the
action was promised as a separate action in each particular case, but at a later stage
it was made applicable to all cases of *iniuria*. At the same time, a series of edicts
induced an expansion in the meaning of *iniuria* to include not only physical assaults
but also an ever-growing range of offences against a person's honour or reputation.[180] The injury-causing act had to be committed intentionally or deliberately
and had to be unlawful in the sense that it was committed without a recognized
justification or defence.[181] Delictual liability for *iniuria* could arise directly or
indirectly, for example by insulting the wife, children or other dependants of
another and thereby injuring the husband, father or master.

### 3.4.2.5  Praetorian Delicts

The above-mentioned delicts were regarded as belonging to the *ius civile* and
praetorian interventions were only aimed at extending or improving redress. However, the praetor went further and introduced new actions in respect of some
conduct for which the *ius civile* made no provision. The cases for which such
actions were created were consequently referred to as praetorian delicts. There were
numerous such delicts, but the most important were duress (*metus*) and fraud
(*dolus*).

*Metus* came to the fore when a person was induced by threats of violence to enter
into a legal act to his own detriment. If the legal act originated in the *ius civile*, the
duress had no effect on it and the act remained perfectly valid in all respects. To

---

[180] Examples of such offences included assault and battery, defamation, trespass, public abuse
against another, malicious prosecution, the exercise of a servitude without a claim of right, the
violation of the chastity of a woman or child, threatening, throwing rubbish on a neighbour's
property, causing nuisance with water or smoke, and making a false announcement that someone
owes one a debt.

[181] Such defences included self-defence, the lawful exercise of disciplinary authority, mistake,
incapacity, and acting in jest or joviality.

rectify this unsatisfactory situation, the praetor intervened and a number of legal remedies were made available to persons subjected to duress, provided the force or threat of force used was of such nature that a reasonable person would have feared imminent danger to his person, property or family. Thus, a person forced by duress to conclude a legal transaction arising from the *ius civile* was granted the *exceptio metus causa* as a defence against any person seeking to profit from the transaction in question. Where the transaction had already been executed and loss had been suffered as a result, the praetor made available to the aggrieved person a *restitutio in integrum* whereby the latter could request the restoration of the legal situation that existed prior to the conclusion of such transaction. A much stronger remedy was the *actio metus causa*, a penal action applicable whenever someone incurred financial loss as a result of duress and that pursued a payment of four times the value of such loss. With the introduction of this action towards the end of the republican age, *metus* was granted recognition as an independent delict.

*Dolus* denoted any fraud, deceit or contrivance employed to induce a person to enter into a legal transaction to his own detriment. Just as in the case of duress, *dolus* did not invalidate a transaction that arose from the *ius civile* and the victim had no remedy against the defrauder. However, in the first century BC the praetor intervened and granted the *exceptio doli* to the person who had been conned into concluding a legal transaction as a defence against an action aimed at enforcing such transaction. When the transaction had been executed and loss had already been suffered, the praetor granted *restitutio in integrum* to the defrauded party. This remedy was apparently assimilated at an early stage by the *actio doli* and *dolus* was elevated to the status of an independent delict. The *actio doli* was applicable whenever somebody suffered financial loss as a result of fraud and lay for redress for the actual loss suffered.[182] It should be noted, however, that this action was a subsidiary action (*actio subsidiaria*) since it could be employed only if no other remedy of any kind was available.

### 3.4.2.6   Quasi-Delicts

The term quasi-delict (*quasi-delictum*) denoted a wrongful act that did not qualify as a *delictum* but which nevertheless engendered an obligation between the aggrieved person and the actor, even though the latter may not in fact be blameworthy. Justinian enumerates four kinds of wrongdoing under the heading of quasi-delicts: the judge who gave a wrong judgment either deliberately or negligently (*iudex qui litem suam facit*, meaning literally 'the judge who makes a suit his own') was liable to the party who was thereby prejudiced; the occupier of a dwelling was liable for double the damage caused by anything thrown or poured out of the dwelling (even without his knowledge) on to a public place (*res deiectae vel effusae*); the occupier of premises incurred liability when something was suspended

---

[182] The *actio doli* was introduced by the praetor and jurist Aquilius Gallus in *c.* 66 BC.

or placed in such a way as to be a danger to passers-by (*res suspensae vel positae*); and, finally, a ship-owner or the keeper of an inn or stable was liable for any theft or damage to the property of their clients committed by their slaves or employers or, in the case of the innkeeper, of permanent residents.

### 3.4.2.7   Noxal Liability

When a son *in potestate* or slave committed a delict without the knowledge of the *paterfamilias* or master, the victim could institute the action that arose from the delict against the latter in the form of an *actio noxalis*.[183] When such an action was instituted, the paterfamilias or master had two alternatives: he could deliver the wrongdoer to the aggrieved party (*noxae deditio*); or, defend the action and, in the case of condemnation, pay the penalty and/or damages claimed. A special form of *actio noxalis* was the *actio de pauperie*, an action that under certain circumstances lay against the owner of an animal. When an animal acted contrary to its nature and caused damage in circumstances in which the owner could not be held at fault, the victim could institute the *actio de pauperie* against the owner. The latter then had the option to either pay for the damage done or to surrender the animal.[184]

## 3.5   The Law of Succession

As previously noted, the Romans considered the law of succession to be part of the law of things, since succession was construed as a mode of acquisition of rights over things in a mass (*per universitatem*). Since, however, it was not merely the assets of the deceased that passed to the heirs but also his debts or obligations, the law of succession is more appropriately treated as an independent section of private law.

The Law of the Twelve Tables already recognized a distinction between intestate and testamentary succession. The rules of intestate succession determined who would be heir, when a person died without a valid will. The law of testamentary succession, on the other hand, consisted of the rules whereby a testator could by way of a will himself determine the devolution of his estate after his death.

---

[183] If, for example, a slave committed theft, the *actio furti noxalis* could be instituted against the slave's master.

[184] If the damage was caused by a wild animal, the *actio de pauperie* did not apply as it was considered to be in the nature of such an animal to cause damage. It should be noted, however, that the aedilician edict gave an action where a wild animal was kept near a public road and caused damage.

### 3.5.1  Intestate Succession

Roman law knew three main systems of intestate succession: the old civil law system which, subject to some modifications, remained formally in force until the age of Justinian; the praetorian system, which was superimposed upon it; and finally the entirely novel system with which Justinian replaced both, and which was to supply the basis of much of the modern law of succession in civil law systems.

The Law of the Twelve Tables established the first order of succession on intestacy. For the freeborn, the *sui heredes*, that is those who fell under the *potestas* of the deceased and who became *sui iuris* on his death, came first.[185] The *sui heredes* had to inherit whether they wanted to or not and were, therefore, referred to as *heredes sui et necessarii*. If there were no *sui heredes*, the estate was transferred to the nearest agnatic relatives (*proximi agnati*), i.e. those related to the deceased through males.[186] Otherwise than in the case of the *sui heredes*, the *proximi agnati* could lawfully refuse to accept the succession (hence they were described as *heredes voluntarii*). If there were no *proximi agnati* the estate devolved on the *gentiles*, members of the clan of the deceased. It should be noted that the identification of the nearest agnate was made very narrowly, so that if he died or declined the inheritance the estate did not go to the next nearest agnate but to the *gentiles*.

As Roman society evolved, the system of intestate succession elaborated by the Law of the Twelve Tables proved inadequate in several respects. Thus, by way of a series of edicts the praetor gradually developed a new system of intestate succession, which gave rights first to the descendants of the deceased (including emancipated children and children given in adoption); next to the *legitimi*, i.e. those persons that could inherit in accordance with the Law of the Twelve Tables (*sui heredes*, *proximi agnati*, *gentiles*); then to blood relatives up to the sixth degree (*proximi cognati*)[187]; and finally to the husband or wife.

Although the praetorian intestate succession was initially retained by the drafters of the Justinianic codification, Justinian in the late stages of his reign introduced a completely new system by means of two important enactments (*Novellae* 118 and 127). Under the new system, the descendants (*descendentes*) of the deceased were the first to succeed, regardless of whether they were related through the male or female line. Failing the descendants, the estate devolved on the ascendants (*adscendentes*) and the brothers and sisters of the deceased. If there were no members of the second group, the nearest other collaterals inherited *per capita*. Finally, although it was not expressly stated, it would appear that if there were no

---

[185] If a freedman died intestate, in the first instance his *sui heredes* succeeded and failing them his patron.

[186] As a rule, this group included the brothers and sisters of the testator as well as his uncles and aunts.

[187] Blood relationship followed the male as well as the female line in contrast to *agnatio*, which followed only the male line.

blood relatives at all the surviving spouse could succeed as a last resort. If the deceased left no intestate heirs, the estate went to the imperial treasury (*fiscus*).

## 3.5.2   Testamentary Succession

The law of testamentary succession consisted of the rules relating to the making of a valid will, what dispositions could be made in a will and what effect these dispositions had.

The earliest form of will known to Roman law was the *testamentum calatis comitiis*, a will created in a strictly formal manner in the *comitia calata*, a special gathering of the popular assembly convoked twice a year for this purpose. Originally the assembly had to grant its approval in the form of a legislative act, but in later times the people's role in these cases was confined to merely witnessing the relevant procedure. Another early form of will was the *testamentum in procinctu*: a will created through an oral declaration by a soldier to his fellow soldiers when they were in battle array. Both the above forms of will became obsolete and fell into abeyance before the end of the Republic.[188] A third form of will that emerged at an early stage and continued to be used for a relatively long period was the *testamentum per aes et libram*, which developed from the practice of using a modified form of *mancipatio*. The *testamentum per aes et libram* consisted of the formal transfer of the testator's estate by way of *mancipatio* to a trustee (*familiae emptor*) with oral instructions that the latter should divide it among the persons nominated as heirs after the testator's death. In early law the trustee stood in place of an heir and could, in theory, govern the estate in whatever manner he wished as though he were the heir. At a later stage, however, he was considered to be no more than an executor of the testator's wishes and could be compelled by the beneficiaries to give effect to the will. The relevant procedure was modified by the praetor in the later republican age: if a written will were produced with the seals of those necessary for a *mancipatio* (i.e., the *familiae emptor*, the *libripens* and the five witnesses), then the praetor granted possession to the person nominated as heir. Finally, the *testamentum tripertitum* was introduced in the later imperial period and became the principal form of will in Justinian's time. This form of will was called 'tripartite' because its requirements had been derived from three sources: the *ius civile*, which required that the whole will had to be created at one and the same time in the presence of witnesses; the *ius praetorium*, according to which the will had to be sealed by seven witnesses; and imperial legislation, which determined that the

---

[188] G. 2. 101: "Originally there were two kinds of wills: parties either made a will at the *comitia calata*, which were assembled twice a year for that purpose; or in the face of the enemy, that is to say when the testator took up arms for the purpose of making war, for the term [*procinctus*] refers to an army ready for battle. Hence, persons made one kind of a will in time of peace and tranquility, and another when about to go into battle." And see *Inst* 2. 10. 1.

testator and the witnesses should each write a *subscriptio*, i.e. a short formal declaration on the will for identification purposes.[189]

The term *testamenti factio* denoted the legal capacity of a person to create a valid will under Roman law.[190] Originally, only male Roman citizens could make a will, but in later law foreigners with *ius commercii* and, since the time of Augustus, women could also act as testators. The testator had to be *sui iuris*, over the age of puberty and of sound mind.

In principle, any Roman citizen was eligible to be named as heir, over or under the age of puberty, *sui iuris* or *alieni iuris*, sane or insane. Furthermore, slaves of Romans could also receive under a will. When a testator instituted his own slave as heir, the slave became free and was compelled as a *heres necessarius* to inherit. This event often occurred where a testator wished to liberate his slave, but it could also happen when the testator's estate was so encumbered with debts that he did not wish to burden his natural heirs with it. On the other hand, if the slave of another person was instituted as heir, the slave could only accept on the instruction of his master who actually acquired the inheritance. For a certain period in history, women were restricted in their capacity to inherit[191] but this restriction fell into abeyance during the Principate. Undetermined persons (*personae incertae*) could not inherit at all and this category embraced those whose juristic personality could not be precisely determined in the mind of the testator. Originally, this meant that legal persons like the state, municipalities and religious or charitable organisations could not be instituted as heirs nor could persons not yet born at the time the will was composed (*postumi*). In the course of time, however, the disqualification of *postumi* was removed through modification of the ban on the institution of *personae incertae*.[192]

To avoid the danger of dying without an effective will, the testator could appoint a substitute, or line of substitutes, to succeed in the event that the instituted heir could not inherit. Where the instituted heir was a *suus heres* of the testator and under the age of puberty, the will was so written that the substitute would take even if the instituted heir took but died before reaching the age of puberty.[193]

---

[189] On this form of will consider *Inst* 2. 10. 3 & 4; C. 6. 23. 29; *Nov* 119. 9.

[190] The legal capacity to create a will is referenced in later literature by the term *testamenti factio activa*. This is distinguished from the legal capacity to be instituted as heir in a will, referred to as *testamenti factio passiva*. The term *testamenti factio relativa* denotes the legal capacity to act as a witness to a will. It should be noted, however, that these terms do not appear in the Roman juridical sources.

[191] Under the *lex Voconia* (*c.* 169 BC), a woman could not be instituted as heir by a testator whose estate had a value greater than a fixed amount (probably 100,000 *asses* or sesterces). See G. 2. 274.

[192] Similarly, exceptions in favour of the state, municipalities, charitable institutions and other corporate bodies were gradually admitted. Thus, in Justinian's time it was possible to institute the state, the Church and religious or charitable organizations as heir but private associations could only be instituted as heir by special licence. Evidence from the sources suggests that Justinian issued a constitution that finally abolished the general principle that a *persona incerta* could not inherit.

[193] The relevant formula was as follows: "Let my son Titius be my heir; if my son Titius shall not be my heir, or shall be my heir and die before he becomes his own master (i.e. before reaching puberty), then let Seius be heir." See *Inst* 2. 16 pr.

In addition to nominating an heir, a will could contain legacies and trusts and appoint guardians (*tutores*). A legacy (*legatum*) was a particular form of testamentary disposition whereby the testator left one or more specific objects to some person who was not one of his heirs. Otherwise than in the case of the heir, the legatee (*legatarius*) benefited under a special title which meant that he only acquired certain individually designated objects (*res singulae*). Insofar as the legacy amounted to a diminution of the estate's assets, it may be described as a burden on the heirs.[194] Legacies, like institutions of heirs, had to be created by the use of special formal words, and were of different kinds depending on the words used. The two most important kinds of legacy were the *legatum per vindicationem* and the *legatum per damnationem*.[195] The *legatum per vindicationem* was used to make the legatee owner of the thing bequeathed on the death of the testator and without intervention of the heir. The *legatum per damnationem*, probably the most important form of legacy, had a wider scope. By means of this form the legatee acquired a claim, supported by a strong personal action, against the heir or heirs for payment of the legacy. The effect was that the legatee was in almost the same position as a creditor of the deceased estate. A trust (*fideicommissum*) was a disposition whereby a testator made an informal request to a person (*fiduciarius*) to convey a benefit from the estate to a third party (*fideicommissarius*). In republican times, trusts were not legally enforceable but were binding only on the conscience of the heir. They were employed primarily as a means of evading certain restrictions in the law of succession relating to the institution of heirs and legatees. However, in the time of Augustus they became legally enforceable in some cases by means of an extraordinary procedure that took place before a specially appointed praetor (*praetor fideicomissarius*). Furthermore, in some situations codicils (*codicilli*), informal documents giving directions for the disposal of a deceased estate, were recognized as having legal force. A distinction was drawn between two kinds of *codicilli*: the *codicillus testamento confirmatus*, a codicil confirmed in a will, and the *codicillus testamento non confirmatus*, the independent codicil. In the former codicil any disposition that could be made in a will, except for the institution of an heir and disinheritance, could be effected, while in the latter only *fideicommissa* could be created. In the time of Justinian, when legacies and *fideicommissa* were placed on an equal footing, legacies could also be established by means of such a codicil.

---

[194] In D. 30. 116 pr, a legacy is defined as "a diminution of the inheritance whereby the testator directs that something that would otherwise form part of the estate going to the heir is to go to some other person." See also *Inst* 2. 20. 1: "A legacy is a kind of gift left by a deceased person." It is interesting to note that both Gaius and Justinian shared the opinion that the legacy did not fall within the field of the law of succession because it was not a form of acquisition of ownership of things *per universitatem*. Since, however, the topic of legacy was closely connected with testamentary succession, they felt that they could deal with it as a sub-division of the law of succession. See G. 2. 191 and *Inst* 2. 20 pr.

[195] G. 2. 192.

## 3.6   The Law of Actions

Roman private law developed from the law of procedure, otherwise recognized as the law relating to actions. This derived from the fact that the Roman jurists were concerned not so much with the formulation of general principles regarding the rights and duties of individuals, but with establishing the factual circumstances under which an aggrieved person should be granted a legal remedy. As a remedy in Roman law existed only where there was an appropriate action, the law as a whole had little import for the Romans unless a recognized form of action existed whereby an individual could enforce a claim. From the decisions given in individual cases general rules and principles were distilled at a later stage in the development of the law.

The law of procedure became applicable when a person claimed that his rights had been infringed upon and he wished to remedy this situation. In the earliest times, when no comprehensive system of remedies existed to assist an aggrieved person in the enforcement of his rights, the obvious course for him was self-help. It is clear, however, that this method could lead to all manner of irregularities as the stronger person could coerce a weaker one without the latter having an opportunity of having their objections heard. With the development of the Roman state, rules were introduced limiting the application of self-help by subjecting it to certain requirements. Thus, self-help became permissible only after the state had satisfied itself that there had indeed been an infringement of one's rights and, to prove this, a judicial decision was frequently necessary. In the course of time, self-help was eliminated and a more sophisticated system of rules evolved to provide remedies for a variety of infringements of Roman citizens' rights.

The Roman law of procedure is generally distinguished by three stages of development: the period of the *legis actio* procedure, the period of the formulary system and the period of the *cognitio extraordinaria*. The *legis actio* procedure was employed during the Republic; the formulary system was in use from the second century BC to the third century AD; and the *cognitio extraordinaria* prevailed during the Empire.

The two principal types of legal procedure up to and including the Principate age, namely the *legis actio* and the formulary procedures, were both divided in two stages. The first stage, known as procedure *in iure* ('before the law'), took place before a jurisdictional magistrate[196] and terminated when issue was joined (*litis contestatio*—in modern law the equivalent of closing of pleadings). The magistrate did not himself pronounce the final judgment, but merely determined whether the case was sufficiently strong for referral to a judge for trial and, if so, declared the applicable law. The second part of the procedure took place before the judge or

---

[196] Originally this was probably a pontiff, then the consul and from 367 BC the praetor. From 242 BC cases involving disputes between foreigners, or between foreigners and Roman citizens, were assigned to the *praetor peregrinus*.

judges and was known as *apud iudicem* ('before the judge').[197] During this phase the judge (*iudex*) conducted the trial based on the evidence produced within the frame established by the magistrate and pronounced a formal judgment.

### 3.6.1  *The* Legis Actio *Procedure*

The *legis actio* procedure (literally, an action based on the law) was the earliest procedure known to Roman law. The principal characteristic of this procedure was the use of certain prescribed formal declarations and ritual acts, through which each party and the magistrate had to proceed. These formalities originated in religious rituals, but were later embodied in laws. Some of the *legis actiones* were aimed at resolving disputes, while others were applied for the purpose of executing a judicial decision that had been pronounced in respect of a dispute.[198] But regardless of the purpose for which the *legis actio* procedure was applied, the formalities had to be strictly observed and the slightest deviation could nullify the whole procedure.[199] The *legis actio* procedure could accommodate only a limited number of cases and its exaggerated formalism did not allow for the possibility of bringing the growing number of new disputes within the sphere of law. Consequently, as Roman society advanced, this procedure gradually fell into disuse and a new flexible procedure based on writing, the formulary (*per formulam*) procedure, came into existence in the later republican epoch.

### 3.6.2  *The Formulary Procedure*

The formulary procedure was probably first used by the *praetor peregrinus*, who relied on the *ius gentium* and was therefore not bound by the strict formalism of the *ius civile*. Its application was subsequently extended to cases where both parties to a dispute were Roman citizens and the *legis actio* procedure was not available by the *lex Aebutia*, enacted in the second century BC. The reform of civil procedure was

---

[197] The judge was a private citizen chosen by the parties from the official list of judges (*album iudicum selectorum*).

[198] Five different types of *legis actiones* are mentioned in the sources: the *legis actio sacramento*; the *legis actio per iudicis arbitrive postulationem*; the *legis actio per condictionem*; the *legis actio per manus iniectionem*; and the *legis actio per pignoris capionem* (see G. 4. 12–29). The first three were applied to resolve a dispute, whilst the last two were used to enforce the execution of a judgment.

[199] This is illustrated by a case reported by the jurist Gaius where a man sued another for chopping down his vines. The aggrieved party lost his suit because he used the words 'vines' (*vites*) instead of 'trees' (*arbores*) as prescribed by the Law of the Twelve Tables. See G. 4. 11.

completed by the *leges Iuliae* of Augustus in *c.* 17 BC, which abolished the *legis actio* procedure altogether, with minor exceptions.

The formulary procedure derives its name from the *formula*, a written document prepared in the *in iure* (before the praetor) stage of the procedure, which contained a formal statement of the claim that if proved before the judge (in the *apud iudicem* stage) led to the condemnation in damages of the defendant. The available *formulae* were published by the praetor in his edict, but whenever a new case arose for which no *formula* and hence legal remedy existed, the praetor could introduce a new *formula* by issuing the appropriate decree in his edict. In this way he created a new action and, indirectly, extended the scope of the law. The forms of action connected with these *formulae* were termed *actiones honorariae*, i.e. actions derived from the *ius honorarium*.[200]

The principal forms of action employed by the praetor to deal with cases not covered by the existing law were the *actiones in factum*, the *actiones utiles* and the *actiones fictitiae*. An *actio in factum* (action based on the facts of a particular case) was an 'ad hoc' new action granted to an aggrieved person in a case where neither the *ius civile* nor the praetorian edict were useful and the case situation justified the furnishing of a remedy on equitable grounds. When such an action was allowed, the actual facts of the case were incorporated into a new formula (*formula in factum concepta*). An *actio utilis* ('adapted' or 'analogous' action) was devised by the praetor to tackle a case not covered by the existing law that was analogous to another case with an available legal remedy. Finally, an *actio fictitia* (action based on a fiction) enabled the praetor to extend the operation of an existing action by using a fiction so that a particular case not covered by the action was placed within its scope. The relevant *formula* instructed the *iudex* to assume that certain facts were present or absent in the presented case.

The formulary system featured an important division of actions that had a correlation with the judge's discretion: the division between *actiones stricti iuris* and *actiones bonae fidei*. In actions *stricti iuris* the relevant *formula* had to be strictly construed and the judge could only consider the matters it contained. This category embodied actions based on unilateral contracts, such as the *stipulatio* where the promisor was bound to the precise object promised. On the other hand, the actions *bonae fidei* presented the judge with a greater latitude of discretion whereby he could take into equitable consideration all facts relative to the case whether or not these were stated in the *formula*. Actions *bonae fidei* encompassed those arising from real or consensual contracts, such as sale (*emptio venditio*), hire (*locatio conductio*), mandate (*mandatum*) and partnership (*societas*).

In the altered conditions of the late Republic the formulary procedure permitted the jurisdictional magistrates to introduce new legal remedies to accommodate the

---

[200] The vast majority of the *actiones honorariae* were praetorian creations, although several important actions were created by lesser magistrates such as the curule aediles. The *actiones honorariae* were distinguished from the *actiones civiles*, i.e. the actions originating from the *ius civile*.

socio-economic relations of an increasingly sophisticated society. For a great span of time after the establishment of the Principate the normal jurisdiction of the magistrates was maintained and the formulary procedure remained the principal method for initiating a legal action in disputes relating to private law. The only element that changed during the Principate epoch was the function of the praetorian edict. As previously noted, in the closing years of the Republic the productive strength of the praetorian edict as a source of law faded and praetorian initiatives became increasingly rare. This trend prevailed during the Principate age and as the praetor's ability to develop new legal remedies diminished, the changes to the edict were based on measures introduced by other law-making agencies, such as imperial enactments and senatorial resolutions.

### 3.6.3   *The* Cognitio *Procedure*

During the imperial epoch the emperor and his bureaucracy gradually asserted themselves in the field of the administration of justice and introduced a new system of procedure known as *cognitio extraordinaria* or *cognitio extra ordinem*. This procedure could be employed not only in cases involving private disputes, but also in criminal cases and disputes between private citizens and state organs. As the role of the praetor as a judicial magistrate waned, the formulary procedure fell into disuse and the *cognitio* procedure became the exclusive mode of procedure during the Dominate age.[201] The most significant feature of the *cognitio* procedure was that the two phases *in iure* and *apud iudicem* were abolished and the whole process took place before one official only. This had the effect that litigation could take place in a simpler and more convenient fashion while at the same time most of the judicial and administrative functions of the state fell under a central authority. A further innovation introduced by the *cognitio* procedure was that a hierarchy of courts came into existence and, consequently, the possibility of appeals, which had not existed under the previous systems, was recognized.

---

[201] The *per formulam* procedure was abolished by an edict of Emperors Constantius and Constans in AD 342. See C. 2. 57. 1.

# Chapter 4
# Criminal Law and Criminal Justice

## 4.1 Introduction

In modern law a distinction is drawn between delict (or tort) and crime, or between the delictual (or tortious) and criminal aspects of an act. In general, the distinction is between an act that violates an individual's rights to his person, property or reputation and one that endangers the order or security of the state. The difference between delict and crime corresponds to the difference between the two principal objects the law is concerned with, namely redress and punishment. With respect to delict, the chief aim of the law is to compensate the injured party rather than punish the wrongdoer. With respect to crime, on the other hand, the principal aim of the law is to punish the wrongdoer with a view to preventing him and others from committing the same or similar crimes in the future and/or satisfying the public sentiment that wrongdoing must be met with retribution. As previously noted, in Roman law the corresponding distinction was between *delictum* and *crimen*. The term *delictum* or *maleficium* denoted an unlawful act that caused loss or injury to the person, property, honour or reputation of another. From this act there arose an obligation on the part of the wrongdoer to pay a penalty or compensate the victim for the harm suffered. The word *crimen*, on the other hand, signified a wrongful act that was directed against the state, or the community as a whole, and was prosecuted and punished by state organs. However, in Roman law the two concepts to some extent overlapped, since the law of delicts, besides being concerned with compensation for the victim, sought also to inflict punishment on the wrongdoer. This can be explained on the ground that the relevant penalty (*poena*) originated as the formalization of the primitive right to exact revenge and was imposed as a punishment on the wrongdoer that went not to the state, as in the ordinary criminal process, but to the victim. In Roman law the distinction between delict and crime mainly derived from the fact that with respect to the former case the victim could

© Springer International Publishing Switzerland 2015                    159
G. Mousourakis, *Roman Law and the Origins of the Civil Law Tradition*,
DOI 10.1007/978-3-319-12268-7_4

recover compensation *and* inflict punishment on the wrongdoer by means of a private action in civil proceedings and not through prosecution by state organs.

It should be noted that the criminal law holds a secondary place on the Roman legal scene. It was private law to which the Roman jurists devoted their main interest, and it was the private law that gave Roman law its great importance as a basis of much of modern law. It was not until the second century AD that Roman juridical literature began giving serious attention to matters of criminal law. Prior to that we have to rely mainly on literary sources, whose focus of attention is largely on the upper social classes. The test was whether a criminal case made a good story, and the best stories were those involving persons in positions of power. This leaves us in the dark as to how the ordinary citizen fared, in particular when prosecuted for common (as opposed to political) offences. Nevertheless, even with this qualification, the sources give valuable insight into how the Romans thought about crime and criminal justice.

## 4.2    Crime and Criminal Justice in the Archaic Era

In the earliest period of Roman history, many acts that in modern law are treated as offences against the state and prosecuted by public authorities were regarded as private wrongs that presented the injured party or their family with a rightful claim to seek vengeance on the wrongdoer. Moreover, certain wrongful acts directed against the community as a whole were regarded as public crimes and were pursued and punished by the state itself. However, during this period the list of crimes was invariably short and embraced offences that directly threatened the existence and security of the community, such as treason (*proditio, perduellio*)[1] and murder (*parricidium*)[2]; and religious offences of a particularly heinous nature, such as blasphemy and other sacrilegious acts, which, unless duly punished and atoned

---

[1] The crime of treason was committed when a Roman citizen acted in a way that rendered him an enemy of the Roman state. Its scope embraced acts such as assisting an enemy in time of war, inciting an enemy to attack the Roman state, delivering a Roman citizen to an enemy and inciting an internal rebellion.

[2] It seems that initially *parricidium* was as a rule treated as a matter to be settled between the offender and the deceased's kin, whether by regulated vendetta or by judicial process. This view derives support from a law attributed to King Numa, according to which if anyone killed a man by accident he could atone for the deed by sacrificing a ram before the dead man's agnates at a public meeting. One might perhaps surmise that there were two concurrent procedures, private and public. It should be noted, further, that avenging the killing of a kinsman was regarded as a religious duty. This notion was so deeply rooted, that long after murder was established as a crime against the state, a kinsman was bound to initiate a prosecution against the killer; if he failed to do so, he was not allowed to obtain any of the deceased person's inheritance.

for—as a rule by the sacrifice of the offender to the deity concerned (*consecratio capitis*)[3]—were liable to provoke the gods' wrath against the entire community.[4]

With the exception of treason, which was always regarded as a public crime, there is uncertainty as to which offences were treated as crimes and which as private wrongs in the Law of the Twelve Tables. This legislation made some provision, the nature of which is unclear, on infaming incantations, which was treated as a capital offence. An adult who pastured his animals on another's land or took another's crops by night was to be sacrificed to the goddess Ceres, but a child might only be flogged and either made bondsman to the victim or fined. A person who willfully set fire to a building or an adjacent stack of hay was to be scourged and burned to death, but a fine or a flogging was sufficient penalty for an accidental fire. It was considered lawful to slay a thief by night, or an armed thief in daytime, provided that this was not done privily. Thieves caught in the act were scourged and delivered as bondsmen to their victims if they were freemen; if they were slaves, they were scourged and hurled from the Tarpeian Rock. Children who committed theft were scourged at the praetor's discretion and reparation was made. A corrupt judge or arbiter was subject to capital punishment and a person who gave false testimony was to be flung from the Tarpeian Rock. A point to note here is that from a very early period the Romans drew a distinction between the responsibility of an adult and that of a child, and between deliberate and negligent acts. In general, the penal provisions of the Twelve Tables combined archaic and more progressive aspects. Like all ancient legal systems, their starting-point was the notion of revenge, although priority was now given to retaliation through state-supervised procedures. The state intervened and imposed penalties only in cases of treason or certain religious offences that directly affected the welfare of the community. However, it is not until we come to the period of the late Republic that the list of recognized crimes (*crimina publica*) begins to resemble a system of criminal law.

According to Roman tradition, in the Monarchy era the king, who possessed all jurisdiction in principle, was accustomed to delegating his criminal jurisdiction in cases of treason to a pair of judges (*duumviri perduellionis*), who were specially appointed for each occasion, and in cases of murder to a pair of standing judges called *quaestores parricidii*. Regarding the capital sentences pronounced by either of these pairs of judges, the king had the discretion to allow an appeal to the people

---

[3] Such punishment served to restore the harmony between the community and the gods (*pax deorum*) by eliminating the state of collective impurity created by the commission of the offence. In later times the sacrifice of the offender was replaced by the milder penalty of outlawry and the confiscation of goods. As this penalty involved the exclusion of the offender (referred to as *sacer homo*) from the community and from the protection of human and divine law, anyone could kill the offender with impunity; his killing was regarded as a sacrifice to the deity he had sinned against. Offences against the gods were dealt with by the *pontifices*.

[4] It should be noted, however, that in the earliest period of Roman history the distinction between secular and religious crimes was not clearly made. Treason, for example, was also construed as an offence against the gods protecting the community, and the execution of the offender as a sacrifice to them. A strong religious element can also be traced in the crime of murder.

(*provocatio ad populum*), and could endorse their judgment on whether the offender should be killed or freed.[5] However, it is impossible to ascertain the entire truth in the traditional account.[6]

After the establishment of the Republic, jurisdiction over the major crimes was vested in the consuls. The authority to adjudicate (*cognitio*) derived from their right of supreme coercion (*coercitio maior*) derived from their *imperium*. If a case of treason (*perduellio*) arose, the consuls nominated two judges (*duoviri perduellionis*) to conduct the inquiry and pronounce the sentence.[7] In cases of murder (*parricidium*) the two quaestors acted as judges and in this capacity were designated *quaestores parricidii*.[8] The jurisdiction of the curule and plebeian aediles encompassed cases involving offences against the public order or public morals, and contraventions of statutory enactments. From the third century BC, jurisdiction in cases involving persons belonging to the lower classes and slaves was assigned to the *tresviri capitales*, lower magistrates who exercised police functions in Rome. A criminal prosecution could be based on a statutory enactment (such as the Law of the Twelve Tables), an established customary norm or an order of a state organ. Originally, criminal proceedings had an entirely inquisitorial nature. As soon as the commission of a crime captured a magistrate's notice, he had the responsibility to initiate such investigation of the case as he deemed necessary. There was no such thing as a third party participating formally in the proceedings as prosecutor or accuser and producing evidence to establish the accused's guilt. It was the duty of the magistrate to both instigate a charge against an individual and take steps to procure the necessary evidence and thus, in a sense, he acted as prosecutor as well as judge.

According to Roman tradition, the *lex Valeria*, a statute passed in the first year of the Republic, stipulated that a Roman citizen could not be slain pursuant to a magistrate's sentence without a right of appeal to the people (*provocatio ad populum*). The Law of the Twelve Tables confirmed this rule that a capital

---

[5] The notion of *provocatio ad populum* first appears in the sources that elaborate the trial of Horatius, under King Tullus Hostilius. See Livy 1. 26.

[6] Modern scholars have expressed doubts as to whether the *duumviri perduellionis* and the *quaestores parricidii* originated from the period of the kings, and there is evidence suggesting that the right of appealing to the assembly was first granted by a *lex Valeria* enacted soon after the establishment of the Republic.

[7] However, since the middle of the third century BC cases of *perduellio* were usually tackled by the *tribuni plebis* and the appointment of *duoviri perduellionis* became virtually obsolete. Furthermore, a less grave crime of a similar nature, the *crimen laesae maiestatis* (or *maiestas*) was recognized, which consisted in acts that tended to impair the power, renown and dignity of the Roman state. It should be noted that the dividing line between *perduellio* and *maiestas* was never precisely drawn.

[8] The original title of the quaestors seems to have been *quaestores parricidii*, which indicates that their duties in the administration of criminal justice came first in order of time. As their financial duties assumed increasing prominence, they were designated as *quaestores parricidii et aerarii*, and finally as *quaestores* simply. This, at any rate, is a possible explanation for an obscure matter.

sentence[9] pronounced by a magistrate could not be executed unless on appeal it had been ratified by the people. A provision of the same statute rendered the *comitia centuriata* (therein referred to as *comitiatus maximus*) uniquely competent to deal with appeals against capital sentences. On the other hand, appeals against pecuniary sentences were tackled by the *comitia tributa* or the *concilum plebis*, depending on whether the relevant sentence was pronounced by a magistrate of the *civitas* or the *plebs*.[10]

However, we may observe after the enactment of the Law of the Twelve Tables the invariable practice of magistrates *cum imperio* to refrain from pronouncing a sentence that could be challenged on appeal to the people. The reason is that only the assembly of the centuries had authority to impose a death sentence once a person was declared guilty of a capital offence. Accordingly, criminal jurisdiction was exercised by magistrates alone only in cases involving less serious offences.[11]

The rules concerning appeals and the restrictions imposed on the magistrates' judicial powers by legislation entailed the exercise of criminal jurisdiction by the Roman people in important cases during most of the republican period.[12] The procedure adopted in trials before the people (*iudicia populi*) is only discoverable in the descriptions of writers from a later date and a great part remains obscure. Sources reveal that the magistrate who resolved to impeach a citizen, after duly summoning the accused, held a trial in (at least) three successive public meetings (*contiones*). During these meetings he investigated the case and determined matters of fact and law based on the produced evidence.[13] If the accused was found guilty, the magistrate issued an order summoning the appropriate assembly to meet on the

---

[9] The term *poena capitalis* denoted not only the sentence of death inflicted in one or another of different ways, but also a sentence entailing the loss of liberty.

[10] The right of appeal was re-confirmed and extended by the *lex Valeria Horatia* of 449 BC, the *lex Valeria* of 300 BC and the *leges Porciae* (first half of the second century BC). The *lex Valeria* is declared to have extended this right to corporal punishment, while under the *leges Porciae* an appeal could be raised against capital sentences and sentences of scourging (*verberatio, castigatio*) pronounced on Roman citizens anywhere (originally, the right of appeal lay only against sentences pronounced within the city of Rome or a radius of one mile therefrom). By the latter legislation the magistrate who refused the *provocatio* was probably rendered liable to a charge of treason. The question of whether the right of appeal was available to citizens serving as soldiers has been a source of difficulty to historians. Although in theory it appears that under one of the *leges Porciae* every citizen soldier had this right, in practice it is unlikely that a military commander would allow an appeal where the exigencies of military discipline called for an immediate execution of the sentence.

[11] As early as the middle of the fifth century BC, a series of legislative enactments (*lex Aternia Tarpeia, lex Menenia Sextia*) established the maximum limits for fines imposed by magistrates. As regards imprisonment, it should be noted that in republican times this was normally regarded as a means of preventing escape and not as a form of punishment, though no doubt a magistrate with *imperium* or a tribune of the plebs might employ it by way of *coercitio*.

[12] The jurisdiction of the popular assemblies embraced in particular political crimes or offences that affected the interests of the state.

[13] The magistrate might include more than one charge in the same accusation and could withdraw or amend the charge (or a charge) at any stage of the trial.

expiry of the regular interval of 3 market days (*trinum nundinum*).[14] During this period (3 market days amounted to 24 days) the citizens would have ample opportunities to discuss with one another the case and the issues it involved. When the assembly congregated on the appointed day, the magistrate presented a motion in the form of a bill (*rogatio*) for confirmation of the verdict and sentence. In response to this motion and without any preliminary debate, those in favour of confirmation voted '*condemno*' ('I condemn') while those against it voted '*absolvo*' ('I absolve').[15] If the majority in the assembly was in favour of condemnation, the presiding magistrate pronounced the sentence.[16] A notable feature of Roman legal procedure was the right of the accused to flee Rome as a voluntary exile at any time before the assembly's final vote. Selection of this option entailed the enactment of a decree of outlawry, or interdiction from water and fire (*aquae et ignis interdictio*). This practically meant banishment accompanied by loss of citizenship and property. The individual declared an *interdictus* was deprived of legal protection and, if he returned to Rome without permission, could be killed by anyone with impunity.

## 4.3  The Development of Criminal Justice in the Late Republic

Adjudication of public crimes by the people may have been efficacious in the context of a small city-state composed of conservative farmers and middle-class citizens. However, as socio-economic and political conditions became more complex, especially in the period following Rome's wars of expansion, comitial trials proved increasingly inadequate to deal with the complicated issues that criminal prosecutions frequently invoked. Quite aside from the fact that trials by the people were cumbersome and time-consuming, the escalating number of cases made adjudication of public crimes by the assemblies very difficult.[17] Inevitably, popular

---

[14] Where the accused was found guilty and sentenced to death or other severe punishment, he said '*ad populum provoco*': 'I appeal to the people'. Even if the accused failed to say this, it appears certain that he was assumed to have said it. For the rule was that a sentence that could be appealed against could not be carried out unless and until it had been confirmed by the people on appeal, and surely a convicted person could not be allowed to escape punishment simply by remaining silent.

[15] The voting procedure was governed by the same rules as those applicable when the assembly had to decide on a legislative proposal.

[16] It should be noted that the assembly could not alter the sentence; for example it could not reduce a capital sentence to one of fine or lower the amount of a fine. This means that if any citizen, though convinced of the accused's guilt, considered the sentence too harsh and was not prepared to uphold it, he had no alternative but to vote for absolution. Furthermore, if the assembly was prevented from meeting at all (e.g. because of a tribunician veto) or proceedings were halted before voting was completed (e.g. because of the appearance of an ill omen), the accused had to be released.

[17] The immense concentration of impoverished citizens in Rome during this period was accompanied by a rapid increase in crime, especially violent crime. At the same time, the lure for money tempted the greedy and malfeasance in office gained appeal with its anticipated high rewards. As

criminal justice eventually had to be replaced by a new and more functional court system. The gradual evolution commenced in the early second century BC with the creation, by decision of the people, of special *ad hoc* tribunals (*quaestiones extraordinariae*) for the investigation of certain offences of a political nature. These embraced offences such as abuse of power or dereliction of duty by magistrates and provincial officials, and conspiracies against public order and the security of the state. Moreover, the senate, on occasions of emergency, assumed (or usurped) the power of setting up, by its own authority alone and without the sanction of the people, special courts from which there was no appeal.[18] A tribunal of this kind consisted invariably of a magistrate *cum imperio* (i.e. a consul or a praetor) surrounded by a body of assessors (*consilium*) selected by the magistrate or the senate. The court's decision was determined by the majority of the assessors and no appeal against it was allowed as the court was regarded to represent the people. An early illustration of a special *quaestio* was the commission established by the senate in 186 BC to investigate and punish the crimes committed by members of the Bacchanalian cult.[19]

In the transformed socio-political conditions of the later Republic, the *quaestiones extraordinariae* provided a more efficient means of dealing with public crimes than the *iudicia populi*, whose role in the administration of justice gradually diminished. However, it was only with the introduction of standing courts of justice that a stricter regulation of criminal procedure was finally realized.

---

no regular police force existed in Rome, the detection of criminals was usually relegated to the injured parties or common informers, and this made the prosecution of offenders very difficult.

[18] However, in 123 BC a statute passed on the initiative of C. Gracchus (*lex Sempronia de capite civis*) reaffirmed the principle that no citizen could be punished for a capital crime without the sanction of the assembly. This law seems to have forbidden the establishment of special tribunals by senatorial decree alone and without the approval of the people. Nevertheless, the senate was able to circumvent this prohibition by making use of the so-called *senatus consultum ultimum* authorizing the consuls to apply any extraordinary measures deemed necessary to avert an imminent threat to the state. In the politically turbulent years of the late Republic, the *senatus consultum ultimum* was often employed by the senatorial nobility as a weapon against their political opponents (known as *populares*). Although the latter strongly denounced this practice, they did not hesitate to resort to it themselves when there were in a position to coerce the senate.

[19] The adherents of this cult, which was based on the worship of the wine-god Bacchus, had formed secret associations and were engaged in orgiastic religious rites. After a number of cult members had been found guilty of criminal and immoral conduct, the senate issued the *senatus consultum de Bacchanalibus* declaring membership of the Bacchanalian cult to be a capital offence and instructing the consuls to hold an investigation *extra ordinem*. During the persecutions that followed more than four thousand people were put to death. The senate's action seems to have been motivated by genuine aversion to conduct that was taken to offend public morals and reflected a policy against religious associations operating in secret (the worshipping of Bacchus and other deities was permitted if done in the open and under official supervision). For the text of the *senatus consultum de Bacchanalibus* see FIRA I, 30; A. C. Johnson, P. R. Coleman-Norton, F. C. Bourne (eds), *Ancient Roman Statutes* (Austin 1961), No. 28.

### 4.3.1  The Permanent Jury Courts

A turning-point in the history of Roman criminal law was the creation of standing courts (*iudicia publica* or *quaestiones perpetuae*) authorized to adjudicate crimes of a specific nature. The first of these courts was instituted to investigate allegations of abuse of power by senatorial magistrates charged with provincial administration and tax collection on behalf of the Roman state. In 149 BC the tribune L. Calpurnius Piso initiated the *lex Calpurnia repetundarum*, a plebiscite that established a standing tribunal (*quaestio de repetundis* or *repetundarum*) composed exclusively of members of the senatorial class and chaired by the *praetor peregrinus* that tried cases involving extortion (*crimen repetundarum*)—an offence frequently committed by provincial magistrates against the people of their provinces.[20] The proceedings in this court bore a strong resemblance in form to a civil action,[21] and a defeated defendant was obliged to return the illicit gain to those affected.[22] No appeal from the court to the *comitia* was allowed, nor could its decisions be suspended by tribunician veto.

The establishment of the *quaestio repetundarum* later inspired the creation of other standing courts by special statutory enactments *ex post facto* for individual crimes,[23] especially crimes committed by high-ranking magistrates or army officers during performance of their duties. Thus, by the end of the second century BC, four permanent courts had been established: for extortion (*de repetundis*); for high treason (*de maiestate*)[24]; for electoral corruption (*de ambitu*)[25]; and for embezzlement of public money (*de peculatu*).[26]

---

[20] The money and other effects that were allegedly extorted, and would be restored if the prosecution proved successful, were known as *pecuniae* or *res repetundae*, or simply *repetundae*. One should note that a charge of extortion could only be instituted against a provincial magistrate after he had demitted office.

[21] As in civil actions, proceedings were initiated by the injured party, who in this case were the aggrieved provincials.

[22] In later years, the person found guilty of extortion was condemned to pay twice the value of the illegally appropriated property; other penalties that could be imposed included the expulsion of the offender from the senate and the declaration that he was an *infamis*.

[23] The Romans neither shared the modern reluctance to create extraordinary or special tribunals nor did they espouse the principle enshrined in many contemporary legal systems against retroactive legislation.

[24] In the later republican era, treason meant the betrayal of Roman citizens to an external enemy; the same offence also encompassed certain acts of provincial governors, such as waging war or leaving one's province without authorization. The scope of treason was considerably broadened during the imperial age.

[25] *Ambitus* was a vaguely defined crime because it consisted in going beyond understood but unstated limits on what could properly be expended in attracting votes.

[26] The crime of *peculatus* was distinguished from the theft of private property, termed *furtum*. The punishment for embezzlement of public funds was normally a fine that usually amounted to four times the value of the stolen property.

Under Sulla's government (82–79 BC), the standing court system was extended further and the entire machinery of the *quaestiones perpetuae* was overhauled to place the administration of criminal justice on a more firm and consistent basis. The *quaestio repetundarum* was reorganized by the *lex Cornelia de repetundis*, and the *quaestio de maiestate* instituted by Saturninus in *c.* 103 BC was recognized as the principal court for high treason by the *lex Cornelia de maiestate* of 81 BC.[27] The court dealing with electoral corruption (*de ambitu*) was also retained, while Sulla's own *lex Cornelia de ambitu* introduced heavier penalties for this crime.[28] As regards homicide, a court for hearing cases of poisoning (*quaestio de veneficis*) was apparently established before the time of Sulla. A court attending to cases of assassination (*quaestio de sicariis*) had been created as early as 142 BC, but it appears to have operated only as a *quaestio extraordinaria*. Under Sulla's *lex Cornelia de sicariis et veneficis* of 81 BC, both forms of homicide were dealt with by the *quaestio de sicariis et veneficiis*, which thus became a general murder court. The same court also tried those who attempted to procure the unlawful conviction of another person.[29] One of the permanent courts established by Sulla tackled certain forms of injury (*iniuria*) caused by acts of violence, such as beating (*pulsare*), striking (*verberare*) and the forcible invasion of another person's house (*domum introire*).[30] Sulla also introduced a *quaestio de falsis* that functioned as a court dealing with cases involving the forgery of official documents, wills and the counterfeiting of money.[31] After Sulla's

---

[27] Before the enactment of this law the tribunes could still convene the *comitia* to hear charges of treason. Sulla terminated this practice by restricting the powers of the tribunes. At the same time, he broadened the definition of the *crimen maiestatis* to encompass any act performed by a Roman citizen that impaired the safety and dignity of the state. The scope of this crime then embraced wrongdoings that were previously treated as *perduellio* or *proditio*, such as sedition, unlawful attacks against magistrates, desertion and the like. Moreover the *lex Varia* of 92 BC stipulated that treason was committed by those who 'by help and advice' (*ope et consilio*) induced an allied state to take up arms against Rome. In the closing years of the first century BC, two further statutes on the crime of *maiestas* were enacted: the *lex Iulia maiestatis* of Julius Caesar (46 BC) and the *lex Iulia maiestatis* of Augustus (8 BC). Several later imperial laws were based upon these statutes. The *crimen maiestatis* was punishable by death, although the person charged with the offence was usually allowed to go into exile before the court pronounced the sentence (in such a case, he was subject to an *aqua et ignis interdictio*).

[28] A series of laws devised to repress corrupt electoral practices were introduced during the second and first centuries BC, such as the *lex Cornelia Baebia* (181 BC); the *lex Cornelia Fulvia* (159 BC); the *lex Maria* (119 BC); the *lex Acilia Calpurnia* (67 BC); the *lex Tullia* (63 BC); the *lex Licinia* (55 BC); and the *lex Pompeia* (*c.* 52 BC). The last law on *ambitus* was the *lex Iulia de ambitu* passed under Augustus in 18 BC.

[29] According to sources, the first chapter of this law gave the court capital jurisdiction over those who carried weapons with the intention of killing or stealing, or who killed. The fifth chapter dealt with poisoning, i.e. the making up and selling of a drug as well as its fatal administration. See D. 48. 8. 1; C. 9. 16.

[30] This court was created by the *lex Cornelia de iniuriis* of 82 BC. Of course, *iniuria* was also a delict, and the criminal and delictual procedures operated side by side. Consider D. 3. 3. 42. 1; D. 47. 10. 5 pr.

[31] This was instituted by the *lex Cornelia testamentaria* or *de falsis* of 81 BC.

era more *quaestiones perpetuae* were implemented such as the *quaestio de vi* for crimes of violence[32]; the *quaestio de plagiariis* for kidnapping, treating a free man as a slave and inciting a slave to leave his master[33]; the *quaestio de sodaliciis* for electoral conspiracy[34]; and the *quaestio de adulteriis* for adultery.[35]

Generally, the permanent courts were governed by rules similar to those governing the extraordinary courts and, like the latter, were regarded as operating under the authority of the people.[36] It is germane to mention that the supreme jurisdiction of the *comitia* remained unaffected, in principle, by the establishment of the standing court system. In practice, however, the old comitial procedure was seldom engaged when trial by a *quaestio perpetua* was available. As the system of the *quaestiones perpetuae* approached completion, the role of the assemblies in the administration of criminal justice thus ceased.

According to the statute of 149 BC that established the *quaestio repetundarum*, the members of this court were recruited exclusively from among the senators. As provincial magistrates invariably belonged to the senatorial nobility, the above rule could engender some favour for the provincial magistrate charged with extortion. A magistrate who was retired from office and charged with extortion had the benefit of a trial by his peers and his chances of acquittal were thus greatly increased. As new permanent courts were brought into existence, this would naturally hold good in their case also. As a result of the senate's understandable reluctance to punish members of its own class, the new court system became a convenient instrument of self-protection for the senatorial oligarchy. It is thus unsurprising that the organization of the jury courts surfaced as one of the most highly contested issues in the later Republic.

In 123–122 BC Gaius Gracchus, seeking to implement his basic policy aim of curbing the senate's powers, procured the passing of a statute (*lex Acilia*) whereby

---

[32] This court was established by the *lex Lutatia de vi* in 78 BC; that law was supplemented by the *lex Plautia de vi* passed around 63 BC. There were two kinds of violence: *vis publica* and *vis privata*. The former covered various forms of seditious conduct that fell outside the scope of the *crimen maiestatis*, as well as the organisation and arming of gangs for the purpose of obstructing the activities of state organs. The punishment for such offences was banishment. On the other hand, *vis privata* covered acts of violence against individuals and, like theft, was considered a private offence (*delictum*). The distinction between the two forms of violence was confirmed by two laws of Augustus, the *lex Iulia de vi publica* and the *lex Iulia de vi privata*. See D. 48. 6 & 5; C. 9. 12.

[33] This court was instituted by the *lex Fabia de plagiariis* (of unknown date, but probably first century BC). D. 48. 15; C. 9. 20.

[34] Established by the *lex Licinia de sodaliciis* of Crassus in 55 BC.

[35] Installed by the *lex Iulia de adulteriis* of Augustus in 18 BC. Consider D. 48. 5; C. 9. 9. It should be noted here that adultery in a strict sense was sexual intercourse between a married woman and a man not her husband. Other sexual offences, including rape or the seduction of a freeborn boy or man, were referred to as *stuprum*. Male homosexual behavior as such was not considered illegal.

[36] In the last century of the Republic, *quaestiones extraordinariae* were still occasionally instituted by special statutes to deal with certain offences falling outside the jurisdiction of the permanent courts.

the right of sitting as members of the *quaestiones perpetuae* was transferred from the senators to the equestrians. At first, eradicating the senatorial monopoly on the administration of criminal justice appeared to be a move in the right direction. It meant that if members of the senatorial nobility controlling the provincial administration were accused of abuse of power, they would face a tribunal composed of *equites*. But in reality the transfer of control over the court system to the *equites* did not diminish the deleterious influence of factional politics on the administration of justice. It simply allowed a class whose political role was once largely neglected to participate in what was originally regarded as an 'in-house' affair. Naturally, the senatorial nobility refused to acquiesce in this situation. Thus, the issue of membership within the standing courts persisted as a prominent apple of discord and the subject matter of various legislative measures throughout the last century of the Republic. Sulla's short-lived reform restored the senate's control of the court system, which was expected in view of his general policy trends. After this event, the *lex Aurelia* of 70 BC established a more equitable balance in the composition of the juror lists. This law provided that each *quaestio perpetua* was to consist by one-third of senators, one-third of *equites* and one-third of *tribuni aerarii* (the latter are commonly understood to have been *equites* but with a lesser property qualification). In the last decades of the Republic, when the internecine strife between the senatorial factions peaked, it may appear that the equestrians had the upper hand in the standing courts.[37]

As previously noted, each *quaestio perpetua* was competent to deal only with a particular category of offence. The nature of this category was defined in the statutory enactment establishing the *quaestio*, as amended possibly by subsequent legislation. A court of this type embodied a considerable number of non-official members and was chaired by a president referred to as *quaesitor*. According to the system finally adopted, the president was normally a praetor. However, any other magistrate or even a private citizen (usually an ex-magistrate) invested with magisterial powers could be appointed president.[38] The members of the court

---

[37] Under the *lex Pompeia* of 55 BC, the jurors were still chosen from the three groups mentioned in the *lex Aurelia* but only the richest men within each group were eligible. The *lex Iulia iudiciorum* of Caesar, passed probably in 46 BC, excluded the *tribuni aerarii* from the lists of jurors. Finally, Augustus restored the three classes of the Aurelian law and added a fourth that represented the lower classes of the community. As Augustus exercised control over the senatorial and equestrian classes, it may be safely assumed that during his time criminal courts decided cases in line with the official, that is Augustan, policies.

[38] After the enactment of the *lex Calpurnia* (149 BC) that established the court of *repetundae*, the duty of presiding over the relevant proceedings was assigned to the *praetor peregrinus* as most claimants were foreigners. As the caseload increased and new standing courts were created, the number of praetors was later enlarged to eight and six of these presided over the courts. The praetors were assigned to the different courts by lot after the senate decided which courts should be presided over by a praetor. Usually praetors were allocated to courts dealing with offences of a political nature, such as extortion, electoral corruption, conspiracy against the state, treason and embezzlement. Aediles were usually assigned (also by lot) to courts addressing murder, violence and fraud. The presiding magistrate had to swear that he would abide by the statute that installed the court and could be liable to punishment if found guilty of corruption.

were not the president's nominees but were chosen in accordance with the provisions of the statute establishing the particular *quaestio*. Generally, a large body of qualified citizens was summoned and a complicated process involving challenges on both sides reduced this body to the prescribed number.

The form of the proceedings in the permanent courts was essentially accusatorial, as opposed to inquisitorial. This meant that no action could be initiated unless a citizen laid a formal accusation against another and thereby undertook to prosecute at the trial.[39] The sole function of the court was to hear and assess the evidence and arguments presented by the prosecution and the defence respectively, and thereafter to convict or acquit. The president publicly announced the verdict, which was thus nominally his verdict. Nevertheless, he was bound to decide the case in accordance with the opinion of the majority of the members as ascertained by a ballot. Hence, it was the members who constituted the actual adjudicators. Note that no sentence was pronounced as the penalty for the particular offence was stipulated by the statute that established the *quaestio*, and liability to this penalty ensued automatically from the conviction. A person found guilty by a *quaestio perpetua* could not appeal to the people against the court's decision.

The first step in a criminal prosecution was the *postulatio*, which constituted an application by a citizen to the magistrate directing a particular *quaestio* for permission to instigate charges. This was an essential preliminary requirement, as the applicant might be precluded by law from laying charges against any person, or against the particular person he intended to prosecute.[40] After permission to prosecute was granted, the accuser stated the name of the accused and the offence committed (*nominis et criminis delatio*) in a formal and written manner while the accused was present.[41] The document containing the accusation (*inscriptio*) was then signed by the accuser and by all those supporting his claim (*subscriptores*). Moreover, the accuser had to swear an oath that he did not issue a false accusation out of malice (*calumnia*) or in collusion with the accused (*praevaricatio*).[42] After the magistrate had formally accepted the indictment (*nominis receptio*), the accused became technically a defendant (*reus*) and the trial date was set. The accuser was granted sufficient time to prepare his case (*inquisitio*)—in most cases, 10 days

---

[39] Initially only the aggrieved party or his closest relatives were entitled to initiate an indictment, but in later times almost every citizen of good repute had the right to launch an indictment and conduct a prosecution. However, accusers motivated by the prospect of personal gain often abused the indictment procedure. Despite the possibility of a suit of slander against false accusers, some people even carved a profession from accusing wealthy fellow-citizens.

[40] Where two or more persons applied at the same time for leave to institute an indictment against the same individual, a panel of jurors determined who had priority by considering the cases of all those seeking permission to prosecute (*divinatio*).

[41] D. 48. 2. 3. pr.

[42] *Calumnia* (*crimen calumniae*) was committed when a person launched charges against another knowing that the latter was innocent. False accusers were liable to severe penalties that entailed infamy and exclusion from public office. *Praevaricatio* referred to the collusion between the accuser and the accused in a criminal trial for the purpose of obtaining the latter's acquittal. A person found guilty of *prevaricatio* was harshly punished and branded with infamy.

appears as the minimum period but in certain cases (especially when evidence had to be gathered from overseas) a longer period might be allowed. The accuser might also request the summoning of witnesses (a maximum of 48) by the magistrate, although the latter was free to summon as many as he thought fit (*testimonium denuntiare*). The next step in the process was the selection of the members of the court designated to try the case.[43] These were chosen by lot (*iudicum sortitio*) from the annual list of jurors (*album iudicum*) prepared by the praetor at the beginning of each year.[44] After the required number of jurors was selected in this way (50 and 75 were typical), both the accuser and the defendant had an opportunity to disallow a specified number of jurors (*iudicum reiectio*).[45] The presiding magistrate then replaced the disqualified jurors by drawing more names from the *album iudicum* (*iudicum subsortitio*).

During the trial, the accuser and the defendant dominated the scene, with their advocates and witnesses engaged in cross-examinations that were often rancorous.[46] The jurors listened in silence, while the presiding magistrate was mainly responsible for the orderly progress of the proceedings.[47] Both oral and documentary evidence was admissible.[48] Witnesses (*testes*) testified under oath and were examined by their own side and cross-examined by the other.[49] After all the evidence was presented and the closing speeches delivered, the magistrate

---

[43] Under the *lex Acilia* the jury had to be empanelled immediately after the *nominis delatio*. But this exposed the jurors to the dangers of intimidation and corruption. Thus subsequent to Sulla's judicial reforms, juries were empanelled after the *inquisitio* and shortly before trial day.

[44] Under the *lex Acilia* the *album iudicum* comprised 450 persons, but in later years the number was increased (probably to 900). The praetor was required to publicize the list of jurors and to swear an oath that only the best men had been chosen.

[45] Roman legal procedure was governed by the principle that a person could not be appointed as a juror without the consent of the parties concerned. The rules governing the *iudicum reiectio* were settled by the *lex Vatinia* of 59 BC.

[46] The accused stood in a particularly strong position, as he was entitled to as many as six advocates and was granted twice the total speaking time allocated to the prosecution. It should be noted that if the accuser failed to appear in court on the day of the trial his case was dismissed. On the other hand, the absence of the accused did not preclude the proceedings. However, in such a case it was required (under a law of Augustus) that a condemnatory verdict be unanimous.

[47] The magistrate's role was largely formal – he did not decide points of law, summarise the evidence and so on in the manner of a modern judge sitting with a jury.

[48] The category of documentary evidence comprised records of various kinds, such as account books (*tabulae accepti et expensi*), letters (*epistolae*), written notices (*libelli*) and, in some cases, the account books of those entrusted with the collection of public revenues (*publicani, tabulae publicanorum*). The written evidence also included the statements of witnesses who were unable to appear in court in person for various reasons (ill health, old age, absence from Rome and so on). It also incorporated certain public statements relating to the case issued by state organs (*testimonia publica*).

[49] Witnesses for the defence were often invited to speak not only about facts but also about the accused's character – those who testified to the good character of the accused were referred to as *laudatores*. Character evidence carried special weight and the absence of *laudatores* was regarded as in itself damning.

convened the jury and placed the question of the defendant's guilt or innocence to the vote. In early times the vote was open, but the enactment of the *lex Cassia* in 137 BC entailed the use of a secret ballot (*per tabellas*) to determine the court's decision. Each juror was given a small tablet marked on one side 'A' (*absolvo*) and on the other 'C' (*condemno*). He then erased one or the other and cast the tablet into an urn (*sitella*). Jurors also had the third choice of 'NL' (*not liquet*: not proven) if they were unable to reach a decision.[50] The verdict was determined by the majority of the votes: if there was a majority of 'C's the accused was pronounced guilty by the presiding magistrate; if the 'A's predominated or if there was an equality of votes, he was pronounced not guilty. If the majority of the jurors voted '*non liquet*' the presiding magistrate announced the necessity for a more thorough investigation into the case and fixed a day for a new hearing (*ampliatio*).[51]

As previously noted, the penalties imposed by the standing courts were specified in the statutes that instituted these courts, and liability to these penalties routinely followed upon conviction. There existed two kinds of penalties: capital and monetary. In theory, most crimes of a serious nature were capital but it was practically unknown to inflict the death penalty (*poena mortis*) on a Roman citizen deriving from a condemnation on a criminal charge in normal circumstances. The reason is that persons tried by these tribunals enjoyed a statutory right of fleeing into exile before the court pronounced its final sentence.[52] When, as invariably happened, a condemned person invoked this right, a resolution passed by the vote of the people declared his legal status as an exile and interdicted him accordingly from using water and fire (*aquae et ignis interdictio*).[53] The normal effect of this interdiction rendered the culprit liable to summary execution if discovered on Roman territory, which after the Social War (91–88 BC) covered the whole of Italy.[54] Hence, condemnation by a standing court on a capital charge virtually amounted to a sentence of banishment. It is feasible that some late republican statutes expressly substituted interdiction from fire and water with death as the penalty for certain crimes.

---

[50] In such a case, jurors probably had to erase both 'A' and 'C' and scratch in the letters 'NL'. Just to erase 'A' and 'C' counted as no vote.

[51] After the enactment of the *lex Servilia Glauciae* (*c.* 101 BC), proceedings in trials for extortion (*de rebus repetundis*) were divided into two distinct parts (*comperendinatio*). In the first part (*actio prima*), the parties elaborated their arguments and witnesses on both sides were called upon to testify. The second part (*actio secunda*) occurred after a day's interval and the parties were granted the opportunity to comment on the evidence presented and provide additional information. After this second hearing the jurors issued their verdict, which now only assumed the form of 'guilty' or 'innocent' (the 'not proven' option was not available).

[52] Naturally, in times of unrest persons regarded as dangerous were ruthlessly put to death. It may have been routine practice to eliminate malefactors from the lower classes by irregular means. Moreover, it should be noted that no immunity from the death penalty was ever enjoyed by non-citizens.

[53] The phrase *aquae et ignis interdictio* implies a denial of the necessaries of life to the individual in question.

[54] The relevant resolution might, however, specify an extended area within which the interdiction was operative.

The modern observer can hardly fail to form an unfavourable appraisal of the Roman administration of criminal justice. A survey of civil law and procedure would fare better as this field early displayed logical categorization and generally produced adequate results. Roman criminal justice appears as haphazard, capricious, opportunistic and remote from the contemporary standards of equal protection of the laws. Proceedings in the standing courts were cumbersome and trials could be protracted as cases were often heard more than once. Although a jury of less than a 100 members could grasp complicated evidence and assess the parties' credibility better than a crowd of thousands, jurors were often as susceptible to corruption and bribery as the people in the turbulent *iudicia populi*. A less unfavourable appraisal of the Roman criminal justice system is formed if one contemplates the immense pressures of a rapidly expanding empire. Further, the adverse circumstances of a largely haphazard evolution engendered many new concepts and categories of criminal wrongdoing (such as crimes against public order and the security of the state, various types of fraud, corruption and abuse of office) that furnished the framework for the subsequent development of the criminal law.

## 4.4   The Administration of Criminal Justice in the Principate Age

At the end of the republican era, the jurisdiction of the assemblies in capital crimes had entirely disappeared. The ordinary mode of criminal trial for serious offences featured a prosecution before a standing court (*quaestio perpetua*). Less serious offences were dealt with in a summary fashion by lower-grade magistrates, the *tresviri capitales*. Shortly after the establishment of the Principate, the tasks of the *tresviri capitales* were assumed by imperial officials (*vigiles*) acting under the supervision of the *praefectus vigilum*.[55] On the other hand, the standing jury-courts remained in operation for quite a long time after they were reorganized by the *lex Iulia iudiciorum publicorum* of Augustus (17 BC). This enactment drastically revised the composition of the jury-courts in the spirit of broadening the socio-economic basis of public participation, and prescribed the rules of procedure governing the conduct of trials. A general list of jurors was established comprising four categories based on status and property qualifications: senatorials; equestrians; the *tribuni aerarii*; and finally, a new class formed by the owners of property worth 200,000 sesterces (*duocentenarii*) who would be summoned in cases of minor importance. Moreover, the minimum age for jury service was lowered from 30 to 25, so that there always existed sufficient citizens to serve as jurors. In 18 BC,

---

[55] Offences falling within the jurisdiction of the *praefectus vigilum* included arson, robbery, burglary and theft. The most serious cases were tackled by the *praefectus urbi*. See D. 1. 15; C. 1. 45.

Augustus completed the system of *quaestiones perpetuae* by creating two new tribunals of this kind: the *quaestio de adulteriis* and the *quaestio de annona*. The jurisdiction of the first court encompassed cases of adultery (*adulterium*), extra-marital relationships involving women of a high social standing, and procurement.[56] The second court dealt with accusations against merchants who endeavoured to raise the market prices of foodstuffs, or who engaged in unfair practices relating to the supply or transportation of food.[57]

However, since trial by jury was not readily amenable to official control, the system of the *quaestiones perpetuae* was contrary to the spirit of the new imperial regime. Apart from this fact, the standing court system had several deficiencies that were not adequately addressed by the Augustan legislation. Firstly, each *quaestio* was constituted in a specific manner according to the statute that originally established it (or possibly according to some subsequent statute), and could only tackle a particular offence category as specified in such statute. Hence, frequently a wrongful act that merited punishment as a crime was not punished as it did not precisely fulfill the definitional requirements of any of those offence categories for which *quaestiones* had been instituted. Secondly, the statutory enactment establishing a *quaestio* (or possibly a subsequent statute) prescribed the punishment for the specific category of offence in question, and this punishment automatically attached on conviction. Thus, the tribunal had no power to either increase or mitigate such punishment to address the circumstances of the individual case. In general, the penalties imposed for offences captured by the jurisdiction of the jury-courts were often regarded as too mild and therefore disproportionate to the gravity of the offences committed. In addition, proceedings in the jury-courts were expensive, laborious and even protracted as the cases were often heard more than once. Thus, since the early years of the Principate the work of the jury-courts was supplemented by the new extraordinary jurisdiction (*cognitio extraordinaria*) of the emperor and those officials to whom he delegated his judicial powers. At the same time, the *princeps*-emperor sanctioned the senate's assumption of an extraordinary criminal jurisdiction. In a sense, the senate may be construed to have replaced the popular assemblies' jurisdiction and this body was resorted to mainly in cases involving offences with a political nature or any case where the accused was a senator. In principle, these two jurisdictions were concurrent but reality exposes the more extensive nature of the emperor's jurisdiction from the start. As more offences fell within the sphere of the new tribunals' jurisdiction over time, the *quaestiones perpetuae* faded into the background and finally disappeared in the early years of the third century AD.[58]

---

[56] D. 48. 5; C. 9. 9.

[57] D. 48. 12.

[58] No doubt the rules governing the *quaestiones perpetuae* were still used as guides by magistrates exercising extraordinary jurisdiction, even though many rules were quite inadequate to serve as a basis for a mature system of criminal law.

### 4.4.1   The Criminal Jurisdiction of the Senate

The criminal jurisdiction of the senate originated in the early years of the Principate period when the senate evolved as a court of law on a par with the *iudicia publica*.[59] Initially, it dealt with cases connected with the *crimen laesae maiestatis*, wrongful conduct that diminished the majesty of the emperor and the people of Rome. It also addressed cases involving abuse of power perpetrated by provincial governors. In the time of Tiberius (AD 14–37), the senate's jurisdiction was enlarged to encompass not only crimes against the security of the state (such as treason) but also a wide range of serious crimes (including adultery, murder and forgery) committed by members of the senatorial order. In this way, the senate by the end of the first century AD had developed into a *forum privilegiatum* with exclusive jurisdiction over the crimes of senators.

Trials before the senate were conducted in accordance with a procedure that blended the old rules of senatorial debate with those of the *iudicia publica*. A prosecution was launched by an application to a consul for leave to initiate an accusation (*postulatio*), followed by the accuser's formal announcement of the charge (*nominis delatio*). The magistrate to whom the application was submitted then formally registered the name of the accused (*nominis receptio*) and the trial date was established. On the appointed day, the senate was convoked and the trial commenced under the presidency of a consul. After the arguments of the parties were presented and the evidence heard, individual members submitted their motions and presented opinions. The verdict was attained by a majority vote without the involvement of the presiding magistrate. The emperor frequently participated in the judicial sessions of the senate and, as *princeps senatus*, cast the first vote that presumably carried decisive weight. The sentence became valid in law upon the final announcement of the verdict and its insertion in the official record as a senatorial resolution. No appeal to the people was available against a death sentence imposed by the verdict. Since the late second century AD, the jurisdiction of the senate was curtailed both substantially and procedurally. By the middle of the third century AD, the senators were no longer involved in the administration of criminal justice.

### 4.4.2   Imperial Jurisdiction

Since the era of Augustus, the operation of the emperor's domestic tribunal started to resemble a public criminal court. In time, the emperor assumed jurisdiction not

---

[59] During the Republic the senate did not have independent criminal jurisdiction. Its role in the administration of justice was limited to instituting, under certain circumstances, temporary courts of inquiry (*quaestiones extraordinariae*) and introducing in times of emergency any measures deemed necessary for the security of the state.

only over matters affecting him personally, such as conspiracies, but also over common-law crimes. He possessed the power to withdraw at his discretion any criminal case from the ordinary judicial authorities. In the early years of the Principate, this seems to have occurred on rare occasions. Despite any endeavours of an individual *princeps* to avoid determining cases directly as a judge, he was inevitably drawn into this activity by the appeals against court decisions and the increasing number of citizens' petitions for justice. Moreover, juristically inclined emperors, like Claudius, always sought to extend the imperial court's radius of competence by introducing cases to this court and determining them in the final instance.[60] However, a long time passed before the jurisdiction of the jury-courts and the senate was superseded by the imperial *cognitio*, especially in cases involving capital charges.

In the exercise of his criminal jurisdiction, the *princeps*-emperor was not bound by the general rules governing ordinary criminal law proceedings and had complete freedom in the composition of his council of advisors (*consilium*). He also had a free hand in the definition of offences, the choice of penalty, the mode of punishment and the degree of its severity. As the decisions of the imperial court gradually acquired the status and force of laws, criminal law evolved from its static form to broaden in scope and complexity. However, criminal law was never the subject of scientific study to the same extent as private law. As a result, the administration of criminal justice was pervaded by an element of arbitrariness that easily rendered it an instrument of oppression.[61]

In Italy, the highest criminal jurisdiction under the emperor was assigned to the city prefect (*praefectus urbi*) and the praetorian prefect (*praefectus praetorio*). By the late second century AD, the former had jurisdiction over all crimes committed in Rome and in a zone within a radius of 100 miles from the city[62]; offences committed outside that delineated area fell within the jurisdiction of the latter. These two high-ranking imperial officials had the unrestricted power to inflict any recognized form of punishment, capital or otherwise, on any offender. They could try any case in the first instance, but they also dealt with appeals against sentences of lower magistrates (central or local) endowed with an inferior criminal jurisdiction. In principle, a judgment of the *praefectus urbi* or the *praefectus praetorio* could be appealed against before the emperor. Of course, the latter could refuse to entertain such an appeal and deem the judgment in question as final. By the Severan period (late second century AD), the magistrate responsible for the maintenance of security in the capital (*praefectus vigilum*) had acquired jurisdiction in criminal

---

[60] Similarly, Augustus is reported to have devoted much of his time to hearing cases *extra ordinem*. See, e.g., Cassius Dio 55. 7. 2; 56. 24. 7; Suetonius, *div. Aug.* 33. 1. and 2; 51. 2.

[61] A novel and, from the modern viewpoint of the Rule of Law, highly objectionable feature of the new criminal jurisdiction of the emperor was its emancipation from the general precepts of criminal law. Thus, acts that under the common criminal law were not at all punishable could be punished as crimes and trials for acts with mandatory punishments under the general criminal statutes could result in acquittal.

[62] See D. 1. 12. 1. pr. and 4; Cassius Dio 52. 21. 1-2.

matters such as arson, burglary, robbery and theft, though he probably referred particularly grave cases to the city prefect.[63] A specialized jurisdiction over offences connected with the food supply of Rome was assigned to the *praefectus annonae*.[64] Moreover, some criminal jurisdiction was assigned by decree of the senate or imperial constitution to the consuls and praetors who tried cases *extra ordinem* assisted by a body of assessors (*consilium*).

As regards the senatorial provinces, the governor was the highest criminal (as well as civil) judge in the province. He could attend to cases either in the first instance or on appeal from lower courts. With respect to non-Roman citizens (*peregrini*), his power to inflict punishment was unfettered and no appeal against his sentences was allowed. However, his authority was fairly limited in cases involving Roman citizens: he was not entitled to pronounce the death sentence on citizens unless the latter were first granted the opportunity to have their case judged in Rome. In the imperial provinces, criminal justice was administered by imperial officials acting as representatives of the emperor (*legati Augusti*). From as early as the first century AD, the emperors started to grant those *legati* who commanded troops in their province the power to execute soldiers (Roman citizens). The latter did not possess the right to present their case before a court in Rome. In the course of time, the mass of Roman citizens living in the provinces greatly increased and it was practically impossible to send all those charged with capital offences to Rome for trial. As a result, this power (*ius gladii*) was granted to all provincial governors and was made applicable to civilians as well. However, whether or not a governor was also entitled to execute a death sentence without first applying for and receiving special authority from the emperor to do so seems for a long period to have depended on the precise terms of the particular grant. After the *constitutio Antoniniana* of AD 212 extended the Roman citizenship to all the free inhabitants of the empire, all provincial governors could wield their own authority to order the death of Roman citizens. This action was averted if a condemned person successfully appealed against the sentence. Indeed, whenever a provincial governor had duly pronounced a capital or non-capital sentence on a Roman citizen it was always theoretically possible for the latter to appeal to the emperor despite the great practical difficulties that this could entail.[65] If provincial appeals were allowed, they were usually delegated by the emperor to either the *praefectus urbi* or the *praefectus praetorio* whose decision in most cases was regarded as final.

In trials before extraordinary criminal tribunals the adopted procedure differed from that engaged under the system of the *quaestiones perpetuae* in some important respects. As we have discerned, proceedings in the latter system were set in motion

---

[63] D. 1. 2. 2. 33; 1. 15. 3, 1 and 4.

[64] D. 48. 12. 3. 1.

[65] A number of legal restrictions were placed on the freedom of appeal, especially after the introduction of the *constitutio Antoniniana* in AD 212. In general, on appeals the governor had a degree of discretion: he could order the execution of offenders found guilty of certain grave crimes (e.g. sedition) and refuse appeals that were only initiated to delay execution when the applicant's guilt was manifest. See D. 28. 3. 6. 9; 49. 1. 16.

by a private citizen (not a state organ) who assumed the role of the accuser by filing a charge against the alleged offender with the magistrate presiding over the competent jury-court. The *cognitio extraordinaria*, on the other hand, had a predominantly inquisitorial character. A criminal prosecution was initiated by a state organ (such as a police official or other public official) acting on information provided by the injured party or a private informer, so no formal accusation by a citizen was necessary. The magistrate in charge of the proceedings had a more active part in the trial than the president of a jury-court. The former could resort to inquisitorial methods at any time if the supposed interests of justice so demanded. Moreover, in contrast to the system of the *quaestiones perpetuae* where the guilt or innocence of the accused was determined by a panel of jurors, both the verdict and the sentence were now determined by the magistrate at his discretion. As there were no fixed penalties, the magistrate was in principle free to impose any penalty he deemed appropriate by considering the nature of the offence, the particular circumstances, and the offender's personal and social position. Over time, a body of norms developed from imperial enactments, juristic opinions and the practice of the courts. These norms more definitely fixed the scope of offences and matters relating to criminal liability and punishment. Some norms were concerned with procedural matters while others pertained to the requirements of criminal responsibility, such as conduct, intent and defences.[66]

### 4.4.3   Criminal Offences, Responsibility and Punishment

The criminal law of the Principate age contains elements indicative of a system that had advanced considerably beyond the system that prevailed during the Republic. This is evident from consideration of the list of criminal offences and related criminal liability requirements. Treason and sedition were serious crimes, as were various forms of abuse of power by state officials. Within the scope of treason (*perduellio*) fell the betrayal of Romans to foreign enemies, inciting allies into becoming enemies and, from the fifth century, instructing barbarians how to build ships. It was also treason for a provincial governor not to relinquish his province on the arrival of his successor. However, during this era the most common form of treason was *maiestas* or *crimen laesae maiestatis*: conduct involving a threat to the safety or dignity of the emperor and his family. Of abuses by state officials, the most common was the extortion of money or other forms of property (*res repetundae*) by provincial governors and other magistrates from provincials. Similarly liable were persons in a position of authority, such as judges, who took money to deliver or withhold a particular decision. Other offences of this kind included *peculatus*, the embezzlement of public money, usually by a person in a position of responsibility; and *de residuis*, the failure to account for all the money with which such a person

---

[66] Many of these norms had their origins in the republican period.

had been entrusted. In the early imperial age, the crime of public violence (*vis*) embraced the conduct of a magistrate who ill-treated a respectable citizen. In the same period, electoral corruption (*ambitus*) ceased to be of real significance, since magistrates were no longer elected by the popular assemblies but by the senate in accordance with the wishes of the emperor.

The law relating to murder was in general terms similar to modern law. The crime of parricide, however, normally defined as the murder of an ascendant, involved a separate and particularly harsh form of punishment, the *culleus* (*poena cullei*) or sack: the person found guilty was sewn up in a leather sack, probably together with snakes and other animals, and thrown into a river or the sea. Adultery, strictly speaking the sexual intercourse between a married woman and a man not her husband,[67] was a crime whilst, in contrast, male homosexual practices were not, unless they involved the rape or seduction of a freeborn boy or man.[68] The rape of women is difficult to detect in the Roman sources, partly because it was closely connected in some parts of the empire with abduction marriage. Such an offence could have been classed as serious assault (*vis*), outrage (*iniuria*) or *stuprum* (a general term for sexual crime). Incest was an abhorrent crime, based on custom, not statute. Offences against property, such as theft and damage to property, continued to be treated as delicts, although certain aggravated forms of theft, such as cattle stealing (*abigeatus*), burglary and theft at the baths, constituted criminal offences. The forgery of documents (*falsum*), especially wills, and the forging of money were serious crimes, and so was kidnapping.[69] The criminal law of this period also encompassed offences against good morals or public order, including usury and interference with the officially organized supply of cereals and other foodstuffs (*annona*). An important aspect of the criminal law pertained to the need to control the conduct of private accusers in a system that lacked a public prosecution service, and where such right of accusation was never fully replaced by a magistrate's initiative. The relevant procedural offences were calumny, prevarication and tergiversation, all regulated by the *senatus consultum Turpillianum* of AD 61. As previously noted, calumny (*calumnia*) was the bringing of a false accusation from malice. Prevarication (*praevaricatio*) involved the collusion between the accuser and the accused for the purpose of weakening or eliminating undesirable evidence or supporting spurious defences, perhaps from friendship of influence. Tergiversation (*tergiversatio*) was the withdrawal of the charge without authorization by the court, including failure to take any steps needed to continue the action. Perjury could also fall under the *senatus consultum Turpillianum*. Roman law

---

[67] A man was just as much an adulterer as a woman was an adulteress, but he could not be so labeled for being unfaithful to his wife, or for having intercourse with a slave woman or a prostitute or someone considered disreputable (e.g. an actress), but only with a respectable woman. The prior right to lay an accusation of adultery belonged to the husband. The woman's father and third parties, members of the public, could also bring such an accusation.

[68] Male homosexuality became a crime during the later imperial period.

[69] Kidnapping usually involved the confinement of a free person or slave. Someone who knowingly 'bought' a free person was also liable for this offence.

recognized that persons accused of crimes should be duly notified of the charges and granted the opportunity to defend themselves in a court of law.[70]

Criminal responsibility presupposed that the accused met certain requirements relating to age, sex and mental capacity. Children below the age of 7 years (*infantes*) were excluded from criminal liability as they were deemed incapable of forming the requisite criminal intent (*dolus*). Children below the age of puberty (*impuberes*—boys under 14 and girls under 12) were also presumed incapable of forming such an intent, although this presumption was construed to be rebuttable, particularly if they were approaching puberty.[71] Insane persons were also incapable of committing a crime, but this was attributed to the misfortune of their condition, which required proving, since insanity might be feigned. Moreover, they could be subject to restraint if they posed a threat to public safety.[72] A person was not criminally liable if he accidentally caused a prohibited harm.[73] Mistake or ignorance as to the law, contrary to mistake of fact, did not preclude culpability as it was held that citizens had a duty to know the law.[74] The law also recognized various defences and mitigating pleas that negated or reduced culpability for a criminal act, such as self-defence[75]; superior orders[76]; loss of self-control caused, for example, by justified anger or intoxication[77]; and duress and necessity.[78] Higher magistrates were immune from criminal prosecution during their term in office, but their immunity ended with this term.

An overt act was necessary for the commission of a crime; this could include speech (such as incitement to sedition or to murder), but a person could not be held criminally liable for thoughts alone.[79] A person who counseled the commission of a crime might be treated as committing the offence, or as being an accomplice. Accomplices were usually liable to the same penalty as the principal; they too

---

[70] See D. 48. 2. 3. and 7; 48. 19. 5. Slaves were in general not subject to prosecution under the system of the *ordo iudiciorum publicorum*, as the system of standing jury courts was called, largely because the relevant penalties, such as exile, were inappropriate. They could be tried, however, by the courts exercising *cognitio*.

[71] Consider D. 9. 2. 5. 2; 48. 8. 12; 29. 5. 14; 21. 1. 23. 2; 47. 12. 3. 1; 48. 6. 3. 1; 48. 10. 22 pr; C. 9. 47. 7.

[72] See D. 21. 1. 23. 2; 29. 5. 3. 11; 48. 4. 7. 3; 1. 18. 13. 1; 1. 18. 14.

[73] D. 48. 19. 11. 2; C. 9. 16. 4 (5).

[74] D. 39. 4. 16. 5; C. 9. 16. 1. Foreigners (*peregrini*) could not be expected to know the law, but these had no formal protection against the *coercitio* of the Roman magistrates and imperial officials. They were not entitled to due process, although it was often granted to them.

[75] D. 48. 8. 9; 9. 2. 45. 4; 48. 8. 1. 4.

[76] The defence of superior orders was open to a person who assisted someone under whose authority he stood, for example a son or a slave acting under his *paterfamilias'* or master's authority respectively. However, this was normally only a ground for mitigating the prescribed penalty and did not negate liability, unless the deed was not obviously criminal. See on this issue D. 48. 10. 5; 50. 17. 4; 9. 2. 37. pr; 44. 7. 20.

[77] D. 48. 8. 1. 5; 48. 5. 39 (38). 8; 48. 3. 12. pr; 49. 16. 6. 7.

[78] D. 19. 2. 13. 7.

[79] See D. 48. 19. 18.

must have possessed *dolus* and must have aided the principal with physical help, serious planning or concealment.

As previously observed, during the later Republic capital punishment practically ceased to be inflicted on Roman citizens except in times of civil unrest or strife. In cases falling within the jurisdiction of the standing jury-courts, the accused ostensibly enjoyed a statutory right of fleeing into exile within a short period after he was found guilty of a capital crime. On availing himself of that right, he was then denied fire and water by a vote of the people (*aqua et ignis interdictio*). Such an outcome essentially amounted to a sentence of banishment from Roman territory, which after the Social War (91–88 BC) meant banishment from Italy. After the establishment of the Principate, the foregoing position remained practically unchanged in the case of condemnation on a capital charge by a *quaestio perpetua*. On the other hand, when a Roman citizen was declared guilty of a capital crime by an extraordinary tribunal this often entailed death. In the third century AD, the standing jury-courts virtually vanished and proceedings before extraordinary tribunals became universal. This period also featured the extension of the Roman citizenship to all the free inhabitants within the empire. As a result of these events, the capital punishment of Roman citizens became widespread. Moreover, different forms of punishment according to social status were securely in place by this time.

In the Principate era, the social distinction between the upper and lower classes found a clear expression in the legal notions of *honestior* and *humilior*. The *honestiores* ('honourable') were comprised of the privileged members of the governing class (senators, equestrians, civil servants, soldiers and members of the provincial town councils), whilst those belonging to the lower classes of society were collectively referred to as *humiliores* ('humble'). The *humiliores* had a distinctly inferior standing in the eyes of the law and were subject to heavy and degrading punishments. By contrast, the *honestiores* were exempted from punishments of a shameful nature, and the pronouncements of death and other severe penalties against reputable citizens were rarely enforced.[80]

In relation to capital punishment the force of the distinction between *honestiores* and *humiliores* is exhibited by the fact that offenders belonging to the former group were as a general rule decapitated or conferred some other form of relatively painless and honourable death,[81] while offenders attached to the lower classes were usually subjected to cruel and degrading modes of execution, such as crucifixion, impalement, exposure to wild beasts and burning at the stake.[82] A similar distinction between the *honestiores* and the *humiliores* applied in connection with the non-capital punishments.[83] The most common forms of punishment imposed upon members of the *honestiores* class were deportation (*deportatio*) usually to an

---

[80] Senators and members of the equestrian order convicted of crimes, which would have brought ordinary persons heavy sentences, were only required to withdraw into exile.

[81] D. 48. 19. 8. 1.

[82] D. 48. 19. 9. 11; 8. 2; 28. pr. 11-12. and 15; 38. 1.

[83] Apart from fines (*multae*), which might be imposed on anyone.

island or oasis, and expulsion (*relegatio*) entailing the offender's exclusion from residence in a specified territory (normally Italy and one's own province). The former punishment had a more serious nature and it was accompanied by the loss of citizenship and property, though not of personal freedom.[84] The punishment of expulsion was a mild form of exile involving simple internment in an island without further consequences.[85] Other forms of punishment often inflicted on members of the upper classes included expulsion from the *ordo* to which the offender belonged, exclusion from holding civic office[86] and prohibition from pleading in the courts of law.[87]

The next focus is the non-capital punishments commonly imposed on offenders attached to the class of *humiliores*. These punishments embraced penal servitude in or around the mines[88]; confinement accompanied by some form of hard labour for the public benefit[89]; flogging; flagellation; and branding.[90] Condemnation to confinement for life with hard labour in the mines (*ad metalla*) was eventually held to involve loss of liberty. On the other hand, condemnation of a Roman citizen to confinement accompanied by some lesser form of hard labour for the public benefit (*in opus publicum*) was ultimately deemed to entail loss of citizenship but not personal freedom.[91]

## 4.5   Crime and Criminal Justice in the Dominate Period

In the late Empire, the scope of existing offence categories was extended and several new offences were introduced by imperial legislation to tackle new forms of wrongdoing induced by societal changes. For example, the crime of extortion (*crimen repetundarum*) was defined in a broader manner to encompass all kinds of infractions perpetrated by state officials in the course of their administrative or judicial tasks.[92] The ambit of crimes such as treason (*crimen maiestatis*) and corruption (*ambitus*) was likewise expanded,[93] and more severe penalties were

---

[84] *Deportatio* could only be imposed by the emperor in his judicial capacity or the *praefectus urbi* with the approval of the emperor. D. 48. 19. 2. 1; 48. 22. 6. 14.

[85] The *relegatio* was usually imposed for only a specified period. D. 48. 22. 4. 7. 14. 18.

[86] D. 48. 22. 7. 20-22; 48. 7. 1.

[87] D. 48. 19. 9.

[88] D. 48. 19. 8. 4; 48. 19. 36.

[89] D. 48. 19. 8. 11.

[90] Imprisonment (*carcer*) was used as a method for ensuring that a person would appear for trial, but it was not regarded as a legal penalty. See D. 48. 3. 2. pr; 3. 3.

[91] The chief aims of criminal punishment were declared to be general deterrence, rehabilitation, retribution and the satisfaction of the victim's family. Consider, e.g., D. 48. 19. 20; D. 48. 19. 28. 15; D. 48. 19. 16. 10; 48. 19. 38. 5; 50. 16. 131.

[92] See D. 48. 11. 1. pr.

[93] *Ambitus* now covered any attempt to climb faster or hold a rank longer in the imperial civil service contrary to established regulations. See C. Th. 9. 26 passim. The scope of *maiestas* encompassed offences such as coining or maintaining a private prison. See C. Th. 9. 11. 1; 9. 21. 9. and C. 9. 24. 3.

instituted for the offence of misappropriation of state property (*peculatus*).[94] Diverse offences were subsumed under the crime of sacrilege (*sacrilegium*) and these involved neglect or violation of imperial orders or enactments.[95] The concept of violence (*vis*) was also extended to cover acts of violence and various kinds of abuses committed by private individuals and state officials.[96] After the recognition of Christianity as the official religion of the empire, acts of opposition to the established religious doctrine were punished as crimes. The relevant offences included acts such as adherence to sectarian beliefs or to a dissident religious sect; the propagation of heretical doctrines; and refusal to observe religious holidays.[97] Moreover, an assortment of disabilities was imposed on renegades, pagans and Jews.[98]

Overall, criminal legislation in the later imperial age was fragmentary and often inconsistent, with little attention devoted to the subjective requirements of criminal liability such as *dolus* or *mens rea*.[99] The removal of all limitations on the emperor's power entailed the non-existence of safeguards in practice against the arbitrary exercise of power (except perhaps through the Church). It also meant no restrictions on the punishments that could be inflicted with the emperor's authority. The statement of the jurist Hermogenianus that interpretation should be used to mitigate rather than aggravate the penalties of the laws,[100] and the notion that it is better to let the guilty go unpunished than to condemn the innocent,[101] mentioned in the Digest of Justinian, meant very little in the later imperial era. In this savage and degenerate age, only the wealthy and powerful individuals who could corrupt or intimidate state officials and judges were relatively safe from arbitrary punishments.

### 4.5.1  The Court System

In the bureaucratic state of the late Empire, imperial officials exercised practically all traditional powers and functions relating to the administration of justice. Most

---

[94] C. 9. 28.

[95] C. 9. 29.

[96] In the field of criminal law, the distinction between *vis publica* and *vis privata* was fundamental but not always clear. The original distinction was probably based on whether an offence committed with violence affected direct interests of the state (*vis publica*) or those of a private person (*vis privata*). In the later imperial period, *vis publica* was generally understood to be committed by officials and *vis privata* by private persons. Both forms of *vis* constituted crimes against public order and were subject to severe punishment.

[97] Consider C. Th. 16. 2. 31. and C. 1. 3. 10.

[98] C. Th. 16. 10. 4. and C. 1. 11. 1. and 9; C. Th. 16. 9. 1. and C. 1. 10. 1; C. Th. 9. 7. 5. and C. 1. 9. 6; C. Th. 16. 5. 1. and C. 1. 5. 1; 1. 5. 20.

[99] In the sphere of criminal law, the term *dolus* was used to denote the intention of the wrongdoer to commit the offence and this presupposed his knowledge of the unlawful character of the act.

[100] D. 48. 19. 42.

[101] D. 48. 19. 5. pr.

officials had little or no legal training, and therefore were often assisted by legal advisers (*adsessores*) who had received legal education and had usually belonged to the legal profession. Moreover, it was quite common for senior officials to perform their judicial functions through delegates (*iudices dati* or *pedanei*); the latter were usually low-ranking officers and their decisions could be appealed against before the officials who appointed them. In general, the system of appeals corresponded directly to the hierarchical structure that was observed with regard to the administrative tasks performed by the various state officials.

At the lowest level of jurisdiction were the municipal courts (*curiales*), which possessed an extremely small sphere of competence. In the field of criminal law their powers were restricted to punishing minor offences and, in the case of other offences, to conducting the preliminaries of the trial that would normally proceed before the provincial governor.[102] In both criminal and civil cases, the provincial governors functioned as the regular (i.e. normally competent) judges of the first instance (*iudices ordinarii*) and, in addition, dealt with appeals against sentences passed by municipal courts.[103] According to the circumstances, appeals against the governor's decisions were managed by the *praefectus praetorio* of the prefecture or by the *vicarius* of the diocese that encompassed the province in question.[104] A further appeal from a *vicarius* to the emperor was feasible, but a judgment passed by a *praefectus praetorio* could not be contested on appeal as the latter was deemed the personal representative of the emperor.[105] Under exceptional circumstances, the *praefecti praetorio* and the *vicarii* could hear cases as judges in the first instance such as when a litigant suspected that a powerful adversary would intimidate the provincial governor. As regards Rome and Constantinople, the *praefectus urbi* was the highest judge within the city and the surrounding territory enveloped by his authority, and he heard appeals from ordinary judges officiating within these bounds. In theory, the emperor could exercise jurisdiction in all kinds of criminal or civil cases as a judge of first instance and on appeal. However, in practice he rarely tried cases in person as the nature of the imperial office during this period did not permit close contact between him and his subjects (cases submitted to him were usually managed by the *praefectus praetorio* or another state official authorized to act in the emperor's stead).

The system of courts outlined above dealt with the ordinary array of cases, whether of a criminal or civil nature. In addition to the ordinary courts, there existed

---

[102] In civil matters, these courts could only tackle cases where the amount of money at stake was trivial unless their jurisdiction was extended by agreement between the relevant parties.

[103] The primary assignment of the governors was the administration of justice as during the later Empire they did not possess military powers and the size of their assigned territories had been considerably reduced.

[104] The decisions of governors with proconsular rank were appealable only to the prefect or the emperor.

[105] In later times, a special form of appeal (*supplicatio*) against the decisions of the prefects could be submitted to the emperor. The petitioner requested the emperor for a renewed examination of a matter that normally did not permit an appeal. See C. 1. 19.

many special courts that addressed particular types of cases (usually administrative) or cases involving individuals from a particular group or class. Most of these courts had their roots in the established principle that a magistrate had administrative jurisdiction over matters connected with his departmental tasks and a disciplinary jurisdiction over his subordinates. In the fourth century AD, the sphere of competence of the special courts tended to expand at the expense of the regular courts and this provoked frequent clashes of jurisdiction. The category of special courts encompassed, for example, the court of the *rationalis* (the official who represented the public treasury in a diocese) that handled disputes relating to taxation and other fiscal matters.[106] Furthermore, the *praefectus urbi* dealt with cases involving violations of public order and breaches of building regulations. Illustrations of special jurisdictions that applied to certain categories or classes of persons included the disciplinary jurisdictions of military commanders and heads of government departments over soldiers and members of the bureaucracy respectively.[107] Members of the senatorial order fell within the exclusive jurisdiction of the *praefectus urbi* if they domiciled at Rome or Constantinople, or within the jurisdiction of their provincial governor.[108] In such cases, the decisions of provincial governors were subject to review by the emperor or the urban or praetorian prefects. Members of the clergy also enjoyed certain jurisdictional privileges in the sphere of civil law, although in criminal cases they remained subject to the jurisdiction of the secular courts. In the middle of the fourth century AD, Emperor Constantius decreed that bishops accused of criminal offences could be tried before a council of bishops with an appeal to the imperial appellate courts.[109] However, this privilege seems to have been revoked in later years.[110]

## 4.5.2   The Criminal Justice Process

After the disappearance of the standing jury courts (*quaestiones perpetuae*) in the third century AD, the *cognitio extraordinaria* emerged as the regular procedure for

---

[106] A decision issued by the court of the *rationalis* could be appealed against before the *comes sacrarum largitionum*, the minister in charge of state finances.

[107] In the fifth century AD, all crimes other than adultery committed by members of the armed forces (including officers and commanders) were not encompassed by the cognizance of the ordinary courts, but were only tried by military courts. See C. Th. 2. 1. 2.

[108] Until the time of Constantine, members of the senatorial class were deemed to be domiciled at Rome or Constantinople no matter where they actually lived. Therefore, they were regarded as falling within the jurisdiction of the prefects of the two capitals.

[109] C. Th. 16. 2. 12.

[110] See C. Th. 16. 2. 23 and 16. 11. 1. If a cleric's conduct constituted both an ecclesiastical and a secular offence, it would invoke two separate processes: disciplinary proceedings by the ecclesiastical authorities and a criminal prosecution by the secular authorities. A cleric's establishment of a sect advocating heretical doctrines is an illustration of such an offence.

criminal trials. Nevertheless, many rules of the old statutes that instituted the *quaestiones perpetuae* and clarified particular offence categories were still deemed relatively authoritative.

In most cases, criminal proceedings were set in motion by a public prosecution conducted by a judicial magistrate. Proceedings by *accusatio*,[111] where the prosecution was conducted by any competent member of the public, were still feasible.[112] However, these proceedings were now rare due to the high risks they entailed for the accuser (if the prosecution was unsuccessful the accuser faced the same punishment that the accused would have suffered, if convicted).[113] Proceedings by *cognitio* were instigated in one of three ways: (a) following a report by a minor official (e.g. a municipal officer) charged with security duties; (b) following a denunciation by the injured party or a private informer; and (c) at the initiative of a judicial magistrate. In the first case, the official who lodged an incriminating report had to appear in court to present the case against the accused. To some extent, his role corresponded to that of a private accuser in the *accusatio* proceedings. Like a private accuser, an official who laid a charge was liable to punishment if the trial did not entail the conviction of the accused; however, unlike a private accuser, he was only liable if he had initiated a false accusation knowingly and maliciously. In the second case, a private citizen informally denounced another to a judicial magistrate. The latter was obliged to act on such denunciation and to officially institute and conduct criminal proceedings against the suspect.[114] The denouncer did not play a formal role during the trial, and could not be prosecuted if the charge was unsubstantiated.[115] In the third case, an official vested with judicial functions initiated the collection of incriminating information and launched criminal charges against those detected as offenders by his agents.

In the *cognitio* proceedings, the judge at his discretion determined the date of the trial.[116] Once the trial date was established, the judge had a duty to summon the accused (this could be done either by personal notice or by edictal citation) and arraign all the witnesses required to testify in the case. In the majority of cases

---

[111] As elaborated previously, in the republican and early imperial periods the *accusatio* procedure was adopted in trials conducted before the *quaestiones perpetuae*.

[112] However, the incorporation of certain inquisitorial features substantially derogated from the presumed disinterestedness of the judge and the accusatorial nature of the proceedings. These features embraced, for example, control by the judge rather than the accuser over the questioning of the witnesses and the accused.

[113] On the other hand, the practice in the Principate period was to punish only the person who accused another in full knowledge of the latter's innocence.

[114] C. Th. 16. 5. 40. 8.

[115] Private denunciations devised as a basis for a criminal prosecution were not generally permissible – indeed, issuing such a denunciation could be punished as a crime (see C. Th. 10. 10.). However, as the gravity of the crime increased the range of available procedures widened to include the possibility of private denunciations.

[116] This was also the case in proceedings by *accusatio*, although it was customary for the judge to determine the date in consultation with the accuser.

(especially those involving offences of a serious nature), the alleged offender would be detained in a state prison[117] and could languish there for months waiting for the commencement of his trial.[118] At the hearing, the officer who reported the crime to the judicial magistrate was required to appear before the court and elaborate the matter, in a similar manner as an accuser addressed the court at the beginning of an accusatorial hearing. The remainder of the hearing also essentially corresponded to the equivalent stages of an *accusatio* trial, although the inquisitorial element was more pronounced than in the latter. On the other hand, when the prosecution was galvanised by information supplied by private denunciators or reports submitted by agents of the judicial magistrate, the hearing would essentially have comprised a purely inquisitorial interrogation of the accused and an examination of the available evidence. But the judge had the discretion to select the manner of these details. The judge was only constrained by the rules relating to the collection and submission of evidence.[119] It was recognized that a suspect could only be sentenced if the court was convinced of his culpability; if uncertainty predominated, the suspect was granted the benefit of doubt and absolved with a release from all restraints. A suspect's confession was deemed to constitute conclusive proof of guilt, and judges were not allowed to pass a death sentence unless the suspect had confessed or the witnesses were unanimous in identifying him as the wrongdoer. In these circumstances, judges were tempted to use torture in a limitless manner to extract

---

[117] Witnesses arraigned by the judge could also be secured by detention, especially in the case of witnesses destined to be examined under torture, i.e. those from the lowest strata of society, or those who were likely not to render truthful evidence of their own accord. See C. Th. 9. 37. 4.

[118] A number of imperial constitutions issued during this period were concerned with the treatment of prisoners awaiting trial. It was decreed that such prisoners (as opposed to those already convicted) had to be treated humanely (according to the perceptions of the age) – this directed, for example, that prisoners could not be manacled but only lightly chained; were granted access to the open air during daytime; not starved; and the reasons for their prolonged detention regularly investigated. However, it is doubtful whether these provisions were implemented effectively as evidenced from the recurrent references to prison malpractices in contemporary sources. Moreover, as there were always too many prisoners on remand Justinian limited the detention period to six months for a prisoner awaiting trial (or in some cases, a year) and made provision for bail. Consider, e.g., C. Th. 9. 1. 7 and 18; C. Th. 9. 3. 6. and C. 9. 4. 5; C. 9. 4. 6; C. Th. 9. 3. 1 and C. 9. 4. 1.

[119] The testimony of witnesses and the depositions of slaves were accepted as evidence only if they were factual and related to the personal experience of the witness or slave concerned. Hearsay evidence did not carry any weight, while evidence as to a person's character was permissible but accorded limited significance. The testimony of one person only was normally not admitted as proof. If there were conflicting statements before the court, their veracity was assessed by regarding the credibility of the witnesses. Congruent evidence from a number of witnesses was accorded great weight. Circumstantial evidence could probably be relied on, whether as subsidiary to other forms of evidence or as sole evidence where there were no eyewitnesses who could testify that the alleged offender actually committed the offence in question.

concordant evidence or, best of all, a confession during interrogation[120] when the accused or the witnesses belonged to the lower classes (*humiliores*).[121]

After weighing the presented evidence, the judge announced his verdict that either declared the accused guilty or absolved him of the crime. If the accused was convicted, the judge proceeded to determine the punishment to be imposed and the trial procedure ended with the passing of the sentence.[122] The law stipulated the penalties that a judge could impose. Once the judge determined that the accused's conduct conformed with the description of the relevant crime, he was obliged to impose the prescribed punishment regardless of any mitigating or aggravating circumstances.

As regards the available forms of punishment, the position was not ostensibly different from that in the later years of the Principate. However, the penalties now imposed were generally harsher than those in earlier times. The most severe punishment in Roman criminal law was the death penalty (*poena mortis*). As a rule, condemned criminals were executed in public immediately after the passing of the sentence if no appeal was lodged.[123] This usually occurred in the locality where the crime had been committed. There were four general forms of execution that the sentencing judge could impose. The most lenient of these forms was decapitation by the sword (*decollatio, capitis amputatio*). The remaining three forms of execution were the aggravated ones: garotting (*ad furcam, patibulum damnatio*), death at the stake (*vivi crematio*) and execution at the public games.[124] Other severe forms of punishment included forced labour in the mines (*ad metalla*)[125]; gladiatorial

---

[120] The decision whether or not to subject the accused or a witness to interrogation under torture vested in the judge, who also specified the method and degree of torture and where it would be performed. In principle, the judge could only order the accused's torture if the latter's guilt could not be proved by any other means and if a prima facie case against him had been established.

[121] Persons belonging to the upper classes (*honestiores*) were exempt from interrogation under torture.

[122] As already noted, in principle a person convicted of a crime could appeal to a higher court against the judge's decision. In practice, however, the right of appeal was subject to certain limitations. For example, leave to appeal might be refused by the trial judge if he was convinced, by virtue of an admission of guilt or other cogent evidence, that there was no merit in the appeal, or that the attempt to appeal was merely a dilatory manoeuvre; leave to appeal could also be refused to those whose actions had endangered public safety. Consider C. Th. 11. 36. 1; 11. 36. 4; 9. 40. 4. and C. 9. 47. 18.

[123] There was no general mandatory waiting period that had to elapse before the execution could occur. The only exception to this was when a death sentence was pronounced by the imperial court acting as a court of first instance; in this case, at least thirty days had to pass before the sentence could be executed (C. Th. 9. 40. 13). However, this limitation was not absolute as the emperor could, and often did, override this restriction.

[124] Emperor Constantine abolished death by crucifixion that was used for slaves and individuals of the lower class (*humiliores*) convicted of particularly grave crimes.

[125] In practice, this amounted to a deferred death sentence as most people succumbed to the terrible living conditions in the mines. A milder form of this punishment was *damnatio ad opus metalli* (condemnation to mine labour).

combat (*ad ludum*)[126]; forced labour in the public works (*opus publicum*) for life[127]; and deportation (*deportatio*).[128] The less severe, non-capital punishments embraced banishment without loss of citizenship (*relegatio*)[129]; forced labour in the public works for a fixed term; confiscation of property[130]; corporal punishment[131]; and fines (*multae*). Incarceration was not recognized as a regular form of punishment; as in earlier times, the sole function of a prison was to secure temporarily those persons awaiting trial, or convicted criminals anticipating the execution of a severe sentence.[132] A judge had to contemplate certain factors when selecting the form of prescribed sentence to impose (e.g. the death penalty or another capital punishment) or determining the appropriate penalty in exceptional cases where his discretion governed the sentence. The essential factors encompassed whether the convicted person had a free or servile status and, in the former case, the offender's social class. Generally, a servile status and inferior social status operated as aggravating factors.[133] On the other hand, persons with a higher rank (*honestiores*) enjoyed certain penal privileges: they were not sentenced to death by garrotting or at a public game, nor condemned to the mines or subjected to flagellation or forced labour in the

---

[126] This form of punishment was abolished in AD 399. Before this event, imperial constitutions had installed some restrictions on its imposition. A related form of punishment was *damnatio ad ludum venatorium* (a fight with wild animals), which still existed in Justinian's time.

[127] This was regarded as a less severe form of punishment than the foregoing categories, as it did not entail enslavement as a public slave but only loss of Roman citizenship. Moreover, those subjected to this sentence were not consigned to work in a high-mortality industry. Rather, they were employed in merely ignoble, debasing works, such as road building or labour in the public bakeries, the imperial weaving establishments or one of the other compulsory guild industries. See e.g. C. Th. 9. 40. 3. 5. 6; 9. 40. 7. 9; 10. 20. 9.

[128] This entailed the offender's retention of his free status accompanied by a deprivation of his Roman citizenship and banishment for life to a specific locality (usually, a small island or a desert oasis). The loss of citizenship meant the loss of all civil law rights and capacities and, in principle, the confiscation of the deportee's estate. However, in practice this was mitigated by the norm to concede all or part of the estate to his family and by the custom of granting the deportee a subsistence allowance.

[129] There were two forms of *relegatio*: *relegatio simplex* and *relegatio qualificata*. The former entailed banishment *from* a specific locality, while the latter (the more severe form) invoked banishment *to* a specific locality. Both forms of *relegatio* could be imposed for life or for only a certain period of time. The *relegatio* could be combined with additional punishments, such as the confiscation of the whole or a part of the condemned person's property.

[130] The confiscation of an offender's estate (or a part thereof) operated mainly as a subsidiary punishment that was auxiliary to the capital punishments and to *relegatio* for life.

[131] This was often imposed in cases involving minor crimes committed by slaves or by persons who were too poor to afford any fines.

[132] The conditions of imprisonment were generally appalling: convicts were kept in fetters; confined in narrow, windowless cells; never permitted into the open air; and maltreated by the prison guards. The legislative reforms initiated by Emperor Constantine to improve prison conditions related only to the treatment of prisoners awaiting trial and excluded those who had already been convicted. See C. Th. 9. 3.

[133] Slaves found guilty of grave crimes were usually sentenced to death (by one of the aggravated forms of execution), or condemned to the mines.

public works. Aggravating factors embraced transgression in office, the high incidence of the crime at issue in a particular area, and recidivism. On the other hand, the facts that the offender was youthful, a minor participant in the crime and a slave who committed the offence on the order of his master all served as mitigating factors.


### 4.5.3  Judicial Protection of the Lower Classes

The society of the late Empire was a non-egalitarian and rigidly stratified society where the mass of the common people (*humiliores*) were exposed to the arbitrariness of an all-powerful and deeply corrupt administrative apparatus that favoured the upper classes. Yet members of the lower classes were not entirely bereft of protection against the abuses of an arrogant officialdom. The *defensor civitatis* or *plebis* was one of the institutions established by the state for the redress of grievances suffered by the poor and lowly. The office first appeared in the diocese of the Oriens during the early fourth century AD and by the end of that century it had been extended throughout the whole empire.[134] The *defensores* were probably chosen initially by the citizens from among persons with a high social status (*honorati*) deemed sufficiently qualified to contest their peers' excesses, and this selection then awaited confirmation by the praetorian prefect or the emperor. These individuals were entrusted with the special duty of protecting the common people in a municipality against acts of extortion and oppression committed by the bureaucracy and the mighty landowners (*potentiores*, *possessores*). This authority enabled them, for example, to prevent torture in criminal proceedings; veto the arrest of a person suspected of a crime; and intercede against unfair fiscal exactions and enforced military service. Moreover, they were endowed with a minor jurisdiction in criminal and civil matters that was subject to an appeal to the provincial governor, and could arrest and transfer to the governor those accused of serious crimes.[135] For a phase, the *defensor* and his court were apparently successful in providing cheap and swift justice to members of the lower classes. However, in the long term the institution failed to achieve its goal of alleviating the conditions of the poor and the underprivileged. Probably the greatest difficulty was to locate, in this degenerate age, strong and upright men willing to undertake the burdens of the office and capable of resisting the pressures of the powerful. Hence, different methods for appointing holders of the said office were engaged now and then. Ultimately, the *defensor civitatis* became simply another extraordinary magistrate

---

[134] The *defensor civitatis* is the first recorded instance of what is today known under the name of ombudsman, a civil commissioner entrusted with the protection of citizens against maladministration and other acts contrary to law.

[135] The jurisdiction of the *defensor* pertaining to civil matters, although initially small, gradually expanded and attained considerable dimensions under Justinian.

and an instrument of the bureaucracy and the land-owning elite whose abuses he was originally destined to curb.

As the institution of the *defensor civitatis* proved short-lived, oppressed people increasingly sought protection from the Christian bishops whose influence in the administration of secular justice tended to intensify. From the perspective of the civilian population, the operation of the administration became increasingly oppressive and Christianity assuaged this situation. The faith embodied an egalitarian ideology that viewed all humans as equal before God and it exercised a mitigating influence in several fields on the conditions of the oppressed classes and groups. For example, bishops could frequently defend refugees who pursued sanctuary in churches, or intervene in favour of the accused or the convicted in criminal trials. Moreover, these bishops as religious heads of their towns were more effective than the *defensores* in protecting impoverished citizens against the unfair demands of imperial officials. One may declare in conclusion that during a period featuring the most lawlessness thus far in Roman history, the influence of the Church constituted an important element of civil stability and protective justice.

# Chapter 5
# The Codification of Roman Law

## 5.1 Introduction

In the later imperial era, a great problem that confronted the administration of justice was the vast and diffuse nature of the legal materials that constituted the fabric of law. The Roman imperial government was always inefficient in collecting and harmonising the enactments of emperors, the opinions of the jurists and the other legal sources recognized by the courts. The relevant records embodied material that was inconsistent with current legal practice or outdated. Further, they existed as a disordered mass scattered in archives of the central and provincial administration, as well as in the libraries of law schools and jurists. Under these conditions, it was difficult to ascertain the current state of the law. Even the central administrators and judicial magistrates had only a very imperfect knowledge of the law and precedents that were engaged as the basis of their decisions. The legal history of the late Empire is marked by the successive efforts of the imperial government to remedy this situation. The high-handed methods adopted to achieve legal certainty are characteristic of both the autocratic form of government and the totally dependent attitude and unquestioning subservience to authority that prevailed among the judges and jurists in this period.

### 5.1.1 Early Codifications

During the Principate age, imperial edicts (*edicta*) were posted in the principal towns of the empire and remained in view for a short period (probably a month). In all likelihood, the decrees (*decreta*) were not officially published but could be ascertained from the record of the case issued to the successful litigant. The rescripts (*rescripta*) were also recited in court and preserved in the court record,

© Springer International Publishing Switzerland 2015
G. Mousourakis, *Roman Law and the Origins of the Civil Law Tradition*,
DOI 10.1007/978-3-319-12268-7_5

while the mandates (*mandata*) were communicated to and retained by the officials to whom they were issued. The enactments of the emperors were thus accessible to lawyers and the general public when they were issued, but no permanent central record of imperial legislation was retained. On the other hand, private lawyers from as early as the second century AD started to compile collections of imperial constitutions. For example, we know of a collection of 13 rescripts of Septimius Severus published in AD 200, and a collection of decrees produced by the jurist Paulus in the closing years of the Principate.[1]

During the reign of Diocletian, the lack of any official collection of imperial constitutions was partly remedied by the publication of two private or 'semi-official' collections of law: the *Codex Gregorianus* and the *Codex Hermogenianus*. The former collection, published towards the end of the third century AD (probably in AD 291), contained imperial constitutions (mostly rescripts) from Hadrian (AD 117–130) up to and including Diocletian.[2] These materials were arranged by subject matter in books and titles according to the traditional scheme observed by the classical jurists in their *Digesta*, and chronologically within each title. Around the same time (probably in AD 295), Hermogenianus[3] published a supplementary collection of constitutions that were issued during the reign of Diocletian. His book was subdivided into only titles, while the constitutions it contained were arranged in chronological order. The Hermogenian Code was re-edited several times and new constitutions were added; but both this code and the preceding Gregorian Code remained as unofficial collections. On the other hand, some evidence divulges that the production of these codes was approved or authorized by Diocletian's government. This is corroborated by the fact that their authors enjoyed regular access to the archives of the imperial chancery, which suggests that they held senior positions in the imperial administration and performed their work under official supervision. The extraordinary authority that the Gregorian and Hermogenian Codes acquired after their publication is a more significant fact that distinguishes them from all private collections of legislation. The courts recognized these codes as authoritative and exhaustive records of all imperial legislation existing up to the date of their publication. Moreover, the codes were included among the principal texts of legal education and served as models for the first official law code produced in the fifth century AD on the orders of Emperor Theodosius II. As neither of the above-mentioned codes survived, information on their content is based on extracts

---

[1] Moreover, the Digest of Justinian references an early collection of rescripts (mainly of Marcus Aurelius and Lucius Verus) that formed part of Papirius Justus's *libri XX constitutionum*, a work that appeared in the late second century AD.

[2] Of the author of this collection very little is known, not even if, as is usually accepted, his name was Gregorian.

[3] He is probably identified with the Hermogenianus whose *Iuris Epitomae* was a minor source for Justinian's Digest. Hermogenianus appears to have held the office of *magister libelli* during the reign of Diocletian. In this capacity he was responsible for the framing of legislation in the emperor's name.

incorporated in subsequent compilations of law such as the *Fragmenta Vaticana*, the *Collatio* and, especially, the Code of Justinian.[4]

## 5.2 The Theodosian Code

A considerable degree of uncertainty still prevailed in legal practice as to which constitutions and opinions were authoritative, despite the existence of the Gregorian and Hermogenian Codes and various collections of juristic material. In AD 321–322 Emperor Constantine enacted a number of statutes designed to provide guidance to judicial authorities on the use of the classical literature. Nearly a century later (AD 426), the so-called 'Law of Citations' issued by Theodosius II and Valentinian III aspired to establish a veritable hierarchy for the opinions of celebrated jurists. On that basis, it installed a body of juristic opinion alongside the existing collections of imperial constitutions. However, this law apparently proved insufficient or otherwise was possibly devised merely as a provisional measure. This prompted the same emperors in AD 429 to appoint a commission of distinguished lawyers and officials to rectify the situation. First, they had to compile a collection of all the imperial constitutions produced since the time of Constantine that were still in force. The next task was to combine this new collection with the Gregorian and Hermogenian Codes and classical juristic texts to create a code that would constitute a harmonious and comprehensive statement of the law. However, the execution of this project seems to have encountered insurmountable difficulties. Finally, in AD 435 a second commission was appointed to assemble all the extant constitutions issued since the reign of Constantine into a single compendium. The principal rationale for this new project appears to have been the government's desire to enable the legal practice to access the imperial legislation, which existed in a disorganised state.[5] The commission completed their assignment within a period of 3 years. The new collection was published in AD 438 under the name *Codex Theodosianus* and acquired the force of law first in the East and, shortly afterwards, in the West.[6] It was declared that the new code would be valid "in all cases and in all

---

[4] For a reconstruction of the Gregorian and Hermogenian Codes see P. Krüger, *Collectio librorum iuris anteiustiniani* III (Berlin 1878-1927); FIRA II, pp. 653-665. And see A. Cenderelli, *Ricerche sul 'Codex Hermogenianus'* (Milan 1965); D. Liebs, *Hermogenians Epitomae* (Göttingen 1964), 23 ff.

[5] Only the constitutions issued since Constantine's era had to be collected in an authoritative, exclusive compendium as imperial legislation issued prior to this period already existed in the Gregorian and Hermogenian Codes.

[6] Some questions have been invoked as to whether the Theodosian Code was actually promulgated in the Western Roman Empire, as required for attaining formal statutory force there. In any event, it is clear that the Code was accorded full practical effect, and was also regarded as an authoritative source of law in the West. See on this B. Sirks, "From the Theodosian to the Justinian Code", *Atti dell'Academia Romanistica Costantiniana (VI Convegno Internazionale)* 1986, 275 ff.

courts and shall leave no place for any new constitution that is outside itself, except those constitutions which will be promulgated after the publication of this code."[7] The Theodosian Code was essentially an extension and continuation of the Gregorian and Hermogenian Codes that were used as its models and still engaged by the courts. Moreover, the new code did not affect the application of the Law of Citations that prescribed the weight of authority accorded to the works of classical jurists.

The Theodosian Code embodied over 3,000 constitutions from the time of Constantine (*c.* AD 312) to AD 438. The material was arranged in 16 books, each of which was divided into titles relating to specific topics. The germane parts of all the constitutions addressing a particular subject were inserted under the appropriate title in chronological order. While the code also comprised constitutions that were already abrogated by the time of compilation, it was easy to apply the rule of statutory construction whereby earlier legislation was repealed by later, inconsistent legislation, thus rendering it a simple matter to determine which constitutions represented valid law. The first five books focus on private law; books 6–8 address matters of constitutional and administrative law; criminal law is the subject of book 9; books 10–11 contain the law relating to public revenue; books 12–14 stipulate the rules governing municipalities and corporations; book 15 includes provisions pertaining to public works and games; and book 16 elaborates provisions on ecclesiastical matters. As the above description evinces, the majority of the constitutions embodied in the code are concerned with matters of public law.

The Theodosian Code has been transmitted virtually in its entirety with only some minor lacunae. Modern reconstructions are based partly on later collections, particularly the *Lex Romana Visigothorum* and the Code of Justinian, and partly on two manuscripts, one dating from the fifth century AD and the other from the sixth century AD.[8]

## 5.3  The Germanic Codes of Roman Law

We have observed that the early fifth century AD featured the gradual detachment of Western Europe from the control of imperial officials and its capture by the power of various Germanic kings. The latter did not attempt to impose their own laws and customs upon the Romans residing in their territories, nor did they adopt Roman law for their own subjects. Thus, as the Roman Empire in the West disintegrated the

---

[7] C. Th. 1. 1. 6. 3.

[8] Several reconstructions of the Theodosian Code have emerged since the sixteenth century. The most important early edition is that of Gothofredus (*Codex Theodosianus, cum perpetuis commentariis*), published in Lyons in 1665. Other editions of the Code were published by Hanel (Bonn 1837) and Th. Mommsen (Berlin 1905). Mommsen's edition (*Theodosiani libri XVI cum constitutionibus Sirmondianis*) is the one most widely used. For an English translation see C. Pharr (ed.) *The Theodosian Code and Novels and the Sirmondian Constitutions* (Princeton 1952).

once universal system of Roman law was replaced by a plurality of legal systems. The Roman part of the population continued to be governed by Roman law (*leges romanae*), while the newly settled Germanic peoples observed their own laws and customs (*leges barbarorum*). This entailed a revival of the ancient principle of the 'personality of the laws' that had fallen in abeyance after the enactment of the *constitutio Antoniniana* in AD 212: within every community, some groups would claim as their right the application of one of several existing bodies of legal rules. For the Romans in these western communities, the old forms, legal rules and statutes were still in force. The magistrates were now responsible to Germanic chiefs and administered legal justice in a familiar manner. However, the courts in this period encountered serious difficulties with the administration of justice that derived from the uncertainty regarding the content and authority of imperial and juristic law, and the general decline of legal culture in the West. To rectify this problem, some Germanic kings considered it necessary to order the compilation of legal codes containing the personal Roman law that applied to their Roman subjects. The most important codes were the *Lex Romana Visigothorum*, the *Lex Romana Burgundionum* and the *Edictum Theoderici*. Although much of the law embodied in these collections is a crude reflection of the classical system, they possess great importance for legal historians: besides depicting the state of the law and society at the dawn of the Middle Ages, they preserved several Roman legal texts that cannot be located in any of the extant Roman sources.

In AD 506, the King of the Visigoths Alaric II promulgated the *Lex Romana Visigothorum*—hence, it is also known as the Breviary of Alaric (*Breviarium Alarici*). It contains extracts from the Gregorian, Hermogenian and Theodosian Codes; a number of post-Theodosian constitutions; an abbreviated version of Gaius' Institutes (*Epitome Gai*); sections of the *Sententiae* by Paulus; and a short *responsum* of Papinianus as a conclusion. Some of the texts are accompanied by interpretations (in the form of paraphrases or explanatory notes) aimed at facilitating their understanding and application.[9] As the code was devised to replace all other sources of law, it was proclaimed that imperial constitutions and juristic opinions not included in it had no binding force in the courts of law.[10] The *Lex Romana Visigothorum* remained in force in Spain until the seventh century[11]; in

---

[9] These interpretations are clearly influenced by the so-called 'vulgar law' and were probably derived from earlier sources.

[10] The surviving copy of the Visigothic Code of Roman law is addressed to a Count (*comes*) named Timotheus and officially certified by Anianus, presumably a royal secretary. The aims of the code are proclaimed to be the correction of what seems unfair in the laws; the clearing up of the complexities which are present either in the written Roman laws or in the unwritten principles of ancient law; the removal of all abstruseness and the gathering within a single book of selected extracts from the works of earlier jurists.

[11] In the middle of the seventh century, the gradual shift from the system of personal laws to a territorial system prompted its replacement with another law book, the *Lex Visigothorum*. This was intended to apply to both the Roman and Gothic subjects of the Visigothic kingdom in Spain.

Southern France, its application prevailed (even though no longer as an official code) until the twelfth century.[12]

The *Lex Romana Burgundionum* was composed during the reign of King Gundobad of the Burgundians and was promulgated by his son Sigismund in AD 517 for use by the Roman inhabitants of his kingdom. It is based on the Gregorian, Hermogenian and Theodosian Codes; a shortened version of the Institutes of Gaius; and the *Sententiae* of Paulus. Unlike the Visigothic Code mentioned above, it does not contain any extracts from the original Roman sources. Instead, the materials are incorporated into a set of newly formulated rules that are systematically arranged and distributed over 47 titles.[13] The *Lex Romana Burgundionum* never possessed the importance or the popularity of the Visigothic Code, and apparently became obsolete soon after the Burgundian kingdom was conquered by the Franks in the middle of the sixth century.[14]

In the late fifth century, King Theodoric II (AD 453–466), ruler of the Visigothic kingdom of Southern France, enacted the *Edictum Theoderici* that was applicable to both Romans and Visigoths.[15] It has 154 titles and contains materials distilled from the *Sententiae* of Paulus; the Gregorian, Hermogenian and Theodosian Codes; and post-Theodosian legislation.[16]


## 5.4   The Codification of Justinian

### 5.4.1   *Introductory*

As we have already observed, Justinian's desire to achieve unity in law prompted his far-reaching legislative programme that was designed to transform the legal world of his realm. The imperial government had already endeavoured in the fifth century to create some order in the mass of laws claiming validity in the empire. However, the Theodosian Code as the first official codification of the law was from the outset incomplete as it ignored the important part of Roman law based on the writings of the classical jurists. Furthermore, many new imperial constitutions were issued after the enactment of that code and several constitutions it embodied became obsolete. On the other hand, the Law of Citations (AD 426) may have

---

[12] For a modern reconstruction of the Visigothic Code of Roman law see G. Hänel, *Lex Romana Visigothorum* (Lipsiae 1849, repr. 1962). See also FIRA II, 667 ff. (appendices only). And see R. Lambertini, *La codificazione di Alarico II* (Turin 1990).

[13] The order of the topics is the same as in the *Lex Condobada*, an earlier compilation issued for the Germanic part of the population.

[14] For a modern reconstruction of the *Lex Romana Burgundionum*, see R. L. De Salis, MGH, *Leges* I. 2 (Hanover 1892); and see FIRA II, 711 ff.

[15] In the past this law code was believed to have been promulgated by Theodoric the Great (AD 493-526), ruler of the Ostrogothic kingdom of Northern Italy, for his Roman subjects.

[16] See F. Bluhme (ed.), MGH, *Leges* I. 5 (Hanover 1875-1889); FIRA II, 681 ff.

provided a partial solution to the problem caused by the unwieldy mass of classical legal literature. It enhanced the chances for uniformity and predictability in judicial decision-making. Yet from the viewpoint of scientific arrangement and thoroughness, it was obviously inadequate. This situation urgently dictated the formulation of a comprehensive and authoritative statement on the entire Roman law that had legally binding force, clarified the changes induced by the post-Theodosian legislation and removed the uncertainty surrounding the content and authority of juristic works. One of Justinian's first tasks after his ascension was the production of such a statement that would replace all former statements of law in juridical literature and legislation. At the same time, he resolved to improve the quality of legal instruction by introducing an educational system based on dependable legal sources that would present the law clearly, thoroughly and systematically. A key figure in this undertaking was Justinian's legal adviser, Tribonianus, a man of exceptional talents who successively occupied the most illustrious offices in the imperial administration.[17] Significant contributions also emanated from Theophilus, professor (*antecessor*) at the law school of Constantinople, and Dorotheus and Anatolius, who taught at the law school of Beirut. As noted previously, their new insight into the operation of the classical law enabled the jurists from these two schools to enhance the standards of legal scholarship and supply the methods that made the projected legal reform possible.

## 5.4.2   The First Code

On 13 February AD 528, Justinian, by means of the *Constitutio Haec*, entrusted a ten-member commission chaired by the *quaestor sacri palatii* with the task of consolidating all the valid imperial constitutions into a single code. The commission consisted of seven senior state officials that embraced Tribonian, who was then *magister officiorum*; two distinguished advocates; and Theophilus, a professor at the law school of Constantinople. The commissioners were instructed to draft a collection of imperial enactments by drawing on the Gregorian, Hermogenian and Theodosian Codes, and on the constitutions issued between AD 438 and 529. They were empowered to delete outdated or superfluous elements from the texts,

---

[17] Tribonian was born in Pamphylia (in southwestern Asia Minor) and was probably educated at the law school of Beirut. He began practice as an advocate in the court of the praetorian prefect of the East – the most important court after that of the emperor. After the completion of the *Codex Iustinianus* in 529, he was nominated minister of justice (*quaestor sacri palatii*). However, his unpopularity during the Nika riots prompted his discharge from this office and appointment as chief of the administration (*magister officiorum*). After the publication of the first parts of Justinian's codification, he once more became minister of justice (535). As *quaestor* he drew up several new laws or novels that introduced significant reforms, especially in the field of public administration. He died in AD 546 and thereafter Justinian's legal activity showed a marked decline. See Procop. *Anecd.* 13. 12. and 20. 16-17.

eliminate contradictions and repetitions, and effect any necessary amendments to update the material. The constitutions were to be arranged systematically according to the subject matter and listed in chronological order under appropriate titles. The new collection was published on 7 April 529 under the name *Codex Iustinianus* and came into force on 16 April 529 (by virtue of the *Constitutio Summa rei publicae*). It replaced all earlier codes, and any omitted imperial enactments could not be quoted in the courts of law (with a few exceptions). As imperial constitutions were copiously issued after 529, this first code was soon outdated and replaced in 534 by a revised edition. The only surviving material from Justinian's original code (designated *Codex vetus*, the old Code) is an index discovered on a fragment of papyrus in Egypt during the early nineteenth century.[18]

### 5.4.3   The Digest or Pandects

After the completion of the first Code, Justinian directed his attention to the goal of systematising the part of the law based on the works by the classical jurists (*ius*). During their work on the Code, the compilers encountered many questions on points of law that had invoked different opinions from the classical authorities and these could not be settled under the Law of Citations. A condensation and simplification of the entire juridical literature was urgently required and, as a preparatory step, Justinian arranged the publication of a collection of 50 constitutions (the so-called *quinquaginta decisiones*) on 17 November 530. In this collection, he endeavoured to provide solutions to controversies that had arisen among the classical jurists and to abrogate obsolete legal concepts and institutions.[19]

After the Fifty Decisions, Justinian issued the *Constitutio Deo Auctore* on 15 December 530 whereby he instructed Tribonian (then minister of justice) to institute a commission of 16 members. The objective was to collect, review and present in an abridged form the entire mass of Roman law contained in the writings of the classical jurists. Tribonian selected one senior imperial official, Constantinus; two professors from the law school of Constantinople, Theophilus and Cratinus; two professors from the law school of Beirut, Dorotheus and Anatolius; and 11 distinguished advocates. The commissioners were to scrutinize and assemble extracts from the works of the old jurists who were conferred the *ius respondendi* by the emperor, and those juristic works that were recognized or relied upon by later

---

[18] *P. Oxy.* XV 1814. See B. P. Grenfell, A. S. Hunt, *The Oxyrhynchus Papyri* (London 1898). And see P. E. Pieler, *Byzantinische Rechtsliteratur* in H. Hunger, *Die hochsprachliche profane Literatur der Byzantiner*, Bd. 2 (Munich 1978), 412 ff. Consider also P. de Francisi, 'Frammento di un indice del primo Codice Giustinianeo', 3 *Aegyptus* (1922), 68-79; P. Krüger, 'Neue juristische Funde aus Agypten', 43 *SZ* (1922), 560-3.

[19] No copy of the original collection has been preserved, but its content is integrated in the new Code of 534.

authorities.[20] Next, the selected materials had to be harmonized and systematized within the limits of a single comprehensive work that comprised 50 books subdivided into titles.[21] Like the compilers of the first Code, the commissioners were granted wide discretionary powers: they were free to determine which juristic writings to incorporate; remove superfluous or obsolete institutions; resolve contradictions; and shorten or alter the texts to adapt them to contemporary requirements. The collection was to exist as a correct statement of the law at the time of its publication and the only authority in the future for jurisprudential works (and the embodied imperial laws).[22]

It was anticipated that the work would require at least 10 years for completion, yet the commission worked with amazing speed and produced the collection in only 3 years. The work, known as *Digesta* or *Pandectae*,[23] was confirmed on 16 December 533 by the *Constitutio Tanta* (in Latin) or *Dedoken* (in Greek) and came into operation on 30 December 533. From that date, only the juristic texts embodied in this work were legally binding; references to the original works were declared superfluous and the publication of commentaries on the Digest was prohibited.[24] As Justinian states in the introductory constitution, nearly 2,000

---

[20] All the juristic works had to be considered (i.e. not only those of the five jurists mentioned in the Law of Citations) on their own merits, and no special weight was accorded to the opinions of any jurist because of his personal reputation or earlier influence. Justinian stipulated that the commission must avoid inserting matter that already existed in the *Codex* and always indicate the original source of a jurist's extract.

[21] The arrangement of the materials had to adopt the divisions and subdivisions of the Commentary on the Edict.

[22] "We therefore command you to read and work upon the books dealing with Roman law, written by those learned men of old to whom the most revered emperors gave authority to compose and interpret the laws, so that the whole substance may be extracted from them, all repetition and discrepancy being as far as possible removed, and out of them one single work may be compiled, which will suffice in place of them all." *Constitutio Deo Auctore* 4.

[23] *Digesta* (from *digerere*) means 'that which has been arranged or systematised'; *Pandecta* (from the Greek phrase '*pan dehesthe*') signifies 'an all embracing work' or 'encyclopedia'.

[24] "No skilled lawyers are to presume in the future to supply any commentaries [on the Digest] and confuse with their own verbosity the brevity of the aforesaid work. . ." *Constitutio Deo Auctore* 12. Literal translations from Latin into Greek, short summaries (*indices*) and collections of parallel texts (*paratitla*) were permitted. "No one, of those who are skilled in the law at the present day or shall be hereafter, may dare to append any commentary to these laws, save only insofar as he may wish to translate them into the Greek language in the same order and sequence as those in which the Roman words are written (kata poda, as the Greeks call it); and if perhaps he prefers to make notes on difficulties in certain passages, he may also compose what are called paratitla. But we do not permit them to put forward other interpretations – or rather, perversions – of the laws, for fear lest their verbosity may cause such confusion in our legislation as to bring some discredit upon it. This happened also in the case of the commentators on the Perpetual Edict, who, although the compass of that work was moderate, extended it this way and that to diverse conclusions and drew it out to an inordinate length, in such a way as to bring almost the whole Roman legal system into confusion. If we have not put up with them, how far can vain disputes be allowed in the future? If any should presume to do such a thing, they themselves are to be made subject to a charge of fraud, and moreover their books are to be destroyed. But if, as we said before, anything should appear

books containing 3,000,000 lines were digested and reduced to 150,000 lines while 'many things and of highest importance' were altered in the process.[25] The work integrated the writings of 39 jurists that spanned a period from about 100 BC to AD 300.[26] However, some four-fifths of the work consisted of extracts from the writings by the five great jurists from the late Principate period (Ulpianus, Paulus, Papinianus, Gaius and Modestinus),[27] while the remaining 34 jurists contributed only one-fifth of the entire collection. This disparity may be explained by the fact that the works of the five classical jurists mentioned above were the most recent and widely used, and therefore the best preserved.

The Digest consists of 50 books and each is sub-divided into titles (*tituli*),[28] fragments (called *leges*) and, where necessary, sections or paragraphs, the first of which is called the *principium* (or *proemium*). In accordance with Justinian's instructions, the titles were placed, as far as possible, in the same order as in the *Codex vetus* and the *edictum perpetuum*.[29] The beginning of each fragment enumerates the name of the jurist quoted, together with the title and section of the book from which the excerpt was taken. Four numbers are thus required to identify a citation in the Digest: book, title, fragment and section (or three, if the fragment is short, or if a reference alludes to the first paragraph).[30]

An enduring question that has puzzled Romanist scholars is how the compilers of the Digest successfully completed an enormous work within such a remarkably

---

doubtful, this is to be referred by judges to the very summit of the empire and made clear by the imperial authority, to which alone it is granted both to create laws and to interpret them." *Constitutio Tanta* 21.

[25] There is some doubt as to whether these remarks should be understood literally.

[26] The earliest writers excerpted were Quintus Mucius Scaevola and Aelius Gallus. The latest was Arcadius Charisius, who apparently lived in the late third or the first half of the fourth century AD.

[27] Ulpianus presented the largest contribution (about 40 per cent of the entire collection), with Paulus in second place.

[28] With the exception of books 30, 31 and 32.

[29] In the *Constitutio Tanta* or *Dedoken* that introduced the Digest, Justinian refers to a further division of the materials into seven parts (paras 2-8). The first part, entitled '*Prota*' (Books 1-4), contains general rules relating to the administration of justice (public officials, jurisdiction, the treatment of certain categories of persons and such like); the second part (Books 5-11) is entitled *De iudiciis* and deals with real actions and judicial proceedings; contracts and personal actions is the subject-matter of the third part, entitled *De rebus* (Books 12-19); the fourth part (Books 20-27) bears the title *Umbilicus Pandectarum* and is concerned with matters such as marriage, guardianship and the rights of mortgagees; in part five (Books 28-36), various rules relating to wills, legacies and testamentary trusts are included under the heading *De testamentis*; these are followed in part 6 (Books 37-44) by rules governing the acquisition of ownership and possession of property, intestate succession, interdicts, exceptions and such like; finally, part seven (Books 45-50) covers matters such as obligations and civil injuries, local government, public works, appeals, criminal offences (included in Books 47 and 48 entitled '*libri terribiles*'), the meaning of legal terms and maxims of the law. This division seems to have been introduced mainly for instructional purposes.

[30] An example of a reference taken from the ninth book of the Digest, title 2 ("On the Aquilian Law"): D. 9. 2. 11. 2. or D. 9. 2. 24. or D. 9. 2. 13. pr.

short time. Friedrich Bluhme, a German legal historian, presented an answer to this question in the early nineteenth century and his theory (known as "*Massentheorie*") is still accepted by most scholars today.[31] Bluhme asserts that the structure of the texts within the various titles suggests that the extracted juristic writings were divided into three sections or parts ('masses'), and that each section was the subject of the work of a separate sub-committee. Bluhme refers to the first section as the 'Sabinian mass' and this consisted mainly of extracts from the commentaries of Ulpianus, Paulus and Pomponius on the *ius civile*. Its arrangement conformed with the system devised originally by the classical jurist Masurius Sabinus in his work *Libri tres iuris civilis*. The second section, known as the 'edictal mass', concentrated on the commentaries of Ulpianus and Paulus on the *edictum perpetuum* (*ad edictum*) and other closely related texts. The third section displayed a far more casuistic nature than the other two and contained juristic opinions (*quaestiones, responsa, epistulae*) of Paulus, Ulpianus, Papinianus and other jurists. Bluhme designated this part the 'Papinian mass' because of the special weight assigned to the *responsa* of Papinianus. Bluhme also distinguished a fourth, smaller section that he referred to as the 'post-Papinian' or 'appendix mass' and this embodied materials from the works of less famous writers. After the different sub-committees completed their work on each group of juristic texts, their members convened to assemble, arrange and consolidate the selected fragments into a coherent whole.[32]

When Justinian ordered the preparation of the Digest, he was concerned with preserving the substance of the classical juristic law and producing a body of law that would fulfil the needs of his own time. However, accomplishing both these objectives was an impossible enterprise. In reviewing and arranging the juridical literature, the commissioners discovered that many problems had been highly controversial among the past legal experts and remained so for centuries. Moreover, many rules and institutions were palpably antiquated and no longer functional or incompatible with contemporary legislation or with altered conceptions of equity (particularly in view of the fact that meanwhile Christian ethics had become prevalent). Such obsolete material had to be either eliminated or adapted to contemporary requirements. The changes (additions, suppressions, substitutions) to the classical texts initiated by the commissioners are known since the sixteenth century as interpolations (*interpolationes* or '*emblemata Triboniani*'). These alterations did not always attain their purpose and unavoidably obscured the meaning of

---

[31] F. Bluhme "Die Ordnung der Fragmente in den Pandektentiteln", *Zeitschrift für geschichtliche Rechtswissenschaft* 4 (1820), 257-472; also in *Labeo* 6 (1960), 50 ff. 235 ff. 368 ff.

[32] H. Peters proposed a different hypothesis on the construction of the Digest in his work "Die oströmischen Digestenkommentare und die Entstehung der Digesten" (*BerSachGW*, 1913, 65). Peters declared the existence of a work on the *ius* (a kind of 'pre-Digest') in the Eastern law schools that was assembled for instructional purposes, and relied upon as a model by the compilers of Justinian's Digest. Although this theory attracted some attention in the past, scholars now believe that it is not adequately supported by historical evidence.

the original works, and misrepresented the intentions of their authors.[33] As a result, much of the law contained in the Digest was neither the authentic law of the classical period nor an accurate statement of the law in Justinian's own day. Rather, it existed as a layered amalgam that ignored many of the post-classical changes.[34] The problem was further exacerbated by Justinian ordering a ban on any commentary addressing his codification.

As early as the sixteenth century, a perception of Roman law as a historical phenomenon evolved from the influence of the Humanist movement. Thereafter, scholars have endeavoured to detect the interpolations in the codification of Justinian to uncover the true character of classical law. The problem attracted a great deal of attention, particularly in the late nineteenth and early twentieth centuries when many scholars in Germany and Italy elaborated techniques (based largely on a linguistic analysis of the texts) for the identification of the interpolations. However, the search for the interpolations ultimately acquired a cult-like fervour that entailed great exaggeration over the nature and extent of the alterations introduced by Justinian's compilers. Nowadays, scholars recognize that not all contradictions and inconsistencies in the Digest are attributable to the codifying commission. Undoubtedly, the works relied upon originated from the classical era. However, when these materials reached the commission they had already been altered (either consciously or unconsciously) by earlier copyists and editors. In general, a text is likely to be deemed interpolated if it deviates from another version of the same text that has been transmitted to us via an earlier reliable source, such as the Vatican Fragments or the Institutes of Gaius. Moreover, texts dealing with legal concepts or institutions that are confirmed as obsolete in Justinian's time are presumably interpolated because the compilers had to adapt them to contemporary requirements. In any other case, a hypothesis of interpolation must be treated with great caution.[35]

---

[33] One should note that the texts had probably been changed to some extent in the period that preceded the Justinianic codification. This may have derived from errors during the copying of the original manuscripts, modifications initiated during the re-editing of the works by post-classical compilers and the insertion of marginal or interlinear notes into the texts.

[34] As Barry Nicholas remarks, "in seeking to preserve the greatness of the past Justinian failed to produce a practical codification which his own subjects could use, and in seeking to present the law of his own day he distorted what he was trying to preserve". *An Introduction to Roman Law* (Oxford 1962, repr. 1991), 44.

[35] The Digest frequently cites Gaius with several quotations originating from Gaius' Institutes, a work transmitted to us through a manuscript dating from the fifth century but believed to reflect the law of the classical period. Generally, if one compares the extracts contained in the Digest with the relevant sections of the Institutes there are no major changes. However, assorted passages in the former work were evidently interpolated. For example, the Institutes 98-99 elaborates: "Adoption takes place in two ways, either by the authority of the *people* or by the *imperium* of a magistrate, [such as the praetor]. By the authority of the *people* we adopt those who are *sui iuris* (independent); this kind of adoption is called adrogation, because the person who is adopting is asked (*rogatur*) whether he wishes to have the person adopted as his lawful son, the person who is adopted is asked whether he is consents to this, [and the people are asked whether they bid this be so]." This also appears in the Digest 1. 7. 2, but with certain changes: the phrases in brackets were omitted and the

The Digest was preserved for posterity in various manuscript copies that mainly derive from the eleventh century and later—the period that featured the revival of Roman law in Western Europe. The oldest manuscript dates from the sixth century (*c.* 550) and was probably one of the approximately 80 copies produced in Constantinople for use by various government departments. A note on this manuscript indicates that it was in Italy in the tenth century and it is known to have been kept in Pisa since the middle of the twelfth century (hence its alternative name *Littera Pisana*). In 1406, Pisa was captured by the Florentines and the document was transferred to Florence where it has since been stored (bearing the name of *Littera Florentina* or *Codex Florentinus*). The medieval manuscripts are almost all copies of the *Codex Florentinus*.[36] Parts of the Digest have also been conveyed to us in the Greek language through the *Basilica*, a Byzantine law code issued in the tenth century by Emperor Leo the Wise.[37]

## 5.4.4   *The Institutes*

As previously noted, an important goal of Justinian's program was to enhance the quality of legal education that had been largely haphazard, unsystematic and based on fragmentary sources. In connection with this goal, the Digest as an authoritative and comprehensive statement of juristic law had a central role in legal practice and was also designed to serve as the basis for higher instruction in the law schools. However, Justinian realized before the work was even completed that it was too extensive and complex for students to use (especially for those in their first year of

---

word 'emperor' replaced the italicized word 'people'. Furthermore, the word '*generalis*' (in general) has been inserted at the beginning. The comparison of these two passages clearly exhibits the kind of interpolation devised by the compilers of the Digest. In Gaius' era (second century AD), it was accepted that theoretically the emperor was a magistrate whose authority derived from the will of the people and that the people continued to perform all their ancient functions through their delegates. In Justinian's time, this theory was abandoned due to the transformation of the imperial power into an absolute monarchy. Moreover, in the second century AD, the praetor was still an active magistrate but in the sixth century he was merely an honorary official divested of all his traditional powers. This explains the deletion of the reference to the praetor as a magistrate with *imperium* by the compilers of the Digest. Finally, in inserting the word '*generalis*' the compilers were simply indicating their introduction of a new topic.

[36] These are known as *Litterae* or *Codices Bononienses* as they were used in the law school of Bologna, or *versio vulgata* (the 'common' or 'popular version').

[37] For a photographic copy of the *Codex Florentinus* see A. Corbino and B. Santalucia (eds), *Justiniani augusti Pandectarum Codex Florentinus* (Florence 1988). The most important early editions of the Digest embrace those of Gothofredus (1583) and Spangenberg (1776-1791). The most complete edition is that of T. Mommsen and P. Krüger, under the title *Digesta Iustiniani Augusti* (Berlin 1868-1870, repr. 1962-1963). For a shorter version, see T. Mommsen and P. Krüger, *Iustiniani Digesta* in *Corpus Iuris Civilis* I (pars 2a), 16th edn (Berlin 1954, repr. Dublin and Zurich 1973). For an English translation see A. Watson, *The Digest of Justinian* (Philadelphia 1985).

their studies). Moreover, the Institutes of Gaius that had served for centuries as an
introductory textbook was now outdated in several respects. It was requisite to
produce a textbook that would present beginners with a good foundation in the
basic principles of contemporary law before progressing to the more detailed and
weightier aspects of the legal system. In response to this need, Justinian ordered in
533 the preparation of a new official legal manual for use in the empire's law
schools. The task was entrusted to a three-member commission consisting of
Tribonian and two of the four professors engaged in the preparation of the Digest
(Theophilus from Constantinople and Dorotheus from Beirut). The commissioners
were instructed to produce a book that reflected the law of their own time, omitting
any obsolete matter and incorporating any necessary references to the earlier law.
The completed work was confirmed on 21 November 533 under the name
*Institutiones* or *Elementa* (by virtue of the *Constitutio Imperatoriam maiestatem*)
and came into force as an imperial statute, together with the Digest, on 30 December
533 (by way of the *Constitutio Tanta* or *Dedoken*).[38]

The compilers of Justinian's Institutes relied heavily on the Institutes of Gaius
(about two-thirds of the entire work consists of materials gleaned from the latter
text). They also used the *res cottidianae* ('everyday matters'), a rudimentary work
attributed to Gaius; elementary works by jurists such as Ulpianus, Paulus,
Marcianus and Florentinus; imperial constitutions (including many of Justinian's
own enactments); and any accessible parts of the Digest.

Justinian's Institutes retained Gaius' division of the subject matter into three
parts, i.e. the law relating to persons; the law relating to property; and the law
relating to actions. It also replicated his division of the work into four books.[39]
Otherwise than in Gaius' Institutes, each book is subdivided into titles and the titles
into paragraphs.[40] Unlike the Digest's presentation of the material as a collection of
extracts, the compilers of the Institutes adopted a narrative style. They sacrificed
citations and attributions, but produced a blended, continuous essay under each title

---

[38] It has been suggested that the work on the Institutes was probably divided between Dorotheus
and Theophilus, with Tribonian acting in a supervisory capacity. However, this view has been
questioned by some scholars who argue that Tribonian played a more active role in the preparation
of the book. See H. Ankum, "Gaius, Theophilus and Tribonian and the Actiones Mixtae", in
P. Stein and A.D.E. Lewis (eds), *Studies in Justinian's Institutes in Memory of J.A.C. Thomas*
(London 1983), 4 ff.

[39] Book one deals with the law of persons, except for an introductory preface on jurisprudential
matters and the sources of law; the second book explores the law of property and part of the law of
succession; book three addresses the remainder of the law of succession and the major part of the
law of obligations; and book four concerns the remaining part of the law of obligations and the law
of procedure. In book four, Gaius' discussion of the *legis actio* and the formulary procedures was
replaced by a brief description of the *cognitio extraordinaria*, the procedure used in the post-
classical period. It was followed by two titles on the duties of a judge (*de officio iudicis*) and on
criminal law (*de publicis iudiciis*).

[40] The first paragraph is the *principium* or *proemium* (pr). Thus, to identify a citation in the
Institutes one must indicate the number of the relevant book followed by the number of the title
and the paragraph (or by the abbreviation 'pr' if reference is made to the *principium*).

to increase its comprehension. On the other hand, the method of composition does not appear considerably different from that engaged by the compilers of the Digest. The provenance of the individual passages is discoverable, although creating the impression of a continuous text would have involved a different management of the extracts than that required in the preparation of the Digest. In its presentation, the Institutes are couched in the form of a dogmatic, mechanical lecture. It has much less colour and character than those of Gaius—features that may well be attributed to the largely derivative nature of the work.

Numerous manuscript copies of the Institutes were produced in Justinian's time, but none have survived.[41] We have inherited the work through various manuscripts that nearly all date from the tenth century or later. The *Codex Taurinensis* of the tenth century is the most famous of these manuscripts and it incorporates notes (*scholia*) that apparently originated from the time of Justinian. These manuscripts, combined with the text of Gaius' Institutes discovered in 1816, furnished the basis for most of the modern reconstructions of Justinian's Institutes.[42]

### 5.4.5   The Second Code

As noted previously, the Code of 529 soon became antiquated mainly due to the fresh legislation issued by Justinian subsequent to its enactment. Thus, at the beginning of 534 the preparation of a new edition was assigned to Tribonian, Dorotheus and three of the advocates who had participated in the compilation of the Digest. The commissioners were instructed to adapt the Code by inserting the new constitutions, including the 'Fifty Decisions' (*quinquaginta decisiones*) mentioned earlier. In this task, they eliminated obsolete or superfluous provisions, removed contradictions and repetitions, and filled in the gaps in the texts. It would appear that the commissioners worked with great speed as on 16th November 534 the *Constitutio Cordi* confirmed the refashioned Code under the name *Codex repetitae praelectionis* and it came into force on 29th December 534. It was declared the sole authority with respect to all imperial legislation that had been issued up to the date of its publication.[43]

The Code is divided into 12 books, each consisting of several titles dealing with specific legal topics. The titles present the relevant constitutions in chronological order; the headings of the constitutions list the names of the emperors who issued

---

[41] Only one fragment dating from the sixth century has been preserved.

[42] The earliest printed edition of the Institutes appeared in 1468 but Cujas in 1585 produced the first scholarly edition. The definitive modern edition of the Institutes is P. Krüger's *Iustiniani Institutiones, Corpus Iuris Civilis* I (pars 1a) (Berlin 1872). For English translations see J. A. C., Thomas, *The Institutes of Justinian* (Cape Town 1975); P. B. H. Birks and G. MacLeod, *Justinian's Institutes* (New York 1987). See also E. Metzger (ed.), *A Companion to Justinian's Institutes* (London 1998).

[43] Although it was provided that further enactments may be later introduced when necessary.

them and the persons to whom they were addressed; the constitutions are subdivided into paragraphs with the first labelled as the *principium*. The first book addresses jurisdictional and ecclesiastical matters; books two to eight elaborate private law; book nine pertains to criminal law; and books 10–12 deal with administrative law issues. The oldest of the approximately 4,500 enactments contained in the Code dates from the era of Hadrian (early second century AD), while the majority (approximately 1,200 constitutions) originate from the reign of Diocletian (late third/early fourth century AD). The Code incorporates around 400 enactments produced by Justinian.[44]

Shortly after the Code came into force, several manuscript copies were produced that, despite Justinian's prohibition, embodied commentaries and abbreviations of contemporary jurists. The *Codex Veronensis* is the oldest manuscript copy that has been preserved and it probably derives from the sixth or seventh century AD. It is only fragmentary and has been supplemented by reference to other manuscripts. It appears that a complete manuscript copy was never used in the early Middle Ages. In certain manuscripts the Greek constitutions have been removed, while in others the last three of the Code's 12 books have been omitted. From the ninth century AD, the text of the Code was supplemented by reference to complete manuscripts that were apparently still extant. However, the last three books were not restored to their original position until the eleventh century when together with Justinian's Institutes and the *Authenticum* (one version of Justinian's Novels) they were incorporated into a volume designated the *Volumen Parvum*. In the sixteenth century, the influence of the humanist movement prompted Cujas and Agustin to restore the Greek constitutions. Dionysius Gothofredus published the complete Code in his *Corpus Iuris Civilis* in 1583.[45]

### 5.4.6   The Novels

After the enactment of the *Codex repetitae praelectionis*, Justinian's legislative activity persevered unabated as political and social developments dictated changes in the law unforeseen by earlier legislation. As the new enactments were introduced after the Code, they acquired the name of *Novellae constitutiones* or *Novellae leges* (new laws) and this is the derivation of the modern name, 'Novels'. Before the end of Justinian's reign, over 150 such enactments were issued with the great majority

---

[44] The sources of the extracted materials included the *Codices Gregorianus, Hermogenianus* and *Theodosianus*; certain collections of post-Theodosian constitutions; Justinian's own enactments; and, to some extent, the *Codex Vetus*. The Code is written in Latin; only a very small number of constitutions (mainly issued by Justinian) appear in Greek.

[45] Modern scholars usually rely on the new complete edition (*editio maior*) of the *Codex Iustinianus* published last century by P. Krüger (Berlin 1877). For the *editio stereotypa* (*minor*) see P. Krüger, *Codex Iustinianus*, in *Corpus Iuris Civilis* II, 11th edn (Berlin 1954, repr. Dublin and Zurich 1970).

dating from the period prior to Tribonian's death in 546. Most of these enactments addressed matters of administrative and ecclesiastical law and certain areas of private law (particularly family law and the law of intestate succession).[46] In the *Constitutio Cordi* of 16th November 534, Justinian expressed his intention to compile an official collection of these later laws when a sufficient array had been issued—but he never executed this intention. Information on this material is gleaned from a few private and unofficial collections created during and after Justinian's reign, and assembled by later editors.

The oldest collection of Novels that we know of is the *Epitome Iuliani*, an abridged version of a collection of 124 constitutions dating from the period 535–555. Iulianus, a professor at the law school of Constantinople, compiled this collection during the reign of Justinian. It was probably intended for use in the recently recaptured Italy, as indicated by the fact that the Greek constitutions it contains were translated into Latin.[47]

Another work also written in Latin is the *Authenticum* (or *liber Authenticorum*), an anonymous collection of 134 constitutions originating from the period 535–536. The exact date of its publication is not ascertained—it may have been composed in the sixth century AD, but the oldest manuscript copies date from the eleventh century. Irnerius, a leading representative of the School of the Glossators (11–13th cent.), regarded it as an authentic, official collection of Novels ordered by Justinian for use in Italy (hence its designation as *Authenticum*). The prevalent view today is that Irnerius was mistaken and that it was likely designed as a teaching aid for use in the law schools of the empire. The collection embodies the Latin Novels in their original text and the Greek ones in a faulty Latin translation.[48]

The most extensive collection of Novels is the so-called *Collectio Graeca*, consisting of 168 constitutions issued in Greek by Justinian and his successors Justin II (565–578) and Tiberius II (578–582).[49] It was published after 575, probably during the reign of Tiberius II, and is accessible to us through two

---

[46] The majority of Justinian's new laws were issued in Greek, the language of business in the East. Some laws were composed in Greek and Latin, and some only in Latin (mainly those addressed to the western provinces of the empire or containing supplementary provisions to earlier enactments that had been drafted in Latin).

[47] The oldest manuscript copies of this work date from the late seventh or early eighth century. For a modern reconstruction of Julian's collection see G. Hänel, *Iuliani Epitome Latina Novellarum Iustiniani* (Leipzig 1873).

[48] For a modern edition of this collection see G. E. Heimach, *Authenticum, Novellarum constitutionum Iustiniani versio vulgata*, I-II, (Leipzig 1846-1851). And see P. E. Pieler, *Byzantinische Rechtsliteratur*, in H. Hunger, *Die hochsprachliche profane Literatur der Byzantiner*, Bd. 2 (Munich 1978), 409 ff. 425 ff. N. van der Wal and J. H. A. Lokin, *Historiae iuris graeco-romani delineatio. Les sources du droit byzantin de 300 a 1453* (Groningen 1985), 37-38.

[49] Four constitutions of Justin II and three of Tiberius II were incorporated into this collection. It also contains some further texts that are not imperial constitutions but decrees of *praefecti praetorio*.

manuscripts originating from the thirteenth and fourteenth centuries.[50] Although the *Collectio Graeca* was prevalently used in the Byzantine East,[51] it was apparently unknown in the West until the fifteenth century. It was introduced in Western Europe by Byzantine scholars who fled to Italy shortly before and after the fall of Constantinople to the Ottoman Turks (1453) and was brought to light by the humanist scholars of the fifteenth and sixteenth centuries.[52]


### 5.4.7  *The* Corpus Iuris Civilis

Justinian's legislative work is mainly comprised of the Code (*Codex repetitae praelectionis*), the Digest, the Institutes and the Novels. All four compilations together constitute the material known as *Corpus Iuris Civilis*. The latter term did not originate in Justinian's time[53]; it was invented by Dionysius Godofredus (1549–1622), who produced in 1583 the first scholarly edition of Justinian's codification that remained the standard edition until the nineteenth century.[54]


### 5.4.8  *Concluding Note*

The outstanding feature of Justinian's reign was its focus on the idea of unity—unity in territory, religion and law. In this respect, the legal codes compiled under his authority should be viewed as interconnected parts of an organic whole. Recognizing the role of law as a tool of integration, Justinian aspired to produce a comprehensive, systematic and authoritative statement of the existing law based on the legal inheritance of the classical period. It was designed to replace all former statements of law in both legislation and jurisprudence. This goal is particularly

---

[50] In one of these manuscripts (retained in Venice) there is an appendix containing thirteen edicts of Justinian (two of these are also traced to the other manuscript); these thirteen enactments are sometimes regarded as forming a separate collection referred to as *Edicta Iustiniani*.

[51] It was one of the sources used by the compilers of the *Basilica*, the most important Byzantine law code.

[52] The *Collectio Graeca* furnished the basis for the modern standard edition of the Novels produced by R. Schöll and G. Kroll in 1895 (in this edition the Novels are divided into chapters and paragraphs). See *Novellae, Corpus Iuris Civilis* III, 10th edn (Berlin 1972). For the Novels that survived in various papyri and inscriptions see M. Amelotti and L. Migliardi Zingale, *Le costituzioni Giustinianee nei papiri e nelle epigrafi* (Milan 1985).

[53] In the Code, Justinian refers to his work as pertaining to the 'whole body of law' ('*in omni corpore iuris*'). C. 5. 13. 1. pr.

[54] The modern standard edition is that of T. Mommsen, P. Krüger, R. Schöll and W. Kroll, consisting of three volumes: Volume One contains the Institutes (ed. Krüger) and the Digest (ed. Mommsen, revised Krüger); Volume Two elaborates the Code (ed. Krüger); and Volume Three embodies the Novels (ed. Schöll and Kroll).

evident in the Digest, the largest and definitely the most important part of his codification. The accomplished work fell short of this objective, and this is unsurprising owing to the magnitude of the task and the swift completion of the work. Perhaps a more important rationale for this shortcoming was the general intellectual climate of the age—an intellectual climate that was unfavourable to the kind of creative legal thinking that constitutes the hallmark of the classical age.

From the viewpoint of legal history, Justinian marks the end of the ancient world. Compared to the achievements of the classical period, his legislation may perhaps be regarded as the product of an era of decay. Yet Justinian did succeed in assembling and preserving most of the Roman legal heritage for posterity—an immense body of legal materials spanning hundreds of years of legal development. But his work was not a mere compendium of the Roman legal experience, nor a mere revision of existing law. The Code and the Novels contained a great deal of reformatory legislation that impressed almost every branch of the law. The immediate use of Justinian's legislation was hindered by its continued employment of Latin and its complexity. Both these problems were addressed in the law schools, for which the emperor had provided a detailed curriculum. Thus, in practice, the courses offered aimed first at facilitating linguistic understanding and, subsequently, at legal construction. This led to the emergence of an extensive literature consisting of translations, summaries and commentaries in the form of lecture notes or separate treatises.[55] In the course of time, the various Greek renderings of the Latin texts replaced the original works, although an official translation was not produced until the publication of the *Basilica* in the early tenth century.[56]

The influence of the Justinianic codification has been tremendous. In the Byzantine East, it prevailed as a basic document for the further evolution of the law until the fall of the empire in the fifteenth century. In Western Europe, it remained forgotten for a long period but was rediscovered in the eleventh century. Initially treated as the object of academic study, it later experienced a far-reaching reception—a reintegration as valid law that led to its becoming the common foundation upon which the civil law systems of the Continental Europe were built. As a historical source, Justinian's Corpus comprehensively depicts the way that Roman law and legal thinking evolved from the first century BC until the sixth century AD. It also reveals a great deal on the state of the law and society at the dawn of the Middle Ages.

---

[55] One of the best known examples is the 'paraphrase' of Justinian's Institutes by Theophilos.

[56] See relevant discussion in Chap. 6 below.

# Chapter 6
# Roman Law and Byzantine Imperial Legislation

## 6.1 The Historical Context of Byzantine Law

As observed in Chap. 1, the end of the fourth century featured a virtual split of the Roman Empire into two states (even though contemporaries did not regard this as a formal division). After a long period marked by economic and cultural decay, foreign invasions and internal strife, the Western Empire finally collapsed in AD 476 when the last emperor of the West was overthrown by his German mercenaries. The loss of the western provinces transferred the centre of gravity in the empire from the Latin to the Greek element and accelerated the transformation of the Eastern Empire into the medieval Byzantine Empire. Byzantium inherited from Rome a great deal of her political, social and cultural institutions. Roman law remained in force as a living system and the concept of *imperium Romanum* (now in the form of *imperium Christianum*) furnished the basis of all Byzantine political theory. Though the elements of continuity between the Byzantine world and the world of antiquity are clear and undeniable, so too are the differences. Byzantine civilization was a new cultural synthesis based on the classical traditions of antiquity infused with important new elements introduced by the upheavals of the later imperial era and by the rise of Christianity. Justinian surpassed other rulers as he proactively established the finished forms and set the tone of the Byzantine society. The distinctive features of the emerging Byzantine culture are clearly manifest in his political, religious and artistic programs. Although his legislation displays classical leanings, it also naturally shows traces of Greek and Eastern influences.

As already noted, Justinian executed his schemes to reconquer the provinces lost to invaders. His reconquest of the West was a fleeting achievement that shattered the empire economically and militarily, contributing further to the weakness arising from sectarian and cultural diversity. After his death, the empire quickly lost its briefly regained strength and the very existence of the Byzantine state was threatened by internal disruptions, economic decay and foreign invasions. As the empire's defences crumbled, the Visigoths regained control of Spain and another Germanic

© Springer International Publishing Switzerland 2015
G. Mousourakis, *Roman Law and the Origins of the Civil Law Tradition*,
DOI 10.1007/978-3-319-12268-7_6

tribe, the Lombards, invaded Italy from the North conquering most of the peninsula. At the same time, Persian armies advanced through the eastern provinces while the Slavs and Avars besieged the Balkans. In 627, the capable Emperor Heraclius launched a campaign that finally succeeded in stemming the Persian tide and expelling the Slavic assaults. The Moslem conquests then ensued around 630 that entailed the Arab capture of Egypt, Syria and a large part of Asia Minor. But as the imperial boundaries receded, retrenchment produced a comparative strengthening of the state and the Byzantine Empire acquired the homogeneity that the policies of Justinian had failed to produce. This occurred due to the new borders corresponding more closely with ethnic and religious lines, as the inhabitants of the empire were now largely Greek-speaking and Orthodox Christian. During these years, the empire fully entered its Byzantine period embracing the Greek language and displaying a deep orientalisation with Christianity engrained in its thought and ethos.

The Arab threat was held in check and the empire entered a period of recovery in the early eighth century during the reign of Leo III the Isaurian (717–740). Leo strengthened imperial authority, reorganized the government and the law, and introduced measures aimed at stimulating commerce and industry. However, the considerable benefits the empire derived from his rule were to some extent negated by the great iconoclastic controversy—the quarrel over the admissibility of images in religious art—that he initiated and had consumed Byzantine society for more than a century. The recovery from the crisis of the seventh century and the resultant consolidation in the eighth century produced a strengthened empire that attained new heights during the Macedonian dynasty (867–1057). During this period, the internal organization of the Byzantine state was strong enough for the emperors to embark upon a program of territorial expansion. By the early eleventh century, the empire had been cleared of foreign enemies and its boundaries stretched from the Danube to Crete and from Southern Italy to Syria. The peace and prosperity that followed served as a powerful stimulus to art, literature and educational activity in the capital and the provinces.

However, both the Macedonian dynasty and the ensuing prosperity disappeared within merely half a century after the death of Basil II (976–1025), the last great Macedonian emperor. The cause of the decline was a remarkable confluence of internal ills that exhausted the body of the empire as it endured external attacks from powerful new foes (such as the Seljuk Turks and the Normans). Probably the most virulent of these illnesses was the strife between the military establishment and the imperial bureaucracy. The successes of the Byzantine military machine in the tenth and eleventh centuries bred a great arrogance in the military class and an ambition to overthrow the hegemony of the bureaucrats within the government. Basil II restrained these ambitions through military action and persecution[1]; but he was succeeded by weak rulers who were unable to control the army, and the

---

[1] One of the principal concerns of tenth-century imperial legislation was that land and fiscal resources of the state should be kept out of the hands of the predatory 'powerful' – usually Anatolian aristocratic landowners. The power of these families was broken when Basil II defeated the two major eastern aristocrats, Bardas Skleros and Bardas Phokas, in 989, and then issued the last great anti-powerful novel in 996.

prolonged struggle between the generals and civil officials undermined the empire's strength at a critical period. At the same time, a growing economic crisis provoked by a decline in state revenues (largely due to the abandonment of arable land in the provinces) compounded the empire's difficulties. In spite of a limited recovery under Alexius I Comnenus (1081–1118), the ills of Byzantium so weakened the empire that its disintegration was virtually inevitable at the end of the twelfth century and thereupon Constantinople fell to the forces of the Fourth Crusade in 1204. Although the capital was recaptured by the Byzantines and the empire was restored about half a century later (1261), the political splintering of the Byzantine world prompted by the Latin conquest hastened the final collapse.

The fourteenth and fifteenth centuries featured the reign of the Palaeologan emperors (1261–1453) and an empire ravaged by dynastic competition, social struggles and religious strife. These adverse events played into the hands of the Ottoman Turks who pursued the expansion of their territory. In spite of the civil wars and military disasters, the Palaeologan period witnessed a last great flowering of literary and artistic activity accompanied by a revival of interest in classical studies. The end of this phase transpired in the spring of 1453. After a heroic but hopeless defence, Constantinople was captured by the Ottoman Turks who had already overrun most of the empire's narrow footholds in the Balkans and Asia Minor. During this period, a large number of Byzantine scholars migrated to Western Europe (especially to Italy) conveying important records of the Greco-Roman inheritance in art, philosophy, literature and law. A great deal of the classical knowledge preserved by Byzantium was thus transmitted to the West and it imparted a fresh impetus to the progress of the so-called Italian Renaissance.

## 6.2 Sources of Byzantine Law

It is important to note at the outset that the Byzantines did not recognize a separation between Church and state and, consequently, there was no strict distinction between secular and ecclesiastical legislative authority and jurisdiction. According to Byzantine legal theory, secular and canon law constituted in essence a single legal order: the canons of the Church were received and incorporated into the law of the state; at the same time, the Church gave imperial legislation a 'canonical character' not only by adjusting its own law to the law of the state but also by receiving ecclesiastical law created by imperial authority as its own or by resorting to such law in order to regulate its own affairs. After all, the emperor was the only officially recognized 'universal' legislative authority, even for matters of the Church, after the end of the period of the Ecumenical Councils in the East.

The nucleus of Church law was formed by the decisions (*kanones*) promulgated at Church councils, which have been preserved in a great variety of collections.[2] A

---

[2] It should be noted here that the Church never enacted a comprehensive and authoritative *corpus iuris canonici*.

special type of work are the so-called nomocanons (*nomokanones*), a term alluding to the fact that Church and state were inextricably bound up with one another. The emperor could intervene in the affairs of the Church and vice versa, with the result that both Church and state might have issued legislation on a particular problem, so that both *kanones* and statutes were relevant. From the end of the seventh century the role of the *kanon* in the development of canon law was taken over by the decisions of the patriarch of Constantinople and the authoritative commentary on the existing body of canon law. Although canon legislation did not restrict itself to purely ecclesiastical matters, and the Church courts increasingly concerned themselves with issues of civil law, civil legislation covered a much broader field. In the following paragraphs the emphasis will therefore be on the sources of civil law and in particular the enactments of the emperors, the chief source of law during the Byzantine era.

Until the twelfth century Byzantine imperial legislation was similar in form to the imperial legislation of the Justinianic period[3] and enactments of a general character (*leges generales*) in the form of Novels (*novellae constitutiones* or *nearai diataxeis*) continued to be issued after the manner of the edicts of the Roman emperors.[4] A general law was preceded by a preamble (*praefatio*), in which reference was made to the position of the emperor as God's representative on earth, supreme lawgiver and protector of his people; this was followed by the description of the situation which the law aimed to rectify (*narratio*), the main text of the law (*dispositio*), and the conclusion; the latter contained the penalties (*sanctiones*) which the violation of the law entailed and prescribed the scope of the law and the manner of its publication. Similar to the earlier *mandata* were the *diatyposes*, internal directions given by the emperor to officials in his service (especially to provincial authorities). The earlier *rescripta* were replaced by the *lyses*, answers given by the emperors to inquiries of officials on matters of administrative law, and the *semeioses*, responses of the emperors to petitions concerning matters of civil or ecclesiastical law. From the twelfth century the term *chrysovoullos logos* was used to denote an imperial enactment of a general character, whilst the *lyses* and the *semeioses* were superseded by the *prostagmata* or *horismoi*.[5] The majority of the imperial laws were concerned with public administration and matters of socio-economic policy. Moreover, a number of laws were enacted which introduced innovations in the fields of criminal and family law. In general, Byzantine imperial legislation was 'humanitarian' in character, aiming to

---

[3] From the early sixth century, imperial laws were no longer issued in Latin but in Greek. However, Latin continued to play a part in public administration as well as in the teaching of law until the twelfth century.

[4] One of the last imperial edicts expressly referred to as a *neara* was issued by Emperor Manuel I Comnenus in 1166. See Zepos I. and Zepos P., *Ius Graecoromanum* (IGR) I (Athens 1931, repr. Aalen 1962), Coll. IV, Nov. LXX.

[5] It should be noted here that there is a wide variety in the ways in which imperial laws are described in the sources and so it is only after a careful study of Byzantine history, including diplomatic history, that it would be possible for one to come up with a definite list.

protect those whom it considered weak against those whom it considered strong,[6] and greatly influenced by Christian ethical principles. At the same time it continued the move away from formalism, although this move was accompanied by a decline in technique.

During the Byzantine era custom continued to play a part as a secondary source of law. Despite the general reluctance of Justinian and subsequent emperors to recognise the validity of customary law, numerous customary norms found their way into various imperial enactments and official compilations of the law. Some of these norms had their origin in Greek and Hellenistic institutions of much earlier ages; others were formed in later years, especially after the twelfth century, and reflect the influence of trade practices introduced into Byzantium by the Venetians and other western powers.

## 6.2.1  Legal Development from the End of Justinian's Reign to the Accession of Basil I the Macedonian

In the years following the publication of Justinian's law books, Byzantine legal science flourished. This notably occurred at the two outstanding places of legal learning, the law schools of Constantinople and Beirut (Justinian allowed only these two schools and the law school of Rome to resume under his new program of legal education). As previously observed, Justinian proclaimed that the right to interpret the law pertained only to the emperor[7] and thus he forbade all commentary on his legislation under the threat of punishment. He had only endorsed the composition of summaries of contents (*indices*) and literal (*kata podas*) translations of the Latin texts into Greek. As Justinian declared, the purpose of this prohibition was to protect his legislation from the uncertainty that could arise from disputes as to the meaning of the legal norms it contained.[8] But this prohibition soon fell into abeyance and manuscripts began to circulate containing summaries, commentaries and interpretations of Justinian's texts as well as treatises on individual topics. Most of these works were composed by jurists who taught at the law schools in the East. The most distinguished of these law professors (*antecessores*) embraced Theophilus from the school of Constantinople, and Dorotheus and Anatolius from the school of Beirut. Other notable jurists of the same period were Thalelaeus, Cobidas, Stephanus and Iulianus. Theophilus produced a Greek paraphrase of Justinian's

---

[6] 'Humanity', as conceived by Greek philosophers and construed in the light of Christian religious ethics, was traditionally regarded as a fundamental principle from which all the duties of the imperial office were derived. It furnished an important basis of the legislative activity of the emperor, whose chief aims were supposed to be the accomplishment of justice and the protection of his subjects. It also served as a restraining force, in the sense that the emperor's actions were always kept within certain limits by public opinion.

[7] *Const. Tanta* or *Dedoken* 21; *const. Deo auctore* 12.

[8] *Const. Tanta* or *Dedoken* 21.

Institutes based on an earlier version of Gaius's Institutes that differed to some extent from that used by Justinian's drafters. Theophilus's paraphrase played an important part in the development of Byzantine law and was the first work on Roman law in Greek that was published in Western Europe (1533).[9] We have obtained this work through various manuscripts accompanied by the comments of other contemporary jurists. Fragments of other juristic works of the same period have survived in the form of commentaries incorporated in later Byzantine compilations. These include a commentary on the Digest by Stephanus, a professor from the law school of Beirut; an extensive interpretation of the Code by Thalelaeus, who also taught at the Beirut school; a translation of the Code and accompanying commentary by Anatolius; and an abridgment of the same work by Stephanus. Abridgments of Justinian's Novels were produced by Iulianus, a professor at the law school of Constantinople, and other jurists. In the course of time, the works of the Byzantine scholars largely replaced the original texts of Justinian's codification (whose Latin language made their use very difficult in the Greek-speaking East). Byzantine compilers and commentators in later eras relied upon these works as the chief sources of legal materials.

In the early post-Justinianic period, Byzantine jurisprudence entered a period of decay accompanied by a sharp fall in the standards of legal education. The precise length of time the law schools of Constantinople and Beirut remained open is not known, but it appears that they had probably closed by the end of the sixth century. As the law schools fell into decline, the teaching of law was assumed by teachers of a new kind who were members of professional associations of advocates. Unlike the earlier *antecessores* dedicated to the theoretical study of the Justinianic codification, these new teachers (known as scholastics) were primarily concerned with the legal practice of their own day and its needs. Their teaching was based chiefly on Greek translations of the Institutes and on summaries of the Novels (the part of Justinian's legislative work most relevant to current legal practice), whilst very little attention was paid to the Code and the Digest. A tendency towards simplification and the clarification of all legal subtleties is visible in the surviving works of this period. These include two abridgments of the Novels by Athanasius and Theodorus of Hermopolis, a summary of the Digest by an unknown author (designated in later Byzantine sources as Enantiophanes)[10] and three monographs on special subjects.[11] Theodorus of Hermopolis also produced a summary of Justinian's Code that is revealed from several quotations included in later compilations of law (esp. the *Basilica*).

---

[9] See C. Ferrini, *Institutionum Graeca Paraphrasis Theophilo vulgo tributa*, 2 vols. (Milan & Berlin 1884, 1897).

[10] The name is derived from the title of the relevant work: *Peri enantiophanon* – a Greek phrase meaning 'about what seems to be contradictory'. In this work the author sought to demonstrate that seemingly contradictory passages in Justinian's Digest can be reconciled with each other.

[11] Another work of this period was the *Rhopai*, a collection of excerpts of all passages of Justinian's legislation in Greek referring to the consequences that the passage of prescribed periods of time has had on the substance of law. See F. Sitzia, *Le Rhopai* (Naples 1984).

Of the imperial legislation enacted in the period under consideration only a very small number of novels promulgated by Justin II (565–578), Tiberius II (578–582) and Heraclius (610–641) have been preserved. They are concerned, for the most part, with matters of public, ecclesiastical and private law (especially the law of marriage). The legislation of Tiberius reflects an attempt on the part of the government to curb the excesses of the powerful and improve the economic situation of the small landholders and free labourers. The four novels that have come down to us from Heraclius's reign (dated from the years 612, 617, 619 and 629) deal with matters relating to the organization of the Eastern Church, including the *privilegium fori*. These enactments are the last manifestations of lawgiving in the Justinianic tradition, but, in comparison with Justinian's work, can hardly be regarded as being of far-reaching significance; rather, they represent an interference on the part of the emperor in matters that had been brought to his attention. This is unsurprising in light of the situation the empire found itself in during this period: the wars against the Avars, Persians and Arabs all took a heavy toll and, by the end of Heraclius's reign many eastern provinces had been lost. Although the turmoil the empire was facing is not the only reason why legislation faded into the background, it is clear that the crisis and struggle for survival demanded different priorities.

By the middle of the seventh century, the production of legal works had ceased. Moreover, the disruption of official communications between the capital and the provinces by war undermined the government's ability to ensure the uniform application of the law throughout the empire. As a result, local custom began to play a prominent role as a source of social regulation. The situation was exacerbated further by the fact that Justinian's legislation was written in a language that was foreign in the empire and embodied concepts that both the people and those involved in the administration of justice found difficult to understand. Under these conditions, lawyers and imperial officials found it increasingly difficult to discover the exact state of the law. This prompted the urgent need to introduce a new legislative work that would adapt the Roman law of Justinian to usages actually observed by the inhabitants of the empire and clarify the applicable law in a simple and systematic way. These were the objectives of the compilers of the *Ecloga Legum*, the new legal code enacted in the first half of the eighth century. The enactment of this code attests to the fact that, despite the decline of legal education and scarcity of legal literature, the ideological force of Roman law as a symbol of the state remained unaffected.[12]

---

[12] See on this J. F. Haldon, *Byzantium in the Seventh Century: the Transformation of a Culture* (Cambridge 1990), 279. It should be noted that with the exception of the *Ecloga* and two Novels of Empress Irene promulgated in the 790s, there is virtually no surviving imperial legislation between the closing years of Heraklius' reign and the early years of the Macedonian Dynasty. This does not mean, however, that the emperors of this period did not promulgate any laws. Rather, the legislative forms they employed were different and had a specific and limited purpose (for instance, imperial orders or *prostagmata* were issued instead of *novellae*). Moreover, the scarcity of legislation probably also suggests that there was little or no need for the emperors to enact new laws; they only needed to ensure compliance with the inherited legislation of Justinian.

The *Ecloga Legum* (Selection of Laws) was published in 741 under the authority of Emperor Leo III the Isaurian (717–741) and his son and co-Emperor Constantine V (741–775). A three-member commission headed by the quaestor Nicetas prepared this material. Written in Greek, the work consists of a preface and 18 titles that address the law of marriage, succession, tutelage, contracts and crimes. The preamble declares that the work is based on a selection of laws derived from the Institutes, the Digest, the Code and the Novels of Justinian that were modified, in accordance with Christian ideas, in the direction of greater humanity.[13] As this suggests, the purpose of the *Ecloga* was not to replace the codification of Justinian but to render the embodied law more comprehensible in terms of language and spirit for those involved in the administration of justice (especially in the provinces where the texts of Justinian were hard to find). However, its drafters apparently did not rely on the original texts of the Justinianic codification but on the Greek translations, abridgments and commentaries that had meanwhile replaced Justinian's original texts. Moreover, the *Ecloga* incorporated several legislative enactments issued by emperors of the post-Justinianic era and introduced important innovations reflecting Greek and other eastern influences.[14] In general, the work is characterized by its simplicity and by the special emphasis it attaches to Christian and humanitarian principles. In criminal law the influence of these principles is reflected in the restrictions imposed on the application of the death penalty.[15] Furthermore, the new code introduced more precision and a degree of individualization in the application of punishment, and put some limits to the inequality before the law.[16] It appears that the *Ecloga* was significantly influenced by the

---

[13] In the preamble it is stated that the purpose of law, as a device given by God himself, is to enable men to live by God's word and commandments. God created man and gave him the freedom to determine his own fate. But since man is not always able to exercise that freedom responsibly, God vested in the emperor the authority to follow in the footsteps of the apostle Peter and shepherd the human flock. God gave the law to the emperor for this purpose. As this suggests, the ultimate purpose of the law is to serve as a tool for creating the ideal Christian state. The law derives its force from the authority of the emperor, and that authority is based directly on God's will.

[14] These influences are reflected in, among other things, the exercise of *patria potestas* by the father and mother conjointly; the requirement that both parents consent to the marriage of their children; the right of the surviving party in a marriage to the property of the deceased spouse, their two estates being considered to have become one by the marriage; the absence of the distinction between *tutela* and *cura*; and the rules regulating disinheritance. For a closer look at the character and contents of the Isaurian law book see L. Burgmann, *Ecloga. Das Gesetzbuch Leons III und Konstantinos V* (Frankfurt a. M. 1983). And see L. Burgmann, *Ecloga*, in *The Oxford Dictionary of Byzantium* (Oxford and New York 1991).

[15] At the same time, the recognition of the penalty of mutilation, which was introduced as a form of punishment for crimes that in the past entailed the death penalty, reflects the strong influence of oriental practices on Byzantine criminal law.

[16] Some of the principles of the Byzantine theory of criminal law may be gleaned from various juridical and literary sources, in particular legislative enactments penalizing criminal behaviour. The starting-point was personal guilt, which presupposed the offender to have been capable of understanding what he did. Thus, in principle, young children and the mentally ill could not be held criminally liable. Guilt and the form of punishment were determined by the judge, but the

canons of the Council in Trullo or Quinisext Council of 691,[17] especially in the area
of the law of marriage.[18] However, as the work fell short of addressing all the
practical needs of legal life, attempts were made to fill the gaps in the legislation
primarily through resort to Justinian's *corpus*. In this way, a private manual closely
connected with the *Ecloga* was produced, which is now known as *appendix
Eclogae*, since it is usually found in the same manuscripts with the *Ecloga*.[19]

During the age of the Isaurian emperors, there also emerged three unofficial
compilations dealing with special branches of the law: the Military Code, the Rural
or Farmers' Code and the Rhodian Maritime Code. The Military Code consists
largely of penal provisions aimed at securing discipline in the army. The Rural
Code is believed to have originated in the provinces and was probably based on the
legislation of Justinian and other early sources. It contains provisions of a punitive
character intended to protect small farmers and tenants against exploitation. In the
seventh century, the concentration of land in the hands of a few feudal lords entailed
the gradual disintegration of small-scale land ownership and deterioration in the
living conditions of the rural population. One of the objectives of the Isaurian
emperors was to curb the power of the great landlords and to reorganize the rural
economy to the advantage of peasant communities. The Rhodian Maritime Code
embodies the rules of the customary law of the sea that applied in the East between
the sixth and eighth centuries. This compilation was widely used throughout the

---

privileged (*honestiores*) and common people (*humiliores*) were not punished in the same way.
Even after the enactment of the *Ecloga*, judges in practice had considerable freedom in prescribing
the form and amount of punishment. The list of punishments included the death penalty, loss of
freedom, corporal punishments (such as mutilation, beating and flogging), exile, the confiscation
of property, infamy and various civil disabilities (such as loss of eligibility for public service). In
some cases retaliation in kind was prescribed. Imprisonment was not regarded as a form of
criminal punishment, although this does not mean that it was never used. It should be noted
that, in addition to the public criminal law of the Byzantine state, the Church had its own criminal
law, although the boundaries between the two were not always clear. The penalties used by the
Church included excommunication and, for clerics, deposition from and suspension of office.

[17] So called because it was held in a chamber (in *trullo*), or because it completed the work of the
fifth and sixth Councils of 554 and 681. This Council produced the last extensive conciliar
legislation of the Orthodox Church, including a large number of canons addressing practical
problems caused by the seventh century crisis. However, it was some time before its canons
were received into the standard collections, such as the *Nomocanon of the Fourteen Titles* (*c*. 620).

[18] Canon 54 of the Quinisext Council expanded the impediments to marriage that were provided
for in the legislation of Justinian with respect to both blood relations and relations through
marriage. The *Ecloga* recognized these impediments and expanded them further, introducing
grave penalties against transgressors (besides the dissolution of the illegal marriage). Furthermore,
the *Ecloga* repeated the impediment due to a spiritual relationship (through baptism), which the
Quinisext Council introduced in canon 53. The influence of the Council is also evident in the penal
regulation of prostitution, bigamy and the abduction and seduction of nuns and other women
dedicated to God.

[19] The *appendix* comprises a large number of legal rules derived from various sources based
(directly or indirectly) on the legislation of Justinian. The rules are divided into small groups and,
for the most part, are concerned with Church matters, but with a clear orientation towards
criminal law.

Mediterranean during the Middle Ages and furnished the basis for the further development of the law governing maritime trade.[20]

The seventh century is marked by an important development: the growth of canon law and ecclesiastical jurisdiction at the expense of their secular counterparts. This appears to have been a natural outcome of the conditions of the times. The crisis of the empire hindered the regular activity of the secular judicial authorities especially in the provinces, where the pressure of external enemies was most acutely felt. Bishops and other ecclesiastical authorities must have been under pressure too, but their activities were less directly connected with the Byzantine political and military administration and were supported by orthodox belief. Under these circumstances, it is unsurprising that formal and informal ecclesiastical jurisdiction increasingly took over the role of the secular courts—a development that enhanced the prestige of the Church and its formal or informal law-making functions. One might say that canon law to some extent filled the void left by secular law. At the same time, it formed an integral element of the normative basis of Byzantine society and an important point of orientation for its future development.

### 6.2.2  Legal Development Under the Macedonian Dynasty

The accession to the throne of Basil I the Macedonian (867–886) marks the beginning of the most creative period in the history of Byzantine law since Justinian's reign. The legislation of this period is characterized by a renewed emphasis on the Justinianic codification as the basis of the Byzantine legal system. The return to the Roman law of Justinian was connected with the general revival of interest in the classical tradition. It also reflects the imperial desire to strengthen the image of the Byzantine state as a direct heir of the ancient *imperium Romanum*. A chief objective of the legislative program initiated by the Macedonian emperors was to restore the substance of Justinianic Roman law. To this end, many of the

---

[20] This work provided practical, time-tested regulations for the handling of collision cases between ships and for addressing problems pertaining, among other things, to the relation of the owner of the ship to the cargo owner in the event the cargo was lost. In the course of time, provisions of the code were transmitted, by custom, to the early Italian maritime city-states that were closely related to the Byzantines. It is thus unsurprising that one of the earliest Italian sea codes, that of Amalfi (*c.* 1000), was based on it. As Byzantine maritime trade declined, however, from the twelfth century onwards and the Italian maritime powers dominated the sea routes of the Mediterranean, the Rhodian sea law per se gradually fell into disuse. Nevertheless, some of its more important norms survived and inspired the development of commercial and maritime practices of Venice, Genoa and Pisa, and even of the famous *Consolato del Mare*, an early Catalan legal code (*c.* 1300). On the Rhodian Maritime Code see W. Ashburner, *The Rhodian Sea-Law* (Oxford 1909, repr. 1976); K. M. T. Atkinson, 'Rome and the Rhodian Sea-Law', *Iura* 25 (1974), 46-98; R. Zeno, *Storia del diritto marittimo italiano nel Mediterraneo* (Milan 1946), 96-113.

changes to the law initiated by the Isaurian legislation were removed and the precedence of written law over custom was re-established.[21] At the same time, plans to update the legal system were executed by eliminating matters that had become obsolete.

The first in a series of legislative works aimed at the general revision of the law was the *Eisagoge* (previously known as *Epanagoge*), prepared under the authority of Basil I and his sons Leo and Alexander around 885.[22] It contained a selection of laws drawn from the Greek translations of Justinian's codification and consisted of 40 titles and a preamble.[23] In the preamble, the *Ecloga* of the Isaurians was contemptuously discredited and abrogated as far as necessary (although the criminal law of the *Ecloga* was generally retained).[24] An interesting feature of the *Eisagoge* is that it introduced a system of norms governing relations between Church and state that was markedly different from the one that had existed earlier. According to the approach that had prevailed since the time of Constantine the Great, Church and state were not two separate authorities but rather two aspects of the one and indivisible concept of Christendom. The *Eisagoge* departed from this approach by lending support to the theory of the 'two authorities', which regarded the emperor and the patriarch as equally powerful bearers of the two highest positions within the state.[25] A revised edition of the *Eisagoge*, known as *Procheiros Nomos* or *Procheiron*, was published in the early tenth century by Emperor Leo VI the Wise (886–912). It comprised extracts from Greek translations and abridgments of Justinian's legislation, fragments from the *Ecloga* and enactments of the

---

[21] Although the *Ecloga* was abrogated by the Macedonian emperors, some of its provisions continued to apply in practice, especially in the provinces and among neighbouring peoples in the Balkans and Asia Minor (translations of the *Ecloga* have survived in Slavic, Armenian and Arabic).

[22] Scholars now recognize that Patriarch Photios played a part in the production of this work. The extent of his participation is not known, but certain sections of the work relating to the Church were surely composed by him. His influence is also felt in the criminal law of the *Eisagoge*, which includes several provisions dealing with religious offences, such as apostasy and heresy.

[23] See A. Schminck, *Studien zu mittelbyzantinischen Rechtsbüchern* (Frankfurt a. M. 1986), 4 ff.

[24] The preamble also contains information about the procedure that was followed by the drafters of the *Eisagoge*: first the relevant legislative material was gathered together; then the elements considered obsolete or useless were removed; and finally the remaining material was divided into forty titles.

[25] This new approach is reflected in titles 2 and 3 of the work, the first of which titled 'about the king' and the second 'about the patriarch'. The scope of authority of the two parties is defined in chapter 8 of the third title. According to this, the state is made up of different parts, just like the human body. Among these parts, the most important are the emperor and the patriarch. Concord and unanimity between these two are therefore necessary for the spiritual peace and material prosperity of the state. In this respect, it appears that the task of the emperor was to secure the material well-being of his subjects, while that of the patriarch was to care for their spiritual interests. The authors of the *Eisagoge* proceeded to set out the general principles governing the structure and function of the united Church-state organization, dedicating titles 4-7 to secular authorities (political and military) and titles 8-10 to the Church. Finally, title 11 deals with issues pertaining to the jurisdiction of the secular and the ecclesiastical courts.

Macedonian emperors amending and complementing the law. As in the *Eisagoge*, the materials are divided into 40 titles preceded by a preamble. However, the drafters of the *Procheiron* omitted all the titles of the *Eisagoge* containing provisions on the foundation of the political-ecclesiastical organization, possibly with the purpose of striking out the above-mentioned theory of the 'two authorities'.[26] Both the *Procheiron* and the *Eisagoge* appear to have been given the force of law.

As announced in its preamble, the *Eisagoge* was designed to serve as an introduction to a new, all-embracing code of law that was originally referred to as 'Revision of the Ancient Laws' (*Repurgatio veterum legum*). Work on this project commenced under Emperor Basil I and was completed in the early tenth century during the reign of his son Leo VI the Wise. The original title of the new law book appears to have been *Basilica nomima* (Imperial law), but in later years (from the eleventh century) it was designated *Basilica*. As stated in the preamble, the aim of this work was to collect, update and harmonize the laws contained in the codification of Justinian. It combines into one body of work the materials from the Code, Digest, Institutes and Novels. Although the sequence of the titles is a little different from that in Justinian's books, the contents are largely the same. The vast majority of the extracts were not drawn from the original Latin text of Justinian's codification but from Greek translations and abridgments of jurists from later eras.[27] The *Basilica* also incorporated the Rhodian Maritime Code mentioned earlier. The materials are arranged into 60 books divided into titles, paragraphs and themes. The whole work is comprised of six volumes.[28] The *Basilica* was not intended to replace the codification of Justinian, which retained an unquestioned validity as the ultimate source of law. It aspired to only adapt Justinian's codification to contemporary conditions and needs. However, despite the claim of *repurgatio* (or *anakatharsis*), which suggests an overhaul in order to bring the law up to date, many of the provisions included in the work had hardly any practical importance, and insofar as a certain amount of Justinianic material was 'purged', this was mainly done by omitting rather than replacing the earlier provisions with more recent legislation. Indeed, imperial legislation after the time of Justinian was not

---

[26] As a result, only three titles of the *Procheiron* deal directly with Church matters: Title 15 on *emphyteusis* (ecclesiastical long term lease); title 24 on the wills of bishops and monks; and title 28, on the issue of ordination of bishops and presbyters. However, there was no reduction in the number of provisions that indirectly addressed matters of Church interest, such as the prerequisites of marriage or certain issues of a criminal nature.

[27] Among the chief works utilized by the compilers of the *Basilica* was an abridgment of the Digest by an unknown author, referred to as Enantiophanes; a commentary on the Code by Thalelaeus; and Theophilus's paraphrase of the Institutes.

[28] The text of the *Basilica* is accompanied by a large number of annotations (*scholia*) that include interpretations, examples, explanations and references of various kinds. Some of these comments are extracted from the works of sixth century jurists (old *scholia*), whilst others are derived from juristic works of the post-Macedonian period (new *scholia*). Many of these *scholia* are preceded by the author's name, but otherwise their attribution and dating is a difficult matter. According to some modern scholars, most of both the old and new comments were added to the *Basilica* in the eleventh century at the law school of Constantinople.

included. The number of instances in which we find a contemporary interpolation after the fashion of Justinian's interventions in earlier material is negligible as compared to what might reasonably have been expected if a true 'modernization' of the law had been intended. Only about two-thirds of the *Basilica* have survived throughout the eras in various manuscripts. Our knowledge on the contents of the missing parts derives from later works, such as the *Tipoukeitos* published in the late eleventh century as a legal repertory.[29]

In the years preceding the publication of the *Basilica*, Leo VI issued a number of new laws (*novellae constitutiones*) from which 113 were collected and preserved together with four individual enactments.[30] About one-third of these novels are concerned with ecclesiastical matters, modifying provisions of the civil legislation (for the most part that of Justinian) with a view to adapting them to requirements of canon law. This adaptation was accomplished through an alteration of old laws as well as through the introduction of entirely new rules. Some of Leo's novels were aimed at removing apparent contradictions between the written law and established customary norms. Also originating from the closing years of Leo's reign is the *Eparchiakon Biblion*, an official compilation of rules governing the operation of the various associations of businessmen, tradesmen and craftsmen of Constantinople (*corpora*). One of the most interesting documents that has come down to us from Leo's reign is the *Kleterologion* of Philotheos, a list of the senior military and civil offices of the state, which attests to the growing sophistication of the central and provincial administration during this period.

Among the general laws enacted in the period following the death of Leo VI, reference may be made to two novels issued by Emperor Constantine VII (913–959) dealing with murderers. The first of these novels provides asylum even to persons who committed premeditated murder if they would come forth for confession before their crime is discovered. The second novel then compels the

---

[29] For the standard modern edition of the *Basilica* see G. E. Heimbach, *Basilicorum libri* 60, 1-6 (Leipzig 1833-1850, with prolegomena 1870); and see H. J. Scheltema, D. Holwerda, N. van der Wal, *Basilicorum libri* 60 (Groningen 1953-1988). Consider also P. Zepos, *Die byzantinische Jurisprudenz zwischen Justinian und den Basiliken*, in *Ber. zum* IX *Intern. Byz-Kongr.* V, I (Munich 1958), 1-27.

[30] Leo VI is regarded as the greatest legislator of the Byzantine era, second only to Justinian in terms of legislative output. Leo viewed Justinian as his role model and attempted to imitate and even surpass him as a legislator. But whereas Justinian gathered together and compiled ancient laws, Leo's aim was the purification and amendment of Justinian's legislation. By enacting his own novels and the *Basilika* in close association with each other so that they formed a coherent entity, the emperor hoped to complete the work of Justinian. However, whilst Justinian's authority was vested primarily in imperial dignity, with God as the fount of that dignity, the authority of Leo's laws was thought of as deriving directly from God. Leo held two views of the law: the noble vision of the law as God's instrument, personified in the emperor, for the purpose of imposing order on creation; and the down-to-earth vision that the law must constantly provide practical solutions to concrete problems of everyday life, given the 'variety of human affairs', as Leo states at the beginning of the preface to his collection of novels. For a closer look at Leo's novels see P. Noailles & A. Dain, *Les Novelles de Léon VI le Sage* (Paris 1944); H. Monnier, *Les Novelles de Léon le Sage* (Bordeaux & Paris 1923).

same offenders to become monks. Two other novels by the same emperor deal with matters of intestate succession, providing that one third of the property left behind should be surrendered to the Church for the salvation of the deceased's soul. A number of laws issued during the reigns of Romanos I Lekapenos, Constantine VII, Nikephoros II Phokas, Basil II and Isaac I Comnenus reflect an attempt on the part of the government to protect small-land ownership from the pressures of the powerful landowners. Some of the novels enacted in the second half of the eleventh century by Isaac I, Constantine X Doukas and Nikephoros III Botaneiates were concerned with marriage law, while others aimed at regulating internal matters of the Church, mainly of an administrative nature. Many laws enacted by emperors of the Comnenoi dynasty dealt with the administration of the Church, financial and taxation matters, the judging of disputes and issues concerning marriage.[31]

Besides the official collections of law, there existed several private works (generally legal abridgments or epitomes) composed by jurists for practical use or instructional purposes. Probably the most notable amongst these are two works known as *Epitome Legum* (created in 913 during the reign of Constantine VII Porphyrogenitus) and *Synopsis Basilicorum Maior* (late tenth century). The *Epitome* contains materials drawn from the codification of Justinian, the *Basilica* and the *Procheiron*, as well as several constitutions of Leo VI. The *Synopsis Basilicorum Maior* is a collection of brief abstracts from the *Basilica* arranged in alphabetical order (most of the manuscript copies of this work are accompanied by an appendix containing materials from imperial laws of the tenth and later centuries and other sources). Based on the *Synopsis Maior* and another work (*Opusculum de iure* or *Ponima Nomikon*) written in c. 1072 by the jurist and historian Michael Attaliates, a smaller abridgment of the *Basilica* was composed about the middle of the thirteenth century (*Synopsis Basilicorum Minor*). Three other works can also be mentioned in this connection: the *Experientia Romani* or *Peira* (c. 1050), a collection arranged into 75 titles containing juristic decisions drawn largely from the writings of Eustathius Romanus, a judge at Constantinople[32]; the *Tipoukeitos*, a repertory on the *Basilica* composed by a judge named Patzes in the late eleventh century; and the *Synopsis Legum* (c. 1070), a collection of laws from the codification of Justinian and the *Basilica* prepared by the jurist and philosopher Michael Psellus and dedicated to his pupil, the Emperor Michael VII Ducas.

The revival of literary activity in the post-Macedonian period was facilitated by the establishment of a new law school at Constantinople around 1045 by Emperor Constantine IX Monomachus (1042–1055).[33] The bureaucratization of the imperial

---

[31] Reference may be made in this connection to two novels of Alexios I Comnenus (1081-1118), one dealing with the contracting and dissolution of betrothals and the other with the marriage of slaves.

[32] This work provides a useful insight into the way in which Byzantine normative sources were applied in actual cases.

[33] As previously noted, in the years following the death of Justinian legal learning took a sharp downward trend. How long the old law-schools of Constantinople and Beirut remained open we do

administration in the eleventh century increased the government's need for well-educated officials. Partly in response to this need and partly due to the inadequacy of the current system of legal education (advocates had to teach themselves or learn from private tutors), Constantine founded a school of law and stipulated the conditions governing the work of the professors and students.[34] The constitution of the school specifically declared that no person could practice law until he had finished the prescribed courses and received testimony from the professors as to his competence.[35] Admission to the school was open to capacity and students did not have to pay fees. The emperor appointed and paid the professors (*magistri*) as well as the head of the school. The latter held the office of *nomophylax* that was regarded as one of the highest offices of the state and its holders were admitted to the senate.[36] Until the end of the eleventh century, the teaching of law was based directly on the texts of the Justinianic codification with a step-by-step study and clarification of the contents. In the twelfth century, however, the Justinianic codification appears to have been superseded in the study of law by various abridgments and commentaries. The law school of Constantinople probably remained open until the capture of the city by the Latins in 1204.

## 6.2.3  Legal Development in the Late Byzantine Age

In the thirteenth century, legal culture in the East encountered a sharp downward trend precipitated by the confusion ensuing from the political disintegration of the Byzantine world after the Latin conquest of Constantinople. After the recapture of Constantinople by the Byzantines in 1261, the emperors of the Palaeologan dynasty set themselves the task of reorganizing the administration of justice with an emphasis on reforming the court system.[37] However, no serious effort was directed

---

not know for sure, but it appears that they had fallen into decline and probably closed by the end of the sixth century. About the middle of the ninth century Caesar Bardas, uncle of Emperor Michael III, established a university in the capital in which law was taught, but we know little about the quality of the legal instruction offered. Whatever its contribution to legal learning, Bardas's university was dissolved in the tenth century and legal instruction continued to be given by private teachers, usually members of professional bodies of advocates or notaries.

[34] On Constantinus' enactment by which the school was founded see E. Follieri, *Sulla novella promulgata da Costantino IX Monomaco per la restaurazione della Facoltà giuridica a Costantinopoli*, in *Studi Voltera* II (Milan 1971), 647 ff. see also P. Speck, *Die kaiserliche Universität von Konstantinopel* (Munich 1974).

[35] Lawyers were divided into categories: *synegoroi* (advocates, barristers) and *taboullarioi* (notaries).

[36] The first *nomophylax* of the law-school was John Xiphilinus, a distinguished judge who later became patriarch of Constantinople.

[37] The reform of the court system was the subject of a series of laws issued by Emperors Andronicus II (1282-1328) and Andronicus III (1328-1341). The earliest of these laws provided for the establishment of a High Court consisting of twelve judges in Constantinople. But the

towards improving the quality of legal education that existed at a low ebb after the dissolution of the law school of Constantinople—legal instruction was presented mainly by practitioners in private and was haphazard, unsystematic and based on fragmentary legal sources. The lawyers of this period paid little attention to the codification of Justinian (whose texts were extremely difficult to locate) and instead utilized contemporary Greek summaries and adaptations.[38] The most notable amongst these materials was the *Hexabiblos*, a manual of the entire law in six books that was compiled around 1345 by Constantine Harmenopoulos, a judge at Thessalonica, and designed for the use of judges and court officials. It contains materials drawn from the *Procheiron*, the *Basilica*, the *Peira* and other sources that are all arranged into titles and paragraphs. Private law is addressed in Books 1–5 and divided into five parts: general principles, law of property, law of obligations, family law and law of succession whilst Book 6 is concerned with criminal law. The text is accompanied by a large number of annotations that were mainly created by Harmenopoulos.[39] After the fall of Byzantium, the *Hexabiblos* was still utilized throughout the Ottoman period (with prominence in the ecclesiastical courts) and it contributed significantly to the preservation of the Roman law tradition in the Balkans.[40]

During the later Byzantine epoch, the Church played an increasingly important part in the administration of justice. We observed earlier that since the fourth century the ecclesiastical courts had rights of jurisdiction in cases involving clerics and in civil disputes submitted by the relevant parties. By the end of the twelfth century, the competence of these courts had been extended to a variety of civil cases so that it encompassed all matrimonial cases and cases concerning charitable bequests. The tendency towards widening the jurisdiction of the Church courts

---

reform programme of the Palaeologi was met with limited success. For the relevant legislative enactments see I. Zepos and P. Zepos, *Ius Graecoromanum* I (Athens 1931, repr. Aalen 1962), Coll. V., Nov. XLI-XLIII. On the organization of the state during this period consider L.-P. Raybaud, *Le gouvernement et l'administration centrale de l'empire byzantin sous les premiers Paléologues (1258-1354)* (Paris 1968).

[38] The preponderance of privately held documents proving endowments (e.g. exemptions from taxation) granted by the emperor to local entities (especially monasteries) over general legislative instruments in the last centuries of the empire attests to a 'privatization' of rights and privileges and a change in the relationship between the government, in the form of a ruling dynasty, and the taxpayer and landowner.

[39] For the text see G. E. Heimbach, *C. Harmenopuli, Manuale Legum sive Hexabiblos* (Leipzig 1851, repr. Aalen 1969).

[40] The *Hexabiblos* was also widely known and used in the West, where it underwent several editions during the sixteenth and seventeenth centuries. The existence of a German translation testifies to the fact that the work was used in German court practice throughout the Reception period. The court use of the work in France seems to have been equivalent to that in Germany. Furthermore, the *Hexabiblos* was extensively used by sixteenth century humanist jurists as an important basis for the critical reconstruction of the *Corpus iuris civilis* and the restoration of the text of the *Basilica*. See on this M. Th. Fögen, "Humanistische Adnotationen zur *editio* princeps der Hexabiblos", *Ius Commune* 13 (1985), 213-242. And see the discussion of the Humanist Movement in Chap. 7 below.

accelerated considerably after the interlude of the Latin conquest (1204–1261).[41]
As the ecclesiastical law became closely allied with the civil law, the distinction
between civil and ecclesiastical jurisdictions was evermore blurred. This development is related to the general weakening of the Byzantine state prompted by the
political disintegration of the empire in the thirteenth century, and the parallel
enlargement of Church's role in civil administration (the emperors now increasingly relied upon the Church organization in their effort to maintain imperial unity).
As the importance of canon law increased during this period, there appeared
alongside the various condensations of Roman law several compilations that
combined both canon and civil law, known as nomocanons (or *Syntagmata*).[42]
Works of this kind were produced by Theodorus Bestos (eleventh century);
Theodorus Balsamon (twelfth century)[43]; John Zonaras (twelfth century)[44]; Alexios
Aristenos (twelfth century)[45]; Mathaeus Blastares (fourteenth century)[46]; Constantine Harmenopoulos (fourteenth century)[47] and other jurists. Throughout the Ottoman period, these materials were still produced and utilized by the ecclesiastical

---

[41] It is thus unsurprising that, after 1204, our knowledge of legal practice becomes increasingly
dependent on evidence from various ecclesiastical sources. For the thirteenth century, the works of
Demetrius Chomatenos, Archbishop of Ohrid, and John Apoukaukos, Metropolitan of Naupaktos,
have preserved cases and decisions from their own courts. Moreover, the archives of the monasteries on Mount Athos in northern Greece contain many documents that provide an insight into the
way in which the norms of canon and secular law were applied in practice during the later
Byzantine age.

[42] Among the earliest works of this kind was the *Nomocanon* produced about the middle of the
sixth century by John of Antioch, who later became Patriarch of Constantinople.

[43] Balsamon's commentary on the *Nomocanon of Fourteen Titles* was widely used by lawyers.
Apart from the canons proper, the work included imperial legislation, court cases, synodal decrees
and other relevant materials. The work of Balsamon also includes *responsa*, short treatises on
various aspects of canon law and other theological and philological texts. His influence can also be
observed in canonical literature during both the late Byzantine and post-Byzantine periods.

[44] Of Zonaras' works of special importance is his commentary on the canons of the apostles,
Church fathers and ecumenical and local Councils. Although ecclesiastical sources take precedence over secular ones in his work, it is certain that Zonaras had been educated in law, as it is
evidenced by the hermeneutical methodology he followed.

[45] Aristenos wrote *scholia* on the canons of the apostles and of ecumenical and local Councils.

[46] Blastares' *Syntagma kata stoicheion* (also known as *Alphabetical Syntagma*), a comprehensive
summary of canon law, draws on a variety of canonical and secular sources including the
*Nomokanon of Fourteen Titles*, the commentaries of John Zonaras and Theodorus Balsamon,
the *Ecloga*, the *Eisagoge*, the *Procheiron* and the *Basilica*. The work also contains materials from
many private collections produced between the ninth and fourteenth centuries. The *Syntagma*
gained wide circulation among both canon and secular lawyers, as its rich manuscript tradition
indicates. It was also the object of further reworking as well as a direct source of later compilations
in the post-Byzantine era. The work was widely used in Serbia, Bulgaria and Russia, where it
became an integral part of the basic sources of canon law.

[47] Harmenopoulos, the author of the above-mentioned *Hexabiblos*, also composed a work on
canon law, titled *Epitome of the Holy and Divine Canons*. The *Epitome* is divided into six sections
(corresponding to the six books of the *Hexabiblos*): 1. Concerning bishops; 2. Concerning
presbyters, deacons and subdeacons; 3. Concerning the clergy; 4. Concerning monks and

courts. They also significantly contributed to the preservation of the Greco-Roman legal tradition in countries formerly within the orbit of Byzantine civilization.

## 6.3   The Influence of Byzantine Law

Byzantine law, whether transplanted in its original form or adjusted to local conditions, exercised a strong influence in the Christian East, especially on those peoples who had inherited from Byzantium their political, ecclesiastical and social structure. Thus, Byzantine law, derived largely from the *Ecloga*, was introduced in the Slavic world through the legislative work of the missionaries Methodius and Cyril and through the ninth century *Zakon Sudnyj Ljudem* ('Law for Judging the People'), a Bulgarian law book corresponding closely to the above-mentioned Byzantine code. Particularly influential in the Balkans was the *Procheiron*, which was translated into Slavic in Bulgaria in the eleventh century. In Serbia the reception of Byzantine law commenced with the so-called 'Nomocanon of St. Sava' (early thirteenth century), a compilation of ecclesiastical law containing also the entire *Procheiron*.[48] The reception culminated with the codification of Tsar Stefan Dusan (1349), the greatest work of the Serbian legal tradition. This work was largely an abridgment of the *Syntagma*, a compendium of Byzantine law composed by Mathaeus Blastares in 1335. The Russian canon law code (*Kormčaja kniga*) contains materials from a variety of both canonical and secular Byzantine sources, including the *Ecloga*, the *Procheiron* and the above-mentioned *Zakon Sudnyj Ljudem*. Reference may also be made here to the island of Cyprus where Byzantine law was widely applied both during the period of the Latin kingdom (1192–1489) and during the rule of Venice (1489–1571), particularly by means of the so-called *Constitutio Cypria* or *Bulla Cypria* of Pope Alexander IV.

After the fall of the Byzantine Empire in the fifteenth century, Byzantine law remained the law of the orthodox Christians within the Ottoman Empire, which were under the spiritual and political leadership of the patriarchate of Constantinople. In exercising their administrative and judicial functions, the patriarchate and the ecclesiastic authorities under it applied Byzantine law derived from various manuscript sources in their original form or in the form of abridgments and collections composed by the patriarchate for official or unofficial use and, in later times, from printed works produced in the West (such as the *Ius Graeco-romanum* of Leunclavius and the *Synodikon* of Beveregius).[49] Of much wider use were the

---

monasteries; 5. Concerning the laity; and 6. Concerning women. The work is accompanied by *scholia* that were most probably composed (at least in the greater part) by Harmenopoulos himself.

[48] St. Sava's law book proved influential far beyond Serbia, becoming the basic constitution of both the Bulgarian and the Russian Churches. Furthermore, the rules it contained were applied also to laymen under Church jurisdiction.

[49] The ecclesiastical jurisdiction of the patriarchate of Constantinople, both in the late Byzantine and Ottoman periods, and its regulatory function in matters of Church interest extended far beyond

various nomocanons of the Ottoman period, which mostly drew, directly or indirectly, on the last two systematic manuals of Byzantine law: the *Hexabiblos* of Harmenopoulos and the *Syntagma* of Blastares.[50] Even outside the Ottoman Empire, in countries tracing their cultural origins to Byzantium, the *Hexabiblos* was often used to address gaps in the law, being regarded as the law that was 'naturally' in force when no other rule could be found. In Russian Bessarabia this work was officially recognized as the local civil code in the early half of the nineteenth century and remained in force even after the annexation of Bessarabia to Romania (1918) until Romanian legislation was extended to this region. A Serbian translation of the *Hexabiblos* was also produced for use by the Serb population of the archdiocese of Karlowitz under Austrian rule, as their own native law. In Greece, the *Hexabiblos* was recognized as an official source of law after its liberation in the early nineteenth century and remained in force until a modern civil code was enacted in 1946.

Byzantine legal science and its products in the fields of both secular and canon law were regarded by humanist jurists in the West as integral parts of the Roman legal inheritance and as important sources for its reconstruction. It is thus unsurprising that the editions of the *Corpus Iuris Civilis* from the sixteenth to the nineteenth century included Novels of Byzantine emperors (especially those of Leo VI). It was only with the fragmentation of historical studies and the subsequent adjustment of Roman law to local legal traditions, especially in Germany after the period of the Reception, that Byzantine law would be marginalized and confined to the fringes of Roman law. The general disregard for Byzantium in the Age of the Enlightenment precipitated this outcome. However, since the mid-nineteenth century there has been a renewed interest in the study of Byzantine law as a distinct branch of legal history, even though still outside the general history of Roman law.

---

the boundaries of the Byzantine and Ottoman Empires, to the territories of the East ruled by Venice, to the orthodox Christians of Poland and Ukraine and to the orthodox Christians of the diaspora in the West.

[50] The most widely used work of this kind during the Ottoman age was the *Nomocanon* of Manuel Malaxos (late sixteenth century). Reference may also be made here to the *Staff of the Bishops* of archimandrite James of Ioannina (1645).

# Chapter 7
# The Survival and Resurgence of Roman Law in Western Europe

## 7.1 The Historical Background

With the collapse of the Roman Empire in the West, Europe moved slowly but surely into an era that is generally known as the Middle Ages. This period of transition featured a disintegration of the civilisation and forms of social and cultural life that had been characteristic of the Greco-Roman world. The urban life that had been the ideal of the Greeks and introduced by the Romans throughout the Mediterranean basin declined. Many towns disappeared as new forms of habitation were constructed around fortified manors and small village communities. Although some great urban centres in Italy and Gaul continued to exhibit signs of commercial activity, trade and industry decayed and economic life reverted to an agricultural and pastoral type geared to maintaining local self-sufficiency. As all centralised authority dissolved, political conditions shifted towards the decentralised localism associated with the feudal system and the economically self-sufficient manor became the principal economic and administrative unit. Moreover, general culture in the West declined sharply and illiteracy became widespread. These events derived from the confusion caused by the Germanic invasions and the decay of the cities that had existed for centuries as centres for learning and the propagation of ideas. Nevertheless, vestiges of the classical civilisation remained alive throughout this period and gradually their fusion with the crude culture of the Germanic peoples and the learning of Christianity produced a new cultural synthesis.

By the end of the sixth century, the great Germanic migrations into Western Europe had ceased. Of all the Germanic kingdoms established in the lands of the former Roman Empire, only the Frankish was destined to endure as most of the others disappeared after a brief existence. The first great Frankish dynasty was the Merovingians established by Clovis (481–511). Under the reign of Clovis, the Merovingian rule was transformed from the leadership of a loosely organized tribe to a strong kingship extending over the whole of Gaul. After Clovis' death,

© Springer International Publishing Switzerland 2015
G. Mousourakis, *Roman Law and the Origins of the Civil Law Tradition*,
DOI 10.1007/978-3-319-12268-7_7

this development of the Frankish kingdom was hindered by the political division of the land and the disunity of his successors who continuously intrigued and fought against each other for power. Under these circumstances, the royal authority weakened and the kings increasingly relied upon an independent group of nobles for sustenance, advice and support in war that was rewarded with grants of land, offices and privileges. Despite the feebleness of Clovis' successors, the Frankish kingdom with support from the Catholic Church not only survived as a single realm but also expanded its territory. The most powerful noble in the court was an official designated *maior domus*, or mayor of the palace. From the middle of the seventh century, the gradual decline of royal authority meant the mayors of the palace in the respective courts became the real rulers of the kingdom. In 681, Pippin II of Heristal elevated his position as mayor of the palace of Austrasia (one of the three provinces into which the Frankish domain had been divided) by assuming the mayoralty of the united Frankish kingdom. After Pippin's death, his illegitimate son Charles Martel (714–741) succeeded him in the office of mayor of the palace. Martel gained control of the realm and became the founder of a new line of rulers known as the Carolingians (he did not adopt the royal title himself). Charles' grip on power was secured further after the Battle of Poitiers (732), where he defeated the Arabs who had already besieged Spain, and thus he stemmed their further advance into Western Europe. His son Pippin the Short, who became mayor of the palace after his father's death, deposed the Merovingian for whom he ruled and garnered Church support to reign as the king of the Franks in 751. Church support was requisite to legitimise his role, so Pippin enticed this aid by offering the Pope his protection against the Lombards who threatened Rome. He also ceded to the Pope the Exarchate of Ravenna (in Northern Italy) that he had acquired by conquest from the Lombards after the latter had expelled the last remnants of the Byzantine garrisons. By the time of his death in 768, the borders of the Frankish kingdom had been extended into the Lowlands, Lombardy and the Pyrenees.

The greatest monarch in the Carolingian line was Pippin's son Charles, known to history as Charlemagne (768–814), who became sole ruler of the Franks on the death of his brother Carloman in 771. After a long series of wars, Charlemagne extinguished the Lombard kingdom in Northern Italy and assumed its rulership (774). He quelled the Saxons and thereby added a large tract of territory in Germany to the Frankish realm, strengthened his suzerainty over Bavaria and the area that later became Austria, and repulsed the Arabs beyond the Pyrenees to gain control of Barcelona. Like his predecessors, he followed a policy of close cooperation with the Church. He confirmed the grant of territory in Italy that had been previously presented to the Pope by his father and made it part of his policy to spread the Christian faith in the newly conquered lands. The partnership between the Caro-lingians and the Papacy culminated in Charlemagne's coronation by Pope Leo III as Emperor in Rome on 25 December 800. In internal affairs, Charlemagne exerted great efforts to promote centralised rule. He exercised general supervision over the Church using the Church organization as a vehicle for extending his authority, held the nobles in check (although he often sought their advice in matters of state policy), and ensured closer supervision of the administration by appointing counts and margraves to govern the various parts of his realm. Moreover, he ordered a record of the unwritten laws of the various tribes and the authoritative editing of earlier codes such as the Salic Code of the Franks. Although the legal traditions of each locality were fully respected, Charlemagne engaged his position as head of the empire to issue edicts (capitularies) that were applicable to all his subjects. These statutes were not merely statements of popular customs promulgated by a ruling chief; they were the decrees of a sovereign ruler whose will was the source of law, according to the well-known doctrine of Roman law. Charlemagne's reign also witnessed a revival of learning, and inspired artistic and literary activity. In monasteries and palace schools, the classical texts were once again studied, theological problems pondered, books collected and ancient manuscripts copied. In contrast with these achievements, little progress occurred in the economic sphere as the feudal and manorializing tendencies of the landlord class increasingly escaped from the control of the central government.

The establishment of a Western Empire by Charlemagne was one of the most important events in the rise of a new society in Western Europe. Just as the reign of Justinian had precipitated the emergence of Byzantine civilisation, the achievements of Charlemagne helped to mould the civilisation of Western Europe that began to form in his time. In the years following Charlemagne's death, the unity of the Frankish Empire shattered and political authority everywhere tended to disintegrate. During the ninth and tenth centuries, new invaders—Norse Vikings, Saracens, Magyars and Slavs—threatened Europe from all sides. Charlemagne's successors, weakened by perpetual dynastic struggles, were unable to thwart the advance of these invaders. In the wake of the devastation caused by war and plundering, economic conditions worsened, living standards remained at a low level and learning was stifled. The permanent threat of invasion and the inability of the kings to protect and assert their authority over the local communities of their realms strengthened the centrifugal tendencies in the West. This entailed the proliferation of feudalism with its politically divisive and economically retarding influences.

The feudal system had its roots in later Roman times, but some of its defining characteristics were derived from Germanic traditions. Of particular importance was the custom of Germanic kings and nobles to grant privileges, land or office to persons close to them who were then obligated to serve loyally in the government and in time of war. A hierarchical system gradually emerged: at the top position resided the king and below him, as vassals and subvassals, were the nobles (dukes, counts, barons and knights) while the base consisted of the peasants who provided a livelihood for all by tilling the land. Each vassal had full control over his own territory in return for definite and well-recognized obligations of a personal and military character due to his overlord. This arrangement accorded the vassal his requisite protection, while it provided his overlord with the power and prestige he desired. As medieval kings were not powerful enough to assert their authority over the local communities of their realms, feudal lords acquired a considerable degree of independence. Thus, the fiefs were regarded in economic and political terms as nearly autonomous units. Decentralisation was supreme and remained so until feudalism yielded to the rising tide of nationalism and royal power.

The weakness of central authority enhanced the power of the Church, which adapted itself to the feudal system by accumulating vast landholdings and by extending its influence through its own vassals and serfs. As Church officials became feudal lords themselves, the division of power between Church and state (the former was supposedly supreme in matters of faith and morals, the latter in temporal affairs) became difficult to maintain in practice. Thus, the foundations were laid for the contest between secular and ecclesiastical authorities that transpired during the later Middle Ages.

In the eleventh century, Europe entered a period of political, economic and cultural transformation. The decentralising tendencies that engendered political fragmentation and the expansion of feudalism gradually receded, as political authority grew progressively stronger with the rise of powerful new monarchies. The Holy Roman Empire of the German Nation that was established in the middle of the tenth century by Otto the Great (936–973) asserted its authority throughout the domains of the Carolingian Empire (with the exception of France) and expanded its territories to the East. The kingdom of France consolidated itself under a new line of rulers initiated by Hugh Capet (987–996). Well-organized Norman kingdoms were formed in Southern Italy and in England. In Spain, Arab power declined and Christian rule had extended beyond the centre of the Iberian peninsula by the close of the eleventh century. At the same time, the government of the Church was centralised at Rome and had acquired strength from a series of reforms initiated by Pope Gregory VII (1073–1085) that enabled it to enter into a contest for supremacy with the Empire itself. Improved political conditions and the gradual return of order facilitated economic growth and created a more favourable environment for the development of medieval thought and culture.

One of the most important developments that stimulated the economic and cultural revival of the eleventh and twelfth centuries was the rise of towns and the emergence of a new urban civilisation. Potent factors in urban growth were the rapid expansion of trade and the increase in popularity of fairs, i.e. organized occasions for commercial exchange. During the crusades, the Mediterranean had been reopened as a major West European trading route and new trading possibilities were recognized and exploited. The first to profit from these trade events were the Italian coastal cities (such as Venice, Genoa and Pisa) that gained in strength, independence and prosperity. The increasing number, size and power of commercial cities naturally cultivated the urban middle class and the expansion of its political influence. This new urban class was a powerful force that generated new currents in medieval Europe, as opposed to the inertia of the old agrarian feudal order. The latter was characterised by localism, uniformity and repetition that rendered it inherently stagnant and custom-bound. In contrast, the urban movement was based on diversity and novelty accompanied by a dynamic and more tolerant outlook on life. This promoted the introduction of novel social, economic, political and legal elements into medieval life and stimulated cultural endeavours. As the townspeople struggled for greater economic and political freedom, they redirected the political evolution of Europe and accelerated the decline of feudalism.

The new upward trend of culture manifested itself in a significant increase in literary and artistic output and educational activity, and a revival of classical studies. Alongside the traditional forms of education centred around monasteries and churches, secular education emerged as a vital force in the intellectual development of the European society. Unlike the ecclesiastical schools where teaching concentrated mainly on dialectics and theology, secular schools also focused on practical subjects such as medicine and law. In connection with the study of law, one of the most significant cultural developments occurred: the establishment of the first medieval universities. The organization and administration of the medieval universities varied considerably, but a common element existed as they were structured like guilds under a corporate form of control. In the early medieval schools, such as the famous law school of Bologna, teachers and mature students organized themselves into closely-knit communities to facilitate their pursuit of scholarly interests without any outside interference. From the thirteenth century onwards, an increasing number of universities were established throughout Europe and more than seventy were in existence at the close of the Middle Ages.

The eleventh and twelfth centuries are marked also by the long struggle for supremacy between the Empire and the Papacy. This struggle became known as the 'investiture contest' as it revolved around the right of secular authorities to participate in the choice of bishops and other churchmen and to invest them not only with their secular but also their spiritual authority. Pope Gregory VII (1073–1085) rejected the concept of the Papacy as a bishopric of the emperor, demanding supreme authority in all Church affairs and asserting the supremacy of the Church over the state. Drawing upon the writings of early Church fathers, such as St Augustine, he contended that a ruler (whether a king or an emperor) was subject to the universal power of the Church and could only hold office as long as he performed his duties in accordance with Christian principles. The supporters of monarchical authority countered with the theory of the divine right of kings, arguing that while a king should rule justly and for the benefit of his subjects he was answerable to God alone and not to priests for any failures. Gregory's theories and policies led to conflict with Emperor Henry IV (1056–1106) and war between the papal and the imperial parties raged sporadically throughout Europe until 1122. In that year, a compromise was reached by means of a Concordat signed in the German city of Worms. The Concordat of Worms stipulated that the emperor should abandon the right of investing his bishops with the symbols of their spiritual authority. It recognized the Church as a separate, autonomous body vested with jurisdiction over a defined constituency and governed by a distinct body of law, the canon law. At the same time, non-ecclesiastical political entities and secular legal orders were recognized. The Concordat of Worms was a compromise that reflected a gain for the Papacy. Only when the monarchs had acquired sufficient power during the late medieval period could they effectively challenge the supremacy of the Church.

The period between the thirteenth and the fifteenth centuries witnessed the gradual transition of European civilisation from medievalism to the modern age. The most important factors in the institutional background of the decline of the medieval order was the emergence of strong nationalistic monarchies, the growth of towns and the urban middle class, and the decline of the Roman Catholic Church. After the death of Emperor Frederick II (1250), the medieval concept of emperorship was undermined. Germany transformed into a collection of essentially independent principalities, duchies and bishoprics. A power that could ultimately unify the German states only emerged after the rise of Prussia in the seventeenth century. In France, feudal institutions were gradually abandoned and the country moved towards a centralised state under the authority of the king. During the reigns of Louis IX (1226–1270) and his grandson Philip IV the Fair (1285–1314), the power of the feudal lords was curbed, the administration was centralised and the jurisdiction of the king's courts extended over the entire country. Philip became the first European monarch who could defy the Roman Catholic Church, and his victory over Pope Boniface VIII (1294–1303) meant that the Papacy could never again safely contest the power of the French monarchy. In England, as in France, centralised political authority grew stronger. After the decline of the German imperial influence in Italy, city-states such as Venice, Genoa, Florence and Milan cultivated independence and established themselves as leading financial, commercial and cultural centres. Finally, the closing phase of the Middle Ages featured a sharp decline in the power of the Papacy that had raised its pretensions to the highest level under Pope Innocent III (1198–1216). This derived from the triumph of nationalism and nationalistic political theory over medieval theocratic unity. The end of the fifteenth century exhibited disintegration in the institutional basis of medievalism: the dominant agricultural economy, feudal politics and a universal and omnipotent Church. With the emergence of the Renaissance, the dawn of the modern age was imminent.

The sixteenth century is commonly described as the period of the Renaissance and the Reformation. This period features the revival of the spirit of classical antiquity in the spheres of literature and art, as well as a challenge to existing authority and entrenched tradition. The Middle Ages were over. Gone too was the internationalism that for centuries had been the foundation of political philosophy and ecclesiastical practice. By the close of this period the Holy Roman Empire was an empty shell. The rulers of the territorial states that now existed in the Continent scarcely admitted even a titular allegiance to the emperor. Similarly, the Papacy no longer received the obedience of Western Christendom. Its dominance was called into question by the new churches established in the lands where the teachings of Luther held sway. A new political theory emerged from the ruins of imperial and Church internationalism. In the eyes of Renaissance thinkers, such as Machiavelli and Bodin, the state was not directly concerned with the promotion of religion or morality, but demanded for itself the obedience and loyalty of its subjects. One of the most important developments of this period was that the world burst its bounds. Columbus reached America in 1492, and Vasco de Gama discovered the sea route round the Cape to the Indies in 1497. These discoveries, together with the fall of

Constantinople to the Ottoman Turks in 1453, meant that the Mediterranean was no longer the principal trade route for all Western Europe. As the economic supremacy of the Italian maritime city-states declined, Spain, Portugal, England and Holland, which had been remote from the main flow of commerce, now were in a position to become powerful commercial nations.

In many matters, the seventeenth century saw the continuation of the trends that emerged in the sixteenth: nation states were consolidating their frontiers and establishing their spheres of influence; within states, political power was mainly in the hands of monarchs, who claimed absolute authority over their subjects; religion remained a source of conflict both within and between states; and journeys of exploration continued side by side with the colonization of newly discovered lands. Furthermore, although agriculture continued to dominate economic life, commerce was expanding and industrial production was becoming increasingly significant. On a political level, this century saw the decline of Spain, which yielded to France the position of the most powerful state in Europe, and the rise of the Netherlands into a major commercial and military power. In Germany the century was one of calamity originating in religious conflict: the attempt by Protestant nobles in Bohemia to place a Protestant on the throne triggered the Thirty Years War (1618–1648), which laid the country in ruins. The Treaty of Westphalia (1648), which ended the conflict, accelerated the decline of the Holy Roman Empire as a political organization, although the Empire lingered on as a Hapsburg title until the beginning on the nineteenth century. With the rise of the concept of the nation state, the focus of scholarly and intellectual inquiry shifted from theology to political philosophy. The demand of the age was clear: give us real knowledge of the human condition and of the nature of the relationship between the state and the individual, so that we can create a device to secure social order. Now that the medieval order, centered around the Church and the feudal system of social relationships, has collapsed what form of government could secure order? What mechanism of social control could be devised and on what basis? What is the just foundation of political obedience? Whence comes the authority of the law? These questions no longer admitted of the ready answers that could be given when all princes were assumed to derive their powers from the emperor, who was recognized as the supreme earthly authority in matters temporal. New circumstances now gave rise to new theories, and of those theories important political events were to be born in the period that followed.

The eighteenth century was the period in which the ancient European structures of authority and legitimacy were irreparably fractured. This century saw the American Revolution and the loss of Britain's North American colonies; the French Revolution and the commencement of the Napoleonic wars; and the beginnings of the Industrial Revolution. The century also saw the culmination of the intellectual movement that prepared the ground for revolution, known as the 'Enlightenment'. The Enlightenment brought with it a new sense of optimism, as opposed to medieval pessimism, and a new understanding of human nature based on the notions of rationality and freedom. With the rise of the modern concept of the nation state, intellectual inquiry focused on the nature of the relationship between the citizen and the state, and the question of what rights an individual had, or should have, against the state, especially against a state that acted tyrannically towards its citizens. Two major sets of ideas furnished the intellectual foundations of this period of social and political change: social contract theories and utilitarianism. The essence of the social contract theories is the idea that legitimate government is the result of the voluntary agreement among free and rational individuals. An important point about the social contract theories is that they express the idea that the state rests for its legitimacy upon the consent of its subjects. Laws can legitimately be used to ensure compliance if they have been properly approved by citizens who are party to the social contract. Utilitarianism is primarily a normative, ethical theory that lays down an objective standard for the evaluation and guidance of human conduct. That standard is derived from the assumption that the overriding aim of morality and justice is the maximization of human welfare or happiness. In the field of law, the spirit of the Enlightenment is reflected in the movement towards legal reform, a movement that had its roots in the seventeenth century rationalist natural law thinking. The advocates of reform were convinced that legislation provided an instrument that could be used to remedy social problems, and thus to maximize general happiness according to a rational scheme. This belief that laws and institutions could be reformed to accord with the dictates of reason swept through Europe and led to the codifications of the late eighteenth and nineteenth centuries.

## 7.2   Roman Law the Early Middle Ages

After the collapse of the Roman Empire in the West, the once universal system of Roman law was replaced by what may be described as a plurality of legal systems. The Germanic tribes that settled in Italy and the former western provinces lived according to their own laws and customs, whilst the Roman part of the population and the clergy were still governed by Roman law. This in effect signified a return to the principle of personality of the laws that prevailed in early antiquity (before the third century AD). Accordingly, the law applicable to a person was not determined by the territory in which he lived but by the national group to which he belonged. This arrangement was necessitated by the fact that in the regions under Germanic rule the vast majority of the population remained Roman and the law of the conquerors was too rudimentary to replace the more refined Roman system. The Germanic kings (except those of the Vandals) compounded the situation as they were in reality independent but considered themselves governing under the authority of the Eastern Roman emperors. In this way, a fiction of legal unity between East and West was maintained and Roman law was regarded as perpetual, although, the effective control exercised by the Eastern emperors became evermore shadowy over time. However, the general deterioration of the Roman culture in the West and the confusion ensuing from the application of the principle of personality rendered the administration of Roman law a task beyond the powers of the courts and lawyers of this period. In response to this problem, some Germanic kings ordered the compilation of codes containing the personal Roman law that governed many of their subjects and a written form of the laws that regulated the Germanic part of the population. As previously noted, in the Visigothic kingdom of Gaul, the law that applied to the Romans was elaborated in the *Lex Romana Visigothorum* issued by King Alaric II in 506—hence, this work is also known as the Breviary of Alaric (*Breviarium Alarici*). Other important compilations of this period were the *Edictum Theoderici*, enacted by the King of the Visigoths Theodoric II in the second half of the fifth century that applied to both Romans and Visigoths; and the *Lex Romana Burgundionum*, composed during the reign of King Gundobad of the Burgundians and promulgated by his son Sigismund in 517 for use by the Roman inhabitants of his kingdom.

After the conquest of Italy by the forces of the Byzantium, Justinian's legislation was introduced in that country by a special enactment (*sanctio pragmatica pro petitione Vigilii*) issued by Justinian at the request of Pope Vigilius on 14 August 554.[1] However, shortly after Justinian's death the Lombards invaded Italy and occupied most of the peninsula. Byzantine rule remained over Rome, the area around Ravenna, the southern part of Italy and Sicily. In the territories under their control, the Lombards adopted the custom of reducing their own customs to law and permitting their Roman subjects to live according to their own system. The majority of the Romans were governed by the Roman law of Justinian, whilst a smaller part of the Roman population followed pre-Justinianic (Theodosian) Roman law. The prevalent view among modern scholars is that the only materials of Justinian's legislation that gained practical significance were the Code, the Institutes and the Novels of the *Epitome Iuliani*.[2] The Digest appears to have played no part as a source of law and remained virtually unknown for many centuries.[3] In the areas under Byzantine control, the Roman law of Justinian continued to apply until the middle of the eleventh century when the last of the Byzantine possessions in Southern Italy were lost to the Normans.[4] These areas were also introduced to the

---

[1] Nov. App. VII, 1 in R. Schoell and G. Kroll, *Novellae, Corpus Iuris Civilis* III (Berlin 1972), 799.

[2] In the late seventh or early eighth century the Code was edited into a compendium, which contained only about one-quarter of the first nine books. The last three books (referred to as *Tres Libri*), concerned with the public offices of the Roman Empire, were omitted as being of little relevance to contemporary needs, and were not rediscovered until the middle of the twelfth century. The *Epitome Iuliani* was used until the twelfth century, when it was replaced by a larger collection known as the *Authenticum* (because Irnerius and other Glossators regarded it as an official compilation). Only Justinian's Institutes was known in its entirety, as several manuscripts from this period attest. Like the other parts of Justinian's legislation, these were frequently accompanied by crude and ill-arranged glosses, reflecting the legal ignorance of their authors and the general cultural decadence of the era.

[3] The last known citation to the Digest is found in a letter of Pope Gregory I in 603. After that time and until the eleventh century no reference to this work can be found in literary sources, court records or compilations of law.

[4] The Byzantine rule in central Italy came to an end in the middle of the eighth century with the capture of Ravenna by the Lombards. Sicily was lost to the Arabs in the ninth century, but parts of it were temporarily re-taken by the Byzantines early in the eleventh century.

*Ecloga Legum* of the Isaurians, and the *Prochiron* and the *Eisagoge* of the Macedonian emperors. These furnished the basis for a number of compilations that appeared in Italy during this period, such as the *Prochiron Legum* (also known as *Prochiron Calabriae*) composed in Southern Italy around the end of the tenth century.[5] However, it is uncertain whether the *Basilica* was ever used as a source of law in Italy.

As in Italy, Roman law was preserved in Gaul and Spain in a vulgarised form through the application of the principle of personality and the medium of the Church whose law was imbued with the principles and detailed rules of Roman law. During the Middle Ages, the ecclesiastical courts had rights of jurisdiction over matrimonial cases, matters of succession to personal property and certain aspects of the criminal law. These courts consistently upheld the authority of the Justinianic legislation in cases that fell within their sphere of competence. Moreover, Roman law exercised an influence directly or through canon law on the various codes of Germanic law that appeared in the West during the early Middle Ages but this influence varied greatly between regions and stages of time. The most important Germanic codes embrace the *Codex Euricinianus*, enacted about 480 by Euric the Visigothic king and drafted with the help of Roman jurists; the Salic Code (*Pactus legis Salicae* or *Lex Salica*) of the Franks, composed in the early sixth century; the *Lex Ribuaria*, promulgated in the late sixth century for the Franks of the lower and middle Rhine region; and the *Lex Burgundionum*, issued in the early sixth century for the inhabitants of the Burgundian kingdom. Of the above codes, the Visigothic and Burgundian Codes reflect a stronger Roman influence than the Salic and Ripuarian Codes. Other law codes that exhibited a Roman influence include the Lombard Edict (643), the Alammanic Code (*c.* 720), the Bavarian Code (*c.* 750), the Frisian Code (*c.* 750) and the Saxon Code (*c.* 800).

Over time, the fusion of the Roman and Germanic elements of the population progressed and prompted a dissolution of the division of people according to their national origin. The system of personality of the laws was gradually superseded by the conception of law as entwined with a certain territory or locality. As a result, Roman law as a distinct system of law applicable within a certain section of the population fell into abeyance in most parts of Western Europe. A considerable degree of integration of the Roman and Germanic elements first occurred in the Visigothic territory in Spain. In this region, the *Lex Romana Visigothorum* of Alaric ceased to possess any force and a new code was introduced in 654 under King Recceswinth: the *Lex Visigothorum* (also known as *Forum Iudicum* or *Liber Iudiciorum*: Book of Judicial Actions). This code applied to all the inhabitants of the Visigothic kingdom.[6] In the course of the ninth century, the shift from the

---

[5] This compilation contained materials from the *Prochiron* and the *Ecloga Legum*, as well as several constitutions of Emperor Leo VI the Wise.

[6] The *Lex Visigothorum* follows the structure of the Theodosian Code. It is based on early legislation (especially on a revised edition of Euric's Code issued by King Leovigild) and laws issued by the current monarch (King Recceswinth). Alaric's code continued to be used in southern France, especially in the territory of the Burgundians, and in some countries north of the Alps.

principle of personality to that of territoriality was further precipitated by the development of the feudal system. As noted before, the predominant feature of feudalism was an estate or territory dominated by a great lord (duke, count, baron or marquis) who was often the vassal of an emperor or king. Since the domain of a great lord constituted a quasi-independent unit in economic and political terms, the area that was controlled by a particular lord was decisive as to the form of law that should prevail. However, the intermixture of races meant that the laws recognized in a territorial unit could no longer be those of a particular race. Instead, all persons living within a given territory were governed by a common body of customary norms that varied in regions and periods. In this way, the diversity of laws no longer persisted as an intermixture of personal laws but as a variety of local customs. In all the territories, however, the customary law that applied was a combination of elements of Roman law and Germanic customary law.

By the end of the tenth century, vulgarised versions of Roman law were so intermingled with Germanic customary law that historians tend to describe the laws of this period as either 'Romanised customary laws' or as 'Germanised Roman laws'. Moreover, Roman law exercised a strong influence on the legislation (capitularies) of the Frankish emperors, as well as on the development of the law of the Roman Catholic Church. Thus, Roman law throughout Western Europe sustained its existence and served both as a strand of continuity and as a latent universalising factor. Yet, in comparison with classical Roman law the overall picture of early medieval law is one of progressive deterioration. The study of law, as part of a rudimentary education controlled largely by the clergy, was based simply on abstracts and ill-arranged extracts from older works. As the surviving literature from this period exhibits, legal thinking was characterised by a complete lack of originality.

## 7.3   The Revival of Roman Law

From the eleventh century, the improved political and economic conditions created a more favourable environment for cultural development in medieval Europe. At the same time, a renewed interest in law was prompted by the growth of trade, commerce and industry, and the increasing secularism and worldliness of urban business life.

The legal revival began in Northern Italy. Among the earliest centres of legal learning was the law school of Pavia established in the ninth or early tenth century. Roman law and the customary and feudal law of the Lombard kingdom were taught and developed at this school. As the capital of the Italian Kingdom and the seat of a supreme court with a corps of judges and lawyers, Pavia was the centre of vigorous legal activity. Although legal growth was fostered largely by practical needs, it encouraged the systematic study and interpretation of legal sources and improved standards of legal culture. Indeed, studies were not based solely on practical interests, but were carried out according to the processes of formal logic that were then being developed by the first scholastics. The study of Lombard law was based primarily upon the *Liber Papiensis*, a work composed in the early years of the eleventh century.[7] Other important works of the same period were the *Lombarda* or *Lex Langobarda* and the *Expositio ad Librum Papiensem*, an extensive collection of legal commentaries that embodied materials drawn from both Lombard and Roman sources.[8] The chief source for the study of Roman law was the *Lex Romana Visigothorum*.

By the end of the eleventh century the *antiqui*, the jurists dedicated to the study of ancient Germanic sources, had been superseded by the *moderni*, who were interested primarily in the synthesis of Roman law and Lombard customary law. While the *antiqui* regarded Roman law as a system subordinate and supplementary to Lombard law, the *moderni* sought to rely on Roman law as a basis for the improvement and development of native law. But the Lombard capital of Pavia was not the only Italian city where law was studied and legal works were produced. At Ravenna, the former centre of the Byzantine Exarchate in Italy, there existed in the eleventh century a school of law where Justinian's texts were known and studied. Moreover, Southern Italy remained for a considerable period of time under Byzantine rule and thus Roman legal learning was preserved in this area through the influence of the Byzantine law. After the Norman conquest of Southern Italy in the late eleventh century, Byzantine Roman law continued to apply in that region under the principle of territoriality of the law.

Towards the end of the eleventh century, Roman law studies experienced a remarkable resurgence. It is difficult to assign a single reason for this development, although some writers place central importance on the discovery of a manuscript in Pisa during the late eleventh century. The material contained the full text of Justinian's Digest that had remained largely unknown throughout the early Middle Ages (when the Florentines captured Pisa in 1406 the manuscript was transferred to Florence and hence it is designated *Littera Florentina* or *Codex Florentinus*).

---

[7] The Lombards, like other Germanic peoples, had originally no written law. The first compilation of Lombard law was the *Edictum* of King Rothari, published in 643. This work is considered to be the most complete statement of the customary law of any of the Germanic peoples in the West. The entire body of Lombard law, consisting of the Edict of Rothari and the additions introduced by his successors, is known as *Edictum regum Langobardorum*. Even after the annexation of the Lombard kingdom by the Frankish Empire during the reign of Charlemagne, Lombard law continued to be applied in Northern Italy, where it coexisted with Roman law and the customary laws of other Germanic peoples. To deal with the inevitable inconvenience that the presence of diverse legal systems entailed, the Frankish kings of Italy promulgated a large number of laws referred to as *capitula* or *capitularia*. A private collection of these laws, known as *Capitulare Italicum*, was permanently joined to the Lombard Edict in the early eleventh century. This *corpus* of Lombard-Frankish law, referred to in early sources as *Liber Legis Langobardorum*, is commonly known today as *Liber Papiensis*.

[8] The author of the *Expositio ad Librum Papiensem* distinguishes the various legal interpreters into three groups: *antiquissimi*, *antiqui* and *moderni*. Whilst the *antiqui* very rarely drew on Roman law, the *moderni* strove to discover the spirit of law by relying of Roman legal sources, especially when they encountered gaps in the Germanic (Lombard-Frankish) law.

A second manuscript seems to have been unearthed around the same time but has since been lost. This is referred to as *Codex Secundus* and is believed to have furnished the basis for the copies of the Digest produced at Bologna. The rediscovery of the Digest occurred at a time when there was a great need for a legal system that could meet the requirements of the rapidly changing social and commercial life. The Roman law of Justinian had essential attributes that offered hope for a unified law that could in time replace the multitude of local customs: it possessed an authority as a legacy of the ancient *imperium Romanum* and existed in a book form written in Latin, the *lingua franca* of Western Europe. As compared with the prevailing customary law, the works of Justinian comprised a developed and highly sophisticated legal system whose rational character and conceptually powerful structure made it adaptable to almost any situation or problem irrespective of time or place.

The revival of interest in Roman law had been also fostered by the conflict between the Empire and the Papacy, which was from the outset a conflict of political theories for which the rival parties sought justification and support in the precepts of the law. Roman law attracted the attention of secular scholars seeking intellectual grounds for refuting the papal doctrine of the final supremacy of the Church in temporal affairs. At the same time, the emperors were receptive to this law because its doctrine of a universal law (founded on a grand imperial despotism) provided the best ideological means to support the theory that the emperor, as heir of the Roman emperors, stood at the pinnacle of the feudal system.[9] The supporters of the Papacy argued that as spiritual power was superior to secular power, the Pope was supreme ruler of all Christendom and temporal affairs were subject to the final control of the Church. Scholars supporting the papal party were encouraged to search the ancient texts for legal authority that could support this claim and to develop a science of law on this basis. Opponents of the papal views adopted the same rigorous exploration for supporting materials. Relying upon the despotic principle of Roman law, they argued that the power of the state was absolute and could override the opposition of any group within the state. Roman law was thus construed to uphold secular absolutism—a view utterly at variance with the papal claims to primacy. Through the interpretation of Roman political and legal principles, a new political theory was developed in the course of time that hinged upon the idea of a secular and independent sovereignty founded on law.

---

[9] Charlemagne had been the first to assert that he was in fact heir to the throne of the Western Roman emperors and this claim was again made by Otto when he became German emperor in 962. In the twelfth century, Emperor Frederick Barbarossa employed several Bolognese jurists as his legal advisers in his conflicts with the Italian city-states.

## 7.3.1  The Glossators

The principal centre of Roman law studies in Italy was the newly founded (*c.* 1084) University of Bologna, the first modern European university where law was a major subject.[10] By the close of the thirteenth century, a number of similar schools had been established at Mantua, Piacenza, Modena, Parma and other cities of Northern and Central Italy, as well as in Southern France. The law school of Bologna owed its fame to the grammarian Irnerius (*c.* 1055–1130), who around 1088 began lecturing on the Digest and other parts of Justinian's codification. This jurist came to be regarded as the founder of the school, although he does not appear to have been the first teacher at this institution (the first public course of law at Bologna was delivered in 1075 by the Pavian jurist Pepo (Joseph), who was probably a teacher of Irnerius). Irnerius's fame attracted students from all parts of Europe to study at the Bologna school that had around 10,000 students by the middle of the twelfth century.[11] The jurists of Bologna set themselves the task of presenting a clear and complete statement of Roman law through a painstaking study of Justinian's texts (instead of the vulgarised versions of Roman law contained in the various Germanic compilations usually relied upon in the past). Their object was to re-establish Roman law as a science—a systematic body of principles and not simply a tool for practitioners. However, the ancient texts were unwieldy as they contained an immense body of often ill-arranged materials and dealt with a multitude of institutions and problems that were no longer known. Therefore, the first task to accomplish was the accurate reconstruction and explanation of the texts.[12]

---

[10] By the middle of the twelfth century about ten thousand law students from all over Europe were studying at Bologna. The students had the right to choose their own teachers and to negotiate with them matters such as the place and manner of instruction and the amount of tuition. The students and teachers organized themselves into guilds (*societates*) for purposes of internal discipline, mutual assistance and defence. The various *societates* formed a larger body termed *universitas scholarium*, within which students were grouped by nations.

[11] Irnerius's success is attributed to three principal factors: first, his excellent edition of the Digest, known as *Litera Bononiensis* or the *Vulgata*; second, the new approach to the study of Roman law, which viewed the *Corpus Iuris Civilis* as living law; third, the separation of the study of Roman law not only from the study of rhetoric, but also from the study of canon law and feudal law.

[12] The most important part of their work was the reconstruction of Justinian's Digest. According to tradition, the materials were divided into three parts: the *Digestum Vetus*, embracing the initial twenty-four books; the *Digestum Novum*, covering the last twelve books from books 39 to 50; and the *Digestum Infortiatum*, encompassing books 25 to 38. These three parts of the work were contained in three volumes. A fourth volume comprised the first nine books of Justinian's Code, and a fifth embodied the Institutes, the last three books of the Code and the Novels as found in the *Authenticum*. The fifth volume also incorporated several medieval texts, the *Libri Feudorum* (containing the basic institutions of feudal law), a number of constitutions of the emperors of the Holy Roman Empire and the peace treaty of Constance (1183). These five volumes became known as *Corpus Iuris Civilis*.

The work of interpretation was closely connected with the Bolognese jurists' methods of teaching and performed by means of short notes (*glossae*) explaining difficult terms or phrases in a text and providing the necessary cross-references and reconciliations without which the text would be unusable. These notes were written either in the space between the lines of the original text (*glossae interlineares*), or in the margin of the text (*glossae marginales*). The extended glosses of a single jurist formed a connected commentary on a particular legal topic and this continuous glossing of the texts entailed the emergence of entire collections or apparatuses of glosses that addressed individual parts or the whole of Justinian's codification. By employing the general pattern of scholastic reasoning, the Bolognese jurists (designated Glossators, *Glossatores*) sought to expose the conceptual and logical background of the various passages under consideration and to ascertain the consistency and validity of the principles underlying the legal material upon which they commented. They initiated the process by comparing different passages from various parts of Justinian's work dealing with the same or similar issues, explaining away the inconsistencies and harmonizing any apparent contradictory statements (this method was by no means new as it had been engaged by earlier medieval scholars and resembled the approach used by the jurists of the Constantinople and Beirut law schools during the later imperial era). These successive processes corresponded to the medieval progression in the curriculum of the *trivium* from grammar and rhetoric to logic or dialectic—the content of Justinian's works first had to be understood, and so explanatory notes were used; then the consistency of the texts had to be established through the application of the dialectical method. Logic was the most important element of medieval education. Based on works such as Aristotle's *Organon*, it became the dominant technique of medieval scholasticism.[13]

Apart from the *glosses*, several other types of juristic literature were developed, partly from the teaching of the *Corpus Iuris Civilis* at the law schools. Some deal with the issues in the order in which they are found in Justinian's legislation (*ordo legum*), such as the *commenta* or *lecturae*, reports written down by assistants or experienced students and sometimes revised by the teacher himself.[14] Another form of literature is the written record of a *quaestio disputata*, an exercise in which a

---

[13] Scholasticism as a system of philosophy was based on the belief that reality exists in the world of abstract ideas, generally independent of the external sensual world. Its chief assumption was that truth is discoverable if pursued according to the norms of formal logic. From this point of view, the only path to wisdom was the avoidance of logical fallacies rather than observation of commonplace nature. The formal logic that was applied was largely based on the work *Sic et non* ('Yes and No') of the French philosopher Peter Abelard (1079–1142), composed around 1120. In this work Abelard applies the principles of logic, as laid down by Aristotle, to texts of the Church fathers. The relevant texts are grouped by reference to their similarity (*similia*), or contrariety (*contraria*) and reasoning *per analogiam* or *a contrario* is applied, while distinctions (*distinctiones*) are introduced explaining the differences between the texts. This so-called scholastic method, which could be applied to any authoritative text, whether in the field of theology, philosophy, medicine or law, prevailed throughout the Middle Ages and remained influential even after the end of this period.

[14] The *commentum* was rather condensed, whilst the *lectura* was a full report on the lecture that included all that was said and done in the lecture hall.

teacher posed a question, either a theoretical one or one derived from legal practice, and his students offered opposing views. This was meant to teach students to analyse a legal problem and to argue their case in a logical and structured way. A further type of commentary, which did not originate in the classroom, was the *summa*. The *summae* are synopses or summaries of contents of particular parts or the whole of Justinian's work.[15] Unlike the above-mentioned *commenta* or *lecturae*, these are systematic works that do not follow the order of the issues in the original texts but establish their own order with respect to the fragments within the title they treat. Other forms of juristic literature included: works clarifying conceptual distinctions arising from the texts (*distinctiones*)—these comprised a series of divisions of a general concept into subcategories that were carefully defined and explained until all the implications of the concept were elucidated; collections of conflicting juristic interpretations (*dissensiones dominorum*—the term *domini* referred to medieval jurists); anthologies of opinions on various legal questions connected with actual cases (*consilia*); cases constructed to exemplify or illustrate difficult points of law (*casus*); collections of noteworthy points (*notabilia*) and statements of broad legal principles drawn from the texts (*brocarda* or *aphorismata*); and short monographs or treatises (*summulae* or *tractatus*) on specific legal topics, such as the law of actions and legal procedure.[16]

The interpretation and analysis of Justinian's legislative works was the exclusive preoccupation of the Bolognese jurists until the late thirteenth century. Among the successors of Irnerius, the most notable were Bulgarus,[17] Martinus Gosia,[18] Jacobus and Ugo (renowned as the 'four doctors of Bologna'), Azo, Rogerius, Placentinus, Vacarius, John Bassianus, Odofredus and Accursius. Azo became famous for his influential work on Justinian's Code, known as *Summa Codicis* or *Summa Aurea*.[19]

---

[15] The *summae* were similar to the *indices* composed by the jurists of the law schools in the East during the late imperial era.

[16] Of particular importance were works dealing with the law of procedure (*ordines iudiciarii*). Since the *Corpus Iuris Civilis* does not contain a comprehensive section on the law of procedure, these works sought to record and compile all the relevant material on legal procedure in general and on specific actions, and to provide guidance on how to initiate a claim in law. One of the best-known works of this kind is the *Speculum iudiciale* of Wilhelmus Durantis (*c.* 1270).

[17] Bulgarus advocated the view that Roman law should be interpreted according to the strict, literal meaning of the text. From the beginning of the thirteenth century, this approach seems to have prevailed. Among Bulgarus's followers were Vacarius, who went to teach in England, and Johannes Bassianus, the teacher of Azo.

[18] In contrast to Bulgarus, Gosia held that the Roman law texts should be interpreted liberally, that is, according to the demands of equity and the needs of social and commercial life. Bulgarus also recognized the role of equity, which for him pertained to the 'spirit' of the law or the intent of the legislator; Gosia, on the other hand, understood equity in the Aristotelian sense, that is as a corrective principle of the law in exceptional cases. Gosia's followers included Rogerius and Placentinus, who had been students of Bulgarus.

[19] The importance of Azo's *Summa Codicis* was reflected in the popular saying: '*Chi non ha Azo, non vada a palazzo*', which means that in some places a man could not be admitted as an advocate unless he possessed a copy of Azo's *Summa*.

In the late twelfth century, Rogerius founded a law school at Montpellier in France (probably together with Placentinus) and this institution became an important centre of legal learning. Vacarius, a Lombard, travelled to England around the middle of the twelfth century and commenced teaching civil law at Oxford. In *c.* 1149 he composed his famous *Liber pauperum* that comprised a collection of texts from the Code and the Digest of Justinian accompanied by explanatory notes. The aim of this work was to introduce the Roman law of Justinian to the poorer students in England.

The greatest of the late Glossators was the Florentine Franciscus Accursius, a pupil of Azo's, who dominated the law school of Bologna during the first half of the thirteenth century. Accursius produced the famous *Glossa Ordinaria* or *Magna Glossa*, an extensive collection or *apparatus* of glosses from earlier jurists covering the entire Justinianic codification and supplemented by his own annotations.[20] The *Glossa Ordinaria* both summarised and made obsolete the whole mass of glossatorial writings from the preceding generations of jurists. It represented the culmination of the Glossators' work and gained rapid acceptance in Italy and other parts of Europe as the standard commentary on Justinian's texts, providing guidance for those engaged in the teaching and practice of law.[21] The *Glossa Ordinaria* was regularly published with editions of the *Corpus Iuris Civilis*, so that they were received together throughout the Continent. With the publication of Accursius's Great Gloss, the contribution of the School of the Glossators to the revival of Roman law ceased but their methods were still applied in the teaching of law at Bologna and elsewhere for a long time.

The Glossators' approach to Roman law is characterised by its lack of historical perspective. Neither the fact that Justinian's codification had been compiled more than 500 years before their own time, nor the fact that it comprised extracts of an even earlier date meant much to them. Instead, they perceived the *Corpus Iuris Civilis* as one body of authoritative texts and paid little attention to the fact that the law actually in force was very different from the system contained in Justinian's texts. This attitude was reinforced by the theory that the Holy Roman Empire was a successor to the ancient Roman Empire—a theory that the Glossators tended to support.[22] It was also associated with the fact that the Glossators' interest in law was chiefly academic and their learning was quite remote from practical affairs.[23] Being true medieval men, the Glossators regarded Justinian's texts in much the same way as theologians regarded the Bible or contemporary scholars viewed the

---

[20] The work comprised about 96,000 glosses.

[21] The importance of Accursius's gloss was manifested in the popular saying: '*Quod non adgnovit glossa, non adgnoscit curia*', which means that a rule unknown to the *Glossa Ordinaria* was also not recognized by a court.

[22] This is evidenced by the fact that the Glossators added to the *Codex* constitutions of the German Emperors Frederick Barbarossa and Frederick II.

[23] The general attitude of the Glossators was not affected by the fact that their teachings exercised an influence on the statutory law of Italian cities and entered the practice of law through their graduates who were appointed to the royal councils or served as judges in local courts.

works of Aristotle. Just as Aristotle was treated as infallible and his statements as applicable to all circumstances, the texts of Justinian were regarded by the Glossators as sacred and as the repository of all wisdom. The Glossators have been subjected to the criticism that they neglected both the developing canon law and the statutory law enacted by local political bodies, especially in the Italian city-states. They were entirely preoccupied with the study of Roman law, which for them represented a system of legislation more fully developed than either the nascent canon law or the contemporary statutory law. Nevertheless, the Glossators did succeed in resurrecting genuine familiarity with the whole of Justinian's codification and their work prepared the ground for the practical application of the legal doctrines it contained. Their new insight into the workings of Roman law led to the development of a true science of law that had a lasting influence on the legal thinking of succeeding centuries.[24]

## 7.3.2  The Commentators

By the close of the thirteenth century, the attention of the jurists had shifted from the purely dialectical analysis of Justinian's texts to problems arising from the application of the customary and statute law and the conflicts of law that emerged in the course of inter-city commerce. The enthusiasm for the study of the ancient texts that had enticed many students and scholars to Bologna in the twelfth century now waned, and the place of the Glossators was assumed by a new kind of jurists known as Post-glossators (*post-glossatores*) or Commentators (*commentatores*). The new school with chief centres at the universities of Pavia, Perugia, Padua and Pisa, reached its peak in the fourteenth century and remained influential until the sixteenth century.

The rise of the Commentators' school was not unrelated to the new cultural and political conditions that emerged in the later part of the thirteenth century. Of particular importance was the gradual erosion of the traditional dualism of a universal Church and a universal Empire as a result of the crises affecting both institutions[25]; and the growing strength of nation and city-states in Europe, which

---

[24] On the school of the Glossators see O. F. Robinson, T. D. Fergus and W. M. Gordon, *European Legal History* (London 1994), 42 ff. P. Vinogradoff, *Roman Law in Medieval Europe* (Oxford 1929, repr. 2001), 32 ff. J. A. Clarence Smith, *Medieval Law Teachers and Writers* (Ottawa 1975); R. L. Benson and G. Constable (eds), *Renaissance and Renewal in the Twelfth Century* (Cambridge Mass. 1982); D. Tamm, *Roman Law and European Legal History* (Copenhagen 1997), 203–6; P. Stein, *Roman Law in European History* (Cambridge 1999), 45 ff. E. Cortese, *Il rinascimento giuridico medievale* (Rome 1992); W. Kunkel and M. Schermaier, *Römische Rechtsgeschichte* (Cologne 2001), 230 ff. H. Lange, *Römisches Recht im Mittelalter,1: Die Glossatoren* (Munich 1997); H. Schlosser, *Grundzüge der Neueren Privatrechtsgeschichte, Rechtsentwicklungen im europäischen Kontext* (Heidelberg 2005), 36–53.

[25] The last emperor of this period who was able to maintain a unitary view of the Empire was Frederick II of Swabia (1194–1250). His successors concentrated their efforts on consolidating

were able to develop their political structures with little interference from higher universal entities. During the same period, scholastic philosophy reached its pinnacle with the work of the catholic theologian Thomas Aquinas (1225–1274), who synthesized Aristotelian philosophy and Christian theology into a grand philosophical and theological system. The new dialectic that this philosophy forged was not restricted to theological-metaphysical speculation but permeated the study of both public and private law.

Unlike the Glossators, the Commentators were not concerned with the literal reading and exegesis of Justinian's texts in isolation but with constructing a complete legal system by adapting the Roman law of Justinian to contemporary needs and conditions. The positive law that applied in Italy at that time was a mixture of Roman law, Germanic customary law, canon law, and the statute law of the empire and the various self-governing Italian cities. The Commentators endeavoured to integrate these bodies of law into a coherent and unitary system. In executing this task, they abandoned the excessive literalism of the early Glossators and sought to illuminate the general principles of law by applying the methods of rational inquiry and speculative dialectics—thereby building an analytic framework or 'dogmatic construction' of law. Furthermore, in their roles as legal consultants and administrators, they contributed significantly to the development of case law, which also provided a fertile ground for the progressive refinement and testing of their concepts and analytical tools. Indeed, many of their theoretical propositions and dogmatic constructions evolved out of the pressures of actual cases. On the other hand, since the Commentators were mainly concerned with the development of contemporary law, they tended to pay scant attention to the primary sources of Roman law. Thus, the synthesis that occurred was between the non-Roman elements and the Roman law of Justinian as expounded by the Glossators. Systematic treatises and commentaries were written based on this body of law, especially in areas of the law where there was a need for the development of new principles for legal practice.[26]

Among the earliest Commentators was Cino of Pistoia (1270–1336), a student of the French masters Jacques de Revigny and Pierre de Belleperche. Cino began his teaching career at Siena, having been for about 10 years active in practice, and moved to Perugia in 1326. There he composed his great commentary, the *Lectura super Codice*, which continued to be read and cited for more than a century.[27]

---

their rule in Germany rather than on governing the Empire as a universal political entity. The crisis that affected the Church is evidenced by, among other things, the transfer of the papal seat to Avignon, where the Pope remained subject to the control of the French kings for about seventy years (1309–1377).

[26] The increased attention to the needs of legal practice is evidenced in the development of the *quaestio disputata*: from the middle of the thirteenth century onwards, jurists increasingly based their *quaestiones* on local statute law or even local custom, which were then analysed by means of the methods of the civil law.

[27] Cino's method consisted of several successive stages: (a) the literal rendition of a legislative text (*lectio literae*); (b) the subdivision of the text into its component provisions (*divisio legis*); a summary of the content of the text (*expositio*); examples of practical cases to which the text was

At Perugia Cino was the master of Bartolus of Saxoferrato, the most influential of the Commentators and one of the great jurists of all time.

Bartolus (1314–1357) obtained his doctorate at Bologna and lectured at Perugia and Pisa, where he also served as judge. He produced a monumental commentary on the entire *Corpus Iuris Civilis*, which, like Accursius's Great Gloss, was acknowledged as a work of authority and extensively used by legal practitioners and jurists throughout Western Europe. Bartolus also dictated legal opinions and composed a large number of monographs on diverse subjects. His reputation among his contemporaries was unsurpassed and his writings came to dominate the universities and the courts for centuries. In Italy, where the doctrine of *communis opinio doctorum* operated (whereby the solution supported by most juristic authorities should be upheld by the courts), the opinions of Bartolus were regarded to possess the same weight as the Law of Citations had accorded to the works of Papinian.[28]

Another influential jurist of this period was Baldus de Ubaldis (*c.* 1327–1400), a pupil of Bartolus. Baldus taught at Bologna, Perugia and Pavia and was also much involved in public life. Unlike Bartolus, he was a canonist and a feudalist as well as a civilian.[29] He was best known for his opinions (*consilia*) that proposed solutions for problems arising from actual cases, especially cases involving a conflict between Roman law and local laws and customs.[30]

The Commentators were remarkably flexible in their interpretation and application of the Roman texts regardless of the original context. They did not hesitate to apply a text to address a current issue, no matter how obsolete they might know its real meaning to be, if its use could be fruitful. However, when they derived arguments from materials that had little or no relation to current affairs, they were not recklessly distorting Roman law to fit their own needs but were consciously adopting its principles to develop new ideas. Their use of the Roman texts was partly due to a feeling that it was important to support a conclusion by reference

---

relevant (*positio casuum*); significant observations derived from the law (*collectio notabilium*); possible counter arguments (*oppositiones*); and, finally, an exposition of the problems that might arise (*quaestiones*). By applying this method, Cino sought to subject a legislative enactment to a dialectical process and a systematic analysis that would bring to light the rationale of the relevant law, while being aware that the pursuit of logic could lead to arguments irrelevant to the actual application of the law.

[28] In Portugal, his writings were declared to have the force of law in 1446. Moreover, lectures on his work were established at Padua in 1544 and at Ferrara in 1613. The extent of Bartolus's influence is expressed in the saying: '*nemo jurista nisi Bartolista*', which means one cannot be a jurist unless one is a follower of Bartolus.

[29] His work includes commentaries on the Decretals of Gregory IX and the *Libri Feudorum*. In this connection, it should be noted that in the time of Baldus there was a closer connection between civil law and canon law. It was customary for a student to engage in the study of both subjects and thus become doctor of both laws (*doctor utriusque iuris*).

[30] The *consilium*, the advice given by a law professor on a practical problem, evolved as the most important form of legal literature during this period, as judges were often obliged to obtain such advice before delivering their decision. In the *consilia* problems caused by the interplay between diverse sources of law (local statutes, customs, etc) are tackled through the Roman law jurists' techniques of interpretation and argumentation.

to some authority, no matter how reasonable in itself the conclusion might have been.

The reconciliation of the scholarly Roman law and local law that was achieved though the Commentators' work produced what is referred to as 'statute theory', the notion that in the fields of legal practice local statutes were the primary source, while Roman and canon law were supplementary. However, in spite of the priority bestowed on statutory law, the Roman law-based civil law could prevail in various ways. First, a statute might expressly embody elements of Roman law, and to that extent Roman law shared in the statute's primary authority. Second, a statute might contain technical terms or concepts, which would in almost all cases be construed in the civilian sense, especially since it was accepted that statutory enactments had to be interpreted in such a way as to involve the least possible departure from the civil law. Even when a statute required strict interpretation of its text, it could often be argued that it required declaratory interpretation in light of other available legal sources.

The Commentators succeeded both in adapting Roman law to the needs of their own time and in imbuing contemporary law with a scientific basis through the theoretical elaboration of Roman legal concepts and principles.[31] Of particular importance was their contribution to the development of criminal law, commercial law, the rules of legal procedure and the theory of conflict of laws. It was the Commentators who constructed on the basis of the Roman texts on criminal law a legal science and who created a general theory of criminal responsibility. It was they who developed commercial law in such areas as negotiable instruments or partnership; who articulated the concept and principles of international private law; who devised the detailed rules of romano-canonical procedure on the basis of the Roman *cognitio* procedure; who formulated doctrines of legal personality for entities other than human beings; and who gave substance to the notion of the rights of a third party to a transaction and to the law of agency. The work of the Commentators played a major part in the creation of the *ius commune* and enabled the reception of Roman law throughout Western Europe in the fifteenth and sixteenth centuries.[32]

---

[31] In the words of the German jurist Paul Koschaker, "[the Commentators] drew from the treasures of Roman wisdom and legal technique that could be used at the time and made of it a basic part of the law of their time, thus preparing the unification of Italy in the field of private law; they in addition made of Roman law the substratum of a legal science, which was later to become European legal science." *Europa und das Römische Recht* (Munich and Berlin 1953), 93.

[32] On the school of the Commentators see O. F. Robinson, T. D. Fergus and W. M. Gordon, *European Legal History* (London 1994), 59 ff. P. Stein, *Roman Law in European History* (Cambridge 1999), 71–74; D. Tamm, *Roman Law and European Legal History* (Copenhagen 1997), 206–8; F. Wieacker, *A History of Private Law in Europe* (Oxford 1995), 55 ff. W. Kunkel and M. Schermaier, *Römische Rechtsgeschichte* (Cologne 2001), 232 ff. N. Horn, "Die Legistische Literatur der Kommentatoren und der Ausbreitung des gelehrten Rechts" in H. Coing (ed.) *Handbuch der Quellen und Literatur der neueren europäischen Privatrechtsgeschichte. I: Mittelalter (1100–1500), Die gelehrten Rechte und die Gesetzgebung* (Munich 1973), 261–364; G. Wesenberg and G. Wesener, *Neuere deutsche Privatrechtsgeschichte* (Vienna and Cologne

## 7.4    The Development of Canon Law

During the fifth century, the weakness of imperial authority in the West led to the strengthening of the Church and its acquisition of greater political power. As the Roman system of administration disintegrated everywhere, the Church assumed many of the functions of the civil government. Since there was nobody left in Rome who could wield greater power, the bishop of Rome rose to a position of supreme authority. In the course of time, the Roman Catholic Church evolved into a grand international organization that was united, disciplined and thoroughly centralised, with an elaborate administrative structure and a comprehensive system of law courts and officials. In its early formative period, the institutionalised Church borrowed freely from the structure, general concepts and detailed rules of Roman law. It endeavoured to formulate laws to regulate its constitution and to govern the conduct of its members as precisely and as carefully as did the Roman emperors. Therefore, the Church functioned as a means for preserving and disseminating much of the Roman legal system. The growth of the Church and the sustained use of Roman law were interconnected: the Church organization was shaped by Roman law whilst the development of Roman law in the West was affected by the medium (the Church) through which it was transmitted. Out of the interaction between Roman law and Christian ideas, there emerged the law of the Church or canon law. Until the revival of Roman law in the eleventh and twelfth centuries, the Church law was the most important universalising factor in Western Europe. Elements of Church law were incorporated into the various legal codes promulgated by Germanic kings in the West and into the legislation of the Carolingian and Holy Roman Empires. Moreover, during the early Middle Ages the Church claimed and acquired jurisdiction for its own courts (either exclusive or concurrent with that of secular authorities) over certain categories of persons and areas of the law.[33] Throughout the Middle Ages the limits of the jurisdiction granted to the Church tribunals was a matter of constant dispute between Church and secular authorities. Eventually, the ecclesiastical courts were deprived of their civil jurisdiction but meanwhile many of the rules and procedures they had applied were adopted by the secular civil courts.

The chief sources of Church law were the decretals of the Popes (the acts through which the Popes, as heads of the Church, exercised their legislative, administrative and judicial powers), the canons of the Church councils, and various patristic writings concerned with matters of administrative policy and Church doctrine.[34] From the fourth century, several compilations of Church law appeared

---

1985), 28–39; H. Lange and M. Kriechbaum, *Römisches Recht im Mittelalter. Band II, Die Kommentatoren* (Munich 2007).

[33] The jurisdiction of ecclesiastical courts embraced, for example, matrimonial causes and disputes relating to hereditary succession.

[34] The Church drew a distinction between two fundamental categories of law: divine and human. Divine law is thought to have its origin in God's will and is further divided into positive law

in the West and the most important were the *Collectio Dionysiana* (composed in Rome by the monk Dionysius Exiguus on the basis of Apostolic and conciliar canons) and the *Hispana* that were compiled in the early sixth and early seventh centuries respectively. Early in the ninth century an extended version of the *Collectio Dionysiana*, known as *Dionysio-Hadriana* (attributed to Pope Hadrian I), was declared by Charlemagne as the chief code of Church law that applied throughout his empire. In the ninth century, there also appeared a collection of both fictitious and genuine canons that became known as the *False Decretals* (this included the so-called 'Donation of Constantine', a forged document that alleged Emperor Constantine had transferred considerable secular power to the Pope). The aim of this work was apparently to strengthen the claim of Papacy and Church authorities to temporal power. Its legal importance lies in the fact that both the spurious and the genuine materials it contained were utilized by later canonists in their development of the canon law system. Another important collection of the same period was the *Lex Romana canonice compta*, which embodied the rules of Roman law adapted and applicable to the ecclesiastical legal system.[35] Reference should also be made to the *Collectio Anselmo dedicata* (*c*. 882), the first compilation to contain the canonical and Roman texts of Justinian's age arranged in a systematic form. The last two works testify to the process of mingling, interaction and mutual influence of Roman and canon law. This interrelationship may be described as a true reception, through which Roman law norms came to be part of the legal system of the Church.

As noted, the eleventh and twelfth centuries witnessed the revival of legal studies in Western Europe. During the same period, canon law also became the object of systematic study. The task of the canonists was to amalgamate and harmonize the mass of canons contained in earlier canonical collections, and this involved eliminating contradictions and updating matters as necessary. Their ultimate aim was to develop, expand and systematise canon law as an independent body of law and not merely as a set of rules for ecclesiastics. The work that succeeded in transforming canon law into a complete system was the *Decretum* or *Concordia discordantium canonum*, composed by Gratian (a monk at the monastery of Santi Felice e Naborre in Bologna) around the middle of the twelfth century. The *Decterum Gratiani*, as this work became known, was both a code of and a treatise on canon law. It presented in a systematic way and without inconsistencies and contradictions the rules governing priesthood, ecclesiastical jurisdiction,

---

(embodied in the Bible and in tradition) and natural law (the rules derived from nature, discovered by human reason and applicable equally to all human beings). Human law is divided into canon law, consisting of decretals and canons, and civil law. The earlier collections of Church law were mainly composed of Apostolic and conciliar canons; in the later works, the Papal Decretals comprised the bulk of the material.

[35] The principal sources of this work are the Institutes, the Code and, to a greater extent, the Novels of Justinian.

Church property, marriage and the sacraments and services of the Church.[36] Gratian's method of arranging the materials was similar to that followed by the drafters of Justinian's Institutes.[37] Although it was published as an unofficial private work, Gratian's *Decretum* was soon recognized as an authoritative statement of the canon law as it stood in his era. Like the codification of Justinian, it became the object of systematic study in the universities.[38] Students could obtain their degree either in civil law or in canon law, or they could qualify as bachelors of both civil and canon law.

The canon lawyers initially welcomed the revival of the study of civil law, since canon law, it seemed, could learn much from the civil law. In time, however, the two systems became rivals. Civilian and canonist jurists were ranged on opposite sides in the great struggle for supremacy between the empire and the Papacy, which in one form or another lasted throughout the greater part of the Middle Ages. Just like the supporters of the empire endeavoured to buttress the doctrine of the supremacy of the state over the Church by utilizing principles derived from Justinian's texts, the supporters of the Papacy relied on the *Decretum* and earlier patristic writings to defend the hegemony of the Church and to justify the papal claims to temporal power.[39]

In the period following the publication of the *Decretum*, a number of compilations supplementary to Gratian's work were issued by the Popes. These embraced the *Liber Extra*, also known as *Liber Extravagantium*, of Gregory IX, published in 1234[40]; the *Liber Sextus Decretalium*, published by Boniface VIII in 1298[41]; and the *Constitutiones Clementinae* of 1317.[42] In 1501, a private collection of decretals that were not included in earlier compilations was published under the title

---

[36] The official title of this work (*Concordia discordantium canonum*) expresses very clearly its purpose: to reconcile apparently conflicting texts so as to form one authoritative whole. This was done with the help of the well-established dialectic method: through arguments *per analogiam* and *a contrario* and by devising *distinctiones* capable of explaining the similarities and differences between the relevant texts.

[37] The work is divided into three parts; these, in turn, are subdivided into *distinctiones* or *causae*, with the latter again divided into *canones*.

[38] Canonist jurists added an extensive body of *glosses* and commentaries, which were later synthesized in the *glossa perpetua* of the canonists Giovanni Teutonico and Bartolomeo da Brescia.

[39] In this debate the canonists had one advantage. As F. Tout has observed, "While the civilian's Empire was a theory, the canonist's Papacy was a fact. As living head of a living system, the Pope became a constant fountain of new legislation for the canon law, while the civil law remained as it had been in Justinian's time." *The Empire and the Papacy* (London 1921), 220.

[40] This was an official collection, in five books, of papal constitutions and decretals, composed by the Spanish Dominican monk Raymond of Peñafort along the lines of Justinian's compilation. The work was promulgated by the papal bull *Rex pacificus* on 5 September 1234, and was sent to the Universities of Bologna and Paris to be studied and to be used in the courts.

[41] The *Liber Sextus* was promulgated by the bull *Sacrosanctae Romanae Ecclesiae* on 3 March 1298.

[42] This collection was composed by order of Pope Clement in 1313 and was completed and promulgated (by the bull *Quoniam Nulla*) under Pope John XXII in 1317.

*Extravagantes*. All the above works were republished in 1580 by Pope Gregory XIII as parts of an official collection comprising the entire body of canon law (*Corpus Iuris Canonici*), which became the ecclesiastical equivalent of Justinian's *Corpus Iuris Civilis*.[43] Like Roman law, canon law played an important part in the development of law in Europe. Its influence is particularly noticeable in the areas of the law of marriage, the law of succession and the law of obligations. Moreover, canon law has had a considerable influence in the fields of criminal law and the law of procedure.[44]

## 7.5 The Growth of Commercial Law

As observed earlier, from the twelfth century onwards there occurred a large-scale expansion of economic activity. The development of towns into major commercial and industrial centres, first in Italy and later in other parts of Europe, stimulated maritime and overland trade, and engendered the introduction of new forms of business enterprise.[45] Since the existing systems of law were no longer adequate to meet the needs of commercial life, informal tribunals were established in many cities by guilds[46] and merchants' associations. These tribunals heard cases by summary process and in accordance with rules that were practical, fair and based upon the usages actually observed by businessmen in their dealings with one another. These rules were recognized and applied by secular and ecclesiastical authorities as customary law, and they evolved into a body of internationally

---

[43] Each body of law retained its distinctive character, content and field of application. Intrinsic to both systems was a claim of universality, a factor that helps to explain their wholesale reception as elements of the common law (*ius commune*) of Continental Europe.

[44] On the development of canon law see O. F. Robinson, T. D. Fergus and W. M. Gordon, *European Legal History* (London 1994), 72 ff. P. Stein, *Roman Law in European History* (Cambridge 1999), 49–52; J. A. Brundage, *Medieval Canon Law* (London and New York 1995); F. Wieacker, *A History of Private Law in Europe* (Oxford 1995), 47–54; K. W. Nörr, 'Die kanonistische Literatur' in H. Coing (ed.), *Handbuch der Quellen und Literatur der neueren europäischen Privatrechtsgeschichte. I: Mittelalter (1100–1500), Die gelehrten Rechte und die Gesetzgebung* (Munich 1973), 365–382; E. J. H. Schrage, *Utrumque Ius. Eine Einführung in das Studium der Quellen des mittelalterlichen gelehrten Rechts* (Berlin 1992), 90–109.

[45] Since international trade was for a long period dominated by such Italian cities as Venice, Florence, Genoa and Pisa, it is unsurprising that most of commercial institutions, if they did not originate in Italy, had their modern development there.

[46] The guild was an autonomous corporation with monopolistic powers over a particular trade or craft: only those enrolled (the masters of the crafts, their co-workers and apprentices) could legally practice the trade. Furthermore, it alone had the power to adjudicate commercial disputes among its members. In the course of time guilds became, in many towns, the basic units of the communal government and thus enrolment in a guild was often an important prerequisite to participation in public life.

recognized law, known as the Law Merchant, which succeeded in penetrating areas where even Roman law met with resistance.[47] This common commercial law, like Roman law and canon law, formed another vital strand in the law of Western Europe, not excluding in this case the law of England.[48]

## 7.6   Feudal Law

Feudal law comprised the body of rules governing the relationship between a feudal lord and his vassal and the tenure by which the vassal held the land he received from the lord. The system originated in Germanic customary law and was developed in France during the Carolingian era. The three greatest monarchs of the late twelfth and early thirteenth centuries—Henry II of England and Normandy (1154–1189), Philip Augustus of France (1180–1223) and Frederick Barbarossa of Germany (1152–1190)—all promulgated important laws dealing with diverse feudal matters. In the thirteenth and fourteenth centuries, treatises on feudal law were composed by Romanist jurists and several works appeared that recorded local customs in various parts of Europe. It is important to note here that in France and England feudal law was woven into the whole legal fabric, whilst in Germany it was treated as a distinct system whose rules were applicable only to certain estates or individuals and were administered by special courts. However, in all three countries feudal law did not operate independently of other bodies of law: all secular systems (feudal, mercantile, urban and royal) influenced and overlapped one another.

One of the most distinctive features of feudal law was its combination of political and economic rights: the right of government, the right of jurisdiction and the right to use and dispose of land.[49] The point of departure was the legal situation that arose when a person, the vassal, received a piece of land from the lord as a *beneficium* and, in return, undertook to provide personal service, usually of a military character. The personal bond that was created entailed duties as well as rights for both sides: the vassal owed the lord whatever good faith required, usually aid and counsel (*auxilium* and *consilium*), and the lord in his turn undertook the duty to protect and maintain the vassal. The term tenure is used to describe the grounds of a continuous possession of land, or of anything that could be equated

---

[47] For example, in England, where Roman law was unable to displace the common law, the merchant law was adopted as part of the law of the land because it was better suited to the needs of domestic and international commerce.

[48] For a closer look at the development of the Law Merchant see O.F. Robinson, T. D. Fergus and W. M. Gordon, *European Legal History* (London 1994), 90 ff.; D. Tamm, *Roman Law and European Legal History* (Copenhagen 1997), 228–30; J. Kirschner (ed.), *Business, Banking and Economic Thought in the Late Medieval and Early Modern Europe* – Selected studies of Raymond de Roover (Chicago 1974).

[49] An important distinction in this area was that between the greater and the lesser right of jurisdiction, depending on whether capital punishment was available as an option or not.

with land.[50] In a purely feudal society land was not owned by anyone; it was held by superiors in a ladder of tenures leading to the king as the supreme lord. Thus, a person could have certain rights in land valid against his lord, and the lord could have certain rights in the same land against his lord, as well as other rights valid against that lord's lord, who might be the king. The rules concerning feudal hierarchy and rights of succession were an important part of feudal law. Moreover, from an early time, it had been recognized as a rule of customary feudal law that if a vassal broke faith with his lord the fief reverted to the lord.[51] Important rights associated with feudalism were the right to exercise governmental and administrative powers, and the right to hold court and declare the law. Besides the immunities in matters of taxation and jurisdiction granted to local lords, the later also possessed powers of policing, judging and inflicting punishment in the territories under their control, especially during the ninth and tenth centuries. In Germany where, as previously noted, feudal law (*Lehnrecht*) remained distinct from the law of the land (*Landrecht*), the feudal courts developed and operated side by side with the other courts. By contrast, in France legal procedure became totally feudalized after the death of Charlemagne in the early ninth century.[52]

The move towards the systematization of feudal law began in the twelfth century, when the Lombard feudal law that applied in Italy became the subject of academic inquiry. The Lombard sources of law, such as the *Lombarda* and the *Liber Papiensis*, were explained and commented on by jurists at Pavia and Bologna and around 1150 a collection of feudal law, the *Libri Feudorum*, appeared in Milan.[53] In the period that followed the study of feudal law became part of the study of Roman law and the *Libri Feudorum* were commented on and systematized by several legal scholars, such as Pillius of Medicina, James de Ardizzone and Accursius. The latter produced an authoritative gloss to the *Libri* in the 1220s, which were eventually included in the final volume of the *Corpus Iuris Civilis*, which contained Justinian's Novels. In this way, the main body of feudal law became part of the *libri legales*, the legal books of the learned law, and continued to be studied by scholars and used by practitioners until the end of the sixteenth century or even later.[54]

---

[50] 'Tenure' is derived from the Latin work *tenere*: to hold.

[51] The Norman word for such a breach of faith was 'felony'. In England the most serious crimes came to be referred to as felonies, because they were considered to involve breaches of the fealty owed by all people to the king as guardian of the peace of the realm.

[52] In England after the Norman conquest the local courts came under the control of the kings and thus royal justice was able in a fairly short period of time to supplant feudal justice.

[53] The *Libri Feudorum* was based mainly on imperial legislation in the kingdom of Italy but also embodied other materials, including decisions from various feudal courts.

[54] In the later half of the twelfth century, a book attributed to Glanvill appeared in England, which contained the customary feudal law of the realm, with references to the Institutes of Justinian. Nearly half a century after Glanvill, the German Eike von Repgow published an account of feudal law as part of his *Sachsenspiegel* (1235). Moreover, feudal and common law were often combined, as we can see in the famous *Customs of Beauvaisis* (a region north of Paris), published by the French jurist Philippe de Beaumanoir in about 1280.

Once feudal law became systematized, the specificity of its norms increased and the uniformity of its general principles gradually overshadowed local differences. The reification of the relevant rights and obligations superseded the personal aspects of the lord-vassal relationship and also gave the vassal a greater degree of economic autonomy in managing his fief. Special emphasis was now placed on the reciprocity of the rights and obligations between the parties, as well as on the participation of the parties in the proceedings through which disputes over such rights and obligations were adjudicated. In a word, the characteristic features of feudal law were formalized as elements of its autonomous development in time. Nevertheless, in comparison with Roman and canon law, feudal law was less systematic, less integrated and less scientific. It was largely customary law and as such was treated with more skepticism and as more open to correction and even repudiation than the learned law pertaining to Justinian's main *Corpus* and Gratian's *Decretum*.[55]

## 7.7   The Reception of Roman Law

The thousands of students from all over Europe who had studied at Bologna and other Italian universities conveyed to their own countries the new legal learning based on the revived Roman law. Throughout Western Europe (in France, Spain, the Netherlands, Germany and Poland), universities were established where scholars trained in the methods of the Glossators and the Commentators taught the civil law on the basis of Justinian's texts. Their students formed a new class of professional lawyers whose members came to occupy the most important positions in both the administrative and judicial branches of government. Before the twelfth century, justice was administered by untrained jurors and based on local legal sources. In contrast, justice was now administered by professional judges appointed by a sovereign who could apply Roman law if local sources (either customary or statutory) were deficient. Through the activities of university-trained judges and jurists, the Roman law expounded by the Glossators and the Commentators entered the legal life of Continental Europe. It formed the basis of a common body of law, a common legal language and a common legal science—a development known as the 'Reception' of Roman law.

Like the Latin language and the universal Church, the received Roman law served as an important universalising factor in the West at a time when there were no centralised states and no unified legal systems but a multitude of overlapping and often competing jurisdictions and sources of law (local customs and statutes,

---

[55] On the development of feudal law see O.F. Robinson, T. D. Fergus and W. M. Gordon, *European Legal History* (London 1994), 26 ff.; D. Tamm, *Roman Law and European Legal History* (Copenhagen 1997), 199–201; M. Bloch, *Feudal Society*, 2nd ed. (London 1962); P. Stein, *Roman Law in European History* (Cambridge 1999), 61–62.

feudal, imperial and ecclesiastical law). However, the course of the reception was complex and characterised by a lack of uniformity. This derived from the fact that the way in which Roman law was received in different parts of Europe was affected to a great extent by local conditions, and the actual degree of Roman law infiltration varied from region to region. In areas of Southern Europe that had incorporated Roman law as part of the applicable customary law, the process of the reception may be described as a resurgence, refinement and enlargement of Roman law. This occurred, for example, in Italy where the influence of Roman law had remained strong and in Southern France where the customary law that applied was already heavily Romanised. In Northern Europe, on the other hand, very little of Roman law had survived and the process of the reception was prolonged with a much more sweeping impact in some regions at its closing stages. The common law (*ius commune*) of Europe that gradually emerged towards the close of the Middle Ages was the result of a fusion between the Roman law of Justinian (as elaborated by medieval scholars), the canon law of the Church and Germanic customary law. The dominant element in this mixture was Roman law, although Roman law itself experienced considerable change under the influence of local custom and the statutory and canon law.

The universal *ius commune* was juxtaposed with the *ius proprium*, the local laws of the diverse medieval city-states and other political communities. Local law sometimes assumed the form of statute or, especially in earlier times, grew out of custom.[56] But the universal and local laws were not necessarily antithetical; they were complementary and each interacted with and influenced the other. Statutory enactments born out of the need to address situations not provided for by the *ius commune* were often formulated and interpreted according to the concepts developed by scholars of the *ius commune*. The scholars, in turn, with their concern for concrete problems of social and commercial life and the need to deal with the law as it actually existed, took the local law into consideration. In their roles as judges, lawyers and officials, jurists trained in Roman law at Bologna and other law schools regarded local law as an exception to the *ius commune*, and therefore as something

---

[56] The first compilations of city customary law appeared in the second half of the twelfth century in Venice and Bari. These collections were subsequently superseded by statutory enactments, i.e. legislation issued by a local legislative body. An enactment of this kind (*statutum*) was distinguished from a law of theoretical universal application (*lex*), which could be promulgated only by the emperor. In principle, a *statutum* was subordinate and could only supplement but not alter or derogate from a *lex*. In fact, however, local statutes that were irreconcilable with imperial laws often prevailed in the legal practice of the area or city in which they had been enacted. An important example of legislation issued by a monarch is the *Liber Constitutionum Regni Siciliae*, also known as *Liber Augustalis*, a legal code for the Kingdom of Sicily promulgated by Emperor Frederick II in 1231. This code remained the principal body of law in the Southern Kingdom until the eighteenth century. Royal legislation was also enacted in the County (later Duchy) of Savoy, the provinces of Sardinia, the Patriarchate of Aquileia and many other areas. In the domains of the Church, the most important legislative enactment was the *Constitutiones Sanctae Matris Ecclesiae*, also informally known as *Constitutiones Aegidianae*, issued in 1357 by Cardinal Gil of Albornoz, the legate to the papal state during Pope's residence in Avignon.

requiring restrictive interpretation. Furthermore, they tended to interpret local law based on concepts and terminology derived from Roman law, thereby bringing it into line or harmonizing it with the *ius commune*.[57]

## 7.7.1   The Reception of Roman Law in France

In the period between the sixth and the ninth centuries, three bodies of law applied in France: under the system of the personality of the laws, the Germanic sections of the population were governed by their own laws and customs, whilst the Roman inhabitants of the country continued to live according to Roman law; at the same time, everyone in France (irrespective of ethnic origin) was bound by the laws promulgated by the Frankish monarchs. In the course of the ninth century, the personal system of laws began to disintegrate (as the fusion of the different races made its application virtually impossible) and yielded to a territorial system. The shift from the system of personality to that of territoriality coincided in time with the expansion and consolidation of the feudal institutions in France. Whilst the territory of every feudal lord was governed by its own customs, the customary law that applied in an area generally tended to derive from the predominant ethnic group. And since the Roman element was dominant in Southern France and the Germanic element prevailed in the North, the whole country was divided into two broad regions: the country of the written law (*Pays du Droit écrit*) in the South, where Roman law as embodied in various sources, such as the *Lex Romana Visigothorum* and later editions of the *Corpus iuris civilis*, prevailed; and the country of customary law (*Pays des Coutumes, droit coutumier*) in the North that featured the application of a variety of local customs with a Frankish-Germanic character. In both zones, the law in force also included elements derived from royal, feudal, and canonical sources.

In the South of France, the land of written law, the common law of the region was essentially Roman law (notwithstanding local differences). The Roman law of Justinian was rapidly received in Southern France and accepted as the living law of the land. This favourable reception was facilitated by the revival of Roman law in the late eleventh and twelfth centuries, and the spread of its study from Bologna to

---

[57] Even in parts of Europe where Roman law was not received in a normative sense, the conceptual structure created by the Glossators and the Commentators was sometimes employed to give a Roman form to indigenous customary rules. Thus, although the *ius commune* was not adopted in Norway and Hungary, local legislation exhibited a certain Roman influence. For example, the Norwegian Code of 1274 of King Magnus VI, while intended to be a written statement of ancient Viking custom, reflects an influence of Roman-canonical law in its organization and many of its institutions. Similarly, in Hungary the spirit of Roman law exercised an influence on the structure of Hungarian law and the character and development of legal thought. In areas as far off as the Ukraine and Belarus, where there was no reception, doctrines and practices of Roman law were introduced through the influence of Byzantine law.

Montpellier and other parts of France. In the early twelfth century, a summary of Justinian's Code was produced in Southern France with the designation *Lo Codi* and based on the work of the Glossators. The study of Roman law received a fresh impetus with the establishment of new law schools at Toulouse and Orleans in the thirteenth century. In these schools and the many others that sprang up in the years that followed the civil law was taught on the basis of Justinian's texts.[58]

In the northern regions of France, the country of customary law, a multitude of Germanic customs were in force. Some of these customs applied over a wider area (*coutumes générales*), whilst others were confined to a particular town or locality (*coutumes locales*)—there were 60 general customs and 300 special or local customs. In this part of France, Roman law was regarded as a supplementary system invoked when the customary law was silent or ambiguous. Moreover, in certain areas of the law (such as the law of contracts and the law of obligations) the Roman system had been adopted and perceived as superior to customary law as well as better suited for tackling many new problems that emerged from the expansion of economic activity.

The administration of justice fell in the province of regional judicial and legislative bodies referred to as Parliaments (*Parlements*). In the country of customary law, the case law of the Parliament in Paris acquired special significance. Advocates attached to this body fostered legal development by means of an intensive literary activity that pertained, largely, to the study of case law.[59]

From the beginning of the thirteenth century, the customs of many regions of Northern France began to be recorded. Several collections of customary law appeared, written in the vernacular but modelled on Roman law compilations. Some of these works, such as the *Les Livres de Jostice et de Plet* (The Books of Justice and Pleading), composed around 1260, reflect a strong influence of Roman law. In other works, such as the *Coutumes de Beauvaisis* (the customs of the county of Clermont in Beauvaisis) written in the late thirteenth century, the impact of Roman law is much less noticeable. Moreover, some of these compilations were private whilst others were issued under the authority of various feudal lords (*chartes de coutumes*). In general, the purpose of these works was to compile and present in a clear form the rules of customary law that applied in one or more regions so that these rules could more easily be proved in the courts of law.

---

[58] The *Ultramontani*, as the jurists at Toulouse, Orleans and Montpellier were referred to, employed essentially the same methods and composed the same types of legal work as their Italian colleagues at Bologna. The first professors of these universities were Frenchmen who had studied at Bologna, but later there were some who had received their training in France (such as Jacques de Revigny and Pierre de Belleperche, both of whom taught at Orleans). These later jurists were more interested in legal theory than the Italian Glossators, and adopted a more historical and more liberal approach to the study of the Roman legal sources. Moreover, they made a significant contribution to non-Roman areas of law, such as penal law and international private law.

[59] In the course of time, the works of the Parisian advocates formed the basis of an extensive body of jurisprudence that was built upon the comparative study of the diverse local customs – a study that also paid attention to the great tradition of Roman law in France.

In order to reduce the confusion caused by the multiplicity of customs, King Charles VII ordered the compilation of the customs of all regions of France in his Ordinance of Montils-les-Tours in 1453. Although the direction proved largely ineffectual, it was repeated by subsequent monarchs and most of the customary law had been committed to writing by the end of the sixteenth century. The consolidation of customary law through its official publication precluded the wholesale reception of Roman law in Northern France, although elements of Roman legal doctrine entered the fixed body of customary law by way of interpretation. Moreover, Roman law continued to apply in areas of private law on which customary law was silent. This interaction of Roman and customary sources infused the law that prevailed in Northern France with a distinctive character.

Although the publication of the customs removed much of the confusion caused by local differences, legal unity was certainly not achieved. In addition to the differences between Northern and Southern France, considerable regional diversity persisted even within each of the main territorial divisions. Legal unity was finally established in France with the introduction of the Napoleonic Code in 1804.

In the course of the 150 years prior to the enactment of the French Civil Code, the academic study of Roman law reached a climax—a development associated with the writings of jurists such as Jean Domat (1625–1695) and Robert Joseph Pothier (1699–1772).

Domat was born in Clermont-Ferrand, where he served as judge until 1681. His best-known work is his *Les loix civiles dans leur ordre naturel*, published in three volumes between the years 1689 and 1694. After an examination of the entire recorded body of legal material (*droit écrit*) of his region (Auvergne), Domat concluded that it was permeated by an internal logic and rationality that pointed to the existence of certain universal or immutable legal principles (*loix immuables*). He noted that these natural principles are reflected best in the norms of private law; public law, on the other hand, is composed to a much larger extent of statutory laws of a changeable or arbitrary character (*loix arbitraries*). Domat asserted that the general principles of Roman law, as embodied in the codification of Justinian, met the criteria of the *loix immuables* and could be ascribed the status of a system. He argued, further, that contemporary French language was capable of expressing this system in a clear and precise way.[60]

Pothier was born and studied in Orleans, where he served as judge and, from 1749, as university professor. His first major work, *La coutume d'Orléans avec des observations nouvelles*, published in 1740,[61] was concerned with the customary law of his hometown. His next important work was a comprehensive treatise on Roman private law, titled *Pandectae justineaneae in novum ordinem digestae cum legibus*

---

[60] Domat was the first major academic jurist who challenged the connection between Roman law and its original language, Latin. With respect to the order of the various branches of private law, Domat first treated the general rules of law, then persons, property, obligations and, finally inheritance law. For a closer look at Domat's work see C. Sarzotti, *Jean Domat: Fondamento e metodo della scienza giuridica* (Turin 1995).

[61] A revised edition of this work was published in 1760.

*codicis et novellae* (1748–1752). This was followed by a series of works on a diversity of legal institutions.[62] In his writings, Pothier sought to overcome the problems for legal practice caused by the fragmentation of the law in France by means of a systematic restatement of fundamental Roman law concepts and principles.[63] In this way he contributed a great deal to the process of unification of private law in France.[64]

## 7.7.2  The Reception of Roman Law in Germany

During the early Middle Ages, the law that applied in Germany was customary law that tended to vary regionally as a result of the shift from the system of personality to that of territoriality of the laws. Some of the customs applied over an entire region, whilst others were confined to a single city, village community or manor. After the establishment of the Holy Roman Empire of the German Nation in the tenth century, imperial law (concerned almost exclusively with constitutional matters) contributed as an additional source of law. Although the German emperors regarded themselves as successors of the Roman emperors and imperial legislation was influenced by the idea of a universal empire, initially there was no attempt to render Roman law applicable to all German regions as a form of common law that could replace local customs. In the twelfth and thirteenth centuries, Germans who had studied at the law schools of Italy and France introduced some knowledge of Roman law into Germany. However, the effect of this activity on the applicable customary laws was limited as Roman law scholars were largely ignorant or contemptuous of the local laws, which they regarded as primitive in both form and substance and as unworthy of the serious attention of the learned.

In the thirteenth and fourteenth centuries, there appeared a number of compilations embodying the customary laws observed in certain regions of Germany. The

---

[62] These included his *Traité des obligations I et II* (1761–1764); *Traité du contrat de vente* (1762); *Traité des retraits* (1762); *Traité du contrat de constitution de rente* (1763); *Traité du contrat de louage*; (1764); *Traité du contrat de société* (1764); *Traité de cheptels* (1765); *Traité du contrat de prêt de consomption* (1766); *Traité du contrat de dépôt et de mandat* (1766); *Traité du contrat de natissement* (1767); *Traité du contrat de mariage I et II* (1766); *Traité du droit de domaine de propriété* (1772); and *Traité de la possession et de la prescription* (1772). Pothier's works were widely used by jurists and lawyers throughout the eighteenth and nineteenth centuries. An important collection of these works in 11 volumes was published by Dupin in 1824/25.

[63] For example, in his treatise on the institution of ownership Pothier shows how, in a feudal system that encompassed several forms of property and related entitlements, the fundamental Roman law concept of property could be employed to overcome, in theory at least, many of the discrepancies of the current system.

[64] The Code Civil adopted many of the legal solutions proposed by Pothier, especially in the field of the law of obligations. The drafters of the Code also adopted the systematic structure preferred by Pothier, which goes back to the classical Roman jurist Gaius and was followed by Emperor Justinian: persons; things (including obligations and succession); and actions.

most important of these works were the *Sachsenspiegel*, or the Mirror of the Saxons, composed around 1225 by Eike von Repgow and containing the territorial customary law observed in parts of Northern Germany[65]; the *Deutschenspiegel*, or Mirror of the Germans, published about 1260 in Southern Germany; and the *Schwabenspiegel*, or Mirror of the Swabians, a collection of the customs of Swabia published in the late thirteenth century.[66] These works aspired to provide a basis for developing a common customary law for Germany, but the centrifugal tendencies that prevailed were too strong to be overcome by these works. The formulation of a native common law for the entire country based upon Germanic sources was impossible. This derived from the weakness of the imperial power that was exacerbated by the political splintering of the empire in the late thirteenth century, and the multitude and diversity of the local customs. A further obstacle to the attainment of legal unity was the fact that there was no organized professional class of lawyers interested in developing a common body of law. The administration of justice was in the hands of lay judges, the *Schöffen*, who had the task of declaring the applicable law for a particular issue in court by reference to the customary law that applied in each district. However, the pronouncements of the *Schöffen* were only concerned with particular cases and reflected the personal views of laymen who were not necessarily guided by generally established rules or principles—thus, they added to the uncertainty surrounding the application of customary law.

In the fifteenth century, the problems generated by the fragmented nature of the law in Germany became intolerable as commercial transactions proliferated between different territories. Local custom was no longer adequate to meet the needs of a rapidly changing society, and the weakness of the imperial government meant the unification of the customary law by legislative action alone was unthinkable. If a common body of law could not be developed based on Germanic sources, another system offered a readily available alternative, namely Roman law. The acceptance of Roman law in Germany was facilitated by the idea that the Holy Roman Empire of the German Nation was a continuation of the ancient Roman Empire.[67] In this respect, Roman law was viewed not as a foreign system of law but as a system that continued to apply within the empire as its common law. This idea found support in the newly established German universities, where the teaching of law was based exclusively on Roman and canonical sources[68] whilst Germanic customary law was almost completely ignored. Like the jurists of other countries, German jurists regarded Roman law as superior to the native law and existing in

---

[65] The *Sachsenspiegel*, a work of outstanding quality, achieved great prestige and authority throughout Germany. Modern commentators regard it as the beginning of Germanic legal literature.

[66] Both the Mirror of the Germans and the Mirror of the Swabians reflect some influence of Roman law.

[67] The Emperor of the Holy Roman Empire was at the same time king of Germany and of Italy.

[68] The methods of study and the legal materials used were substantially the same as those employed in Italian universities.

force both as written law (*ius scriptum*) by virtue of the imperial tradition and as written reason (*ratio scripta*) due to its inherent value.

At a practical level, the reception of Roman law in Germany was facilitated by the establishment in 1495 of the Imperial Chamber Court (*Reichskammergericht*) by a legislative act of Emperor Maximilian I (1493–1519). This act focused on the centralisation of the German system of judicial administration and was part of Maximilian's broader political program designed to restore the power of the monarchy and to secure legal and political unity. The new imperial court, which heard appeals from regional and local courts, was directed to decide cases 'according to the imperial and common law and also according to just, equitable and reasonable ordinances and customs'. Since jurists trained in Roman law dominated the composition of the court, the term 'common law' was naturally interpreted as meaning Roman law. The significance of the 1495 legislation was that it formally acknowledged Roman law as positive law in Germany. Pursuant to this law, judges were required to apply Roman law only when a relevant custom or statutory provision could not be proved. In practice, the difficulty in proving an overriding German rule meant that Roman law became the basic law throughout Germany. The model of the Imperial Chamber Court was followed by the territorial courts of appeal established by local princes in Austria, Saxony, Bavaria, Branden-burg and other German states. At the same time, the courts where lay judges still presided increasingly relied on the advice of learned jurists (city advocates, state officials and university professors) for information and guidance concerning local as well as Roman law. In the course of time, the role of the lay judges diminished and the administration of justice was dominated by professional lawyers who had been trained in Roman and canon law at the universities. By the end of the sixteenth century, it had become common practice for judges to seek the advice of university professors on difficult questions of law arising from actual cases. The opinion rendered was regarded as binding on the court that had requested it. This practice (*Aktenversendung*) prevailed until the nineteenth century, entailing the accumu-lation of an extensive body of legal doctrine that applied throughout Germany.

By the end of the sixteenth century, Roman law had become firmly established as the common law of Germany.[69] Germanic law had largely been rejected in favour of the more advanced Roman system and German jurisprudence had become essentially Roman jurisprudence. The Roman law that was received embodied the Roman law of Justinian as interpreted and modified by the Glossators and the Commentators. This body of law was further modified by German jurists to fit the conditions of the times and thereby a Germanic element was introduced into what remained a basically Roman structure. In some parts of Germany (such as Saxony), Germanic customary law survived and certain institutions of Germanic origin were retained in the legislation of local princes and of cities. Legal practitioners and jurists from the sixteenth to the eighteenth century executed the process of

---

[69] German scholars use the phrase '*Rezeption in complexu*', that is 'full reception', to describe this development.

moulding into one system the Roman and Germanic law, which led to the development of a new approach to the analysis and interpretation of the Justinianic Roman law—referred to as *Usus modernus Pandectarum* ('modern application of the Pandects/Digest').[70] This approach continued to be followed in Germany, subject to local variations, until the introduction of the German Civil Code in 1900.


### 7.7.3   *The* Ius Commune *in Italy, the Iberian Peninsula and the Netherlands*


By the close of the fifteenth century, the medieval world of the Italian city-states had evolved into the Kingdom of Naples in the south, the Papal States and Tuscany in central Italy, Piedmont, Lombardy under Milan, the Republic of Venice and a number of lesser states.[71] The Kingdom of Naples was a centralized state with a hierarchy of courts, more akin to France or Spain than the rest of Italy. The continued political fragmentation of Italy did not affect the application of civil law and the working of the courts, which maintained the traditional blending of the Roman law of the Glossators and Commentators, canonical procedure and general and particular custom. The great medieval treatises of Bartolus and Baldus, in particular, continued to enjoy high esteem. The legal literature that emerged in university towns, such as Bologna, Padua, Pavia and Naples, although frequently concerned with local needs, became part of the pan-European *ius commune*—a

---

[70] Although this approach externally appears to be a continuation of the Bartolist method, under the influence of Legal Humanism (see relevant discussion below) it gave rise to a different doctrine about the sources of law: whereas Roman law continued to be regarded as an important source of law, local law was no longer viewed as an aberration from Roman law but as a further development of Roman law through custom. Thus, the *Usus modernus Pandectarum* elevated the importance of local law, which now became the subject of systematic scientific study. As far as Roman law is concerned, the term *Usus modernus Pandectarum* implies that the jurists' purpose was to apply the Roman legal texts in contemporary legal practice. The representatives of this approach may to some extent have been influenced by the work of the Humanist jurists, but they tended to use the Roman texts ahistorically, as just another source of legal norms. However, there was no general agreement among jurists as to which texts actually applied. It should be noted that the methods of the *Usus modernus* movement were adopted by many French and Dutch jurists. Leading representatives of this movement include Samuel Stryk (1640–1710), a professor at Frankfurt a.d. Oder, Wittenberg and Halle; Georg Adam Struve (1619–1692); Ulric Huber (1636–1694); Cornelis van Bynkershoek (1673–1743); Arnoldus Vinnius (1588–1657); Gerard Noodt (1647–1725); and Johannes Voet (1647–1713). On the *Usus modernus Pandectarum* see F. Wieacker, *A History of Private Law in Europe* (Oxford 1995), 159 ff. D. Tamm, *Roman Law and European Legal History* (Copenhagen 1997), 225; A. Söllner, "Usus modernus Pandectarum" in H. Coing (ed.), *Handbuch der Quellen und Literatur der neueren europäischen Privatrechtsgeschichte. II: Neuere Zeit (1500–1800), 1. Teilband, Wissenschaft* (Munich 1977), 501–516; R. Voppel, *Der Einfluß des Naturrechts auf den Usus modernus* (Cologne 1996); H. Schlosser, *Grundzüge der Neueren Privatrechtsgeschichte, Rechtsentwicklungen im europäischen Kontext* (Heidelberg 2005), 76–83.

[71] These included Siena, Ferrara and Mantua.

process facilitated by the invention of the printing press in the late fifteenth century.[72] Italian scholars of the late fifteenth and early sixteenth centuries, such as Giasone del Maino (1435–1519) and Filippo Decio (1454—*c*. 1535), sought to combine the tradition of the *ius commune* with the ideals of the new humanist learning. After the integration of Italy into the Napoleonic state, the French Civil Code was introduced in the country (1806). Even though the *ius commune* continued to exist even after the restoration of the Italian states following the defeat of Napoleon (1815), a growing number of states began to draw up their own law codes (the so-called *codici preunitari*). The earliest among these, the codes of the Kingdom of Naples (1819) and the Duchy of Parma (1820), were modelled closely on the French Civil Code, while the later ones of Piedmont (1837) and Modena (1851) represent a peculiar blend of French style and traditional local elements. In Lombardy and Venice, which had been returned to the rule of the Austrian emperors, the Austrian Civil Code (ABGB) of 1811 was put into force.[73]

Any consideration of the development of law in Spain must take into account the fluid relationships between the different peoples that settled in the Iberian Peninsula and the changing fortunes of the diverse states that evolved in medieval times. As noted earlier, in the second half of the fifth century the Germanic tribe of the Visigoths was successful in establishing a permanent rule on the Peninsula.[74] In the period that followed, Roman personal law, as embodied in the *Lex Romana Visigothorum*, coexisted with the laws of the Visigoths (who never amounted to more that 5 % of the total population). In the course of time, as the two ethnic groups merged, a territorial law, permeated in both substance and form by Roman law, prevailed. This law was embodied in the *corpus iuris* promulgated for all citizens by the Visigothic king Recceswinth in *c*. 654. The new law code, referred to as *Liber Iudiciorum* or *Lex Visigothorum*, remained the basis of law in Spain until the fifteenth century, governing the Christian population even during the long Muslim rule (from 711). During the period when Christian forces were pushing back those of Islam, a diversity of states of varying sizes and significance emerged in the territory of present-day Spain: Castile (later reunited with León), including Galicia and the Basque region; Aragon; Catalonia; Navarre; and the Balearic Islands.

The legal development of Castile-León deserves special mention because of the important role this state played in the unification of Spain. In this realm the king exercised supreme jurisdiction as the natural lord of all his subjects. The growing influence of the court of *alcades de corte*, or of the royal household, composed of professional judges, diminished the importance of local customs of a largely

---

[72] As already noted, the local laws were not necessarily in conflict with the universal ones: many laws born out of the need to address situations not provided for by the *ius commune* were formulated and interpreted in accordance with concepts devised by jurists of *the ius commune*.

[73] The ABGB combined natural law ideas, especially in the fields of the law of persons and family law, with Roman law concepts and principles.

[74] The capital of the Visigothic kingdom was Toledo.

Germanic origin, called *fueros* or *usus terrae*. In the course of the thirteenth and fourteenth centuries men trained in Roman law at the universities (*letrados*) became influential and attained high office in the royal service. A large number of students from Spain attended Bologna, and this trend continued even after the first Spanish universities were established (in Palencia, Salamanca, Seville and Lerida) in the thirteenth century.[75] The Spanish jurists spread the knowledge of Roman law and the methods of the Glossators and the Commentators throughout the Iberian Peninsula. The most significant product of this growth of the study of Roman law was the famous *Libro de las leyes*, commonly called the *Las Siete Partidas* (The Seven Parts [of the Law]), compiled by order of King Alfonso X the Learned during the period 1256–1265. This work, drafted largely by jurists of the University of Salamanca, contains a large number of legal rules on marriage, contracts, inheritance and procedure, derived from a variety of Roman and canonical sources.[76] The enforcement of *Las Siete Partidas* as the common law of Spain was delayed due to the opposition of Spanish traditionalists, who remained loyal to their local customs. Only in 1348 was it promulgated as general law (by the *Ordenamiento de Alcalá*, a compilation of laws enacted by the courts of Alfonso XI in Alcalá de Henares), even though it remained subordinate to local custom. However, as local customs needed to be proved to a court as actually being observed, whilst there was always a presumption in favour of *Las Siete Partidas*, the later work gradually came to prevail as the official law of Spain. The accompanying reception of the learned law of the *ius commune* was so massive that the monarchs decreed that the courts, when faced with gaps in the law, should rely on the authority of the major Glossators and Commentators.[77] Although *Las Siete Partidas* was rearranged at various times as political conditions evolved, it remained the foundation of law in Spain until it was superseded by the *Codigo Civil* of 1889.

In neighbouring Portugal the law that applied was at first derived from the *Liber Iudiciorum* of the Visigoths, as extended in 1054 by King Alfonso V of León, and local customs. But, in the course of time, the *ius commune* was received in this country too, with the principal centres of legal learning being the universities of Coimbra and Lisbon. It is thus unsurprising that the first comprehensive collection of Portuguese laws, the *Ordenações Afonsinas*, enacted by King Alfonse V in 1446, in large part consisted of Roman and canon law. This compilation was followed by the *Ordenações Manuelinas*, promulgated by King Manuel in 1521, and finally in 1603, during the reign of King Philip II, by the *Ordenações Filipilinas*, which remained in force until modern times not only in Portugal, but also in its colonies,

---

[75] So numerous were the students from Spain studying at Bologna that in 1346 a special college was set up for them there by the Spanish Cardinal Gil of Albornoz.

[76] These sources include the *Corpus Iuris* of Justinian, the *Decretum* of Gratian, the *Decretales* of Gregory IX, and the works of some of the most famous of the Glossators, especially Azo and Accursius on civil law, and Goffredo of Trani and Raymond of Peñafort on canon law.

[77] To avoid confusion, in 1427 John II, King of Castile and León, ordained that the courts should not follow, as authorities, the opinions of jurists later that Johannes Andreae (Giovanni d'Andrea) on canon law and Bartolus on Roman law. Later, by a law of 1499, Baldo was also included.

such as Brazil. These enactments embodied the principle that Roman law and the works of the Glossators and the Commentators constituted the common law of the realm that was applicable whenever local legislation or customs were silent or ambiguous.

In the Netherlands, as in most areas of Western Europe, the revival in the study and application of Roman law in the High Middle Ages led to a major reception of Roman legal norms, concepts and principles, so that by the end of the sixteenth century Dutch law bore a heavily Romanised look. This development occurred at a time when the material prosperity of Holland had advanced considerably, owing largely to the growth of trade and commerce, and so a more sophisticated legal system was required to meet the new conditions. Instances of Roman legal influence were particularly evident in the fields of the law of property, contract and delict, as these were the areas where Roman law was considered to be far superior to the indigenous Dutch law. However, in spheres such as the law of persons and intestate succession, local customary laws largely resisted the Roman reception. Moreover, even in the areas of property and contract, Dutch jurists were cautious in their selection of Roman rules, and tended to reject archaic and formalistic concepts. The outcome of this process was thus a hybrid legal system, consisting of Roman and Dutch elements, which came to be known as Roman-Dutch law.[78] The principal centre of Roman legal studies in the Netherlands was the University of Leyden, established in 1575. In the period that followed more universities were founded at Franeker in Friesland (1585), Groningen (1614), Utrecht (1636) and Harderwijk in Gelderland (1648). Legal development in the seventeenth and eighteenth centuries was based largely on the work of the Dutch professors, especially those of Leyden, who, together with the judges of the High Courts of the provinces, created a highly advanced body of law derived from the synthesis of legal science and legal practice.[79] In 1652 Roman-Dutch law was introduced to South Africa, with the result that the Roman and Dutch texts became authoritative sources of South African law.[80]

---

[78] The term 'Roman-Dutch law' was introduced in the seventeenth century by the jurist Simon van Leeuwen, who used it as a title in his principal work, *Roomsch Hollandsch Recht* (1664).

[79] The greatest product of the Leyden law faculty was Hugo Grotius, author of the famous work *De iure belli ac pacis* (1625). Grotius also published a work entitled an Introduction to the Jurisprudence of Holland (*Inleidinge tot de Hollandsche Rechtsgeleerdheid*, 1631), in which he treats the law of Holland as a unique amalgam of Germanic custom and Roman law. Reference should also be made here to Arnold Vinnius (1588–1657), a law professor at Leyden, who established Dutch legal science as a mixture of Roman, customary and natural law elements; Johannes Voet (1647–1714), another Leyden professor, author of the influential *Commentarius ad Pandectas*, published in two volumes in 1698 and 1704; and Ulrich Huber (1636–1694), a professor at the University of Franeker, whose works *De iure civitatis libri tres* (1672) and *Paelectiones iuris civilis* (1678–1690) are built up largely from Roman materials. The widespread influence of the Dutch masters throughout Europe is attested by the large numbers of foreign editions of their principal works in the seventeenth and eighteenth centuries.

[80] It should be noted here that unlike the Continental European legal systems, but like the English common law, Roman-Dutch law in South Africa has not been codified. It is thus unsurprising that law courts and commentators have to grapple, even today, with the historical sources of the *ius*

## 7.7.4   The Influence of Roman Law in Britain

At the end of the eleventh century there was little to distinguish the law in England from that of Germany or northern France. Although England had been a Roman province for more than 300 years, after the invasion of the Angles and Saxons Roman law was superseded by Anglo-Saxon law—a species of Germanic folk-law. The law codes of Ethelbert of Kent (c. 600),[81] Ina (c. 700)[82] and Alfred (c. 890)[83] were of largely the same character as the Continental *leges barbarorum*, although, unlike the latter, they were written in Anglo-Saxon and not in Latin. In general, the substance of the law in England, like elsewhere in northern Europe, consisted mainly of unwritten customary law that was supplemented or superseded in some particulars by canon law. The immediate effect of the Norman Conquest of England in the second half of the eleventh century was to intensify the trend towards particularism by increasing the number of franchise and manorial courts, and by the reintroduction of the old principle of personality of law in favour of the Norman element of the population. But, at the same time, it gave to England alone in the West a strong central government that was capable of imposing a uniform legal and administrative system upon the whole country. Under King Henry II (r. 1154–1189) the royal courts began to encroach on the jurisdiction of the feudal courts, and by the close of the thirteenth century the process towards the construction of a national system of law had been carried a long way.

Three principal elements can be traced in the law of England, as it had developed in this period. The foremost place must be attributed to the function of the *Curia Regis*, or King's Court, the body that under the Normans transacted all the business of the central government.[84] There is nothing in the contemporary history of Continental law that can be compared with the creative activity of this court in the fashioning of the writ system.[85] Second in importance is the Roman and canon

---

*commune* and its Dutch variant. Special attention is given to seventeenth and eighteenth century Dutch authorities, such as Grotius, Voet and Vinnius, although other works from the entire body of learned literature from Bartolus to the German Pandectists, and even the sources of Roman law itself, are regularly consulted in areas like property, contract and succession.

[81] This code, as preserved, contains ninety brief sections dealing with punishments for various wrongs.

[82] This code consisted of seventy-six sections in the form of 'dooms' or penal judgments.

[83] This compilation, known as 'The Laws of King Alfred', contained about 125 sections in all. It draws on earlier Saxon laws as well as on various biblical sources.

[84] King Henry II organized the judicial work of the *Curia Regis*. His judges sat to administer the law on a regular basis, and the practice of sending out itinerant judges, which had been initiated by King Henry I, was re-established and made systematic.

[85] A writ was an order by a court in the king's name directing some act or forbearance. Writs were at first issued only in special cases to meet exceptional circumstances. Something took place that led the king to give a command in writing to a royal official or to some lord who held a franchise court, and this command in writing was a writ. Some of these writs were used to initiate proceedings before a court of law (there were referred to as *original writs*). The use of such writs appears to have become common by the end of the twelfth century. From that time until the

law that came to England in the twelfth century. Thirdly, there is the customary law that survived the Norman Conquest and continued to be applied by the local courts. These latter two sources of law were, as we have seen, those that formed the substance of the private law in much of Continental Europe. The fact that above all others helps to explain why the common law as it evolved in England represents a distinct system from the civil law is the relatively slight influence that these sources had on the content of English law. As commentators have observed, the history of English law has been marked not by the reception of a foreign system of law and its fusion with native customs, but instead by the growth of a body of rules fashioned by the king's justices and developed by their successors in which neither Roman law nor the customary law was a decisive influence. The rigidity of the legal process, the need to conform to the framework that had been developed and the centralized court system, all helped to mould a diversity of local customs and practices into a common law, i.e. a law that was followed by the entire country.

For a century and a half after the Norman Conquest it was by no means obvious that England was destined to develop a distinct legal system. The effects of the revival of Roman law studies in Italy in the eleventh century were early felt in England. Indeed, it is not unlikely that Lanfrancus, a teacher of law at Pavia and subsequently Archbishop of Canterbury, used his knowledge of Roman law in his administrative and legislative reorganization of his realm. The first known teacher of Roman law in England was the Glossator Vacarius, who arrived in the country in the middle of the twelfth century. Vacarius taught at Oxford, where he composed for the instruction of his pupils his famous *Liber pauperum*, a nine-volume compendium of Roman law based on the Code and the Digest of Justinian.[86] Vacarius' success raised the fear that Roman law would be received as the law of the land and provoked a quick reaction from the monarch, who was disturbed by the implication in Roman law of imperial sovereignty. The barons, too, opposed the prospect of Roman law reception since in their eyes Roman law provided a foundation for royal absolutism. Thus, King Stephen prohibited Vacarius from teaching at Oxford and in 1234 Henry III forbade the teaching of Roman law in London. Two years later the barons, gathered in Merton, refused a proposal by bishops to adopt the Roman law principle according to which children born before the marriage of their parents

---

nineteenth century, writs were technical statements of the plaintiff's complaint. There were different writs for different claims: e.g., the writ of right to recover land; the writ of debt, to recover money owing; and the writ of trespass, to complain of a breach of peace. The clerks of the chancery (the secretarial office of the Crown) kept precedents of the writs they issued, and it was not long before it was recognized that unless a man could bring his complaint within one of the forms of writ recorded in the *Register of Writs*, he could have no remedy. Since an action could not be brought without a writ, it became established that the only kinds of harm for which one could seek compensation in law were those that could be described within the narrow and unyielding language of some recognized writ. In later times, attempts were made by Parliament to introduce some flexibility to the law by permitting the issue of new forms of writ, but these were only partially successful.

[86] See F. de Zulueta (ed), *The Liber Pauperum of Vacarius*, Publications of the Selden Society 44 (London 1927).

should be counted as legitimate, on the grounds that they did not wish to alter the laws of England (*Nolumus leges Angliae mutare*). The position adopted corresponded to the practice of the courts and encouraged the autonomous development of English law. Nevertheless, Roman law concepts continued to exert an influence on English doctrine. This influence is clearly reflected in the two most important legal treatises of the era: Glanvill's *Tractatus de legibus et consuetudinibus regni Angliae* (Treatise on the laws and customs of the Kingdom of England) of 1187, and Bracton's treatise of the same title, written about 70 years later.

Glanvill's work, which records the law of the time of Henry II (1133–1189),[87] is partly based on the preface and introductory chapters of Justinian's Institutes, and various Roman legal institutions are referred to or contrasted with English rules. More importantly, the work "shows that Roman law has supplied a method of reasoning upon matters legal, and a power to create a technical language and technical forms, which will enable precise yet general rules to be evolved from a mass of vague customs and particular cases".[88] Bracton's treatise, written in the reign of Henry III (1216–1272),[89] was also clearly influenced by Roman law, which came to him through the Glossator Azo. The scope of his work was the same as that of the French works on customary law, which were being published at the same period: just as the French writers filled out the customary law with importations from Roman law, so Bracton supplemented the meager and inadequate rules of the common law in fields such as the law of personal property and the law of contract by borrowings from Roman sources. Furthermore, Bracton used Roman concepts and distinctions to describe, classify and explain the writs and actions through which the King's Court administered justice.[90] In this respect, his work shows that the common law had considerably progressed: new writs and forms of action had been introduced, and the common law had gone far towards superseding local customs.

The two centuries following Bracton's death saw a sharp decline in the influence of Roman law in England. Though it continued to be studied at the Universities of Oxford and Cambridge, it had little effect on the common law itself. Undoubtedly, the causes were manifold and, in part, political. But one of the principal factors was the fact that English judges and lawyers received their professional training at the Inns of Court and not at the universities.[91] The common law exhibited two

---

[87] Glanvill was at various times Sheriff of Lancashire and of Yorkshire, Justice in Eyre and a general in Henry's army. In 1180 he became Justiciar of England, or Chief Minister of the Crown.

[88] W. S. Holdsworth, *Some Makers of English Law* (Cambridge 1938), 15.

[89] Bracton became a Justice in Eyre in 1245 and, three years later, one of the judges of the *Curia Regis*. Like many other royal judges of that time, he was an ecclesiastic and at the time of his death in 1268 he was Chancellor of the Exeter Cathedral.

[90] As S. E. Thorne observes, "[Bracton] was a trained jurist with the principles and distinctions of Roman jurisprudence firmly in mind, using them throughout his work, wherever they could be used, to rationalize and reduce to order the results reached in English courts." See *Bracton on the Laws and Customs of England* (Cambridge Mass. 1968), 33.

[91] The Inns of Court were self-governing legal societies, products of the medieval spirit of corporate organization that had manifested itself in the trade guilds. Much about their origins is

characteristics in this period: in the first place, it tended to become more fixed and rigid in substance; and, secondly, the rules governing legal procedure became more complex and technical. The legal works of this period consist almost exclusively in commentaries upon the writ system, and the legal education imparted in the Inns of Court was concerned primarily with giving to students an accurate knowledge of the procedural law in whose interstices substantive law was still firmly embedded. Such Roman law as was introduced came not through the courts of common law, but through the ecclesiastical and admiralty courts, and through the Court of Chancery, which owed its origin to the growing rigidity displayed by the common law. At the same time, the growth of the forms of action around which the law of tort and contract later crystallized meant that the fields of law that on the Continent succumbed most readily to the influence of Roman law were secured to the common law.

The sixteenth century was probably the most crucial period in the history of the common law. In the early part of that century the common law came under increasing attack. Many influential voices were raised against it, and there were calls for a wholesale reception of Roman law such as was taking place at the same time in Germany and other parts of Continental Europe.[92] But the common law stood its ground. Four key factors contributed to its survival. First was the character of the Tudor monarchs, who preferred to refashion the medieval institutions of the country and adapt them to the altered conditions of the age rather than to root them out altogether.[93] Second was the fact that new courts, especially the Court of Chancery[94]

---

unclear, but they probably began as hostels in which those who practiced in the common law courts lived. These hostels gradually evolved a corporate life in which benchers, barristers and students lived together as a self-regulating body. The student members were required to take part in moots, attend lectures and study law under the supervision of their seniors.

[92] F. W. Maitland has brilliantly related the story of the sixteenth century pressure of Roman law in England in his *English Law and the Renaissance* (London 1901).

[93] This may be explained by the fact that the principles of the common law constituted at the same time principles of the constitution, and to abolish them entirely would have amounted to a revolution rather than a resettlement.

[94] When, in the fourteenth century, the common law courts were separated from the *Curia Regis*, the judicial power of the monarch and his council was not exhausted. The king continued to receive complaints of wrongdoing and petitions for justice. The king often referred these requests for help to the Chancellor, his chief secretary, who was usually an ecclesiastic. In the course of time, it became customary for petitioners to go directly to the Chancellor, who dealt with cases on a flexible basis: he was more concerned with arriving at a fair result than with the rigid principles of law. As the common law courts became more formalistic and thus more inaccessible, pleas to the Chancellor increased and eventually resulted in the emergence of a special court constituted to deliver 'equitable' or 'fair' decisions in cases that the common law could not address. In a Statute of 1340 (14 Ed III St 1 c 5) a Court of Chancery was mentioned alongside other courts of the age and, by Tudor times, the Chancellor's Court was a firmly established institution whose jurisdiction was expanding and its work was increasing. The term 'equity' came to denote the part of English law administered by the Court of Chancery, as distinct from that administered by the courts of common law. In the seventeenth century conflict arose between the common-law judges and the Chancellor as to who should prevail. King James I, acting on the advice of Bacon and other experts in the law, resolved the dispute in favour of the Chancellor. Whilst the role of equity remained

and the Court of Star Chamber,[95] addressed the deficiencies of the common law.[96] Thirdly, the continuity of the common law was secured by Coke's restatement and modernization of its principles in the early seventeenth century. And, finally, there was the vital role played by the Inns of Court, and by what Maitland has described as "the toughness of a taught tradition".

Since the time of Edward Coke (1552–1634) the common law has never been under serious threat in England. However, the absence of a formal reception did not result in a total absence of impact of Roman law on English law. For instance, Roman law was of some assistance to Lord Mansfield (1705–1793) in the development of English commercial law, and judges have occasionally relied on it, whether in equity or at law, when an analogy was in point. Moreover, to a considerable extent English law had adopted Roman legal terminology. Nevertheless, although Roman legal concepts and doctrines have been woven into the fabric of English law, neither the corpus nor the structure of the latter is Roman.[97]

In contrast to English law, the law of Scotland was affected by the Roman law-based *ius commune* to a significant degree. By the close of the Middle Ages, Scotland had a customary law similar to that of England, although considerably less developed. However, unlike its English counterpart, Scottish law remained open to external influences. The most obvious such influence was that of the Church, and it was through the infusion of canon law that Roman law first influenced Scottish law

---

unchallenged, its application became increasingly regulated through a system of rules and principles based on precedent and gradually developed by a series of Lord Chancellors, all of whom were lawyers as opposed to the ecclesiastics of the earlier era. The Court of Chancery was abolished under the Judicature Acts of 1873–75, which established the High Court of Justice to administer both common law and equity. The Judicature Acts also provided that in cases in which there was a conflict between law and equity, the rules of equity should prevail.

[95] The Court of Star Chamber evolved from the king's Council. In 1487, during the reign of Henry VII, this court was established as a judicial body separate from the Council. The court, as structured under Henry VII, had a mandate to hear petitions of redress. Although initially the court only heard cases on appeal, Henry VIII's Chancellor Thomas Wolsey and, later, Thomas Cranmer encouraged suitors to appeal to it straight away, and not wait until the case had been heard in the common law courts. In the Court of Star Chamber (as in the Court of Chancery) all questions were decided by the court itself, and the granting or withholding of relief was in the discretion of the court and not regulated by rigid rules of law. The Court of Star Chamber was abolished in 1641, but its better rules were taken over by the King's Bench and became a permanent part of the law of England.

[96] As F. W. Maitland noted, "were we to say that equity saved the common law, and that the Court of Star Chamber saved the constitution, even in this paradox there would be some truth." *The Collected Papers of F.W. Maitland* (Cambridge 1911), 496.

[97] As H. E. Holdsworth has remarked: "We have received Roman law; but we have received it in small homoeopathic doses, at different periods, and as and when required. It has acted as a tonic to our native legal system, and not as a drug or poison. When received it has never been continuously developed on Roman lines. It has been naturalized and assimilated; and with its assistance, our wholly independent system has, like the Roman law itself, been gradually and continuously built up by the development of old and the creation of new rules to meet the needs of a changing civilization and an expanding empire." *A History of English Law*, 7th ed. (London 1956–1966), Vol. IV, p. 293.

and procedure. Furthermore, knowledge of Roman law was brought to Scotland by students attending Continental universities from as early as the thirteenth century.[98] In 1532 a permanent court of professional judges, the Court of Session, was established, which used a version of the Continental Romano-canonical procedure. As far as possible, the court relied on native Scots law, but in cases that could not be addressed on that basis, judges had recourse to the Romanist *ius commune*. By the close of the sixteenth century, Roman law had infiltrated many aspects of Scottish law and had become one of the dominant characteristics of the Scottish legal system. However, from the beginning of the eighteenth century, especially after the Act of Union in 1707, by which Scotland and England were consolidated into one kingdom, English law began to exercise a strong influence on the law of Scotland, while the role of Roman law gradually declined.[99]

## 7.8 The Humanist Movement

As previously observed, the Renaissance and the Reformation brought about a broader appreciation of intellectual and cultural accomplishments and an emancipation of human reason from the fetters of traditional faith and dogma. This new outlook and new spirit fostered impatience with the narrow pedantry of the old schools of law. The established doctrine of *communis opinio doctorum*, in its extreme form, hampered the logical development of principles and resolved legal problems by marshalling the opinions of legal scholars on the point at issue and then counting heads. Thus, during this period, the law schools of Italy, which until then had been famous throughout Europe, came to be regarded as the homes of an outworn theory (referred to as *mos Italicus*). The influence of the Renaissance produced a new school of jurists, the Humanists, who brought to legal writing the spirit of the revival of letters.

As has been noted, the rise of the School of the Commentators in the fourteenth century prompted a shift in scholarly attention from the dialectical examination of Justinian's texts to the consideration of the adaptability of Roman law to the needs and conditions of medieval life. The Commentators were primarily interested in developing contemporary law and so they tended to disregard the historical framework and the primary sources of Roman law. From the fifteenth century, the increased interest in the cultural inheritance of classical antiquity cultivated the development of a new approach to the study of Roman law. Scholarly attention now turned to the consideration of Roman law as a historical phenomenon and special

---

[98] The first Scottish university, the University of St Andrews, was founded in 1413, followed by the University of Glasgow in 1451 and the University of Aberdeen in 1495. However, most Scottish students preferred to resort to universities in Continental Europe, especially in France, Germany and, after the Reformation, the Netherlands.

[99] An important factor in this development has been the appellate jurisdiction of the House of Lords.

emphasis was placed on the importance of the techniques of history and philology for its proper understanding and interpretation. The methods used by the Commentators in the study of Justinian's texts had led to the formulation of theories that the Humanists perceived as utterly unwarranted when the texts were studied in their proper historical context; therefore, such theories had to be rejected in favour of interpretations based upon the true historical sense of the texts.[100] The chief aim of the Humanist scholars was thus the rediscovery of Roman law existing in Roman times through the application of the historical method instead of the scholastic method engaged by the medieval Commentators. They thus endeavoured to read the texts of the *Corpus Iuris Civilis* against their historical background, relating them to information provided by non-legal sources from antiquity. A considerable part of the Humanists' work was concerned with the detection of the interpolations in the Justinianic codification as an important step towards uncovering the true character of classical Roman law. An important innovation was that, unlike the medieval jurists, the Humanists were able to read Greek texts, which enabled them to use Byzantine legal sources, such as the *Basilica*, to reconstruct the texts of Justinian.[101] The Humanists also endeavoured to achieve a more systematic treatment of the contents of Justinian's *Corpus*. The medieval *summae* and other works had introduced systematic treatment for one work at a time, but it was now attempted to present the entire *Corpus Iuris Civilis* as one systematic whole.

---

[100] Lorenzo Valla, a fifteenth-century Italian Humanist, criticized the inelegant Latin of the Commentators, arguing that this was proof of their shortcomings as jurists. See P. Stein, *Roman Law in European History* (Cambridge 1999), 75. Stein relates that the French Humanist Guillaume Budé described the earlier jurists' glosses and commentaries as "a malignant cancer on the texts, which had to be cut away." Ibid., at 76.

[101] The Legal Humanists were responsible for the beginnings of what is known as *palingenesia*: the reconstruction of legal texts that have been altered by editors after they were first issued. With respect to the works of the classical Roman jurists, *palingenesia* profited from the fact that every fragment in the Digest is accompanied by an *inscriptio* containing the name of the original author and the title and part of the work from which the fragment was taken. This made it possible for scholars to separate all the fragments contained in the Digest, sort them by jurist and then, for each jurist, sort them by work and then by book (e.g., Ulpianus, *libro octavo decimo ad edictum*). This approach was begun by Jacobus Labittus, a sixteenth century Legal Humanist, in his *Index legum omnium quae in Pandectis continentur [. . .]*, published in 1557. In this work Labittus listed: the texts of the Digest according to their authors, the works in which they appeared, and the books of those works from which they were excerpted; other Digest texts which cited that jurist; those jurists who were not themselves excerpted in the Digest but who were referred to by other jurists therein; and finally those texts in the Codex and Novels which mentioned specific jurists. However, he did not try to restore the original order in the works of individual Roman jurists – this was done in the nineteenth century by Lenel, author of the more extensive *Palingenesia iuris civilis*, I–II (1889). It should be noted here that, as the compilers of Justinian's *Corpus* retained only about 5 per cent of the available texts, a complete reconstruction of the original works was impossible. Nevertheless, with respect to those jurists whose works were extensively used, it is possible to gain a good impression of the scope and structure of a particular work.

The Institutes furnished an important model, since this was the only part of Justinian's codification that contained a real system.[102]

The new school of thought was created in France by the Italian jurist Andreas Alciatus (1492–1550),[103] but its effects permeated throughout Europe. The leading representatives of this school included Jacques Cujas (Cuiacius, 1522–1590)[104]; Hugues Doneau (Donellus, 1527–1591)[105]; Guillaume Budé (Budaeus, 1467–1540)[106]; Ulrich Zasius (1461–1535)[107]; Antoine Favre (Faber, 1557–1624)[108]; Charles Annibal Fabrot (Fabrotus, 1580–1659)[109]; and Jacques Godefroy (Godofredus, 1587–1652).[110] The method adopted by the Humanist scholars in

---

[102] In this connection, reference should be made to the French Humanist Franciscus Connanus (Francois de Connan, 1508–1551), who in his *Commentaria iuris civilis libri decem* attempted to re-order legal material in a more rational way under the tripartite division of law into persons, things and actions derived from the Institutes. Hugues Doneau (Donellus), a sixteenth century French Humanist, in his *Commentarii de iure civili libri viginti octo* (Frankfurt 1595–1597), departed from the traditional approach to law that gave priority to actions and procedure and regarded the rights of the individual as being of greater importance than the methods by which these rights could be defended. This new approach is clearly reflected in the structure of his work. Moreover, Donellus separated the law of obligations from the law of property, both originally considered to constitute aspects of the law of things. See P. Garnsey, *Thinking about Property: From Antiquity to the Age of Revolution* (Cambridge 2007), 202; P. Stein, "Donellus and the origins of the modern civil law", in J.A. Ankum et al (eds) *Mélanges F. Wubbe*, (Fribourg 1993), 448–452.

[103] Alciatus was born at Alzano near Milan and studied in Pavia under the master Jason de Mayno, a prominent member of the Bartolist school. He taught civil law at Avignon and Bourges, which became the principal centre of Legal Humanism in France. Moreover, he established the so-called 'School of the Cultured Men' or 'Cultured Jurisprudence' (*Scuola dei Culti*), which reached its apex with Jacques Cujas in the later sixteenth century.

[104] Cujas was born and studied in Toulouse and taught at Cahors, Valence, Paris and Bourges. Probably the greatest of the French Humanists, he applied his immense knowledge of ancient classical literature and social and political history to elucidating the development of Roman law within its general context. His principal interest was directed at textual exegesis and the doctrinal contributions of individual Roman jurists.

[105] Donellus studied at Toulouse and Bourges, where he taught until the St. Bartholomew's massacre of 24th August 1572, when he fled to Heidelberg. In 1579 he went to Leiden, where he taught law until 1587. He is best known for his extensive commentary on the civil law: the *Commentariorum de iure civili libri viginti octo*.

[106] Budaeus was born in Paris and his university education at his home city and at Orléans centered on the study of law and the classics, especially Greek. His work on Roman law *Annotationes in XXIV Pandectarum libros* (1508) was a milestone in the Humanist challenge on medieval jurisprudence.

[107] Zasius was professor at Freiburg and a member of Erasmus' circle at Basel.

[108] Faber was born at Bourg-en-Bresse and served for some years as president of the Court of Savoy. His most important works include the *Codex Fabrianus* (1606), *De erroribus pragmaticorum* (1598) and *Rationalia in Pandectas* (1604–1626).

[109] Fabrotus was born in Aix en Provence, where he served as advocate to the local parliament and university professor. He is best known for his translation of the *Basilica*, published in 1647. He also edited the works of several Byzantine historians and composed a number of antiquarian treatises.

[110] Godofredus was born in Geneva, where he was appointed professor of law (1619) and, later, councilor of state. His principal work, on which he laboured for thirty years and which was

France for the study of Roman law became known as *mos gallicus* (in contradistinction with the *mos Italicus* of the Bolognese jurists) or *Elegante Jurisprudenz*. From the late seventeenth to the mid-eighteenth century Legal Humanism also flourished in the Netherlands, where it engendered a highly advanced approach to the study of Roman legal sources, referred to as the Dutch Elegant School.[111]

In general, the Humanist movement did not exert much influence on the practice of law as the courts in France and elsewhere remained faithful to the Bartolist tradition.[112] This largely derived from the fact that most Humanists were concerned chiefly with the historical analysis of Roman law and paid little attention to problems relating to the practical application of the law or the need to adapt Roman law to contemporary conditions. At the same time, however, the Humanists' approach to Roman law as a historical phenomenon helped jurists to appreciate the differences between Roman law and the law of their own times. By illuminating the historical and cultural circumstances in which law develops, they prepared the ground for the eventual displacement of the *ius commune* and the emergence of national systems of law.[113]

## 7.9    The School of Natural Law

In the seventeenth and eighteenth centuries, European legal thought moved in a new direction under the influence of the School of Natural Law.

The idea of natural law has its origins in ancient Greek philosophy, but was given a more concrete form by the Stoic philosophers of the Hellenistic and early Roman eras. As previously noted, under the influence of Stoicism, Roman jurists treated natural law as a body of law equally observed by all peoples, and therefore

---

published after his death (1665), is his edition of the Theodosian Code (*Codex Theodosianus cum perpetuis commentariis*).

[111] Among the leading representatives of this School are Gerard Noodt (1647–1725) and Henrik Brenkman (1681–1736).

[112] In Italy the Bartolist method prevailed in legal education throughout the sixteenth and seventeenth centuries. However, this method appears to have lost much of its earlier scientific rigour and was confined mainly to the training of practitioners.

[113] On the Humanist movement see P. Stein, *Roman Law in European Legal History* (Cambridge 1999), 75ff; D. Maffei, *Gli inizi dell'umanesimo giuridico* (Milan 1956); D. R. Kelley, *Foundations of Modern Historical Scholarship: Language, Law and History in the French Renaissance* (New York 1970); O. F. Robinson, T. D. Fergus and W. M. Gordon, *European Legal History* (London 1994), ch. 10; M. P. Gilmore, *Humanists and Jurists* (Cambridge Mass. 1963); F. Wieacker, *A History of Private Law in Europe* (Oxford 1995), 120 ff. W. Kunkel and M. Schermaier, *Römische Rechtsgeschichte* (Cologne 2001), 237–8; G. Kisch, *Humanismus und Jurisprudenz. Der Kampf zwischen mos italicus und mos gallicus an der Universität Basel* (Basel 1955).

also called it *ius gentium*.[114] Stoic philosophy furnished the terminology on the basis of which the early Church Fathers were able to formulate the first conceptions of the Christian natural law and to impart them to the world of their time. The Church Father Aurelius Augustinus (AD 354–430) promoted the idea of a divine origin of law and founded a theory that contributed a great deal to the transition from ancient philosophy to Christian jurisprudence. Augustinus held that the *lex naturalis moralis* is imprinted on the soul, heart, and mind of humankind. Nonetheless, he recognized that temporal or human positive laws are necessary in order that humankind might make manifest that which has been obscured through sinfulness and vice.

The greatest figure in medieval theology is, without doubt, Thomas Aquinas (1225–1274). Aquinas's work is a blending of earlier traditions: the philosophical thought of Aristotle[115] and the theology of the early Church Fathers, especially that of Augustinus. In his most important work, the *Summa theologiae*, a manual for students of theology, Aquinas defines natural law as man's participation in God's eternal law (or God's purpose in creation). Human beings, like all other entities in the universe, are subjects upon which the eternal law moves. However, the crucial difference between human beings and the rest of the created order is *freedom of choice*. This means that people do not necessarily behave in accordance with the eternal law. Thus, two distinct sources of guidance are provided for our benefit: divine law and natural law. These operate by two different means namely, revelation, that is God choosing to make known His will in the Holy Scriptures, and reason respectively. But if we can all know natural law through reason—and we all have reason—how can we account for disputes over fundamental moral issues or differing understandings of right and wrong at different times? Aquinas explains this by the process through which particular natural law precepts are deduced from general principles. He links this process of deduction both with human inclination and with the nature of reason itself. Reasoning about morality is practical rather than speculative. The fact that the conclusions of practical reason are not equally known by everyone does not affect their truth. Furthermore, in the process of application of practical reason to more and more situations, inevitably exceptions to general principles will have to be made and so the result may be variations in the natural law over time and place. Thus, while the primary precepts of natural law (such as the promotion of good and avoidance of evil) are unchanging, the secondary precepts of natural law are variable in content. But if we have Natural Law discoverable by reason why do we need human law? Aquinas defines human law to be an ordinance of reason for the common good, made by him who has care of the community, and explains the need for such law as arising both from unequal knowledge of natural law and the fact that knowledge is not the same as conduct:

---

[114] See relevant discussion in Chap. 2 above.

[115] Aquinas was able to draw on recently made translations of the works of Aristotle by Willem van Moerbeke (*c.* 1215–*c.* 1286), which had made available works that had not been in circulation until that time.

people are free to disobey. Hence, human law can help train us to act in accordance with natural law.[116] Although Aquinas sees human law as deduced from natural law, he recognises that because this deduction depends on practical reason it can lead to more than one possible conclusion. Variations in human laws between societies and over history are partly explicable by variations in the secondary natural law precepts from which they are deduced and partly because the process of deduction allows a measure of freedom and creativity. The doctrines of Aquinas dominated the theological, philosophical and intellectual landscape of Western Europe until the sixteenth century, when the traditional ideas about man and his relationship with God and the world began to be challenged by Humanism, Protestantism and the discovery of the New World. From this period, the natural law discourse began to untie itself from its associations with scholastic theology, and to increasingly use the language of reason. Of particular importance in this development was the work of the Dutchman Hugo Grotius (1583–1645), also known as the founder of modern international law.[117]

In his famous work *De iure belli ac pacis* (1625)[118] Grotius expounded the idea of a purely secular natural law freed from all ecclesiastical authority. He stated that even if we were so bold as to assume that there is no God, or that God is not interested in human affairs, there would still be valid natural law.[119] This freeing of natural law from its religious bonds made it possible for him to place the law outside the bitter opposition that the conflict in matters of religion had engendered since the time of Reformation and Counter-Reformation. What he really did was to return to the common and rational basis of all law, which the Humanist thinkers generally recognized through their rediscovery of the Stoics. It is on this basis that Grotius developed his theory of international law as a law binding all nations by reason. His starting-point in developing out of natural law a set of usable principles for the mutual relations of states (and, so far as applicable, individuals) was the notion that man is by nature sociable: "Among the traits characteristic of man is an impelling desire for society, that is, for the social life _ not of any and every sort, but peaceful, and organized according to the measure of his intelligence, and with those of his own kind."[120] "The maintenance of the social order ... which is consonant

---

[116] Aquinas answers the question of why human laws are necessary by drawing on Cicero and suggesting that human laws must be necessary to ensure the fulfillment of the divine plan because of humankind's limited participation in both natural and eternal law.

[117] The secularism of the natural law of this era accounts for its relative lack of popularity in Italy, where, especially in the seventeenth century, the cultural environment of the Counter-Reformation tended to stifle new ideas. It is thus unsurprising that the famous Italian scholar Alberico Gentili (1552–1608), regarded as one of the founders of the Natural Law School, came under suspicion for heresy and had to seek refuge in England, where he became regius professor of civil law at the University of Oxford.

[118] This work was partly inspired by a desire to devise rules that might lessen the horrors of war, although Grotius sought to formulate a system of law for peacetime as well.

[119] *De iure belli ac pacis, Prolegomena* 11.

[120] *De iure belli ac pacis, Prolegomena,* 6.

with human understanding, is the source of law properly so called. To this sphere of law belongs the abstaining from that which is another's, the restoration to another of anything of his which we may have, together with any gain which we may have received from it; the obligation to fulfil promises, the reparation of a loss incurred through our fault, and the infliction of penalties on men according to their deserts."[121] As the above statement suggests, Grotius viewed the law of nature as essentially the injunction to maintain peace by way of showing respect for the rights of other people.[122] He notes, asserting his own personal faith, that even though this law stems from man's inmost being, it is still deservedly attributed to God, whose will is that the relevant principles should reside within us.[123] And so, summarizing his view, though again without prejudice to the assumption that God might not exist, he writes that "natural law is the command of right reason, which points out, in respect of a particular act, depending on whether or not it conforms with that rational nature, either its moral turpitude, or its moral necessity; and consequently shows that such an act is either prohibited or commanded by God, the author of that nature."[124] Notwithstanding his repeated statement of his own Christian faith, his hypothesis was to be decisive in freeing the doctrine of natural law from the bonds of theology. It should be noted, further, that Grotius employed the comparative method to place his natural law doctrine on an empirical footing. Believing that the universal propositions of natural law could be proved not only by mere deduction from reason but also by the fact that certain legal rules and institutions were recognized in many legal systems, he used legal materials from diverse countries and ages to illustrate and support his system of natural law.

The idea of a rational natural law was developed further by the German philosophers Samuel Pufendorf (1632–1694), Christian Thomasius (1655–1728) and Christian Wolff (1679–1754). For Pufendorf, natural law is purely the product of reason and, as such, has no connection with divine revelation. A fundamental principle is: "Let no one act towards another in such a way that the latter can justly complain that his equality of rights has been violated."[125] More concrete rules derived from reason and thus nature are: not to harm others, and, where harm is caused, to make reparation; to treat others as having equal rights by reason of the dignity of all human beings; to assist others as far as one is able to do so; and to carry out the obligations one has assumed.[126] Pufendorf was the first modern legal

---

[121] *De iure belli ac pacis, Prolegomena*, 8.

[122] According to Grotius, one of the rights derived from the law of nature is the right of self-defence. *De iure belli ac pacis*, 2. 1. 3. Furthermore, a natural right to punish a wrongdoer must be assumed, for otherwise such a right could not be possessed by the state by cession from its subjects. *De iure belli ac pacis*, 2. 20. 1–2. The law of nature is also the source of validity of various forms of acquisition, and underpins rights emerging through promises and contractual agreements. *De iure belli ac pacis*, 2. 3. 4 f. and 2. 11. 4.

[123] *De iure belli ac pacis, Prolegomena*, 11–12.

[124] *De iure belli ac pacis*, 1. 1. 10. 1–2.

[125] *Elementa jurisprudentiae*, 2. 4. 4.

[126] *De officio hominis et civis*, 1. 3. 9. 6–9.

philosopher who elaborated a comprehensive system of natural law comprising all branches of law.[127] His work exercised an influence on the structure of later codifications of law, in particular on the 'general part' that is commonly found at the beginning of codes and in which the basic principles of law are laid down.

Like other natural law thinkers, Christian Thomasius draws attention to the shift from a *iurisprudentia divina*, a theological mode of legal study, to a doctrine of law whose foundation lies in reason and in nature. A central theme in Thomasius's natural law theory is justice (*iustum*): the forbidding of any transgression against the rights of others, in service of which the state is entitled to exercise the right of coercion. This is distinguished from the demands of honesty (*honestum*) and decency (*decorum*). In this way, Thomasius separated the domain of law from that of morality. Drawing on the work of Leibniz and Pufendorf, Wolff proposed a system of natural law that he alleged to make law a rigorously deductive science. His system exercised considerable influence on the eighteenth and nineteenth century German codifiers and jurists, as well as on legal education in German universities.[128]

The School of Natural Law challenged the supreme authority that medieval jurists had accorded to the codification of Justinian. The challenge proceeded on the grounds that the *Corpus Iuris Civilis* was an expression of a particular legal order whose rules, like the rules of any other system of positive law, must be assessed in the light of norms of a higher order that were eternal and universally valid—the norms of natural law. Natural law was construed as rational in its content, since its norms could be discovered only by the use of reason, logic and rationality. It was deemed as common to all men of all times with a higher moral authority than any system of positive law. From this perspective, the practitioners of natural law rejected certain 'irrational' features of the Roman system revealed by the Humanists (such as the remnants of the old Roman formalism detected in the *Corpus Iuris Civilis*) on the basis they were specific to the Roman system of social organization and restricted in time. At the same time, however, they recognized that Roman law contained a large number of rules and principles that reflected or corresponded to the precepts of natural law—rules and principles that they regarded as the product of logical reasoning on the nature of man and society rather than the expression of the legal development of the Roman state. The Roman doctrine of *ius gentium* and *ius naturale*, in particular, seemed to lend support to their own theories. Many legal

---

[127] Pufendorf is best known for his book *De iure naturae et gentium* (on the Law of Nature and Nations, 1672). His earlier work *Elementa iurisprudentiae universalis* (Elements of a Universal Jurisprudence, 1660) led to his being appointed to a chair in the Law of Nature and Nations especially created for him at the University of Heidelberg. As E. Wolf remarks, in his work "Pufendorf combines the attitude of a rationalist who describes and systematizes the law in the geometrical manner with that of the historian who rummages through the archives and who explores historical facts and personalities." *Grosse Rechtsdenker der deutschen Geistesgeschichte*, 2nd ed. (Tübingen 1944), 298.

[128] Other important representatives of the Natural Law School include Gottfried Wilhelm Leibniz (1646–1716) and Jean Domat (1625–1696).

principles espoused by Roman jurists appeared as suitable materials to utilize for building a rational system of law. The Natural Law School, with its system building approach to law, inspired a renewed interest in codification as a means of integrating the diverse laws and customs of a national territory into a logically consistent and unitary system.[129]

---

[129] On the rise and influence of the School of Natural law see A. P. D'Entreves, *Natural Law: An Introduction to Legal Philosophy*, 2nd ed. (London 1970); O. F. Robinson, T. D. Fergus and W. M. Gordon, *European Legal History* (London 1994), ch. 13; F. Wieacker, *A History of Private Law in Europe* (Oxford 1995), ch. 15; P. Stein, *Roman Law in European History* (Cambridge 1999), 107–10; D. Tamm, *Roman Law and European Legal History* (Copenhagen 1997), 231 ff. C. von Kaltenborn, *Die Vorläufer des Hugo Grotius auf dem Gebiete des Ius naturae et gentium, sowie der Politik im Reformationszeitalter* (Leipzig 1848, reprint Frankfurt 1965); H. Thieme, *Das Naturrecht und die europäische Privatrechtsgeschichte*, 2nd ed. (Basel 1954); H. Welzel, *Naturrecht und materiale Gerechtigkeit*, 4th ed. (Göttingen 1962).

# Chapter 8
# Codification and the Rise of Modern Civil Law

## 8.1 The Codification Movement

In the seventeenth and eighteenth centuries, the rise of nationalism and the consolidation of royal power in Europe entailed an increased interest in the development of national law and thereby precipitated the movement towards codification. The demand that law should be reduced to a code arose from two interrelated factors: the necessities to establish legal unity within the boundaries of a nation-state, and develop a rational, systematised and comprehensive legal system adapted to the conditions of the times.[1] The School of Natural Law had a rationalist approach to institutional reform and emphasized comprehensive legal system building. Thus, it provided the ideological and methodological basis to launch the codification movement. The unification of national law through codification engendered the eventual displacement of the *ius commune* and thus Roman law ceased to exist as a direct source of law. But as the drafters of the codes greatly relied on the *ius commune*, elements of Roman law were incorporated in different ways and to varying degrees into the legal systems of Continental Europe. The first national codes designed to achieve legal unity within one kingdom were compiled in Denmark (1683) and Sweden (1734). The process of codification continued in the late eighteenth and

---

[1] Charles-Louis de Secondat, Baron de la Brède et de Montesquieu (1689-1755), taught that laws will only meet the demands of reason if they are capable of accommodating the diverse needs of individual national populations. According to him, laws should be adapted "to the people for whom they are framed, to the nature and principle of each government, to the climate of each country, to the quality of its soil, to its situation and extent, to the principal occupation of the natives... [Laws] should have relation to the degree of liberty the constitution will bear, to the religion of the inhabitants, to their inclinations, riches, numbers, commerce, manners, and customs.... [Laws] have relations to each other, as also to their origin, to the intent of the legislator, and to the order of things on which they are established; in all of which different lights they ought to be considered." (*De l'esprit des lois,* Book 1, Ch. 3.) Montesquieu's ideas captured attention throughout the areas where the *ius commune* prevailed in the eighteenth century.

© Springer International Publishing Switzerland 2015
G. Mousourakis, *Roman Law and the Origins of the Civil Law Tradition,*
DOI 10.1007/978-3-319-12268-7_8

early nineteenth centuries with the introduction of codes in Bavaria (*Codex Maximilianeus Bavaricus*, 1756),[2] Prussia (*Allgemeines Landrecht für die Preussischen Staaten*, 1794) and Austria (*Allgemeines Bürgerliches Gesetzbuch*, 1811). The natural law philosophy exercised a strong influence on both the contents and structure of these codes. However, the most important codificatory event of this period was Napoleon's enactment in 1804 of the French Civil Code (*Code civil des francais*).

### 8.1.1   The Codification of Civil Law in France

At the time of the French Revolution (1789) there prevailed in France two great bodies of law: the customary law in the North with Germanic origins that was deeply influenced, and in some areas replaced, by Roman law; and the written law of the South based on Roman law. At the same time, royal ordinances applied throughout the country.[3] Although a considerable degree of uniformity had been attained within each of these systems, there still existed considerable regional differences within each of the main territorial divisions. The French Revolution ushered in a new phase in French history, underpinned by new philosophical ideas concerning law and its role in society. The Revolution was generally hostile towards the past and treated both Roman law and customary law with suspicion. Frequent demands were voiced by the deputies of the National Convention for the construction of a code of law that would be simple, democratic and accessible to every citizen and whose principles would be derived from reason alone.[4] In the eyes of the revolutionaries, the main elements that had to be eliminated were the feudal system and the control of most of the land by few people; social, political and economic inequalities; and royal and Church despotism. The revolutionary legislation thus abolished feudal rights, the procedural privileges of the clergy and nobility, and most future interests in property; confiscated the estates of the Church; abolished the division of people into social classes; removed the civil disabilities of women, illegitimate children and aliens; and secularized marriage.[5] However, the post-revolutionary period featured a sharp reaction against the excesses of the

---

[2] Although this code formally replaced the *ius commune* as a source of law, the *ius commune* continued to apply as a subsidiary source, as the creator of the code Wiguläus Xaver Alois von Kreittmayr recognized.

[3] The private law that existed at the time of the French Revolution is referred to as *ancien droit*. It was characterized by four chief features: the special role of the Catholic Church in legal matters, especially in the field of the law of marriage; inequality, as a person's position in the eyes of the law varied according to the class to which he belonged; the priority accorded to the social group or the community vis-à-vis the individual; and the special importance attached to landed property.

[4] The Constitution of 1791 stated that a civil code was to be drafted with laws that should be "simple, clear and common to the entire kingdom."

[5] The new revolutionary legislation was introduced in Italy following the arrival of the French armies in 1796 and the establishment of several Italian republics and, later, vassal kingdoms.

Revolution and this is reflected in the law of that period.[6] Thus, the legislation of Napoleon retained much of the old law and only some aspects were apparently influenced by revolutionary ideas. The most important changes occurred in the area of the law of property, where there is no trace of feudal institutions (such as tenure). In other areas of the law, such as family law, we notice a clear departure from revolutionary ideas and legislation.

The French Civil Code of 1804 was drafted by a commission of four eminent jurists: Tronchet, the President of the Court of Cassation and former defence counsel for King Louis XVI; Portalis, a lawyer and provincial administrator at Aix-en-Provence and a close supporter of Napoleon; Bigot de Préameneau, government commissioner for the *Tribunal de cassation* and former lawyer at the Parliament in Rennes; and Maleville, formerly a lawyer at the Parliament in Bordeaux and, later, judge at the Court of Cassation.[7] The chief aim of the commissioners was to fuse the Roman and customary laws into one coherent system that would also embody those ideas of the Revolution that were still approved by public opinion.[8] The three ideological pillars of the Code were private property, freedom of contract and the patriarchal family. The position adopted was that the primary role of the state was to protect private property, secure the enforcement of legally formed contracts and warrant the autonomy of the family. With respect to private property, the Code consolidated the rejection of feudalism and its institutions achieved by the French Revolution. Through private law devices, such as the imposition of limitations on the freedom of testation, the drafters of the Code sought to break up the estates of the once powerful landowners. The formal division of the Code into three parts—Persons, Property and the Different Ways of Acquiring Property—was similar to that adopted by the drafters of Justinian's Institutes. Each part or book is divided into titles, such as Enjoyment and Loss of Civil Rights, Marriage, Divorce, Domicile and Adoptions. These are subdivided into chapters and, in several instances, into sections. Book One covers matters such as marriage, divorce, the status of minors, guardianship and domicile; Book Two deals with property, usufruct and servitudes; and Book Three includes diverse matters such as wills and intestate succession, donations, contracts, torts, matrimonial property settlements, sale, lease, partnership, mortgages, special contracts and such like. Certain parts of the Code (such as that addressing the law of contracts) were to a great extent based on the Roman or

---

[6] With respect to legal development, the period 1789-1796 is sometimes referred to as intermediate period (*droit intermédiaire*). For a closer look see in general C. Petit (ed), *Derecho Privado y Revolución Burguesa* (Madrid 1990).

[7] Portalis, who presented the drafting intentions in the *Discours préliminaire*, was in overall charge. On Portalis' contribution see M. A. Plesser, *Jean Étienne Marie Portalis und der Code civil* (Berlin 1997); M. Long & C. Monier, *Portalis: l'esprit de justice* (Paris 1997).

[8] The first draft of the Code was ready within four months and included a preliminary book entitled *Du droit et des lois* (of law and legislation) inspired by the ideas of the Natural Law School. The draft was assessed by the Court of Cassation and debated in length by the Council of State in 102 sessions, 57 of which were chaired by Napoleon himself.

written law of Southern France, while other parts (such as family law and the law of succession) reflect a stronger influence from the North French customary law of Germanic origin.

The drafters of the Code recognized that a legislator could not foresee all the possible applications of a basic legal principle. Therefore, they opted for the flexibility of general rules rather than for detailed provisions. As Portalis commented, "we have avoided the dangerous ambition to regulate and foresee everything. . . The function of the law is to determine in broad outline the general maxims of justice, to establish principles rich in implications, and not to descend into the details of the questions that can arise in each subject."[9] From this point of view, he identified the main tasks of judges in a codified system of law as being to clarify the meaning of the legal rules in the various circumstances that are submitted to them; to elucidate any obscure facets of the law and to fill its gaps; and to adjust the law to the evolution of society and, to the best extent possible, utilize the existing texts to avoid any potential inadequacy of the law in the face of contemporary problems.

The new code, an expression of the power of the middle class, represented both a substantial and formal departure from the preceding system of law, which it was designed to replace. Even the many pre-revolutionary rules and institutions incorporated into the code were deemed effective only because of their reenactment as part of the new legislation. However, despite the formal rupture with the *ius commune*, the code was of necessity built up of culturally familiar concepts, institutions and ways of thinking about law derived from the preceding system. Thus, much of the earlier legal tradition, with a new ideological basis, was carried over into the code.

The importance of Napoleon's Code is attributed to not only the fact that it fostered legal unity within France, but also the fact that it was adopted, imitated or adapted by many countries throughout the world. This was partly due to its clarity, simplicity and elegance that rendered it a convenient article of exportation and partly due to France's influence in the nineteenth century.

### 8.1.2   The Codification of Civil Law in Germany

In Germany, the French Civil Code attracted a great deal of attention and parts of the country adopted this law as Napoleon extended his rule over Europe. However, the rise of German nationalism during the wars of independence compelled many scholars to express the need for the introduction of one uniform code for Germany to unite the country under one modern system of law and precipitate the process of its political unification. In 1814, A. F. J. Thibaut (1772–1840), a professor of Roman law at Heidelberg University, declared this view in a pamphlet entitled 'On

---

[9] See A. von Mehren and J. Gordley, *The Civil Law System*, 2nd ed. (Boston 1977), 54.

the Necessity for a General Civil Code for Germany'.[10] Thibaut, a representative of the natural law movement, claimed that the existing French, Prussian and Austrian civil codes could serve as useful models for the German draftsmen. Thibaut's proposals encountered strong opposition from the members of the Historical School,[11] headed by the influential jurist Friedrich Carl von Savigny (1779–1861).[12] Savigny elaborated his thesis in a pamphlet entitled 'On the Vocation of our Times for Legislation and Legal Science'.[13] He asserted that law was similar to language, ethics and literature in that it was a product of the history and culture of a people, and existed as a manifestation of national consciousness (*Volksgeist*)—it could not be derived from abstract principles of natural law by logical means alone.[14] From this point of view, Savigny argued that the introduction of a German Code should be postponed until both the historical circumstances that moulded the law in Germany were fully understood and the needs of the present environment were properly assessed. A perplexing question that Savigny had to answer was how to reconcile the idea that the law emanated from the people with the fact that the Roman law operating in Germany was an alien importation. Savigny responded in the following manner: at a certain stage in a nation's development, the creation of law by the people became an overly complex and technical process and further development necessitated the establishment of a professionally trained class of

---

[10] A. F. J. Thibaut, "Rezension über August Wilhelm Rehberg, *Ueber den Code Napoléon und dessen Einführung in Deutschland* (1814)" in *Heidelbergische Jahrbücher der Litteratur*, 7 (1814) at 1-32; and see: *Ueber die Nothwendigkeit eines allgemeinen bürgerlichen Rechts für Deutschland* (Heidelberg 1814).

[11] The rise of the Historical School was one manifestation of the general reaction to the rationalism of the School of Natural Law and the political philosophy associated with the French Revolution and the regime of Napoleon. Savigny officially founded the School in 1815, together with his Berlin colleague Karl Friedrich Eichhorn (1781-1854). They edited the programmatic journal of the School, the *Zeitschrift für geschichtliche Rechtswissenschaft* – the predecessor of the modern *Savigny-Zeitschrift*.

[12] Savigny was born in Frankfurt am Main and became professor in Marburg University in 1803. After a brief period in Landshut (predecessor of the University of Munich), he became one of the founders of the University of Berlin (1810), where he taught until 1842. Furthermore, he was named counselor of the state (*Staatsrat*) in 1829 and held the position of legislative minister in the Prussian cabinet from 1842 to 1848. Notwithstanding his impressive professional career, Savigny's reputation is mainly derived from his academic achievements and the influence they had on 19th century German legal and political thought. The focus of his work was Roman law, as preserved in the codification of Justinian. From 1815 to 1831, he dedicated himself to an extensive and in-depth study of Roman law in the Middle Ages with the view to elucidating the process through which Roman law formed the basis of European legal culture. In his work special attention is given to the contribution of the glossators of the twelfth and thirteenth centuries to the reception of Roman law as the common law of Continental Europe.

[13] F. C. von Savigny, *Vom Beruf unserer Zeit für Gesetzgebung und Rechtswissenschaft* (Heidelberg 1814).

[14] Savigny argued that natural law cannot be imposed upon a people the way the "fathomless arrogance and completely unenlightened drive for education" of natural law legislators had suggested. He believed that the term *Volk* ideally refers to a community united culturally and intellectually by a common education.

lawyers and jurists. In Germany, this stage was reached in the fifteenth century and the jurists who were responsible for the reception of Roman law during that period were true exponents of the German national spirit. Thus, Roman law, as organically received law, is part of German legal history and contemporary legal life; at the same time, it supplies the connecting link between German law and European legal culture in general.

The early proposals for codification were abandoned due to the influence of the Historical School and, perhaps more importantly, the lack of an effective central government. At the same time, scholarly attention shifted from the largely ahistorical natural law approach to the historical examination of the two main sources of the law that applied in Germany, namely Roman law and Germanic law, in order to develop a true science of law. A group of scholars focused on the study of Germanic law, whilst others (including Savigny) concentrated on the study of Roman law and explored beyond the *ius commune* into the *Corpus Iuris Civilis* and other ancient sources. The latter jurists set themselves the task of studying Roman law to expose its 'latent system', which could be adapted to the needs and conditions of their own society. In executing this task, these jurists (designated Pandectists) elevated the study of the *Corpus Iuris Civilis* and especially the Digest to its highest level and produced an elaborate and highly systematic body of law (*Pandektenrecht*) for nineteenth century Germany. Leading representatives of the Pandectists were Georg Puchta, Adolf Friedrich Rudorff, Ernst Immanuel Bekker, Alois Brinz, Heinrich Dernburg, Rudolf von Ihering and Bernhard Windscheid.[15] They produced an elaborate and highly systematic body of law (*Pandektenrecht*) for nineteenth century Germany.

Although the Pandectist movement emerged from the Historical School, it ultimately adopted a rather ahistorical and primarily doctrinaire approach to law. The Pandectists adopted this approach believing in the superiority and eternal validity of Roman law. Their chief objective was to construct a legal system where all particular rules could be derived from and classified under a set of clearly formulated juridical categories and abstract propositions. In this respect, law is approached as a form of logic, a coherent assembly where everything can be reduced to general principles, concepts and conceptual categories. Extra-legal

---

[15] In this connection, the contribution of Puchta (1798-1846) and Windscheid (1817-1892) deserves special mention. Puchta emphasized the academic nature of law and the central role of the jurist in the law-making process at the final stage of the legal development of a people. He drew attention to the study of law as a coherent logical system built from interrelated concepts existing on a purely intellectual level. As the norms of positive law emerge principally through logical deductions from concepts, the legitimacy of legal rules is the result of logical-systematic correctness and rationality. In his works *Lehrbuch der Pandekten* and *Cursus Institutionum*, Puchta applied those ideas to the study of Roman law. Windscheid's *Lehrbuch des Pandektenrechts* (1862), which also applied the systematic approach of the Pandectists to the study of Roman law, had an extraordinarily large circulation in Germany (a seventh edition, revised by the author, appeared in 1891) and became an essential text throughout Continental Europe. Besides its use as a student textbook, the work was highly significant for legal practice in Germany and served as a guide to the drafters of the German Civil Code of 1900 (Windscheid himself played a leading role in the codification as a member of the first commission from 1880 to 1883).

evaluations do not matter, as propositions of law cannot be considered, let alone justified, from an extra-legal point of view. The Pandectists' conception of law as a logical system (*sistema iuris*), distinct from the social, religious, political and economic domains, had a strong impact not only on legal theorists but also on judges: it gave social, ethical, political and economic neutrality to the logical processes that led to specific judicial decisions. In the area of legislation, this approach to law has entailed the use of a technical and abstract language. It also led to a high level of precision in selecting the relevant terms and phrases whose meaning remains fixed throughout the text of the law.

The process of abstraction and generalization is natural and indeed inevitable, if the law is to consist in anything other than a collection of practical rules and solutions to actual problems. However, it involves the danger that once a general rule is formulated it tends to dominate legal life rather than adapt itself to it. The legal genius of the Romans was displayed in their ability not only to create abstract propositions through an analysis of their law, but also to create sufficient flexibility in the abstractions to enable their synthesis into new rules and principles when change was needed. The Roman jurists never made the mistake of over-valuing their abstractions. In contrast, the German jurists became fascinated with the concepts themselves and came to reject as logically unthinkable any change that involved a conflict with the concepts they had formulated. This attitude was particularly dangerous, since the Roman abstractions were formulated as summaries of their own development whilst the German Romanist scholars wished to transpose them to the completely different context of nineteenth century Germany. It was unavoidable that the Pandectists, consciously or unconsciously, considerably distorted the Roman law concepts they revised. Above all, their master concept that law exists to further the realization of the individual will was derived from Hegelian philosophy rather than Roman jurisprudence. The most rigorous attack on the methods of the German legal scholars came from the ranks of the Pandectists themselves in the person of R. Ihering.[16] Ihering asserted that "our Romanistic theory must abandon the delusion that it is a system of legal mathematics, without any higher aim than a correct reckoning with conceptions."[17] Nevertheless, the preoccupation of the Pandectists with the formulation of abstract concepts continued throughout the nineteenth century and their approach played an important part in the process towards the codification of the civil law in Germany.

---

[16] Rudolf von Ihering (1818-1892) held the position of professor in Basel, Rostock, Kiel, Giessen, Vienna and Göttingen. Among his most significant works are: *Der Geist des römischen Rechts* (1852–1865); *Jurisprudenz des täglichen Lebens* (1870); *Der Kampf ums Recht* (1872); *Der Zweck im Recht* (1877–1883); and *Scherz und Ernst in der Jurisprudenz* (1884).

[17] Quoted in M. Smith, *A General View of European Legal History and Other Papers* (New York 1927) at 135. Ihering is regarded as an early representative of jurisprudential trends that emerged as a reaction to the formalism and extreme conceptualism of the Pandectist School, such as *Zweckjurisprudenz*, focusing on the purposes that legal rules and institutions serve, and *Interessenjurisprudenz*, focusing on societal interests as the chief subject-matter of law. These schools of thought were the precursors of legal realism and the sociology of law.

While the Pandectists conceded a central role to the free will of the individual as a participant in law, the jurists of the Germanistic branch of the Historical School emphasized the social aspects of law, giving primacy to collectivism and cooperativism over individualism. This approach was most distinctly represented by Otto von Gierke (1841–1921), who was appointed professor in Berlin in 1887. Other leading exponents of the Germanistic branch were Karl Friedrich Eichhorn, Jakob Grimm, Georg Beseler and Emil Brunner. These jurists erected from the scattered and fragmentary expressions of Germanic legal thought embodied in the legislation and judicial decisions of the German states, and from the history of Germanic legal institutions, a distinct system of law, and strongly championed its principles against those of the Pandectists.

While these historical and theoretical controversies were raging, the political unification of Germany occurred under Chancellor Bismarck and the Second Reich was founded in 1871. However, legal unity did not immediately follow political unity. Throughout the nineteenth century, Germany remained divided into three major areas with respect to private law. The left bank of the river Rhine had been annexed by France in 1794. In this part of the country and other territories under French control, the French Civil Code was in force. Despite the theories of the Historical School, this Code was well received and successfully applied. Prussia and Saxony were territories with codified law, the latter having adopted a Code in 1863. The remainder of Germany was the land of the Roman-canonical law of the Pandectists, modified by particular regional and municipal statutes and customs. But these divisions were clearly no longer tolerable and a commission of 11 members was appointed in 1874 to draft a civil code for the whole of Germany.[18] The code emerged from a 20-year process that involved two drafts.[19] The first draft was published in 1887 and it provoked strong criticism from Germanist scholars who objected to the fact that the work was composed almost entirely from the Roman element of the law. The critics also denounced the abstruse language of the work and its remoteness from everyday social and economic life.[20] In response to these criticisms, a second commission composed of ten permanent members (university professors, lawyers, state officials and professional experts from commerce and industry) and 12 non-permanent ones was appointed by the government to redraft

---

[18] The work of the commission began in 1881 and ended at the close of 1887, when the first draft code was submitted to the chancellor. The chairman of the commission was H. E. Pape, until 1878 president of the Imperial Commercial Court (*Reichsoberlandesgericht*), the highest federal tribunal at the time. Its most prominent members were B. Windscheid and G. Planck (1824-1910), the future president of the Imperial Court of Justice (*Reichsgericht*).

[19] A significant step on the way to the legal unification of Germany was the establishment in 1879 of the *Reichsgericht* (Imperial Court of Justice) as a national supreme court for the entire German empire.

[20] Otto von Gierke, a jurist of rare learning and ability, and a strong believer in the social superiority of Germanic over Roman legal ideas, composed a book entitled "The Draft of a Civil Code and the German Law," which is the clearest and most eloquent summing up of the various objections brought against the proposed Code.

the code in 1890. This second draft, as modified by the Council of State (*Bundesrat*) and a commission of 21 members of the parliament (*Reichstag*), became law on 14th July 1896 with effect from 1st January 1900.

The German Civil Code, the *Bürgerliches Gesetzbuch* or BGB., is marked by two outstanding characteristics: its highly systematic structure and its conceptualism. In both these respects, it owes a great deal to the work of the German Pandectists of the nineteenth century. The Code is divided into five books. The first book contains the general principles of the entire civil law, i.e. the principles that have general application to all legal relations except when special rules are provided. It includes provisions relating to persons (both natural and legal); the nature and classification of things and juristic acts; acting capacity; offer and acceptance; agency and ratification; limitation and prescription; and private means of redressing wrongs and securing rights. The second book is devoted to the law of obligations (*Schuldrecht*), which is concerned with the legal relation between particular subjects of rights. The third book contains the law of property (*Sachenrecht*) that addresses the rights of persons over things by describing the content, acquisition, loss and protection of real rights. The fourth book covers family law (*Familienrecht*) and is divided into two parts: the first part regulates personal relationships in the family; the second regulates the property relationships of family members. Finally, the fifth book deals with the law of succession (*Erbrecht*) that regulates the succession to the rights and liabilities of a deceased person. As already noted, the influence of the Pandectists is reflected in the Code's systematic consistency, succinctness and conceptual clarity. However, the work is not designed to be intelligible to the layman; it is codified jurists' law for jurists, only to be read and understood by them. This did not pose a problem for judges and legal practitioners, who were familiar with the style and methods of the Pandectists through their university legal training.

Notwithstanding their important differences with respect to style and structure, the German and French Civil Codes have a great deal in common. Both codes drew heavily on common sources of law—the *ius commune* and their respective national laws. The influence of the *ius commune* derived from Roman law is particularly evident in the field of the law of obligations, as well as in the way the materials are structured and systematized. On the other hand, native sources of law appear to have exercised a considerable influence in the areas of family law and the law of succession. Moreover, the two codes have a common ideological basis as both are grounded on nineteenth century liberalism and are permeated by the notions of individual autonomy, freedom of contract and private property. As many changes in society transpired during the period of a hundred years that separates the two codes, the German Civil Code is in some respects more advanced or up-to-date than the French one. For example, several important provisions of the German Code recognize that certain private rights are related to certain social obligations and that a subjective right can be misused or abused. In the field of family law, the authority of husbands and fathers is less absolute than in the French Code and the definition of family is not as broad as that adopted by the latter code. Moreover, women have more power in relation to their own property matters. Certain aspects of contract and tort law reflect the effects of the increasing complexity of commercial relationships as well as the advances of industrialization.

In the period following the enactment of the Civil Code, German scholars focused mainly on the task of rendering the Code applicable in practice. This entailed explaining its difficult text, and elucidating and developing its concepts and principles. During the same period, the reaction against the excessive formalism and conceptualism of the Pandectists grew stronger. After the First World War, German legal science began to discard the methods of the Pandectists. While preserving the Pandectists' genius in formulating general concepts, German jurists started to place more emphasis on the examination of detailed facts and the operation of legal principles in concrete factual situations. This process was interrupted, however, by the rise of National Socialism in the post-WWI period and the decline of liberal democratic ideas in Germany. Nevertheless, these new ways to conceptualize the law—associated with legal realism and the sociology of law—entered legal thinking in America and other countries, and exercised a strong influence on the development of legal thought in the twentieth century.

## 8.2   The Civil Law Tradition

Legal scholars use the term 'civil law systems' to describe the legal systems of all those nations predominantly within the historical tradition derived from Roman law as transmitted to Continental Europe through the *Corpus Iuris Civilis* of Emperor Justinian.[21] In the foregoing discussion we have traced the long and intricate process of amalgamation of Roman, Germanic and other bodies of law that form the substance of modern civil law systems. The material also noted the effect thereon of historical developments, cultural factors and the exigencies of legal practice. This process culminated in the codification of civil law in Europe. The codes constitute a new point of departure in the development of the civil law, but its history obviously does not end with their enactment. In the years following the publication of the codes, the dynamics of legal change have worked primarily through special legislation and judicial interpretation, as well as through code revision, constitutional law and the harmonization of law at a European or regional

---

[21] The theme of legal tradition focuses attention on the notion that law and the understanding of law involve much more than the description and analysis of statutes and judicial decisions. Law cannot be fully understood unless it is placed in a broad historical, socio-economic, political, psychological and ideological context. As J. H. Merryman explains, a legal tradition is not simply a body of rules governing social life; it embraces "deeply rooted, historically conditioned attitudes about the nature of law, the role of law in society and the polity, the proper organization and operation of a legal system, and about the way law is, or should be made, applied, studied, perfected and taught. The legal tradition relates the legal system to the culture of which it is a partial expression. It puts the legal system into cultural perspective". *The Civil Law Tradition: an Introduction to the Legal Systems of Western Europe and Latin America*, 2nd ed. (Stanford, Calif. 1985), 2.

level. Legislatures in civil law countries responded to changes in society and the economy by excising large areas of the law from the domain of the civil codes. They also created entirely new areas of law that fall outside the scope of the codes, such as employment law, insurance law, competition law, and landlord and tenant law. Furthermore, legislatures endeavoured to update the civil codes by modifying their texts. Both the French and German codes have been amended several times since their introduction. In general, code revision has been more extensive in the area of family law than in any other areas. Many family law reforms were precipitated by constitutional provisions introduced after the Second World War and by international conventions promoting new ideas of equality and liberty that were at variance with the patriarchal family law of the civil codes. In other areas of the law, legislatures have often encountered difficulty in forging the necessary changes within the structure of the civil codes. To deal with this problem, legislatures have resorted to the introduction of special statutes outside the codes—statutes that could more easily be amended as socio-economic conditions change.

While legislatures created and developed bodies of law outside the sphere of the civil codes, the courts have introduced new rules through the interpretation of the codes' provisions. This judicial adaptation of the codes to new social and economic conditions has produced a new body of law, which is based on the expansion through interpretation of the existing legislative texts. In some civil law countries, such as France, this process has been facilitated by the structural characteristics of the civil code—its gaps, ambiguities and incompleteness. The drafters of the French Civil Code never imagined or anticipated the litigation-producing aspects of modern life such as industrial and traffic accidents, telecommunications, the photographic reproduction of images and mass circulation of publications. Thus, it is no surprise that in essence the modern French law of torts is almost entirely judge-made. Regarding the later codes, such as the German Code, the judicial adaptation of the civil law to changing social and economic conditions was facilitated by the inclusion in the codes of 'general clauses'—provisions that deliberately leave a large measure of discretion to judges. Although traditional civil law theory denies that judges make law or that judicial decisions can be a source of law, contemporary civil law systems are more openly recognizing the unavoidable dependence of legislation on the judges and administrators who interpret and apply it.

### 8.2.1 Geographic Distribution of the Civil Law

As previously noted, the historical origins and development of a legal system is a factor that sets that system apart as a member of the civil law family.[22] Upon closer

---

[22] Contemporary comparative legal scholarship has an extensive tradition of categorizing systems of law into legal families of kinship and descent. The division of legal systems into families fosters the comparative study of law as it allows one to examine legal systems from the viewpoint of their

examination, history is also a factor that explains the internal differentiation within the civil law. It is thus unsurprising that contemporary comparative law scholars identify sub-categories of legal systems within the civil law family, with the Romanistic-Latin or French and the Germanic systems forming two secondary groupings or sub-families.[23] The distinctive French and German legal codifications and juristic styles each exerted a far-reaching influence worldwide, and to some extent their influences overlapped. Indeed, one might argue that the 'typical' civil law systems today are not those of France and Germany, but rather those systems that have undergone a combined influence of both. Nevertheless, in the post-codification period, French law and German legal science have constituted the two main tributaries to the civil law tradition.

The Romanistic-Latin or French group of countries and territorial units share a private law that follows the Napoleonic Civil Code of 1804. In the course of the Napoleonic conquests and the subsequent political and administrative reshaping of many European countries the French Civil Code was introduced into the western regions of Germany, the low countries, Italy, Spain and other parts of Europe. Then, during the colonial age, France extended her legal influence far beyond Continental Europe to parts of the Middle East, Northern and sub-Saharan Africa, Indochina, Oceania, French Guiana and the French Caribbean islands. But the influence of French law both outlived and went beyond the Napoleonic conquests and French colonialism. To this day, the French Civil Code remains in effect, with revisions, in Belgium and Luxemburg. Moreover, the *Code Civil* had a major influence on the Netherlands Civil Code of 1838 (whose spirit has naturally influenced the new civil code of the Netherlands enacted in 1992); the law codes of the Italian federal states prior to 1860 and the first *Codice Civile* of 1865[24]; the Portuguese Civil Code of 1867 (replaced in 1967); the Spanish Civil Code of 1889; the Romanian Civil Code of 1864; and some of the Swiss cantonal codes.[25] Furthermore, when the Spanish and Portuguese empires in Latin America disintegrated in the nineteenth century, it was mainly to the French Civil Code that the legislatures of the newly independent nations of Central and South America looked for inspiration. This is unsurprising, as the language and concepts of the French code were already familiar because of their affinities with the legal institutions and practices that had been introduced by the Spanish and the Portuguese. Moreover, French culture and the French revolutionary heritage were greatly admired in Latin American countries and Napoleon's personality served as an example to many of the early statesmen of these

---

general characteristics, style or orientation. Apart from its practical importance, the division of legal systems into broader families has great value to legal theory, as it requires a more spherical or comprehensive knowledge of law as a general social phenomenon.

[23] Consider on this matter R. David and J. Brierley, *Major Legal Systems in the World Today*, 3rd ed. (London 1985), 35; K. Zweigert and H. Kötz, *An Introduction to Comparative Law*, 2nd ed. (Oxford 1987), 68-75.

[24] See on this C. Ghisalberti, *Unità nazionale e unificazione giuridica in Italia* (Bari 1979), 223.

[25] Even after the Congress of Vienna (1815), the French Civil Code remained in effect in German territories on the left bank of River Rhine and also in parts of the Prussian Rhine Province.

countries.[26] The French legal tradition continues to exist in territories that were first colonized by France but later on taken over by Great Britain or another power with a common law legal system, such as the province of Québec in Canada and the state of Louisiana in the United States of America.[27] With respect to countries that once belonged to the French colonial empire,[28] the current influence of French law varies, depending on the hold of French culture in these countries and the impact of local customs and legal traditions, especially Islamic law.[29]

The Germanic legal family consists of countries that have adopted or are influenced by the German Civil Code and the German Pandectist scholarship (*Pandektenwissenschaft*) that preceded it. Although the German Civil Code appeared on the scene relatively late in the codification era and its highly technical language and complicated structure rendered its direct transplantation difficult, it did play a significant part in the codification of civil law in a number of countries,

---

[26] The Mexican state of Oaxaca promulgated the first Latin American civil code in 1827, following the French *Code Civil*. Bolivia enacted a civil law code in 1830, also modeled on the French Code. This code remained in force until a new code, based on the Italian Civil Code of 1942, was introduced in 1975. The Chilean Civil Code of 1855 was strongly influenced by the French Civil Code, although its principal drafter, Andrés Bello, was also familiar with the work of the German Historical School. Bello's *Código Civil* was adopted by Ecuador (1860), Colombia (1873), Nicaragua (1867), Honduras (1880) and El Salvador (1859), and had an impact on the relevant Venezuelan (1862) and Uruguayan (1868) legislation. The Argentinean Civil Code of 1871 (adopted by Paraguay in 1876) and the Brazilian Civil Code of 1916 (completed by Clóvis Beviláqua in 1899) also reflect the concurrent influences of the Napoleonic Civil Code, French nineteenth century jurisprudence and the German Historical School. See in general C. Stoetzer, *El pensamiento político en la América española durante el período de la emancipación (1789 - 1825)* (Madrid 1966); A. Guzmán Brito, *La codificación civil en Iberoamérica*, Siglos XIX y XX (Santiago, Editorial Jurídica de Chile, 2000).

[27] Although the local population in some of these territories was initially promised that they could retain their French-inspired law, Anglo-American law gradually gained greater importance, largely due to the isolation from legal developments in France, the introduction of numerous English-inspired legal amendments and the transition to English as the language of the courts and the everyday language of the population. This is particularly the case with respect to the US state of Louisiana, where the position of both the French language and French law has become significantly weakened. On the other hand, the legal system of the Canadian province of Québec, where French language continues to be used by the overwhelming majority of the population, has significant legal resources of its own, based on the French legal heritage, which have made it resistant to common-law influence.

[28] This group includes Morocco, Algeria and Tunisia in North Africa; Senegal, Togo, Ivory Coast, the Republic of Congo, Cameroon, Guinea, Gabon, Benin and Burkina Faso in West Africa; Mauritania, Mali, Niger, the Central African Republic and Chad in Central Africa; Madagascar and Djibouti in Eastern Africa; as well as the former Belgian colonies of Congo and Rwanda and Burundi. The language of legal education in such countries is French and many members of the local 'legal elites' have been trained in France.

[29] In combination with Islamic law, French-inspired civil law and jurisprudence remain influential in most North African countries as well as in many Middle Eastern countries.

such as Italy,[30] Greece,[31] Portugal[32] and Japan.[33] Either via Japan or directly, the German civil law influence also spread to Korea,[34] Thailand and partly also China.[35] Furthermore, the legal science that preceded and accompanied the German Code has had considerable influence on legal theory and doctrine in several countries in Central and Eastern Europe, particularly in Austria, Hungary, Switzerland, and the former Yugoslavia. The Austrian General Civil Code of 1811 (*Allgemeines Bürgerliches Gesetzbuch*, or ABGB), also influenced by Roman law, was the product of the Age of Enlightenment and bore the stamp of the School of Natural Law. The German legal influence, especially that of the Historical School, on the Code has been apparent in connection with different legal reforms during the early part of the twentieth century.[36] German legal science had a strong impact in other territories of the Habsburg Empire, especially Hungary, where it led to three civil code drafts (1900, 1911–1915 and 1928). Although none of these drafts attained the status of law, they nevertheless played an important part in judicial practice.[37] The Swiss Civil Code (*Zivilgesetzbuch*) of 1907, drafted by the jurist Eugen Huber, drew upon German and, to a lesser extent, French sources,

---

[30] The BGB was drawn upon by the drafters of the Italian Civil Code of 1942.

[31] The Greek Civil Code of 1940, which came into effect in 1946, was shaped substantially according to the German model.

[32] The drafters of the Portuguese Civil Code of 1967 closely followed the system of the BGB, although individual provisions also reflect French and Italian legal influences.

[33] The Japanese Civil Code of 1898 drew heavily on the first draft of the German Civil Code, but also embodied elements from French and English law. On the codification of civil law in Japan see A. Ishikawa & I. Leetsch, *Das japanische BGB in deutscher Sprache* (Cologne 1985); H. P. Marutschke, *Einführung in das japanische Recht* (Munich 2009).

[34] The Korean Civil Code, enacted in 1960, was drafted by jurists who had studied at universities in Japan and Germany. See Cho, K-C, *Koreanisches Bürgerliches Gesetzbuch* (Frankfurt 1980).

[35] German legal science and the various forerunners of the German Civil Code (e.g. the Dresden Draft and the Saxon Civil Code), as well as the BGB itself exerted a strong influence on Chinese jurists. This influence is reflected in the Civil Code of 1930, parts of which are still applicable in Taiwan.

[36] Many of the ideas of the German Civil Code found their way into Austrian civil law via the so-called Third Partial Amendment, concerning largely the law of obligations, which came into effect in 1916.

[37] Even the first codifications of the civil law in the Soviet Union in the 1920s exhibit similarities to the German Civil Code. Both via Soviet Union and directly, German jurisprudence influenced the legal systems in formerly socialist countries in Central and Eastern Europe. German legal science had a particularly strong influence in the Baltic states of Lithuania, Latvia and Estonia, where a system of private law written by F. von Bunge, a professor at the University of Dorpat in Estonia, in the late nineteenth century was adopted by the independent states in 1918. In the period following WWII, the civil law influence in Central and Eastern Europe subsided when socialist countries adopted new civil codes. Although these code embodied several traditional civil law features, the fundamentally different public law plus significant private law reforms caused most contemporary comparative law scholars to classify the relevant legal systems as part of a new, socialist, legal family. With the demise of the socialist regimes, however, Central and East European nations are once again showing strong affinities to the civil law family.

but was adapted to Swiss circumstances and incorporated significant contemporary reforms.[38]

Civil law survives in so-called 'mixed' or 'hybrid' legal systems, i.e. systems that historically represent a mixture of legal traditions from two or more families of law, such as the civil and common law systems of Quebec, Louisiana, South Africa (Dutch and English influence), Scotland,[39] Puerto Rico and the Philippines.[40] Civil law is also one of the diverse elements in the complex legal systems prevailing in many countries in Asia, such as China, Sri Lanka, Indonesia, Taiwan, Laos, Vietnam and Cambodia.

As the civil law has evolved and entered into combination with other legal elements, its impact has been attenuated. In the aftermath of codification and national law movements, an extraordinary growth of legislative activity was stimulated by the need to modernize the state and address novel problems generated by socio-economic, political and technological developments. Contemporary law-making and law reform are distinguished by a sort of eclecticism. In searching for legal solutions to new problems common to diverse societies, legislatures have been less concerned with provenance than with the promise of new approaches and ideas.[41] The exchange of ideas and models among different legal systems (especially among civil law and common law systems) is gaining momentum and, within the European continent in particular, there is a move towards legal convergence in many areas. At the same time, lawmakers tend to pay more attention to the diversity in society and are more pragmatic in their approach, in contrast with the drafters of the early law codes, who usually upheld one model of behaviour for all people. Thus, private law reform in Europe today is usually preceded by extensive research on contemporary socio-economic conditions and public attitudes. Outside the continent of Europe, the cradle of the civil law, the received European legal norms and institutions never entirely penetrated social life, nor did they ever fully displaced customary and religious norm systems. In light of the above, it is unsurprising that there is probably as much diversity among the responses of civil law systems to legal problems as there is between civil law and common law

---

[38] In 1926, the Swiss Civil Code was adopted, almost word for word, as the Civil Code of the newly formed Republic of Turkey.

[39] The private law of Scotland still reflects a Roman law influence, although contract law, under the influence of the House of Lords jurisprudence, has borrowed much from English law. It should be noted that in Scotland, just like in South Africa, Roman-based civil law survived in uncodified form.

[40] K. Zweigert and H. Kötz, *An Introduction to Comparative Law*, 2nd ed. (Oxford 1987), 74. Civil law is also one of the many elements in the legal systems of Israel and Lebanon.

[41] This tendency is evident, for example, in the new Dutch Civil Code, which came into effect in 1992. In carrying out their work, the Dutch drafters relied not only on a variety of Continental European models, but also on models adopted from common law jurisdictions, as well as on relevant international and transnational conventions and treaties.

countries. It is thus appropriate to ask: what, if anything, besides historical origins, links the civil law systems together and, at the same time, sets the civil law tradition apart from other legal traditions today?

## 8.2.2  Defining Characteristics of Civil Law Systems

One should point out at the outset that it is very difficult to list the defining characteristics of the civil law family of legal systems without resorting to generalizations that would require lengthy qualifications in order for them to be meaningful. In part, the problem is caused by the relatively high level of abstraction that the concept of legal family involves, as well as by the fact that its use as a classification device does not pay sufficient attention to the changes that accompany the individual systems' evolution. According to Zweigert and Kötz,[42] the ultimate distinguishing feature of legal families is their 'style' (Rechtsstil), a multi-faceted notion shaped by the interaction of five factors: (a) history; (b) mode of legal thinking; (c) legal institutions; (d) sources of law; and (e) ideology. All these factors are relevant, albeit to varying degrees, to identifying what sets the civil law apart from other legal families, and in particular the common law family.

As the narrative in this book makes clear, history is a factor that unmistakably sets the civil law tradition apart from other legal traditions. When we refer to the civil law systems as belonging to a single legal family, we are calling attention to the fact that, despite the considerable national differences among themselves, they are characterized by a fundamental unity. The most obvious element of unity is naturally provided by the fact that they are all derived from the same sources, and that they have classified their legal institutions in accordance with a commonly accepted scheme that existed prior to their own development and that, at some stage in their evolution, they took over and made their own. But, as already noted, history is also a factor for the internal differentiation within the civil law, accounting for the fact that the various members of the civil law family may be less homogenous than their common law counterparts.

A characteristic feature of civil law pertains to the mode of legal thinking that it displays. In civil law systems a tendency exists to use abstract terms and, more generally, to employ a conceptual approach to legal problems. Legal norms determine certain patterns of behaviour without regarding the concrete circumstances of particular cases. They are characterized by a kind of optimal generality: they are not too general (as too general norms would complicate the application of law), but general enough for application in certain situations. As a consequence, legal reasoning in civil law countries is basically deductive. Deductive reasoning proceeds from a broad norm or principle expressed in general terms; this is followed by

---

[42] An Introduction to Comparative Law, 2nd ed. (Oxford 1987), 68 ff.

a consideration of the facts of the particular case and the application of the principle to these facts with a view to arriving at a conclusion. Legal reasoning in civil law has a top-down structure, moving from the general to the more specific. By employing this kind of reasoning, the civil law lawyer may present a legal argument as if there is only one right answer to any legal problem. In this respect, any disagreement over the application of the law to the facts is blamed on the presence of faulty logic. This explains why civil law judges do not usually offer dissenting opinions. Every judgment, even in cases decided on appeal, is the judgment of the court as a whole. Under the deductive approach of the civil law, the value of case law is limited as court decisions are viewed as particular illustrations of, or specific exceptions to, the law as embodied in a general norm or principle. In this respect, the material of law may be construed to form an independent, closed system where, at least in theory, all sorts of questions could or should be answered by interpreting existing legal norms.[43] The law in civil law is regarded as 'found' rather than 'made' in each individual case through the application of deductive reasoning or, if necessary, reasoning *per analogiam* or *a contrario*.[44]

Related to the above is the intellectualism and conceptualism that generally characterize civil law thinking—especially German law and the systems it influenced. In civil law systems the study of law is still regarded as a predominantly intellectual pursuit, whilst the practical application of law effectively occupies a secondary place. Notwithstanding the increasing emphasis on the practical implications of the law in recent years, the law in these systems is generally approached as a science, a form of logic, a coherent assembly where everything can be reduced to principles, concepts and categories. In the area of legislation, this approach to law has entailed the use of a technical and abstract language and the formulation of norms with a scope broad enough to cover a wide range of cases. It also led to a high level of precision in selecting the relevant terms and phrases whose meaning remains fixed throughout the text of the law. With respect to the study of law,

---

[43] See on this R. David & J.E,C. Brierley, *Major Legal Systems in the World Today*, 3rd ed. (London 1985), 360-61.

[44] By contrast, in common law systems what is authoritative is what is decided. Law in such systems is seen as open-ended in the sense that new extensions to existing rules can be revealed at any time by the courts. The common law, when viewed through the eyes of a civil law jurist, does not approach law as a science but simply as a method for making distinctions. It is by identifying and distinguishing past cases that the common law lawyer 'discovers' the applicable legal rule in the case at hand. From a civil law viewpoint, this inductive process of discovery in the common law may result in the formulation of a new rule. To the common law lawyer, on the other hand, the deductive approach of the civil law lawyer seems to reverse the natural form of legal reasoning. The common law lawyer adopts as his starting-point the examination of the facts with a view to identifying the precise legal issue raised by the case and the legal rules that should be applied. He does not view law as a set of given rules that can be applied with inexorable logic. When a common law lawyer queries the nature of a case he contemplates facts with a view to identifying the material circumstances of the case and showing that these fall within the scope of one rule rather than another. By contrast, when a civil law lawyer explores the nature of a case, he refers to the legal issues defined in a general and abstract way.

this approach means that one cannot rely on case study alone if one wishes to grasp the essence of the civil law. The study of cases in civil law systems is intended to only illustrate how the law operates in practice, but its essence will necessarily remain abstract. Unlike the common law lawyer, who distinguishes cases on their facts, the civil law lawyer searches for the general principles of law that underpin court decisions.[45] The contrast between the civil law and the common law is traditionally presented as that between case or judge-made law and the essentially doctrinal law of the legal scholars. A great deal of the differences between the two systems are, in one way or another, connected with this contrast between the procedural and the theoretical origin of legal norms. It is therefore unsurprising that legal scholars and academics in civil law countries generally enjoy more prestige than judges, for the duty of the civil law judge is to apply the written law whose meaning is discovered largely through the work of academic scholars. One might say that in civil law the legal scholar is the senior while the judge is the junior partner in the legal process.[46] In modern civil law systems, where court decisions play an increasingly important role in shaping the law, an ever-vigilant academic community observes, reviews and critiques the courts to ensure that any shaping or re-shaping of the law remains a controlled activity. Furthermore, academic scholars continue the tradition of writing textbooks and treatises in their area of expertise. Their works provide the basic source of legal knowledge that is imparted, in an authoritative way, from the scholars to their students and to those entering the legal profession. As the civil law emphasizes the transmission of legal knowledge and as there is so much knowledge to be transmitted, legal instruction in universities takes the form of general overviews of or introductions to the various fields of the law. In

---

[45] As C. D. Gonthier has remarked, the civil law is distinguished from the common law by "a difference in intellectual approach, in the quest and ordering of [legal] knowledge. Each approach reflects one of the modes of functioning of the human intellect, that is, on the one hand, the empirical mode based on specific instances from which one may eventually draw rules and even identify principles and, on the other, the theoretical approach based on established principles from which concrete consequences and applications are drawn." "Some Comments on the Common Law and the Civil Law in Canada: Influences, Parallel Developments and Borrowings", (1993) 21 *Canadian Business Law Journal* 323.

[46] The authority of academic writers in civil law countries can also be explained historically. As previously observed, when the texts of Justinian's legislation were rediscovered in medieval Europe, they appeared so complicated and difficult to understand that it was left to academic scholars (the glossators and the commentators) to decipher and explain them. As a result, the works of academic commentators acquired as much authority as the texts themselves. Judges also came to greatly rely on legal scholars for information and guidance concerning the interpretation and application of the law. By the end of the sixteenth century it was a common practice for judges in Germany and other Continental European countries to refer the record of a difficult case to a university law faculty and to adopt the faculty's collective opinion on questions of law. This practice, which prevailed until the nineteenth century, resulted in the accumulation of an extensive body of legal doctrine. When systematized in reports and treatises the scholarly opinions rendered in actual cases were regarded as a kind of case law and an authoritative source of legal interpretations. See J. P. Dawson, *The Oracles of the Law* (Ann Arbor 1968), 231.

civil law systems the principal source of legal knowledge has always been the textbook, rather than the casebook.

In civil law the tendency prevails to draw a clear distinction between substantive law and legal procedure. This distinction has its historical origins in the work of the humanist jurists of the sixteenth century, who tended to view the law not so much as a body of objective rules but, rather, as a system of subjective rights. In this respect, legal procedure is viewed as a mechanism for enforcing these rights. Whenever substantive law recognizes a right, the law of procedure, as an accessory to substantive law, must provide an appropriate remedy. This shift from law as rules to law as rights was partly due to the fact that in Latin and in all European languages the word for 'substantive law' and the word for right is the same: *ius, droit, diritto, Recht*.[47] In the domain of legal procedure civil law systems generally follow a more dogmatic and formalistic approach to law in contrast to the more empirical approach of the common law. Furthermore, there is a relatively greater scope for an inquisitorial approach to litigation, as opposed to the adversarial approach of the common law.[48] The civil law places greater responsibility on the judge for the investigation of the facts, whilst the common law leaves the parties to gather and produce the factual material on which adjudication depends. One might say that the civil law model of legal procedure is construed to display a preference for 'centripetal' decision-making, determinative rules and a rigid ordering of authority. It also attaches greater importance to written testimony in the form of official documents and reports.[49] However, the usual contrast between the civil law inquisitorial and the common law adversarial mode of trial should not be overstated. As J. Langbein, commenting on German and American procedures, has remarked, "apart from fact-gathering... the lawyers for the parties play major and broadly comparable roles in both the German and American systems. Both are adversary systems of civil procedure. There as here, the lawyers advance partisan positions from first pleadings to final arguments. German litigators suggest legal theories and lines of factual inquiry, they superintend and supplement judicial examination of witnesses, they urge inferences from fact, they discuss and distinguish precedent,

---

[47] In the common law system, on the other hand, legal development focused on remedies rather than rights, on forms of action rather than causes of action. As often said, it was with writs and not with rights that the older English law was concerned. The difference is mainly one of emphasis, but it has the important practical consequence that the agent who controls the grant of remedies also controls the development of the law, for by creating new forms of action or extending existing forms to deal with new facts that agent could in fact create new rights.

[48] Under the adversarial system of legal procedure, the facts emerge through a formal context between the parties, while the judge acts as an impartial umpire. In the inquisitorial system, on the other hand, the truth is revealed by an inquiry into the facts conducted by the judge.

[49] According to M. Damaska, the relatively greater emphasis on certainty in the civil law model of legal procedure is traced to the influence of the rationalist School of Natural Law and in particular the rationalist desire to impose a relatively simple order on the complexities of life. See "Structures of Authority and Comparative Criminal Procedure", (1975) 84 *Yale Law Journal*, 480.

they interpret statutes, and they formulate views of the law that further the interests of their clients". According to this commentator, the chief difference between German and American litigators is that the former are mostly 'law adversaries', while the latter are 'law-and-fact adversaries'.[50]

The civil law has its own distinctive legal institutions. Reference may be made, for example, to the institutions of cause, oblique action, abuse of right, the *actio de in rem verso* and *negotiorum gestio* of the Romanistic sub-family. With respect to the Germanic sub-family one could mention institutions such as the abstract real contract, the *clausulae generales*, the concept of the legal act, the notion of unjust enrichment, the doctrine of the collapse of the foundations of a transaction and liability based on *culpa in contrahendo*. One should point out in this connection that the presence of identical legal terms in different legal families does not necessarily imply that such terms are construed in the same manner. For instance, a term that is used in both civil law and common law systems which has different meanings is 'equity.' Although civil law codes contain several references to it,[51] equity is not clearly defined but civil law judges use the concept whenever they do not wish to follow a formal or rigid interpretation of a legal principle. In English law, on the other hand, the term 'equity' is understood to refer to the body of law that evolved separately from the body of law created by the common law courts.[52] Other examples of identical legal terms that operate in different ways in different systems are those of possession and mistake, which are given different juridical meanings in French and English law.

For largely historical reasons, private law (the law governing relations between private citizens) has had a dominant role in the development of legal institutions, concepts and principles in civil law systems. This is manifested by the fact that the classification of civil law systems focuses on the law canvassed by the civil codes, namely private law.[53] Other branches of law, such as public law (the body of rules concerned with the relationship between public bodies and the resolution of disputes in which the state is a party), developed later, largely on the basis of concepts and principles replicated from private law. A characteristic feature of modern civil law is the sharp distinction drawn between private law and public law. Although this distinction is also recognized in common law countries,[54] in civil law systems it

---

[50] "The German Advance in Civil Procedure", (1985) 52 *U. Chi. L. Rev.*, 823-824.

[51] See e.g. Arts 565 and 1135 of the French Civil Code.

[52] As previously observed, in England the rules of equity were shaped by the Courts of Chancery, which became known as the 'courts of equity.'

[53] As in civil law systems legal relationships are to a large extent organized by forms derived from Roman private law, one might say that the conceptual system of Roman law constitutes a kind of pre-knowledge and a important common denominator (*tertium comparationis*) for these systems.

[54] In common law the difference between private and public law is traditionally regarded as a matter pertaining to the type of remedies available when one of the parties to a dispute is a public body. In other words, the common law is seen as indivisible in the sense that it applies to both the

has far greater practical implications since, derived from it, there are two different hierarchies of courts dealing with each of these categories of law.[55]

The sources of law furnish another criterion for distinguishing between legal families. In civil law systems statutory law (legal codes, statutes, decrees and ordinances) have precedence over custom and judicial decisions. An obvious feature of modern civil law is that it is based on the codification of the law. Codification denotes an authoritative statement of the whole law in a coherent and systematic way. As we saw earlier, the tradition of codification is a product of the rationalist tendencies that prevailed in European political philosophy during the eighteenth and nineteenth centuries. Its roots, however, can be traced to the great codification of Roman law by Emperor Justinian in the sixth century AD. One can trace to Justinian the idea that the code overrides all other legal sources, offering a fresh beginning to the law. In contemporary civil law systems, law codes are integrated documents consisting of comprehensive and systematically stated provisions complemented by subsequent legislation. They govern all major branches of law, including civil law, civil procedure, criminal law, criminal procedure and general commercial law. Even though in civil law systems judicial decisions are studied in order to uncover trends, especially in areas in which there is sparse legislation,[56] court decisions have in principle no binding effect on lower courts. However, despite the absence of any formal doctrine of *stare decisis*, there is a strong tendency on the part of civil law judges to follow precedents, in particular those of the higher courts. In light of this one might say that in practice the difference between *stare decisis* (binding precedent) and what is referred to in France as *jurisprudence constante* (the persuasiveness of judicial trend) is constantly being narrowed down.

Ideology is the least useful criterion when distinguishing between civil law and common law, the other major legal family within the Western legal tradition. The

---

government and the individual citizen, and the same courts deal with matters of both private and public law. The idea of a separate system of public law was developed in England in the latter half of the twentieth century and is associated with the development of the action for judicial review, which is the method for challenging the decisions of public bodies.

[55] It should be noted in this connection that in civil law systems the term 'civil law' is also used to denote the substantive body of private law in contradistinction to commercial law, which is not regulated by a civil code. Commercial law is treated as a distinct body of law that is usually contained in a separate code and administered by a separate court system. It governs, among other things, companies, partnerships, negotiable instruments, trademarks, patents and bankruptcy. In common law systems, on the other hand, no distinction is drawn between civil law and commercial law, the latter being defined in English law as that part of the civil (as opposed to criminal) law that is concerned with rights and duties arising from the supply of goods and services in the way of trade.

[56] Consider, e.g., the administrative practice of the Conseil d'Etat – the supreme administrative court of France.

essence of the philosophical, political, economic and cultural foundations of law in both legal families is too similar for it to be otherwise.[57]


### 8.2.3  Concluding Remarks

Although the oldest legal tradition in the Western world, civil law continues to evolve. In the course of its development it has spawned different sub-traditions and has exported its ideology and legal ideas throughout the world. Furthermore, it has influenced the law of the European Community in structure, style of reasoning and ethos and continues to play an important part in the process of harmonisation of law in Europe. Few would deny that the civil law is gradually converging with the common law, at least to the extent of its growing reliance on case law. Moreover, as already noted, law-making in civil law countries is characterized by a degree of eclecticism: law drafters often look beyond the borders of their own legal family when investigating possible solutions to current legal problems.[58] As the exchange of ideas among civil law, common law and other legal systems gains momentum, some of the differences separating these systems tend to wither away. Nevertheless, significant differences remain. At its heart, civil law remains very much a unique tradition in its own right by virtue of, among other things, its predominant forms of legal reasoning and argumentation, ideas concerning the divisions of law and the organization of justice, reliance on elaborations of statutory and codified precepts,

---

[57] From a purely juristic point of view there exists a system of civil law and a system of common law, but no system of Western law. But if law is seen as an expression of a particular type of civilization, as a condition for a particular form of social organization based on a particular conception of justice, the phrase 'Western law' expresses the fundamental unity that exists between the civil and common law systems. The observer who views law from the perspective of a political scientist, a political philosopher or a sociologist, will discern the basic connections between the civil law and the common law systems: both systems are underpinned by rationalism, individualism and the liberal conception of social order; in both systems the ideal is a society governed by the 'rule of law'; finally, both systems attach primary importance to the autonomy of law, i.e. the understanding of law as conceptually distinct from custom, morality, religion or politics.

[58] According to U. Mattei, the reception of foreign legal rules is usually the end result of a competition where each legal system provides different rules for the resolution of a specific problem. In a market of a legal culture where rule suppliers are concerned with satisfying demand, ultimately the most efficient rule will be the winner. From the viewpoint of a particular legal system, 'efficient' is whatever makes the legal system work better by lowering transaction costs. Mattei's approach, which represents an example of the more recent trend to combine comparative law and economics, may be taken to constitute a narrower version of functionalism focusing not on social functions in general but on a particular function, namely the efficiency of a legal rule or institution in economic terms. See U. Mattei, "Efficiency in Legal Transplants: An Essay in Comparative Law and Economics", (1994) 14 *International Review of Law and Economics*, 3 ff. U. Mattei and F. Pulitini, "A Competitive Model of Legal Rules", in A. Breton et al (eds), *The Competitive State*, (Dordrecht 1991) 207 ff.

and approaches to legal scholarship and education. The changes in the legal universe that have been taking place in the last few decades, associated with the ongoing tendencies of globalization and regional integration, make it difficult for us to predict how the civil law tradition will evolve or how it will be described by future observers. However, we can be reasonably certain that this oldest and most influential of the Western legal traditions has entered a new phase of development and that it will continue to adapt itself to the challenges of an ever-changing world.

# Select Bibliography

Adcock, F. E., *Roman Political Ideas and Practice*, Ann Arbor, The University of Michigan Press, 1964, repr. 1975.

Astuti, G., *Tradizione romanistica e civiltà giuridica europea*, Naples, Edizioni scientifiche italiane, 1984.

Avenarius, M., *Fremde Traditionen des römischen Rechts*, Göttingen, Wallstein, 2014.

Barton, J., *Roman Law in England*, Milan, Giuffrè, 1971.

Bauman, R. A., *Lawyers and Politics in the Early Roman Empire*, Munich, Beck, 1989.

Bauman, R. A., *Crime and Punishment in Ancient Rome*, London and New York, Routledge, 1996.

Bellomo, M., *The Common Legal Past of Europe, 1000-1800*, Washington DC, Catholic University of America Press, 1995.

Berger, A., *Encyclopedic Dictionary of Roman Law*, Philadelphia, APS, 1953, repr. 2002.

Berman, H. J., *Law and Revolution II: The Impact of Protestant Reformations on the Western Legal Tradition*, Cambridge Mass., Harvard University Press, 2003.

Bleicken, J., *Staat und Recht in der Römischen Republik*, Wiesbaden, Steiner, 1978.

Borkowski, J. A. & Plessis, P. du, *Textbook on Roman Law*, 3rd ed., Oxford, Oxford University Press, 2005.

Brundage, J. A., *Medieval Canon Law*, London, Longman, 1995.

Buckland, W. W., *A Textbook of Roman Law from Augustus to Justinian*, edited by P. Stein, 3rd edn, Cambridge, Cambridge University Press, 1963, repr. 2007.

Burdese, A., *Manuale di diritto privato romano*, 4th edn, Turin, UTET, 1993.

Burdese, A., *Manuale di diritto pubblico romano*, 3rd edn, Turin, UTET, 1987, repr. 1994.

Bürge, A., *Römisches Privatrecht*, Darmstadt, Wiss. Buchges., 1999.

Caenegem, R. C. van, *Legal History: a European Perspective*, London, Hambledon Press, 1991.

Caenegem, R. C. van, *European Law in the Past and the Future: Unity and Diversity over Two Millennia*, Cambridge, Cambridge University Press, 2002.

Caenegem, R. C. van, *Birth of the English Common Law*, 2nd edn, Cambridge, Cambridge University Press, 1988.

Cannata, C. A., *Histoire de la jurisprudence européenne*, Turin, Giappichelli, 1989.

Cary, M. and Scullard, H. H., *A History of Rome*, 3rd edn, London, Macmillan, 1975.

Cloud, D., "The Constitution and Public Criminal Law", in *Cambridge Ancient History*, 2nd ed., vol. IX, ch. 13, 491-530, Cambridge, Cambridge University Press, 1994.

Coing, H., *Europäisches Privatrecht*, 2 vol., Munich, Beck, 1985-1989.

Collins, R., *Early Medieval Europe 300-1000*, London, MacMillan, 1991.

Cortese, E., *Il rinascimento giuridico medievale*, Rome, Bulzoni, 1992.

Cortese, E., *Il diritto nella storia medievale*, 2 vol., Rome, Il cigno Galileo Galilei, 1995.

© Springer International Publishing Switzerland 2015

G. Mousourakis, *Roman Law and the Origins of the Civil Law Tradition*,

DOI 10.1007/978-3-319-12268-7

Crawford, M. H. (ed.), *Roman Statutes* (2 vols), London, University of London, 1996.

Crifò, G., *Lezioni di storia del diritto romano*, 3rd edn, Bologna, Monduzzi, 2000.

Crook, J. A., *Law and Life of Rome*, London, Thames & Hudson, 1967; Ithaca, Cornell University Press, 1984.

Daube, D., *Forms of Roman Legislation*, Oxford, Clarendon Press, 1956; repr. Westport, CT, Greenwood Press, 1979.

Dawson, J. P., *The Oracles of Law*, Ann Arbor, University of Michigan Press, 1968.

Declareuil, J., *Rome the Law-Giver*, London and New York, Routledge, 1996; first published 1927.

Drew, K. F., *Law and Society in Early Medieval Europe. Studies in Legal History*, London, Variorum, 1988.

Friedrich, C. J., *The Philosophy of Law in Historical Perspective*, Chicago & London, University of Chicago Press, 1963.

Frier, B., *The Rise of the Roman Jurists*, Princeton, Princeton University Press, 1985.

Garnsey, P., *Social Status and Legal Privilege in the Roman Empire*, Oxford, Clarendon Press, 1970.

Garofalo, L., *Giurisprudenza romana e diritto privato europeo*, Padova, CEDAM, 2008.

Giuffrè, V., *La repressione criminale nell' esperienza romana*, 4th edn, Naples, Jovene, 1998.

Gruen, E. S., *Roman Politics and the Criminal Courts, 149-78 BC*, Harvard University Press, 1968.

Guarino A., *Storia del diritto romano*, 11th edn, Naples, Jovene, 1996.

Guarino, A., *Diritto privato romano*, 12th edn, Naples, Jovene, 2001.

Haldon, J. F., *Byzantium in the 7th Century*, Cambridge, Cambridge University Press, 1990.

Harding, A., *Medieval Law and the Foundations of the State*, Oxford, Oxford University Press, 2002.

Harries, J., *Law and Empire in Late Antiquity*, Cambridge, Cambridge University Press, 1999.

Hattenhauer, H., *Europäische Rechtsgeschichte*, 4th edn, Heidelberg, Müller, 2004.

Honoré, T., *Tribonian*, London, Duckworth, 1978.

Honoré, T., *Emperors and Lawyers*, London, Duckworth, 1981; 2nd edn, Oxford, Clarendon Press, 1994.

Honoré, T., *Law in the Crisis of Empire: 379-455 AD*, Oxford, Clarendon Press, 1998.

Honsell, H., *Römisches Recht*, 5th edn, Berlin & New York, Springer, 2002; 7th edn 2010.

Hudson, J., *The Formation of the English Common Law: Law and Society in England from the Norman Conquest to the Magna Carta*, London, Longman, 1996.

Johnston, D., *Roman Law in Context*, Cambridge, Cambridge University Press, 1999.

Jolowicz, H. F., *Roman Foundations of Modern Law*, Oxford, Clarendon Press, 1957.

Jolowicz, H. F. and Nicholas, B., *Historical Introduction to the Study of Roman Law*, 3rd edn, Cambridge, Cambridge University Press, 1972, repr. 2008.

Jones, A. H. M., *Studies in Roman Government and Law*, Oxford, Blackwell, 1960.

Jones, A. H. M., *The Criminal Courts of the Roman Republic and Principate*, Oxford, Blackwell, 1972.

Jones, A. H. M., *The Later Roman Empire*, Baltimore Md., Johns Hopkins University Press, 1986, originally published 1964.

Karayannopoulos, J. and Weiss, G., *Quellenkunde zur Geschichte von Byzanz (324-1453)*, Wiesbaden, Harrassowitz, 1982.

Kaser, M., *Römische Rechtsgeschichte*, Göttingen, Vandenhoeck & Ruprecht, 1976; 2nd edn 1993.

Kaser, M., *Römisches Privatrecht*, Munich, Beck, 1989; 19th edn (Kaser, M. & Knütel R.) 2008.

Kelley, D. R., *Foundations of Modern Historical Scholarship: Language, Law and History in the French Renaissance*, New York, Columbia University Press, 1970.

Kelly, J. M., *A Short History of Western Legal Theory*, Oxford, Clarendon Press, 1992.

Kisch, G., *Studien zur humanistischen Jurisprudenz*, Berlin, De Gruyter, 1972.

Koschaker, P., *Europa und das römische Recht*, 4th edn, Munich, Beck, 1966.

Kunkel, W., *An Introduction to Roman Legal and Constitutional History*, 2nd edn, Oxford, Clarendon, 1973.

Kunkel, W. and Schermaier. M., *Römische Rechtsgeschichte*, 13th edn, Cologne, Böhlau, 2001; 14th edn 2005.

Laiou, A. E. and Simon, D. (eds), *Law and Society in Byzantium, Ninth-Twelfth Centuries*, Washingdon DC, Dumbarton Oaks, 1994.

Lange, H., Römisches Recht im Mittelalter, 2 vol., Munich, Beck, 1997-2007.

Lawson, F. H., *A Common Lawyer Looks at the Civil Law*, Ann Arbor, University of Michigan Press, 1953.

Lee, R.W., *The Elements of Roman Law: with a Translation of the Institutes of Justinian*, London, Sweet & Maxwell, 1956, repr. 1986.

Lewis, A. D. E. and Ibbetson, D. J. (eds), *The Roman Law Tradition*, Cambridge, Cambridge University Press, 1994.

Lintott, A., *The Constitution of the Roman Republic*, Oxford, Clarendon 1999.

Lobingier, C. S., *The Evolution of the Roman law: from Before the Twelve Tables to the Corpus Juris*, Littleton, Colo., F.B. Rothman, 1987.

Lupoi, M., *The Origins of the European Legal Order*, Cambridge, Cambridge University Press, 2000.

Mehren, A. von and Gordley, J, *The Civil Law System*, 2nd ed., Boston, Little, Brown, 1977.

Merryman, J. H., *The Civil Law Tradition*, 2nd edn, Stanford, Stanford University Press, 1985; 3rd edn 2007.

Metzger, E. (ed.), *A Companion to Justinian's Institutes*, London, Duckworth, 1998, repr. 2002.

Mommsen, Th., *Römisches Staatsrecht* I, Leipzig, Duncker & Humblot, 1887, repr. Graz, Akademische Druck- und Verlaganstalt, 1971.

Mommsen, Th., *Römisches Strafrecht*, Leipzig, Duncker & Humblot, 1899.

Mousourakis, G., *Fundamentals of Roman Private Law*, Berlin and Heidelberg, Springer, 2012.

Nicholas, B., *An Introduction to Roman Law*, Oxford, Clarendon Press, 1962, repr. 1991.

Ostrogorsky, G., *History of the Byzantine State*, Oxford, Oxford U. Press, 1968.

Pieler, P. E., "Byzantinische Rechtsliteratur", in H. Hunger, *Die hochsprachliche profane Literatur der Byzantiner*, Munich, Beck, 1978.

Plessis, P. du, *Borkowski's Textbook on Roman Law*, Oxford & New York, Oxford University Press, 2010.

Radding, C. M., *The Origins of Medieval Jurisprudence*, New Haven and London, Yale University Press, 1988.

Robinson, O. F., Fergus, T. D. and Gordon, W. M., *An Introduction to European Legal History*, 2nd edn, London, Butterworths, 1994.

Robinson, O. F., Fergus, T. D. and Gordon, W. M., *European Legal History: Sources and Institutions*, 3rd ed., London, Butterworths, 2000.

Robinson, O. F., *The Criminal Law of Ancient Rome*, London, Duckworth, 1995.

Robinson, O. F., *The Sources of Roman Law*, London and New York, Routledge, 1997.

Riggsby, A.M., *Roman Law and the Legal World of the Romans*, Cambridge, Cambridge University Press, 2010.

Santalucia, B., *Diritto e processo penale nell' antica Roma*, Milan, Giuffrè, 1989, 2nd edn 1998.

Santalucia, B., *Studi di diritto penale romano*, Roma, L'"Erma" di Bretschneider, 1994.

Scheltema, H. J., "Byzantine Law" in Hussey, J. (ed.), *Cambridge Medieval History* IV, 2, Cambridge, Cambridge University Press, 1967, 55-77.

Schiller, A. A., *Roman Law: Mechanisms of Development*, The Hague and New York, Mouton, 1978.

Schulz, F., *Classical Roman Law*, Oxford, Clarendon, 1951; repr. Aalen, Scientia Verlag, 1992.

Schulz, F., *History of Roman Legal Science*, Oxford, Clarendon Press, 1967, first published in 1946.

Sherwin-White, A. N., *The Roman Citizenship*, 2nd edn, Oxford, Clarendon Press, 1973.

Smith, J. C. & Weisstub, D. N., *The Western Idea of Law*, London, Butterworth, 1983.

Stein, P. G., *Legal Evolution: The Story of an Idea*, Cambridge, Cambridge University Press, 1980.

Stein, P. G., *The Character and Influence of the Roman Civil Law*, London, Hambledon, 1988, repr 2003.

Stein, P. G., *Roman Law in European History*, Cambridge, Cambridge University Press, 1999.

Strachan-Davidson, J. L., *Problems of the Roman Criminal Law*, Oxford, Clarendon Press, 1912.

Tamm, D., *Roman Law and European Legal History*, Copenhagen, DJOF, 1997.

Thomas, J. A. C., *Textbook of Roman Law,* Amsterdam & New York, North-Holland Pub. Co., 1976.

Troianos, S., *The Sources of Byzantine Law*, 3rd edn, Athens, Sakkoulas, 2011.

Troje, H. E., *Humanistische Jurisprudenz: Studien zur europäischen Rechtswissenschaft unter dem Einfluss des Humanismus*, Goldbach, Keip, 1993.

Ullmann, W., *Law and Politics in the Middle Ages*, Cambridge, Cambridge University Press, 1975.

Ullmann, W., *Jurisprudence in the Middle Ages*, London, Variorum, 1980.

Vinogradoff, P., *Roman Law in Medieval Europe*, Oxford, Clarendon, 1929.

Wal, N. van der and Lokin, J. H. A., *Historiae iuris graeco-romani delineatio. Les sources du droit byzantin de 300 à 1453*, Groningen, Forsten, 1985.

Watson, A., *The Law of the Ancient Romans*, Dallas, Southern Methodist University Press, 1970.

Watson, A., *Law Making in the Later Roman Republic*, Oxford, Clarendon Press, 1974.

Watson, A., *Legal Transplants*, Edinburgh, Scottish Academic Press, 1974.

Watson, A., *The Making of the Civil Law*, Cambridge Mass., Harvard University Press, 1981.

Watson, A., *Roman Law and Comparative Law*, Athens Georgia, University of Georgia Press, 1991.

Watson, A., *The Spirit of Roman Law*, Athens, University of Georgia Press, 1995.

Whitman, J. Q., *The Legacy of Roman Law in the German Romantic Era*, Princeton, Princeton University Press, 1990.

Wieacker, F., *Römische Rechtsgeschichte I*, Munich, Beck, 1988.

Wieacker, F., *A History of Private Law in Europe: with Particular Reference to Germany*, trans. T. Weir, Oxford, Clarendon Press, 1995.

Zimmermann, R., *The Law of Obligations: Roman Foundations of the Civilian Tradition*, Oxford, Clarendon Press, 1996.

Zimmermann, R., *Roman Law, Contemporary Law, European Law: The Civilian Tradition Today*, Oxford, Oxford University Press, 2001.

# Index

© Springer International Publishing Switzerland 2015
G. Mousourakis, *Roman Law and the Origins of the Civil Law Tradition*,
DOI 10.1007/978-3-319-12268-7